NEW YORK STATE
AND THE RISE OF
MODERN CONSERVATISM

NEW YORK STATE AND THE RISE OF MODERN CONSERVATISM

Redrawing Party Lines

TIMOTHY J. SULLIVAN

STATE UNIVERSITY OF NEW YORK PRESS

Published by
STATE UNIVERSITY OF NEW YORK PRESS, ALBANY

Printed in the United States of America

For information, contact State University of New York Press, Albany, NY
www.sunypress.edu

Production, Laurie Searl
Marketing, Anne M. Valentine

Library of Congress Cataloging-in-Publication Data

Sullivan, Timothy J., 1959–
New York State and the rise of modern conservatism : redrawing party lines / Timothy J. Sullivan.
p. cm.
Includes bibliographical references and index.
ISBN 978-0-7914-7643-7 (hardcover : alk. paper)
ISBN 978-0-7914-7644-4 (pbk. : alk. paper)
1. Conservative Party of New York State—History. 2. Political parties—New York (State)—History. I. Title.

JK2295.N74S84 2009
324.2747'08—dc22 2007052940

10 9 8 7 6 5 4 3 2 1

To my mother and father

I really am a conservative you know. I've got a lot to conserve.

—Nelson Rockefeller to William F. Buckley Jr.

CONTENTS

ACKNOWLEDGMENTS

This book began as my Ph.D. dissertation in American History at the University of Maryland at College Park. It benefitted during that period from the advice and analysis of numerous faculty members and many of my graduate student colleagues. No member of the College Park community, however, provided such tireless and unselfish assistance as Professor Keith Olson. His confidence in the project was critical in its initial stages. His enthusiasm sustained it through an extended period of research. And in the final phase of the process, his willingness to read and critique an unending series of drafts helped me to identify the essential elements of a complicated narrative.

This book's focus on the party politics of New York State during the 1960s and 1970s stemmed from a suggestion from a personal friend, David G. D. Hecht. As a veteran of those political wars, he understood the richness and significance of the topic before I did.

Archivists and librarians at numerous institutions assisted in the research for this book by contributing their time and expertise. I would especially like to single out the staff of the Special Collections and Archives Department at the University of Albany for their sustained generosity. Additionally, I would like to thank the staffs at the Hayden Library at Arizona State University, the John M. Ashbrook Center for Public Affairs at Ashland University, the Archives and Special Collections Department at the College of Staten Island, the Carl A. Kroch Library at Cornell University, the Hoover Institution Archives, the Library of Congress, the National Archives at College Park, the Manuscripts and Archives Division of the New York Public Library, the Rockefeller Archive Center, the Bird Library at Syracuse University, the Special Collections Department at the University of Maryland, and the Sterling Memorial Library at Yale University.

Finally, the book profited in ways both measurable and immeasurable from the involvement of my wife, Frances. Partly this was due to the wide variety of jobs she assumed and mastered to further its completion. These included editor, fact checker, proofreader, computer consultant, and motivational coach. The book also benefitted, however, because Frances was the first person to read every word that I wrote. The writer Calvin Trillin understood this phenomenon, and readily acknowledged that he showed his wife all of his work not only because he valued her opinion, but also because he hoped to impress her. I wrote a better book because I knew Frances would be its initial reader.

INTRODUCTION

Shortly after 9:00 A.M. on Wednesday, August 11, 1971, two registrars from the New York City Board of Elections arrived at Gracie Mansion on the upper east side of Manhattan. The election officials were escorted into the mansion's living room and introduced to the mayor of New York City, John V. Lindsay, and his wife, Mary. The registrars presented the couple with two blank applications for enrollment, the official document by which voters in the state registered with a political party. The Lindsays sat down to fill out the forms. Both listed Gracie Mansion as their residence. Both indicated their intent to change their party enrollment. And both marked the circle corresponding to membership in the Democratic Party. The two officials then departed Gracie Mansion, taking with them the completed forms, the documentary verification of the morning's business.

That brief bureaucratic procedure ended John Lindsay's theretofore lifelong membership in the Republican Party. The decision had not been easy for the mayor. He had used a family vacation in the Colorado Rockies earlier that month to consider the pros and cons of abandoning the GOP. Lindsay recalled his family's strong Republican roots and how admiration for New York Republican politicians such as Theodore Roosevelt and Fiorella LaGuardia had initially drawn him to a career in politics. A number of fellow Republicans, including longtime financial supporters, had also pleaded with him not to leave the party. At a crowded news conference shortly after meeting with the registrars, Lindsay conceded that becoming a Democrat made him "a little bit sad."[1] Political realities, however, compelled the switch. John Lindsay had to end his lifelong allegiance to the GOP because his liberal policies and views no longer fit into the Republican Party. Lindsay acknowledged that his party switch demonstrated "the failure of twenty years in progressive Republican politics."[2]

Other participants in New York State politics displayed none of the mayor's anguish at this turn of events. Foremost among this group were the leaders of the New York Conservative Party, a state third party dedicated to the demise of liberal republicanism, in general, and its leading proponents within the state such as John Lindsay, in particular. William F. Buckley Jr., the magazine editor, newspaper columnist, and television host who had been the Conservative Party's mayoral nominee against Lindsay in 1965, pronounced the switch sensible, adding, in reference to their earlier campaign, "I told him to do this six years ago."[3] On a tactical level, Buckley and his fellow New York Conservatives welcomed Lindsay's switch as a setback for a political adversary. More strategically, however, Conservatives celebrated Lindsay's switch as a step towards their ultimate goal, an ideological realignment of the two major parties.

Conservatives across the country favored a realignment that would make the Democratic and Republican Parties more ideologically consistent. They complained that two national parties comprised of broad ideological coalitions muddied the political waters and prevented any meaningful party identity. This position reflected both political theory and partisan interest. In the decades following World War II, a majority of Republicans and Democrats agreed on most major public policy issues. Both parties supported a foreign policy aimed at containing the spread of communism, and a domestic program that modestly expanded the size and scope of New Deal social programs. Conservatives, however, belonged to both the Democratic and Republican Parties, but dominated neither on a national level. Divided between the two parties, their minority status in both usually doomed their dissent. Conservatives advocated an ideological reshuffling that would make each party more consistent in terms of its policy and members. This realignment would replace the broad-based coalitions of both major parties with a GOP that was ideologically conservative and a Democratic Party that was consistently liberal. It would provide greater clarity in party identity and a clearer political choice for voters.

New York Conservatives founded a minor party in the early 1960s with the belief that the GOP and the country would benefit from greater ideological consistency within each of the two major parties. The Conservative Party tied its criticism of liberal Republicans to its belief that conservatives, not liberals, belonged in the GOP. "The two party-system has completely broken down in New York," their initial campaign material read. "There are no important differences between the policies advocated by the major parties, and the conservative voters of New York have no place to go."[4] The new party planned to give conservatives in New York a place to go. Initially, that would be a third party. But Conservatives predicted that once the state GOP recognized the cost of these defections, it would make a permanent place for conservative voters.

While the Conservative Party operated within a single state, it aimed to be influential beyond New York. Because the state GOP dominated the liberal wing of the national Republican Party, any modification of the state Republican Party would have national implications. To change politics beyond the state, however, New York Conservatives needed to make the state GOP inhospitable to liberal politicians and unattractive to liberal voters. John and Mary Lindsay's meeting with two election officials in Gracie Mansion that day in August of 1971 demonstrated Conservative success inside the state. Lindsay's attributing his decision to switch parties to the failure of progressive politics within the GOP represented an important victory for New York Conservatives and their ideological brethren outside the state. William Buckley, explaining the Conservative view of this larger significance, characterized Lindsay's move in his syndicated column as "a major contribution to the restoration of meaning to the two-party system."[5]

The Conservative Party's capacity to restore meaning to the two-party system rested on its ability to succeed in New York State politics. At first glance, the party's prospects for success seemed slender. First, it was a third party, an entity regularly consigned to the political margins. Conservative ambitions seemed well beyond the reach of a state third party. Second, it was a third party concerned with the ideological purity of one of the major parties. Exactly why should the GOP take instructions on being Republican from a splinter party? And finally, the party's beliefs seemed to be at odds with its home. In the early 1960s, New York was viewed almost universally as a liberal state. Although not the nation's most liberal state, its size and prominence made it one of the most important liberal states. In addition, New York's liberalism had deep roots. It traced back to the late nineteenth century, when New York was one of the first states to construct a regulatory response to the problems associated with industrialization and urbanization. During that time, New York often led the way with legislation on child labor, workplace safety, and housing standards. In the first half of the twentieth century, the state also became a leader in social welfare programs, adopting measures to assist the unemployed and the needy. With the years following World War II, New York's liberalism expanded to assist a growing middle class through programs such as a state thruway and an expanded university system. This tradition of liberalism suggested an inhospitable environment for a conservative political party.

While the Conservative Party's challenges were readily apparent, it also possessed several important, if less obvious, advantages. Most importantly, minor parties in New York State could and did flourish. In New York, as in no other state, minor parties determined election outcomes, influenced major parties, and survived for decades. The state's minor parties prospered because New York election law permitted one party to cross-endorse the nominee of another political party. Under this system, the cross-endorsed candidate's name appeared on the ballot lines of both parties. The state also allowed disaggregation, whereby the votes received by the cross-endorsed candidate were counted separately on each party's line and then tallied together.[6] Disaggregation ensured that minor parties received credit for the votes cast on their ballot line. By allowing cross-endorsement—known also as fusion and less commonly as cross-filing, multiple party nominations, or joint endorsements—and disaggregation, New York supplied minor parties with invaluable tools.

The practice of fusion was unique to New York by the mid-twentieth century, but it had been common across the country through most of the nineteenth century.[7] In the 1880s, when states began to print election ballots for the first time, they gained the ability to regulate access to the ballot. Capitalizing on this new power, a number of state legislatures passed the first anti-fusion laws in the 1890s. In many states, Republican legislators enacted these measures because candidates cross-endorsed by the Democratic and Populists Parties were winning an increasing number of elections. In 1896, New York also enacted anti-fusion legislation, prohibiting party committees from nominating candidates nominated by another party.[8] In 1910, however, the State Court of Appeals ruled the law unconstitutional, calling prohibitions on cross-endorsement arbitrary limitations on the franchise. The court continued to find subsequent anti-fusion measures unconstitutional.

New York's unique electoral structure meant third parties operated differently within the state. Outside New York, third parties usually formed out of voter dissatisfaction with the major parties' response to some specific issue. When the major parties saw their support diminishing, however, they adjusted by adopting aspects of the upstart party's policy agenda and some of its candidates. Consequently, the third party lost its ability to attract and retain popular support. Richard Hofstadter's Pulitzer Prize-winning book *The Age of Reform* provided a lasting image of the fate of most minor parties in America. "Third parties are like bees: once they sting, they die," he explained.[9] This life cycle, however, did not apply to third parties in New York State. New York election law created a fundamentally different type of minor party with distinct challenges, goals, and life expectancy.

Since New York allowed cross-endorsement, state third parties could nominate or refuse to nominate major-party candidates. This strategy gave minor parties potentially powerful leverage over major parties. They could pursue an adversarial or cooperative relationship, or they could alternate between the two. In addition, the state's ballot access requirements were modest enough to allow minor parties to retain a near-permanent place on the ballot. New York third parties did not sting once and die, but rather they buzzed about irritating major parties for decades. The advantages New York State afforded third parties helped Conservatives achieve their goal of redrawing party lines. They used the leverage that cross-endorsement furnished minor parties to pressure Republicans into becoming more ideologically consistent. In addition, since Conservatives belonged to a minor party and not the GOP, they owed no loyalty to Republicans with whom they had ideological differences. Conservatives could work openly to support like-minded Republicans and to defeat liberal Republicans. Freed from restrictions of loyalty that accompanied membership in a party, and provided the opportunities that New York provided minor parties, Conservatives enjoyed a singular position in trying to change the ideological makeup of the GOP.

The Conservative Party also benefited from its ability to generate grassroots support. The state's liberal reputation obscured its ideological fault lines. Differences between New York City and upstate New York dated back to the colonial era and had been characterized in a number of ways: urban versus rural, industrial versus agrarian, immigrant versus native-born, wet versus dry, and liberal versus conservative. The divisions within the state were never as clean as the many dichotomies made them seem. Upstate contained a number of important industrial cities such as Syracuse, Rochester, and Buffalo. At the same time, parts of New York City, such as Queens and Staten Island, saw themselves as very different from, and frequently in conflict with, Manhattan. Most importantly for a third party in search of supporters, however, New York was home to conservatives. In the decades following World War II, this conservatism expressed itself through skepticism toward many of the state's social welfare programs, especially ones that were seen as benefiting New York City residents disproportionately. A complementary belief in lower taxes and smaller state government accompanied this skepticism towards social welfare programs. These ideological conservatives lived upstate, in parts of New York City such as Queens and Staten Island, and in the growing suburbs on Long Island.

The differences between statewide and local candidates, driven by differences in the nomination process, also provided the Conservative Party with an opportunity to win popular support. New York's candidates for the House of Representatives and the state legislature needed to win party primaries to obtain their party's nomination. Statewide candidates, however, were nominated by party conventions. These conventions allowed party leaders to choose senate and gubernatorial candidates with little grassroots input. In the case of the Republican Party, nominees were often selected for their ability to attract independent and Democratic voters in New York City. GOP leaders adopted this strategy believing that party loyalty would compel most Republican voters, even those ideologically adverse to the GOP nominee, to vote for that candidate in the general election. They used this approach successfully in the 1940s and 1950s to elect statewide liberal Republicans such as Governor Thomas Dewey. So while outside observers characterized New York as liberal partly because of its statewide officeholders, the reality was that the state's undemocratic nomination process concealed significant ideological differences. Conservative Republicans frustrated by this process would provide significant grassroots support for the Conservative Party.

New York Conservatives also benefited from the presence and influence of William F. Buckley Jr. Buckley emerged as an important figure in the conservative movement in 1951 when his first book, *God and Man at Yale*, assailed his alma mater for fostering a liberalism that slighted religious faith. He cemented his leadership of the movement in 1955 when he founded the *National Review* as a forum for conservative thought and opinion. Almost immediately, the magazine became the leading publication of the conservative movement, celebrating the free market, opposing most domestic government programs, and advocating a vigorous anti-communist foreign policy. In terms of American politics, Buckley and *National Review* criticized the liberal republicanism of the Eisenhower administration and the New York GOP. They warned that the GOP's failure to present a clear ideological alternative to the Democratic Party threatened to make the party irrelevant.

Beginning in the mid-1950s, Buckley and his magazine dominated and increasingly defined conservatism in New York State. With its editorial offices in the Murray Hill section of Manhattan, *National Review* not only engaged local conservative writers and editors, it also fostered a community of conservative activists, organizers, and fundraisers. Bill Buckley's conservative network provided leadership and expertise for the Conservative Party. The network gave the party access to writers, election lawyers, campaign managers, and candidates more experienced and more accomplished than most third-party partisans. In addition, Buckley, as a national figure, offered the party entrée into the conservative movement beyond New York. He provided introductions, vouched for the upstart effort, and consistently praised the party in *National Review*, even when many national conservatives regarded it with suspicion.

Finally, New York Conservatives benefited unexpectedly from the state's liberal reputation. Conservatives outside the state did not have to be convinced that New York mattered. Their primary frustration, however, was not the state's tradition of liberal policies. Rather, conservatives across the country resented what they saw as the New York GOP's unfair influence over the national party, particularly in the presidential nominating process. They consistently pointed to the 1944 and 1948 campaigns for the GOP presidential nomination as evidence of the New York GOP's disproportionate influence over the national party. These campaigns, which matched New York governor Dewey against Ohio senator Robert A. Taft, revealed the ideological and geographical divisions within the national Republican Party. Dewey positioned himself as a proponent of "modern republicanism" and New York State as an example of this approach in action. Taft led the party's conservative wing, centered in the midwest, that rejected Dewey's eastern brand of republicanism. Taft's supporters blamed his successive losses on the New York GOP's domination of the national party. Dewey and the state GOP similarly used their influence to ensure that the 1952 presidential ticket also reflected their modern republicanism. In 1951, Dewey and his aides, including the manager of his 1948 presidential run, Herbert Brownell, met with General Dwight Eisenhower in New York to plan Eisenhower's campaign for the GOP presidential nomination against Senator Robert Taft. The 1952 race remained competitive to the convention. With the support of the New York delegation, the convention's largest, and the behind-the-scenes expertise of Herbert Brownell among others, Eisenhower finally won the GOP nomination. Taft and his conservative supporters again felt cheated by the party's eastern wing led by the New York GOP.

The presidential campaigns convinced conservatives across the country that the New York GOP was part of an "eastern establishment" that tyrannized the national Republican Party. In 1964, conservative activist Phyllis Schlafly achieved national prominence with her passionate indictment against liberal Republicans for utilizing secrecy, deceit, and character assassination to control recent GOP presidential nominations. In *A Choice Not an Echo*, Schlafly blamed a group of rich and powerful bankers, Wall Street financiers, and publishers, a group she called the "New York kingmakers," for manipulating the party behind the scenes.[10] While not all conservative Republicans accepted Schlafly's detailed conspiracy, most believed an eastern establishment unfairly dominated their party and maintained its unjust advantage through its financial resources and a biased nominating system. Like Schlafly, conservative Republicans also believed that this eastern establishment resided in New York and included, at various times, the writers, editors, and publishers of the *New York Times*, the *New York Herald Tribune*, and *Time*; the major banks and Wall Street brokerage houses; certain nongovernment organizations such as the Ford Foundation; and the foreign service community based at the United Nations and the Council of Foreign Relations. Conservative Republicans considered the New York Republican Party to be the eastern establishment's political arm, pointing to its conduct in recent presidential nominating campaigns as evidence.

Angry that New York Republicans unfairly dominated the national GOP, conservatives across the country yearned for a way to influence events within the state. The creation of the New York Conservative Party offered them that opportunity. After some initial caution, national conservatives willingly helped New York Conservatives in their struggle with the state GOP. The Conservative Party capitalized on this interest in numerous ways, including fundraising drives that stressed the state conflict's national implications. Ideological conservatives outside New York donated funds to the state party, convinced that any damage to New York liberal Republicans benefited the national conservative cause. Their donations were intended to weaken the liberal wing of the GOP and bring about the ideological reshuffling that would result in the national GOP becoming a consistently conservative party.

The state's liberal reputation also assisted the Conservative Party by magnifying the significance of its achievements. An accomplishment easily dismissed as a parochial matter deserving of little interest became important because it took place in New York. The Conservative Party consistently benefited from the conventional wisdom that it was operating within a uniformly liberal state. Every Conservative achievement was portrayed as unexpected and ground-breaking. Mayor John Lindsay's defection from the Republican Party offered a case in a point. Following Lindsay's move, the major newsweekly magazines all covered the event in depth and all characterized the event as surprising and significant since it occurred in a state as liberal as New York.[11]

The history of the New York Conservative Party in the 1960s and 1970s concerns the ordinary tasks tackled by any political party—drafting platforms, raising money, identifying candidates, and running campaigns. The party addressed these challenges relentlessly in service to its ultimate goal, a more consistently conservative GOP. That vision united candidates, attracted voters and financial donors, and even persuaded a Republican White House to side with a splinter party over the state GOP. As a result, by 1980 the Conservative Party had accomplished more than just drafting platforms, raising money, and running campaigns. It had redefined the GOP, gaining acceptance for ideological conservatives and forcing out the party's liberals. Both in New York State and nationally, the Republican Party became more consistently and more reliably conservative. New York Conservatives helped the state and the nation redraw their party lines.

ONE

A NEW PARTY

In mid-November 1960, a group of Republican Wall Street lawyers met over lunch in a Manhattan restaurant.[1] A discussion of how to respond to the recently completed presidential campaign and election topped the group's agenda. These Republicans blamed the defeat of their party's presidential candidate—Vice President Richard Nixon—on lack of support from the New York GOP and Governor Nelson Rockefeller. Additionally, they saw this act of disloyalty not as an isolated episode, but as part of the state Republican Party's long-term pattern of sabotaging alternatives to its liberal policies and candidates. Over lunch, the men debated potential ways to promote conservatism within the state. Kieran O'Doherty proposed the most radical plan—the formation of a new party, a state conservative party. O'Doherty had already discussed the idea with his brother-in-law, J. Daniel Mahoney. The two men arrived at the lunch convinced conservatives needed to create an independent party, but unsure how to proceed.

Although only Mahoney and O'Doherty supported the creation of a third party, all participants in this political discussion agreed that the liberalism of the New York GOP made life unbearable for state conservatives. While their displeasure was directed at Nelson Rockefeller, it predated the current governor. For decades, New York conservatives had bristled at the state GOP's views and methods. Prior to Rockefeller, conservatives opposed Republican Governor Thomas Dewey and his modern republicanism approach to governing. Dewey considered this approach modern because it accepted the expanded domestic role of government brought about by Franklin Roosevelt and the New Deal in the 1930s, and Republican because it stringently scrutinized government programs to protect the rights of individual citizens, a traditional goal of the GOP. Conservatives mocked Dewey for adopting so much of Democratic agenda that his modern republicanism was actually "me too republicanism."

Paralleling this conflict over the role of government was a divergence over the proper ideological character of the major parties. In contrast with most conservatives, Dewey and other liberal Republicans defended the two national parties being composed of broad ideological coalitions. In a series of lectures at Princeton University on the American political system, the governor warned his audience of the "impractical theorists" who "want to drive all moderates and liberals out of the Republican party and then have the remainder join forces with the conservative groups of the South."[2] Dewey conceded that the result would be tidier, but warned it would also doom the Republicans in every election. "It may be a perfect theory," the governor concluded, "but it would result in a one-party system and finally totalitarian government. As you may suspect, I am against it."[3]

State conservatives also objected to the way liberal Republicans achieved their political goals, believing they relied on undemocratic means. They charged that the GOP abused New York State's system for selecting statewide candidates through party conventions to ignore the wishes of conservative Republicans. In the general election, conservative Republicans were left with the unattractive alternatives of supporting a liberal Republican candidate, defecting to a usually more liberal Democratic nominee, or sitting out the election.

The ability of liberal GOP leaders to deliver statewide nominations to the candidate of their choice sparked an earlier attempt to create a conservative party. In 1956, some New York conservatives wanted to draft General Douglas MacArthur, now a New Yorker residing at the Waldorf-Astoria Hotel, to run as the GOP nominee for the state's open senate seat. Without the general's consent, the Committee of Patriots, a small conservative group run by Eli Zrake in New York City, directed this effort. Zrake ran his own public relations outfit in Brooklyn and participated in numerous conservative campaigns, including Robert Taft's 1952 race. The Committee of Patriots collected forty thousand petition signatures to nominate the still silent MacArthur, and presented its petition at the 1956 state GOP convention in Albany in early September.[4] The state committee, ignoring the petition, voted unanimously to nominate liberal New York City congressman Jacob Javits. Eli Zrake responded with a write-in effort for MacArthur in the general election that proved no more effective than the petition campaign. New Yorkers barely noticed Zrake's efforts for MacArthur as they elected Jacob Javits, a former Liberal Party nominee and proponent of modern republicanism, to the U.S. Senate. Zrake, denied an effective way to promote a conservative candidate within the GOP, began preparations to form a third party the following year. He soon suffered a fatal heart attack, and the effort to create a conservative party withered. The impetus for this conflict, however, the ability of GOP leaders to ignore conservatives when choosing statewide candidates, remained.

While conservatives' frustration with the state GOP predated Nelson Rockefeller, his emergence on the state's political scene intensified their dissatisfaction. In 1958, state GOP Chairman L. Judson Morhouse persuaded Rockefeller, who had served as an appointee in several presidential administrations but had never run for elective office, to enter the race for the Republican gubernatorial nomination. Morhouse considered Rockefeller a formidable candidate, in part because his support for New Deal programs, actively interventionist foreign policy positions, and exuberant personality meant he could win traditionally Democratic votes in New York City. Thomas Dewey had used this electoral strategy to win the governorship three times. More recently, Jacob Javits had adopted the same approach to win his senate seat in 1956. In 1958, however, conservative Republicans hoped to nominate one of their own, state senator Walter Mahoney. *National Review* endorsed Mahoney's candidacy, explaining that while the magazine had nothing against Nelson Rockefeller, he was simply not a Republican.[5] Mahoney's candidacy proved resistible to the state GOP convention, however, which nominated Rockefeller with little controversy. Rockefeller then handily defeated the Democratic incumbent, Governor Averell Harriman, in the fall election.

Rockefeller quickly became the governor conservatives had feared. An advocate of activist state government, he built new housing, authorized new roads, and revamped the state university system. To pay for these initiatives, he and a compliant state legislature raised taxes and instituted a state sales tax and a payroll withholding system. Rockefeller also quickly emerged as a power within Republican circles. He took control of the state party, replacing the existing Republican state committee with new members loyal to him. Jud Morhouse retained his job as chairman of the state GOP because of his support for Rockefeller. On the national level, Rockefeller appointed George Hinman to the Republican National Committee. Hinman, a personal friend, served as Rockefeller's go-between with the national GOP through the 1970s. Finally, Rockefeller used his great wealth to enhance his political power. The governor not only financed his own campaigns, he, along with his family, bankrolled the state GOP. This financial support encouraged loyalty from all but his bitterest enemies within the party.

As much as New York conservatives objected to these actions, they were even more troubled by Nelson Rockefeller's presidential ambitions. In his first year as governor, Nelson Rockefeller conducted a one-million-dollar publicity campaign to raise his national visibility and begin his campaign to win the presidency in 1960.[6] The governor also mobilized the state GOP in this campaign. Long Island Republican congressman Stuyvasent Wainright prepared to enter Rockefeller's name in the 1960 New Hampshire primary, and organized a movement to draft him. Chairman Morhouse traveled throughout the state and across the country to garner endorsements for the governor. Senator Jacob Javits announced that the governor was a better choice for the nomination than front-runner Vice President Richard Nixon.[7] All this effort was short-circuited, however, when, in a surprise announcement in December 1959, Rockefeller withdrew from the presidential race. The governor cited a desire to avoid an internal struggle that would harm the GOP, but observers outside the campaign speculated that he realized he could not match Nixon's support throughout the country. Despite withdrawing from the race, Rockefeller refused to endorse Nixon, the presumptive GOP nominee, and conditioned his support on the vice president's clarifying his position on various policy issues.[8] Rockefeller also prevented New York's convention delegates from supporting Nixon, and indicated his availability for a draft.[9] Faced with resistance from the leader of the New York GOP, Nixon scheduled a private meeting with Rockefeller. Immediately before the Republican national convention began in Chicago, Nixon traveled to New York City to meet with the governor. In Rockefeller's Fifth Avenue apartment, the two men discussed policy issues ranging from civil rights to national security. After several hours, Rockefeller and Nixon worked out an agreement popularly known as the "Treaty of Fifth Avenue" in honor of the meeting's location. The document detailed the policy issues on which the two men agreed, although critics charged that it seemed to reflect the governor's views, especially on civil rights. As part of this compact, Rockefeller announced his support for Nixon as the party's presidential nominee.

Conservative opposition to Nelson Rockefeller eventually spanned three decades and encompassed a variety of the governor's words and deeds. The "Treaty of Fifth Avenue" always remained a principal offense, however. Conservatives disliked the substance of the agreement because its policy positions seemed to represent a wholesale surrender to the Democratic Party. They also objected because the agreement rendered irrelevant the convention's platform committee, where they hoped to prevail. Mostly, however, they considered the agreement another example of GOP liberals, in the person of Rockefeller, unfairly dominating the party. For conservatives at war with the party's liberals, the agreement represented an act of appeasement. Barry Goldwater and other conservatives even referred to the agreement as the GOP's Munich Pact. Conservative outrage with Rockefeller extended beyond the agreement, however. Rockefeller enraged conservatives by tepidly endorsing Nixon in his campaign appearances throughout the state.[10] Richard Nixon's narrow loss to Democratic nominee John F. Kennedy in the general election magnified the significance of Rockefeller's alleged transgression. In an election that close, every variable—especially one as emotional as betrayal of the party—seemed determinative. Conservative resentment was so intense that it forced Jud Morhouse to write state party officials after the election denying that Rockefeller provided less than his full support. The chairman, however, failed to convince conservatives in New York or across the country. For them, Rockefeller's failure to support the ticket—his betrayal of the GOP—became an article of faith. When Barry Goldwater battled Rockefeller for the Republican presidential nomination in 1964, his New York State campaign organization sent state Republicans a list of Rockefeller's transgressions. Rockefeller's sabotage of the Nixon campaign topped the list.[11]

Opposition to the state GOP and Nelson Rockefeller united and energized New York conservatives, including Dan Mahoney and Kieran O'Doherty. The personal history of these two men was intertwined with the political history of New York conservatives. Mahoney and O'Doherty first met in September 1952, when a group of New York supporters of Robert Taft, disheartened by their candidate's treatment by Tom Dewey and Dwight Eisenhower, debated ways to press for a conservative agenda.[12] They shared more than a conservative political viewpoint, however. Both were Irish Catholics in their twenties from the New York City area pursuing law degrees. In 1952, O'Doherty was 26 and attending Columbia Law School. Mahoney, five years younger, was preparing to enter Columbia Law. Over the next few years, the two men became close friends, and then brothers-in-law when Dan Mahoney married Kieran O'Doherty's sister, Kathleen. By the time of that lunch in November of 1960, Mahoney had joined the large Wall Street law firm of Simpson, Thatcher, and Bartlett. O'Doherty practiced anti-trust law at Royall, Keogall, and Rogers, another distinguished Wall Street firm with connections to the Republican Party. Temperamentally, however, the men were very different. O'Doherty, more intense than his brother-in-law, reveled in the give-and-take of a political fight. Years later, William Buckley characterized him as "the sword-militant of the Conservative Party."[13] In contrast, the quieter, more low-key Mahoney adopted a more analytical approach. These differences in style paled in significance, however, to what united the two men. On a personal level, there were common background and family connection. And on the political level, there were a steadfast conservatism and a sense of frustration with the state Republican Party.

But why would these two men decide that creating a new party offered the best response to their political predicament? The answer lay in the unique structure of New York State's electoral system, which allowed a party to cross-endorse the nominee of another political party. The state's history provided numerous examples of minor parties using cross-endorsement or fusion to achieve success. Up through the 1930s, fusion operated primarily as a way to elect reform candidates in New York City by uniting Republicans and disaffected Democrats. Republicans voted for the candidate as the GOP nominee. Democrats, disaffected but unwilling to vote Republican, supported the candidate as the nominee of a temporary paper party. Fusion combined these two pools of votes and every so often elected a candidate. The technique produced a national political figure when voters elected Fiorella LaGuardia, running as the nominee of the Republican and City Fusion Parties, mayor of New York City in 1934. LaGuardia, who served as the city's mayor for over a decade, relied on a paper party that existed only for the purpose of permitting his fusion campaign. Acknowledging the flexibility of party labels in this system, the mayor bragged that he could be elected on a laundry ticket.[14]

For fusion to develop into something less transitory, however, it required a stable third party with true leaders and members. The American Labor Party (ALP), created in 1936, expanded fusion's role. Led by David Dubinsky, president of the International Ladies Garment Workers' Union, the party grew out of the desire of organized labor in New York City to support Franklin Roosevelt's re-election bid free from a Democratic Party tainted by Tammany Hall. The new party secured 275,000 votes to help Roosevelt carry the state in 1936. The ALP then began to cross-endorse acceptable candidates, usually the most liberal Democratic candidates, in state and local elections. In 1944, however, the presence of communists in the party forced some of its leaders to create an alternative minor party. David Dubinsky, with the help of fellow labor leader Alex Rose and such luminaries as Roosevelt advisor Adolf Berle and theologian Reinhold Niebuhr, founded the Liberal Party. The Liberal Party agreed with the ALP on most policy issues, but distinguished itself through opposition to communism at home and abroad. The party's close ties to unions in New York City's garment industry provided the funding and manpower that ensured its vitality.

In considering how to challenge state Republicans in the early 1960s, Mahoney and O'Doherty drew on and went beyond this history of fusion. They understood that New York State provided third parties with a uniquely hospitable environment, but also that fusion could be used far differently. At the time, fusion operated within narrow parameters. First, it mattered only in New York City. Fusion candidates in the nineteenth and early twentieth centuries existed only in New York City politics. Later, the ALP and the Liberal Party began in New York City and continued to attract the vast majority of their support there. More specifically, only opponents of Tammany Hall used fusion. In a city overwhelmingly Democratic, fusion permitted all critics of the Democratic organization to unite on election day. Second, fusion was traditionally linked to labor unions. Union dues from the New York City garment industry funded the two existing minor parties, and union workers provided the necessary manpower. Many contemporary observers considered this support essential to the parties' survival. Finally, fusion parties existed only on the ideological left. Both the Liberal and American Labor Parties were positioned to the left of the Democratic Party. Although none of these characteristics were inherently part of fusion, they defined the practice for most New Yorkers until Mahoney and O'Doherty created a third party that was statewide in appeal, independently financed, and ideologically conservative.

Eager to begin the work of creating a party, Mahoney and O'Doherty recruited four other lawyers and bankers who shared their conservative viewpoint and history of frustration with the state GOP.[15] Like the two brothers-in-law, these men were all mid-level veterans of the 1960 Nixon campaign in New York State who also blamed Nelson Rockefeller for sabotaging their candidate's chances. They all believed that a third party offered the best opportunity to punish the governor for his disloyalty and create an alternative to the state GOP.[16] Meeting twice a month, the group focused on the challenging nuts and bolts of creating a party. New York State law established two requirements to create a new party. First, the party had to gather twelve thousand signatures to place a gubernatorial candidate on the state ballot. This total needed to include fifty signatures from each of sixty-one New York counties.[17] Second, that gubernatorial candidate needed to win fifty thousand votes in the general election. The group quickly recognized the need for a statewide organization capable of canvassing for signatures and raising money.

Mahoney and O'Doherty took the most sensible course of action for any New York conservative facing such a formidable challenge: they contacted William F. Buckley Jr. By 1960, Buckley was already a leader of the conservative movement. He had authored several successful books ranging from an attack on the liberalism of higher education to a defense of Senator Joseph McCarthy. In 1955, Buckley had founded *National Review* and quickly helped it become the pre-eminent publication of conservatism. In September of 1960, Buckley had hosted the gathering of over one hundred young conservatives at his Connecticut home that led to the creation of the conservative organization Young Americans for Freedom. Most important, in the world of New York conservatives, Bill Buckley knew everyone. An earlier attempt to form a third party demonstrated his centrality to conservatism in the state. In 1957, two groups of New York conservatives looked to form a third party. Each group, unaware of the other's existence, approached Buckley for assistance. Buckley persuaded them to join forces, and oversaw their combined effort until Eli Zrake's death shut the project down. Like the leaders of those previous efforts, Mahoney and O'Doherty recognized the value of approaching Buckley with their idea. There was also a personal connection. Mahoney had met Buckley in 1954, when he had invited the young writer to speak at a forum at Columbia Law School. The event never came off, but the two men remained in contact, and Mahoney eventually introduced his brother-in-law to Buckley. Through their friendship with Buckley, Mahoney and O'Doherty also met many of New York's other leading conservatives, including William Rusher, *National Review* publisher, and Marvin Liebman, a leading conservative organizer and fund-raiser.

When Mahoney and O'Doherty appealed for help in creating a party, Buckley, along with Rusher and Liebman, agreed to host the group's meetings.[18] The three prominent conservatives also offered advice and identified others in the movement who could assist. Characterizing his involvement to a friend, Rusher explained that he offered the new party encouragement by attending planning sessions, proposing ways to proceed, and introducing potential financial supporters.[19] While Rusher and Liebman proved valuable, Buckley played a singular role. First, he used *National Review* to assist the new party. The magazine wrote approvingly of the Conservative Party from its inception. Buckley also provided the Conservative Party access to the magazine's mailing list, an extremely valuable resource for fundraising and membership drives.[20] Second, Buckley, already a public personality, generated publicity for the party. The controversial editor's appearance at an event guaranteed press coverage. Third, Buckley served as a conduit between the party and the national conservative movement. His stature in the movement allowed him to assure conservatives that the New York party was responsible and worthy of support. Buckley also introduced the party to wealthy conservative donors from around the country. Finally, Buckley and the writers and editors of *National Review* provided a model for being a conservative. Eventually, the defining characteristics of the magazine—a seriousness concerning policy issues, a willingness to denounce extremists within the conservative movement, and a special taste for battle with GOP liberals—also came to describe the party.

Mahoney, O'Doherty, and the four other members of the original group drafted a political prospectus to send to a small number of prominent conservatives, accompanied by a request for financial support and an invitation to join the party's organizing committee. Buckley, Rusher, Liebman, Frank Meyer, an editor at *National Review*, and conservative writers M. Stanton Evans and Brent Bozell reviewed the prospectus.[21] Mahoney also asked Buckley and Rusher to help identify potential recipients. "Frankly, we are short of big names, and of business and financial types, especially since the purpose of this ad hoc letterhead is to impress potential financial contributors," he complained.[22] To help with this shortage of big names, Buckley asked a number of nationally prominent conservatives to read the prospectus and consider lending their names to the letter publicly introducing the party.[23] The response, however, was disappointing. In a typical reply, Lemuel Boulware, the General Electric executive who directed Ronald Reagan's work with that company, provided a three-page, single-spaced letter explaining the folly of such an effort and advising conservatives to remain in the Republican Party.[24] Buckley relayed these disappointing replies to Mahoney, ridiculing the reasons each gave for declining, and advised him to ignore the responses. "My only position is to go ahead anyway," he wrote. "The older generation hardly qualifies, on the basis of their performance, as preceptors."[25] Buckley closed the letter with the rallying cry "Excelsior," Latin for *higher* and *ever upward*. The difficulty in finding prominent conservatives willing to sign a prospectus typified conservatives' resistance to the new party. Within the state, fusion's limited history as a weapon of Anti-Tammany, liberal parties in New York City discouraged many potential supporters. The potential for a political party without these characteristics to survive, much less bring about an ideological realignment, seemed unlikely. Beyond New York, the effort seemed like an act of disloyalty to the state and national GOP. Since virtually no one outside New York understood fusion or its history in the state, a third party appeared to be a radical and unwise undertaking.

Denied support from the established leaders of the conservative movement, O'Doherty and Mahoney turned to lesser-known conservatives. Through the fall of 1961, they contacted conservative businessmen, college professors, and writers. Buckley or Rusher usually made the initial contact, with Mahoney or O'Doherty following up. Using this approach, they assembled a ten-person organizing committee by November 1961. In a confidential letter, William Rusher characterized the group's members somewhat uncharitably as "New York conservatives of the second rank."[26] Some of these conservatives, such as lawyers Tom Bolan and Godfrey Schmidt, were veterans of the 1958 third-party effort. Others, such as novelist Taylor Caldwell and Anthony Bouscaren, who taught political science at LeMoyne College, were new to the process but equally disturbed that the state GOP effectively neutralized its conservative members. Buckley and Rusher again used their contacts to solicit money for the new party. In order to interest conservatives outside the state, they framed the issue as an opportunity to end the New York GOP's unfair domination of the national Republican Party. These confidential solicitations from Buckley and Rusher raised seven thousand dollars, enough money for O'Doherty and Mahoney to continue.[27] The process, however, took longer than the brothers-in-law originally anticipated. With the November election and December holidays approaching, the group deferred the party's public unveiling until 1962.

A PUBLIC SPECTACLE

Conservative expectations of planning a new party in seclusion did not survive long. On November 15, the Long Island paper *Newsday* exposed a year of discreet political activity with the headline "Rightists Form Anti-Rocky Party."[28] Relying on an unnamed source, *Newsday* correctly reported that the party planned to challenge the liberalism of the state GOP, but got most of the details wrong. Most prominently, the paper ran a picture of Roy Cohn, mistakenly identifying the former aide to Joseph McCarthy as a potential candidate for the party. It also incorrectly identified the party's name and vastly overstated its fundraising capacity. In the party's first public statement, O'Doherty wrote *Newsday* to outline the article's inaccuracies and to warn the GOP of overconfidence in the coming political battle.[29]

The *Newsday* revelation touched off a series of press accounts that highlighted the magnitude of the image problem Conservatives faced. This initial wave of attention uniformly portrayed the group as outside the political mainstream. The *Daily News*, New York City's most ideologically sympathetic paper, referred to the party's leaders as "some far-out conservatives."[30] More significantly, the *New York Times* reported that "[c]ertain of the reputed sponsors of the new conservative group are said to have Birch Society associations."[31] The charge referred to Frederick Reinecke, a Birch supporter and member of the party's organizing committee, who never played an active role in party operations. This and similar stories, however, revealed the new party's vulnerability to being consigned to the extreme right. The John Birch Society, a *cause célèbre* since its existence was revealed in late 1960, combined extreme anti-communism with an unshakable belief in powerful secret conspiracies. Because the society maintained complete secrecy concerning its membership and activities, press accounts speculated about a national reach and huge membership. The *Newsday* story about local conservatives secretly planning to start their own political party triggered fears of a local branch of the Birch Society.

No official relationship existed between the Conservative Party and the John Birch Society. The two organizations differed in approach, world view, and policy positions. The fledgling party also feared being associated with the Society, given its notoriety. But some conservative New Yorkers—how many was unclear—were sympathetic to the Society. They did not belong to the Society or endorse its extreme positions, but they shared its staunch anti-communism and believed the Society suffered undue criticism. The party, at this precarious stage, did not want to alienate these potential supporters. Conservatives hoped to walk the fine line that kept the party structure free from any association with the controversial organization without alienating voters sympathetic to the Society. In public, the party denied any affiliation with the John Birch Society, but refused to denounce the organization and welcomed the support of individual Society members. In private, Conservatives worked to remove any party officials with connections to or sympathies for the Society. Dan Mahoney monitored local party activities for any sign of Birch infiltration and immediately distanced the party from any Conservative official who spoke approvingly of the Society.[32]

The state Republican organization chose to ignore the new party, confident that most attempts to create third parties failed quickly and quietly.[33] A number of GOP politicians, including conservative Republican legislators and congressmen, however, condemned the new party. Conservatives expected resistance from liberal statewide Republicans, such as Rockefeller and Javits, but had hoped for acceptance from the mostly upstate and conservative members of Congress whom they supported. Party loyalty proved a more powerful force, however. Republican State Senate Majority Leader Walter Mahoney argued that a third party was unneeded, and assured his fellow conservatives their home was in the GOP.[34] Other conservatives argued that a "splinter party" would only siphon support from the GOP and elect liberal Democrats. Representative William Miller, an ideological conservative recently elected chairman of the Republican National Committee, denounced the new party as counterproductive. In April, he told

New Yorkers attending the Republican Women's Conference that "[t]he only thing you're going to accomplish by supporting this new party is the defeat of Republican candidates." "Let's go back to New York and forget about the whole thing," he suggested.[35] Given the new party's opposition to Nelson Rockefeller, some of this response was an effort to remain in the governor's good graces. Syracuse mayor Anthony Henninger immediately called Governor Rockefeller when newspaper reports implied he supported the Conservative Party. Henninger denied all the newspaper reports, insisted he was and would remain a Republican, and swore he backed the governor 100 percent.[36]

While Conservatives hoped to win the support of upstate Republican politicians, they expected opposition from liberal officeholders such as Jacob Javits, and the senator did not disappoint. He did, however, take an approach different from that of his fellow Republicans in his criticism. The senator attacked the new party not because it was unneeded or counterproductive, but because it was extreme and dangerous. Javits kicked off his re-election campaign with the charge that Conservatives were "in truth the Radical Right party of New York, similar in philosophy to the Birch Society."[37] Throughout his campaign, he characterized the party as extremist, and, revealing a misconception about conservatism in the 1960s, as isolationist. Javits's attacks were so vehement, they alarmed other Republicans. George Hinman, one of Nelson Rockefeller's senior advisors, wrote the governor about Javits's "stupid politics." "This hurts the whole ticket because you are lumped together with him," he warned.[38] Nelson Rockefeller wanted the support of conservative Republicans in his 1962 gubernatorial campaign, and in his prospective 1964 presidential campaign. As a result, the governor and most of the state GOP carefully criticized the new party in a way that would not alienate conservative Republican voters.

In 1962, New York Conservatives and Republicans worried about Senator Barry Goldwater's response to developments within the state. Representing Arizona in his second Senate term, Goldwater had emerged as the leading conservative politician through his opposition to liberal policies and ideas no matter which party endorsed them. The success of his 1960 book explaining his ideological views, *The Conscience of a Conservative*, indicated the increasing strength of the movement. Goldwater's national prominence guaranteed that if he denounced the third party, it would be effectively marginalized. If, however, the senator embraced the party, he would confer needed legitimacy. A column in a national newsmagazine brought Goldwater into the state conflict. In January 1962, *Newsweek* columnist Raymond Moley predicted the Conservative Party would soon disappear, and criticized conservatives unconcerned about the impact of a "splinter party." He advised loyalty to the GOP because "[c]onservatives should not, like the boy in Lamb's essay, burn the house to roast the pig."[39] Barry Goldwater sent Moley a complimentary telegram expressing the hope that all Republicans would follow the writer's advice.[40] William Buckley responded by sending the senator a telegram vouching for the legitimacy of the new party.[41] This telegram, like all of Buckley's communication with out-of-state politicians, stressed how the party was a necessary response to the state GOP's liberalism. He explained that the Conservative Party opposed the state GOP for betraying true Republican principles, but remained committed to assisting the national GOP. A reassured Goldwater responded with a more favorable, if still skeptical, assessment of the party. Even this partial acceptance was threatened, however, when the senator received an anonymous letter alleging a connection between the Conservative Party and the ultraright publication *Common Sense*. This time, Buckley pledged to Goldwater that the party had no connection with the "berserk right."[42]

Nelson Rockefeller also attempted to secure Goldwater as an ally in the state conflict. In June, the governor's speechwriter drafted a statement for the senator to denounce the "futile splinter movement."[43] Goldwater, however, never delivered the speech, and remained difficult to pin down on the conflict. When Goldwater told a New York congressman that he opposed the new party, a Rockefeller aide doubted that the senator was taking the same position with Conservatives.[44] In July, another Rockefeller aide anonymously attended a dinner at the Brookings Institution in Washington at which Goldwater spoke. In the question-and-answer period, the aide inquired about Goldwater's views on the new party. The senator responded that New York Conservatives should work within the GOP, but stopped short of a denunciation.[45] In September, George Hinman learned that Goldwater responded to individual inquiries about the Conservative Party with a statement that he would vote Republican if he lived in New York, but could not get Goldwater to release the letter.[46] Despite the best efforts of William Buckley and Nelson Rockefeller's staff throughout 1962, neither side in the New York battle got the help they wanted from Goldwater. The Arizona senator remained privately ambivalent and publicly silent about the new party.

Some members of the conservative movement rejected the very idea of a third party as a threat to all Republicans. In March, Douglas Caddy, national director of the newly created Young Americans for Freedom (YAF), wrote the *Wall Street Journal* warning of the dangers of conservative third parties.[47] He argued that the new state party did not promote the interests of conservatives, and called for working within the GOP. Additionally, a major conservative publication essentially imposed a news blackout. *Human Events*, a conservative Washington-based newsletter, failed to mention the party throughout 1962. When a party official traveled to the publication's Washington office to discuss this lack of coverage, the editorial staff explained that the newsletter only supported conservatives who were Republicans. The party responded with an angry letter to Frank Hanighen, the publication's editor and publisher.[48] Hanighen brushed off the complaint, explaining that

Human Events would continue to make its own evaluations.[49] The publication did not mention the new party for another two years.

Throughout this formative period, Bill Buckley's *National Review* was the party's only reliable ally in the conservative movement. The magazine consistently touted the accomplishments and significance of the party. *National Review* wrote about the party seventeen times during 1962 in articles ranging from brief status reports to a full-length piece by the party's eventual gubernatorial candidate. Addressing a national audience, the magazine always paired its support with an explanation that only the uniqueness of New York State politics made a conservative third party necessary.[50] Although Buckley, Rusher, and most of the editorial staff wanted to help the new party, one editor, James Burnham, persuaded the magazine to retain its independence.[51] At an August meeting, the editorial staff decided that the magazine would refrain from formally endorsing the party's candidates, but "would continue to look favorably on the Conservative Party, treating it as an interesting and encouraging development in our state politics."[52] Despite stopping short of formal endorsement, the level of support Buckley and his editorial staff provided New York Conservatives stood apart in a period when criticism of the party was the norm.

PETITIONS AND CANDIDATES

New York Conservatives labored to acquire the tools they needed for success: money and organization. The New York Republican Party and its candidates raised money the old-fashioned way, through major donors, especially the Rockefeller family, and large functions, such as dinners. In contrast, state conservatives used direct mail fundraising. In 1962, Marvin Liebman, one of the most prominent conservative fundraisers in the country, orchestrated a fundraising campaign using mailing lists provided free of charge from Buckley's *National Review*. In February, the party sent its first major fundraising letter, signed by three members of the organizing committee, to fifty thousand conservatives. The letter stressed the lack of opportunity ideological conservatives faced within the state Republican Party.[53] Emphasizing the mainstream nature of the venture, it identified the party's overall goal as persuading the state GOP to act like true Republicans and run more conservative candidates. The fifty thousand dollars raised by the mailing allowed the party to begin building in earnest. Mahoney and O'Doherty immediately hired a small staff and opened an office in midtown Manhattan, not far from *National Review's* offices. The party then began to establish a statewide organization by creating a network of political clubs. With a format mandated by state headquarters, these clubs used a series of committees to raise money, recruit members, and, most immediately, manage petition campaigns.[54]

Throughout most of 1962, the fledgling party worked simultaneously to create an apparatus to gather petition signatures and to field a slate of statewide candidates. Mahoney and O'Doherty considered the requirement that fifty signatures be gathered from each county as the most difficult challenge of the first year.[55] The requirement proved especially challenging because of resistance by upstate voters to the new party. The problem was not the party's conservative ideology or specific policy positions such as opposition to the state's expensive social programs. These were a natural fit for many, perhaps even a majority, of upstate voters. Rather, these voters were troubled by the fact that it was a third party advocating these ideas. Since successful third parties had always been based in New York City, the rest of the state had limited experience with them. Many upstate voters supported the Conservative Party's positions, but viewed the party itself as a betrayal of the GOP.

To oversee the petition campaign, the party hired James Leff, a lawyer who specialized in state election law and had launched successful petition challenges. Mahoney and O'Doherty expected the Republican Party to use New York's byzantine election law to challenge the signatures from the state's smallest counties. New York law stipulated that if the total number of valid signatures in any one county fell below fifty, the entire campaign failed. In addition, state courts had a history of invalidating petitions for the slightest deviation from legal requirements, including matters as trivial as the color of the paper. Hoping to avoid a Republican challenge, the Conservative Party went to court to challenge the requirement of fifty signatures from each county. Leff argued that the statute violated the voting guarantees of the federal and state constitutions by allowing any one county to veto a nominee chosen by the rest of the state.[56] The attempt failed, however, when a State Supreme Court judge upheld the law as a reasonable way for candidates to demonstrate support throughout the state.[57] With the county requirement upheld, the Conservative Party devised and implemented a plan to gather enough signatures to withstand Republican objections. As insurance against likely challenges, Leff wanted at least two hundred and fifty signatures from each county, a goal later reduced to two hundred. Mahoney, O'Doherty, and Leff used the newly created clubs to identify and train volunteers in every county on the proper procedure for collecting the signatures. Looking back, Leff estimated that twenty thousand volunteer hours went into the petition drive.[58]

Success in a petition drive satisfied only the first requirement of New York State election law. The party also needed its gubernatorial nominee to receive fifty thousand votes. Conservatives eventually decided to run candidates for the five statewide offices: governor and lieutenant governor, which were teamed, attorney general, comptroller, and senator. Given the other demands of the year, the party decided against running congressional or legislative candidates. The candidate recruitment process was extremely informal. Mahoney and O'Doherty identified potential nominees and approached them about running for office. Despite the ease of the recruiting process, the party struggled to recruit candidates. During the previous year, Mahoney and O'Doherty had assured backers that several prominent conservatives were considering running for office as Conservative nominees. These potential candidates, however, all found reasons to decline the party's nomination.

Mahoney and O'Doherty eventually recruited Robert Pell, a former career foreign service officer, as the Conservative Party's senate nominee. At the time, Pell taught at Fordham University and served as an editorial consultant to the magazine *America*. When several national conservative journalists praised Pell's distinguished career, state Republicans began to investigate him.[59] Their investigation confused the candidate with another Robert Pell who also taught at Fordham University and who had registered to vote in New York only in 1960. The defective investigation proved irrelevant, however, when Pell resigned the Conservative nomination, citing "differences of opinion as to the conduct of the campaign."[60] In the statement released by party headquarters, he expressed support for the Conservative Party, but offered no explanation of his decision. Kieran O'Doherty refused to elaborate, saying only that Pell and the party had agreed not to air their differences.

The situation deteriorated further when Pell became openly critical of the Conservative Party and its leaders. In a statement provided to his hometown paper, the *Ticonderoga Sentinel*, he called the Conservative Party a "shadow party" and urged conservatives to reject the new party and remain within the GOP.[61] An accompanying *Sentinel* editorial linked the party to the John Birch Society and called on members to "quit this fanatical group."[62] Over the next few weeks, Pell confirmed that his decision was due to the party's relationship with the John Birch Society. The Conservative Party denied the charge, but offered little insight into the controversy. In a bulletin to the party's club chairmen, Dan Mahoney reported that Pell admitted that other considerations prompted his withdrawal. "We had a gentleman's agreement with Mr. Pell not to discuss these considerations publicly," Mahoney explained, "which we will honor as long as it remains possible for us to do so."[63] Pell soon ended his criticism of the party and the controversy disappeared.

The "considerations" that ended Pell's campaign remained undisclosed, but involved the candidate's medical history. GOP Chairman Jud Morhouse attributed Pell's resignation to Birch Society involvement with the Conservative Party, but also claimed that "when Pell indicated his determination to resign from the Party he was threatened with the possibility that embarrassing details of a previous illness would be released to Walter Winchell in an effort to discredit him."[64] William Rusher's history of the conservative movement later recounted the dismay of Conservative Party leaders when they discovered that an unnamed Conservative Party senate candidate with a foreign service background had "years earlier, twice voluntarily committed himself to a mental hospital."[65] Rusher implied the candidate's condition could not be kept secret because the lawyer who handled his hospital commitments served as Javits's campaign manager. The truth remains murky. Faced with Pell's Birch Society charge, the Conservative Party may have threatened to expose his medical record. Or, Pell may have cried "John Birch Society" to punish the party for dropping him as a result of his mental health history. Whichever side prompted the incident, it ended in a stalemate. Both sides upheld the gentlemen's agreement.

The Pell fiasco threatened the Conservative Party's electoral prospects. It confirmed all the negative images—disorganized, secretive, extremist—that the party struggled to overcome at this early stage. In October, Monroe County Conservative Party chairman Raymond Snider publicly resigned, citing disillusionment with the party's leaders and policies. He characterized his resignation as in keeping with Pell's withdrawal.[66] While the Snider resignation attracted little attention statewide, it led a Rochester newspaper to editorialize that the spreading disillusionment throughout the Conservative Party demonstrated the wisdom of rejecting the third party.[67]

Following Pell's resignation, the party needed another senate nominee. With few options and little time, it turned to Kieran O'Doherty. He resisted, citing his inexperience, youth, and other party obligations. On July 21, however, following a meeting at former New Jersey governor Charles Edison's apartment, O'Doherty acquiesced. Conservatives respected Edison for his record in New Jersey and his brief tenure as secretary of the Navy in 1940. But because he had been out of politics for almost two decades, Edison was of little use to the party beyond conservative circles. Several weeks earlier, Syracuse businessman David Jaquith agreed to run for governor on the Conservative ticket. Also initially hesitant given his limited involvement in politics, Jaquith succumbed to the blandishments of former Governor Edison, Eddie Rickenbacker, and the rest of the party's leaders over lunch. The *New York Times* ran the story on the front page with excerpts from Jaquith's statement.[68] With Jaquith and O'Doherty, the party finally had the major candidates it needed for the fall election. The recruitment process, however, revealed the party's inexperience in practical politics and its vulnerability to charges of extremism.

A REPUBLICAN CHALLENGE

Leaders of the New York GOP realized that simply having Republican elected officials denounce the new party was proving ineffective. Despite a unanimously negative response from Republicans, Conservatives had fielded a slate of candidates and were preparing to gather petition signatures. Republican state party chairmen discussed the problem at a regional meeting in July 1962.[69] Jud Morhouse told his colleagues that he feared additional criticism of Conservatives would offend some Republicans and produce sympathy for the new party. He also advised his colleagues to learn from

New York's failure to make ballot access more difficult. The GOP also sent local Republican organizations lists of Conservative clubs with a request to "please investigate and send us data and background material on the leaders."[70] This covert operation produced less than earth-shattering information. Two Monroe County Republican officials, for example, surreptitiously attended a Conservative Party meeting in Rochester. At a meeting hosted by Kieran O'Doherty, the infiltrators were surprised to find "most of the people were articulate, earnest, well-dressed and mature."[71] The group then spent the evening complaining about the state Republican Party without identifying any particular plan of action.

By the summer of 1962, GOP leaders settled on petition challenges as the best opportunity to derail the new party. Initially, Republicans hoped to prevent the Conservatives from gathering the required signatures in several counties. Morhouse sent Rockefeller aide Robert McManus a list of the counties with the smallest vote total. He explained that they "would be the hardest counties for splinter party advocates to gather petition signatures."[72] Republican leaders soon concluded, however, that the Conservative petition campaign was aggressive enough to guarantee the fifty signatures needed from every county. As a result, Republicans planned to selectively challenge and invalidate petition signatures. To create the proper public environment for these challenges, Republicans began to attack the Conservative petition campaign. On September 13, Morhouse charged Conservatives with running a campaign corrupted by Democratic Party and John Birch Society assistance in the collection of signatures.[73] The chairman provided no specific examples of either the Democratic Party or Birch Society role to support his charge.

On September 19, the Conservative Party filed forty-four thousand petition signatures, over three and half times the number required. This number, while insignificant in the context of a state with over seventeen million residents, demonstrated that enough conservative Republicans were alienated from the state GOP to form a third party. There were also enough signatures to seemingly assure success. Later, James Leff estimated that 78 percent of the signatures were safe from challenge.[74] The Republicans responded immediately. Morhouse sent a memo to GOP county chairmen with the names of the petition signers from their county and instructions on how to begin challenges. He asked the chairmen for "help to keep this party from getting on the ballot."[75] The memo listed fourteen possible reasons that a signer could renounce his or her signature. The Republican plan asked county chairmen to select the most appropriate factor when drafting an affidavit. Meanwhile, GOP lawyers scrutinized the petitions for possible errors that could invalidate the petitions. Morhouse reportedly hired a team of outside experts to examine the petitions in what one newspaper account characterized as "a massive GOP drive to knock the Conservative Party slate . . . off the November 6th election ballot."[76] On September 25, Morhouse submitted this material to the court with the request that the petitions be thrown out due to a pattern of error and misrepresentation.

Dan Mahoney asked local party officials to report all Republican efforts to challenge petitions in their county. Mahoney also directed these local officials "to keep a white light of publicity and protest playing on this spectacle."[77] Conservatives hoped to create a public backlash by accusing Republicans of conducting a campaign of intimidation. As part of this public relations campaign, Mahoney claimed that Republicans were using state government departments to threaten petition signers with economic retaliation if they did not recant.[78] The Conservative comptroller nominee charged that Rockefeller used his banking connections in New York State to foreclose mortgages on petition signers.[79] Since most of these allegations relied on anonymous information, they were unverifiable. Still, the campaign proved effective. By casting the GOP as a bully intent on derailing the democratic process, Conservatives used their relative weakness to generate sympathy. The state Democratic Party chairman called on Republicans to answer the charges of coercion and intimidation.[80] By late September, newspaper editorials urged the GOP to end its challenge.

The furor over the petition challenges threatened to impact Republican candidates in the coming election. With his own re-election campaign potentially affected, Rockefeller decided to end the controversy by dropping the challenge. On October 1, Chairman Morhouse withdrew the Republican challenge to Conservative Party petitions. He blamed time constraints, arguing the schedule did not permit a sufficient number of signatures to be invalidated.[81] In reality, Rockefeller and the Republican Party decided to cut their losses. With over forty-four thousand signatures on the petitions, only a full-scale challenge that relied on extremely technical violations could invalidate the petitions. This type of challenge would only increase the negative publicity being heaped on the GOP. Perhaps such a challenge could have been waged against a group seen as politically extreme. But the GOP had not managed to define the new party in this way. As result, Rockefeller dropped the challenge in order to put the party's candidates, himself included, in the best position for the election. By outmaneuvering the Republicans in their first battle, Conservatives guaranteed themselves a place on the November ballot.

THE FIRST ELECTION

For most of 1962, Dan Mahoney and Kieran O'Doherty focused the party's resources on the petition campaign. As a consequence, Conservatives neglected the campaigns of statewide candidates. Kieran O'Doherty, the party's senate candidate, did not begin campaigning in earnest until the petition challenge failed in mid-October. When O'Doherty did become a full-time candidate, he attacked Jacob Javits for a less than vigorous prosecution of the

Cold War, for supporting John Kennedy's New Frontier legislation, but most of all for a poltical career of "un-Republican activity."[82] When the Cuban missile crisis erupted during the closing weeks of the campaign, O'Doherty also criticized Kennedy's blockade of the island as too little too late.[83] But the candidate struggled to keep the focus of his abbreviated campaign on these issues. In the week prior to the election, press attention focused on the fact that he had drawn a salary as a party official for most of the year.[84]

David Jaquith's gubernatorial campaign fared little better. The president of a steel-fabricating company, Jaquith devoted only one-third of his time to campaigning until the final month, and only two-thirds during that month. As a candidate, he charged that the state's high taxes put Nelson Rockefeller in conflict with the ideals of the GOP and created a hostile business environment. Jaquith's and O'Doherty's campaigns reflected the party's policy agenda by stressing opposition to centralized government and deficit spending while advocating lower taxes and the devolution of political power to the local level. Both candidates also struggled to keep the focus of their campaigns on public policy. Jaquith's political inexperience showed in his inability to steer clear of the John Birch issue. When asked about the Society at a rally, Jaquith replied that he hoped his campaign would merit the support of some of its members.[85] Jaquith's failure to distance himself from the Society ensured that the limited press coverage he received concerned his relationship with the Society. The controversy forced the party to continually explain that while it refused to ban Society members from joining the party, it had no relationship with the John Birch Society.[86] Jaquith soon added this explanation to his campaign literature.[87] Still, accounts of his candidacy often ignored this distinction, simply stating that Jaquith welcomed John Birch Society support.

In 1962, the Conservative Party struggled with candidates who were unknown and inexperienced, with little money or time for campaigning, and policies that failed to capture the public's attention. The petition campaign sapped time and effort from the party's ability to raise money or promote its candidates. In the weeks before the election, money grew so tight that the party fired half of its headquarters staff.[88] In addition, press coverage seldom presented the candidates in a flattering light. The big New York City daily papers and most smaller upstate papers were hostile to the Conservative Party. One exception was the *Syracuse Post-Standard*, which prominently featured its hometown candidate, David Jaquith. *National Review* also remained a vocal advocate, but the magazine reached only ideological conservatives. Without money for print, radio, or television advertisements, the campaigns were limited to appearances in front of the party faithful or on public affairs programs. Running against these restricted campaigns, Rockefeller and Javits never responded directly to the attacks launched by Jaquith and O'Doherty.

One bright spot for Conservatives occurred at their only large rally of the campaign, held in New York City's Madison Square Garden in late

October. The rally initially seemed ill-fated. Conservatives began selling tickets for the event only after the petition campaign was resolved in early October. In addition, the rally was held on the night President Kennedy addressed the country on the Cuban missile crisis. Even though organizers delayed the event until after the president's speech, a sizable crowd—estimated at nine thousand by the *New York Times* and at twelve thousand by Mahoney—attended the event to hear a series of speeches attacking New York Republicans.[89] Addressing the events of that October, Kieran O'Doherty charged that liberal Republicans' failure to present a meaningful alternative to Democrats by vigorously prosecuting the Cold War had led to the problems in Cuba.[90] Several newspapers covered the event and expressed surprise at the party's being able to pull off a full-scale political rally under the circumstances.[91]

Another high point for the party resulted from a Republican misstep. In mid-August, Jud Morhouse wrote GOP county chairmen with a plan to appeal to potentially disaffected Republicans. Morhouse sent the chairmen a list of twenty-eight items "for your use in talking to people who feel the Governor is strictly a Liberal."[92] Along with this catalogue of ways Rockefeller saved taxpayer money, the state chairman advised that the information "must be used cautiously and should not be published because we do not want to emphasize the conservative side so much that we lose other votes." The plan fell apart when a GOP official leaked the memo to David Jaquith.[93] On September 19, Jaquith revealed the secret memo at a Queens rally, taunting the governor before a partisan crowd.[94]

Morhouse's memo reflected Rockefeller's strategy to keep conservative Republicans loyal to the GOP. Rockefeller adopted this strategy partly because he wanted a significant statewide re-election victory. Looking ahead to running for president in 1964, he also hoped to neutralize the charge that a portion of his own party would not support him. Consequently, Rockefeller increased the visibility of conservative Republicans during the campaign. He chose his chief antagonist within the state party, Walter Mahoney, as the keynote speaker at the GOP convention. The state GOP also sent out a letter, signed by Mahoney, to every person who signed the Conservative Party petition. Mahoney's letter urged these voters not to splinter the Republican Party since it was the only means of achieving conservative goals. It concluded with the emotional exhortation, "So, come, your place is with me and our Governor. Take your place with self-esteem and honor!"[95] Finally, in the week prior to the election, Rockefeller brought in the country's number one Republican to counter the Conservative appeal. On October 29, former President Dwight Eisenhower addressed a Republican dinner of over seven thousand five hundred party faithful in Syracuse. Press reports speculated that the GOP chose the city to diminish Conservative gubernatorial nominee Jaquith's appeal in his hometown. Eisenhower urged the audience to defend the two-party system and not waste votes on "splinter groups that weaken both parties."[96] A *New York Times* editorial quoted the former president and urged voters to reject Conservatives' "willfully destructive course."[97]

On election day, both Conservatives and Republicans accomplished their principal goals. New York Conservatives succeeded in officially establishing a third party until the next gubernatorial election in 1966. Their gubernatorial candidate, David Jaquith, received just over one hundred and forty thousand votes, greater than the fifty thousand required for official status, but far short of the three hundred thousand predicted by the candidate.[98] At the same time, the New York Republican Party enjoyed an almost complete sweep of the year's races. The party won at every level of state and federal office. It maintained control of both houses of the state legislature and sent all of its members of the House of Representatives back to Washington. Nelson Rockefeller won re-election easily over his lackluster Democratic opponent. The governor's victory margin, however, was smaller than in 1958. In the senate race, Jacob Javits won a landslide victory with a margin of a million votes over his Democratic opponent. O'Doherty's late-starting campaign received just over one hundred thousand votes. Like David Jaquith, O'Doherty drew the bulk of his support from Queens and Staten Island, the most ideologically conservative parts of New York City, and Nassau and Suffolk Counties on Long Island. These areas contained a number of traditionally Republican voters disturbed by the GOP's slighting of conservative concerns. In addition, this part of the state had the most experience with previous third-party efforts. As a result, the idea of fusion did not seem as completely alien as it did to many upstate voters. Conservatives made modest inroads in these areas because they contained a pool of voters supportive of the party's goals—reducing the size of state government, lowering taxes, shifting power to the local level—and of its means—the creation of a minor party.

Conservatives claimed victory in the election, pointing to the party's new official status and Rockefeller's reduced margin of victory. A few news accounts supported this interpretation, including one by a conservative columnist who speculated—without any evidence—that Rockefeller-directed fraud depressed this new party's vote.[99] The editors of *National Review* argued that by reducing Rockefeller's margin, the Conservative Party "has placed an obstacle in Rockefeller running for the Republican nomination as an out-and-out Liberal."[100] Most accounts, however, were far less positive. The *New York Times* stressed that Jaquith's vote total was far less than many, including the candidate himself, had predicted.[101] In his *New Yorker* column, Richard Rovere wrote that, in this first test of ultraconservatism in the state, the new party fell short of attracting enough support to change any politician's mind.[102]

Republicans publicly endorsed this view that the GOP had triumphed in the election. Nelson Rockefeller's 1964 campaign biography boasted that the governor stood up to the far right and exposed its weakness.[103] Following the election, however, Jud Morhouse asked the party's county chairmen for an explanation of Rockefeller's reduced margin of victory. The confidential responses indicated that the GOP needed to be concerned about the now-official Conservative Party, especially in parts of upstate where the trend was more worrisome than the Conservative vote count. The Schenectady County chairman speculated that all of the new party's votes came from Rockefeller supporters.[104] Oswego County's GOP chairman complained that the third party's campaign tapped into conservative sentiment in his area.[105] He also protested that while the new party had no money, it received daily publicity by flooding the local newspapers with letters to the editor. Chemung County's chairman advised Morhouse that he had no adequate answer to the Conservative charge that there were no significant differences between the major parties.[106]

Conservatives ended 1962 successful, if just barely, in all of their critical undertakings. They attracted enough financial support, assembled enough of a statewide organization, collected enough petition signatures, and received enough votes to create a third party. The pressure of all these tasks in the same year limited the level of success achieved in any one. Fortunately for the party, however, the future did not present the same set of diverse challenges. The party's lack of acceptance remained a problem, however. State and national Republican politicians, and most out-of-state conservatives, denounced the new party. The Conservative Party needed to convince members of all these groups of the legitimacy of their effort. And it needed to win much greater support from the state's voters. Barely acknowledging the new Conservative challenge, New York Republicans had won election at every level of public office, and, as the year came to a close, the state GOP looked forward to the next presidential election when its leader, Nelson Rockefeller, would run for the White House.

TWO

JOINING THE MOVEMENT

The New York Conservative Party garnered enough political support in 1962 to guarantee its official existence until the next gubernatorial election. Numerous challenges remained, however, for the party to progress from merely meeting the state's electoral requirements for a party to actually influencing the New York GOP. With two years until the next election, the party focused on winning approval among conservatives nationally and within the state. The party needed to reassure national conservatives about the wisdom of working outside the GOP. Within New York, Conservative leaders attempted to court officeholders and politicians in the state GOP whom they saw as ideologically compatible. Party loyalty, however, proved a barrier to achieving these alliances. The party met with more success, however, when the 1964 presidential campaign allowed it to demonstrate its value to conservatives outside the state who were intent on electing Barry Goldwater president. This acceptance proved a critical first step in the Conservative Party's bringing about political change.

PARTY TRUMPS IDEOLOGY

A week after the 1962 election officially certified the Conservative Party, Dan Mahoney wrote the party's club chairmen to congratulate them. He warned them, however, to remain vigilant during the coming year. "It is easy to stir up enthusiasm before elections," he cautioned, "[b]ut the day-to-day drudgery is what wins them."[1] The Conservative Party faced fewer challenges in 1963 than it had the previous year when its existence depended on simultaneously raising money, establishing local clubs, managing a petition drive, and running statewide electoral campaigns. Party leaders identified only two principal goals for the new year: first, Conservatives needed to convert their clubs throughout the state into a more formal political organization; second, the party needed to create alliances with individual Republican politicians. During the previous year, every elected Republican official, including those who were ideologically conservative, condemned the new party. Conservatives needed to find some friends in the state GOP, especially since they hoped to cross-endorse the majority of Republican legislators and congressmen in 1964.

The party quickly began rechartering its clubs in accordance with state law. New York required each club to approve by-laws, elect party officials, apply for a formal charter, and identify a minimum number of party members in each of the state's twelve thousand election districts. A financially strapped state headquarters generated publicity by staging public enrollment ceremonies with prominent supporters such as former New Jersey Governor Charles Edison. This campaign registered over ten thousand party members in 1963, with the largest number coming from the same parts of New York City and its suburbs that had provided electoral strength in 1962.[2] These residents of Nassau and Suffolk Counties on Long Island and in Queens and Staten Island in New York City tended to be white, middle-class, and former members of the Republican Party.[3] Subsequent academic research demonstrated that individuals who joined the party did so for the reasons articulated by Conservative leaders, as an act of protest against the state GOP's liberalism or because the new party more closely matched their ideological views.[4] While the GOP's enrollment of 2.8 million, and even the Liberal Party's eighty thousand members, dwarfed the Conservative total, the number was sufficient to allow the party to create formal county organizations in a number of key areas.

Conservative leaders expected the party's second goal, forming alliances with individual Republicans, to be easier. Having survived GOP attacks in 1962, Conservatives expected to find ideologically compatible Republicans more receptive. The GOP, however, had not accepted the existence of the new party. Publicly, Governor Nelson Rockefeller said little about Conservatives, dismissing the new party as an unimportant factor in the state's politics when the press asked.[5] In reality, Rockefeller and GOP leaders searched for ways to neutralize the potential danger of a new party. In early 1963, after traveling through the state to speak with party leaders, a GOP official warned that the governor's electoral base was eroding partly because "the Conservative Party is making great strides and is attracting an increasing number of Republicans, both young and old, to its ranks."[6] This threat prompted several GOP politicians to explore changes to state election law intended to threaten the new party. Republican Congressman John Pillion recommended the ultimate sanction, a statewide fusion ban. A month after the 1962 election, Pillion wrote Nelson Rockefeller, Lieutenant Governor Malcolm Wilson, and several other Republicans leaders proposing state legislation to end cross-endorsement.[7] Wilson, aware of state courts' skepticism toward fusion bans, expressed concern about the plan's constitutionality, but promised that his staff would work on developing something "to eliminate the present unwholesome situation."[8] Rockefeller forwarded Pillion's proposal to the relevant Assembly committee, but the legislature never considered the proposal.[9]

In February, however, the state assembly considered an alternative way to counteract the Conservative challenge when it took up a bill increasing the number of votes a party needed for official status from fifty thousand to one hundred twenty-five thousand. The bill passed in the Assembly on a straight party vote with every Republican voting in favor. This unanimous Republican support demonstrated that GOP leaders, most importantly Assembly Speaker Joseph Carlino, backed the measure. Dan Mahoney contended Conservatives could meet the bill's higher threshold, but also called the measure "a clearly hostile act by an important component of the New York Republican Party."[10] Conservatives warned GOP leaders that if the measure became law, they would be forced to field challengers to all Republican incumbents in future elections. For State Senate Majority Leader Walter Mahoney, the legislation went too far in its efforts to make life difficult for the new party. Mahoney assured Conservative Party leaders that the senate would not pass the measure. He proved correct; the bill died in committee.

Walter Mahoney and a few other Republicans offered some encouragement to the Conservative Party. In June 1963, Conservatives announced that Walter Mahoney planned to attend the party's first anniversary dinner that fall. Conflicting interpretations of this first official contact between the two parties quickly emerged. Since Mahoney's appearance had been approved by the state GOP chairman, most commentaries cast the state senator as a missionary. A *New York Times* editorial praised Mahoney as the right choice to bring wayward Conservatives back into the GOP fold.[11] Conservatives, confident they did not require saving, offered a contrasting interpretation. *National Review* touted Mahoney's appearance as "the effective end of the boycott against the Conservative Party by the official GOP."[12] Mahoney's speech at the party's dinner fell somewhere between these two interpretations. He encouraged the crowd by admitting that Republicans had to acknowledge that the Conservative Party was a fact of life. Overall, however, he cautioned the new party to back Republican candidates and avoid acting as a spoiler in future elections. The Conservative Party, eager for acceptance from Republicans, misrepresented Mahoney's message. It publicized the majority leader's circumscribed acceptance of the new party, but ignored his call to support all GOP candidates.[13] Earlier that year, Representative Katherine St. George offered Conservatives similar advice. In January, speaking at a national conservative conference held by *Human Events* in Washington, D.C., St. George advised conference attendees that, in the practical world of politics, they had to support candidates with less than perfect ideological credentials.[14] She outlined the political situation in New York and urged the Conservative Party to recognize reality and back all GOP candidates. Again, the party misrepresented the message. Conservatives consistently emphasized St. George's desire "to see after Republicans' names R-C, which in this instance will mean Republican and Conservative."[15] They neglected to mention that she based her hope on Conservatives simply endorsing every Republican candidate. St. George and Walter Mahoney demonstrated the continued Republican resistance to the Conservative Party. Despite their natural ideological connection to the new party, neither offered Conservatives any support. Instead, they counseled the party to support Republican candidates uncritically. Conservatives heard—or at least repeated—only selected aspects of the Republican response. In its desire to nurture a developing relationship with the state GOP, the Conservative Party mischaracterized the willingness of some Republicans to accept Conservative support as a coalition between the two parties.

Congressman Steven Derounian learned the necessity of caution when dealing with the controversial new party. Dan Mahoney, now Conservative chairman, cultivated a personal relationship with the ideologically conservative politician from Long Island. Beginning in January 1963, the two met in Washington and New York on various matters of mutual interest, such as arranging for a party official to testify before a House committee.[16] In the summer of 1963, Mahoney proposed a meeting between Conservative Party leaders and members of the Republican House delegation.[17] The meeting provided a chance for Conservative leaders to develop personal relationships with members of the state's Republican delegation. Derounian agreed to host the meeting at his Capitol Hill office on August 26. A newspaper reporter, however, learned of this plan and crashed the meeting. The meeting became a major story across the state.[18] The *New York Times* characterized it as a threat to Rockefeller's presidential campaign and reported that several congressmen arrived at the meeting unaware of the participation of Conservative Party leaders.[19] Two days later, the *Times* printed a blistering editorial charging that the Conservative Party and Derounian tricked the state's congressmen into attending. The editorial concluded that the meeting confirmed Senator Javits's assessment that Conservatives were "in truth the Radical Right party of New York, similar in philosophy to the Birch Society."[20] The Conservative Party and Congressman Derounian wrote letters protesting the *New York Times* editorial. The party's letter, drafted anonymously by Bill Buckley, complained that the paper had smeared Conservatives with the Birch label.[21] Derounian's far less combative letter downplayed the significance of the meeting and expressed surprise at the intensity of the paper's reaction.

Derounian wanted Conservatives to display the loyalty to the GOP that Katherine St. George and Walter Mahoney had also advocated. The congressman wanted the new party to abandon its plan to run any challengers to Republican candidates in his home of Nassau County. Conservatives considered these challenges necessary, however, given that all GOP candidates in the county accepted Liberal Party endorsement. Party leaders denounced that alliance for its ideological implications. They also feared the arrangement was the first step in a gubernatorial run by Joseph Carlino, state assembly speaker and chairman of the Nassau County GOP. At the August meeting in his Washington office, Derounian asked the party not to run its own candidates. Mahoney made only minor concessions. Derounian tried again to persuade Conservatives to back down at a party dinner in October. The lobbying effort failed, however, and Conservatives fielded challengers in Nassau County elections that year. Although Republican-Liberal candidates easily won election, Conservatives claimed victory because their candidates out polled their opponents on the Liberal line. "The attempted Liberal Party invasion of the Nassau County Republican Party has been smashed on the beach," Dan Mahoney hyperbolically claimed.[22]

A NEW OPPORTUNITY

Throughout 1963, New York Republicans and Conservatives planned for the following year's presidential campaign. State Republicans knew the 1964 campaign offered an excellent prospect for Governor Nelson Rockefeller to win the White House. Conservatives looked to a run by Arizona Senator Barry Goldwater to promote the cause of conservatism in the country and their party's fortunes in New York. A poll of Conservative Party leadership found 93 percent backing Goldwater for president, with the remaining percentage supporting former vice president and noncandidate Richard Nixon. The state's governor did not register any support.[23] Shortly after the 1962 election, the Conservative Party heralded its ability to influence national politics by denying the state's electoral votes to any Republican presidential nominee it considered unacceptable. Dan Mahoney wanted the party to attempt to veto any unacceptable Republican nominee in 1964. "Our maximum goal will be to achieve this power, and use it to win the Republican nomination for a real conservative (Barry Goldwater, for example)," he explained to his club chairmen.[24] An April 1963 fundraising letter stressed the party's ability to influence the GOP presidential nomination in 1964 as a means of enticing out-of-state donors.[25] This claim of potential influence was at best unproven. When one contributor attempted to inquire about specifics, Mahoney responded that the party was "in a position to be extraordinarily helpful" to Goldwater in securing the nomination.[26]

Throughout 1963, Conservatives assisted the Draft Goldwater Committee headed by former Cornell University professor F. Clifton White and based in midtown Manhattan. When the committee began a petition campaign urging Goldwater to run, the Conservative Party mobilized its clubs. Although the committee initially addressed its correspondence to the "Constitution Party," Conservatives did not allow hurt feelings to dampen their enthusiasm.[27] Their work made New York the leading state in collecting petition signatures. The clubs strongly supported the committee's "Draft

Goldwater" rally in Washington, D.C. New York sent forty-three busloads of Goldwater supporters to the rally, the most in the nation. The party also sold Goldwater campaign material as a way to generate revenue and "promote 'grass roots' Goldwater sentiment in New York State."[28] On a more personal level, the Conservative Party enjoyed a connection with the Draft Goldwater organization, since longtime supporter William Rusher served on its executive committee. After Rusher introduced Mahoney to Clif White, the Conservative chairman joined the Goldwater campaign. By the fall of 1963, Mahoney was providing political intelligence to White.[29]

The 1964 presidential campaign represented an opportunity for the new party to win acceptance from a national conservative movement that had initially regarded it with skepticism. Conservatives across the country supported Barry Goldwater, but New York Conservatives were in a unique position to assist the senator's campaign by frustrating the ambitions of his opponent, Nelson Rockefeller. Their experience as residents of New York ensured their judgment of their governor carried special weight outside the state. To capitalize on its status, the party sent its clubs a list of all newspapers in New Hampshire with instructions to begin a letter-writing campaign criticizing Rockefeller.[30] National conservatives began to accept the party once they realized its unique ability to damage Rockefeller. While *Human Events* still failed to mention the Conservative Party, its executive publisher, James Wick, asked the party for its file on the governor. "Now is the time for all of us to prevent Nelson Rockefeller from getting the Republican nomination," Wick explained. "I am sure that you will play a big part in that activity." Mahoney immediately sent Wick the party's file.[31] The publisher's appeal for assistance represented an early stage in the conservative movement's acceptance of the new party.

The Conservative Party also carefully limited its anti-Rockefeller alliances to mainstream conservatives in the GOP. Kent Courtney ran the Conservative Society of America based in New Orleans, an overtly segregationist organization. Courtney issued a "white paper" criticizing Nelson Rockefeller for financially supporting civil rights groups and for dictating foreign policy through the Council of Foreign Relations.[32] He hoped to unite all of the country's conservative third parties into a national party that Goldwater could use to run as a third-party presidential candidate if the GOP failed to nominate him in 1964. Mainstream conservatives rejected the Society because of its extreme views, especially on civil rights. In April, Courtney wrote William Buckley inviting the New York Conservative Party to join the alliance.[33] Buckley forwarded the letter to Mahoney, who firmly declined the offer.[34] The party wanted to work with the national GOP, not a fringe group like Courtney's organization.

As the Conservative Party worked for Goldwater, Nelson Rockefeller began preparations to run for president. By the spring of 1963, with a campaign organization assembled, Rockefeller campaigned across the country. He actively pursued the support of ideological conservatives, denying he was a liberal and dismissing such labels as anachronistic.[35] Rockefeller soon abandoned this campaign strategy, however. The trigger event was his May 4 marriage to Margaretta Fitler Murphy, commonly known as Happy. With both bride and groom recently divorced from first marriages that had produced children, the wedding created immediate controversy. Many national conservatives used the marriage to savage their political adversary. *Human Events*, for example, ran numerous stories, including a report that 90 percent of Protestant clergymen polled considered the governor's remarriage a legitimate campaign issue.[36] The Conservative Party, however, remained silent throughout the controversy, content to allow national conservatives to make this case against the governor. The party called no press conferences, sponsored no rallies, and instituted no letter-writing campaigns expressing outrage. Instead, it remained in the background as the governor's remarriage generated criticism.

After months of conservative vitriol, Nelson Rockefeller lashed out. On July 14, following a combative Young Republicans' national convention, the governor condemned conservatism and its proponents within the party. He warned that the far right threatened to subvert and destroy the Republican Party. A front page *New York Times* article called Rockefeller's speech a declaration of war on the party's right wing.[37] This statement ended the governor's overtures to GOP conservatives. It also guaranteed a divisive nomination battle with Barry Goldwater. The Conservative Party reacted immediately, criticizing Rockefeller's smear of his political opponents. Dan Mahoney called the action only the latest in Rockefeller's offenses against the GOP and promised a vigorous public response. Speaking on behalf of the party, David Jaquith rallied Conservatives: "Let those of us in New York who know this man's record and his soaring ambitions, sound the warning to Republicans around the country."[38] Still one year away from the Republican convention, the GOP's two presidential candidates began a battle that divided the national Republican Party along ideological lines. The Conservative Party wanted nothing more than to be part of this conflict.

SECRET SUPPORT

In 1964, the Conservative Party assisted Barry Goldwater's presidential campaign in two ways. First, as it had the previous year, the party publicized its version of New York State politics throughout the country in an effort to discredit Rockefeller with Republican voters in other states.[39] The party's executive committee produced a report on the governor's failure to live up to his pledge of "fiscal integrity" for the state. Sent to papers across the county, it found its way into several major conservative papers, including the *Chicago Tribune*.[40] The *Manchester Union Leader*, published by the autocratic and volatile William Loeb, printed the story above its masthead accompanied by a front-page editorial that used the Conservative study as evidence "that money means nothing to a Rockefeller—especially if it's yours, not his."[41] The party also kept up a stream of hectoring press releases and conferences. Some of these simply predicted the governor's defeat. Others highlighted specific charges, such as the governor's improper use of state employees on his campaign. In all of these cases, the fact that the criticism emanated from the governor's home state, and one with an image as liberal as New York, increased the amount of press attention.

Second, the Conservative Party helped the Goldwater campaign make inroads within New York. Since the state GOP supported Rockefeller, the Goldwater campaign needed all the assistance it could secure. By July, the Conservative Party served as a conduit for the national Goldwater organization and state Republicans willing to support the senator. Dan Mahoney and Kieran O'Doherty introduced both of the campaign's eventual state coordinators and other key personnel to the national organization. New York Conservatives also assisted the campaign with its events in the state, most prominently Goldwater's major preconvention rally at Madison Square Garden. In early 1964, Mahoney wrote the senator's campaign staff with several specific logistical suggestions to ensure the rally's success.[42] The rally concerned the Rockefeller campaign enough to dispatch an aide to take notes at the event surreptitiously. This spy prepared a comprehensive memo outlining the speeches and noting the length of positive crowd responses.[43] In subsequent months, Mahoney continued to offer a stream of recommendations concerning the state, most of which were adopted.[44]

Within New York, the Conservative Party worked hardest to help the Goldwater organization win state delegates to the GOP convention. New York sent ninety-two delegates to the San Francisco convention, of which eighty-two—two from each congressional district—were chosen in the party's June 2 primary. Mahoney rallied local leaders to this cause by asserting that Robert Taft lost the 1952 nomination because he failed to make inroads into the New York delegation.[45] In late January 1964, Mahoney outlined a general strategy for the Goldwater campaign in New York and a plan to implement it district by district. The strategy memo found its way to several key Goldwater operatives, including Clif White.[46] The document advised Goldwater to challenge selectively for delegates in the state's most hospitable districts. Mahoney examined each congressional district, assessed Goldwater's chances, and identified potential delegate candidates. In early February, the national Goldwater campaign endorsed this strategy, announcing its plan to run delegate candidates in selected congressional districts. Mahoney also advised the campaign on the best approach to individual delegates.[47]

While the Goldwater campaign accepted Conservative Party assistance and advice, it remained ambivalent about the party itself. The campaign needed to ward off charges of extremism and defend its respectability. An alliance with a third party formed in opposition to the state GOP seemed to send all the wrong signals. In early January 1964, the New York Goldwater committee designated Dan Mahoney as one of the two individuals tasked to identify New York politicians who might support Goldwater. The committee, however, feared the consequences of a public relationship between the Goldwater campaign and the Conservative Party. The campaign assigned Conservatives to the shadows, shielding any support from public view throughout the campaign for the nomination. "The Conservative Party will be of invaluable assistance to the Committee without being overtly represented on it," a committee memo summarized.[48] After a June meeting with Mahoney and O'Doherty, the leaders of the Goldwater state campaign reported, "Conservative Party will continue to help Goldwater movement, but the question of whether our relationship with the Party should be as subterranean as it has been in the past was not resolved."[49]

The Conservative Party, willingly accepting its clandestine role at this stage of the campaign, took steps to assure its support remained secret. Following a Goldwater rally at a New York City hotel, the national Goldwater staff became concerned over the Conservative Party's involvement in the event. Mahoney assured Dennison Kitchell, who headed the campaign, of the party's commitment to discretion. He affirmed that the promotional material used for the rally made no mention of the party, that no party representative talked directly to the press, and that Conservatives at the rally took care not to reveal their party membership.[50] New York Conservatives accepted this clandestine role during the nominating campaign, expecting to be invited out of the shadows for the general election. In April, however, Mahoney learned that, during a conversation with several members of Congress, Barry Goldwater pledged not to accept the endorsement of any third parties. Mahoney recognized that this policy consigned Conservatives to the political margin. The chairman asked Clif White for a meeting with the candidate to discuss the situation. At White's suggestion, Mahoney instead drafted a letter outlining the reasons the Conservative Party should be exempt from this ban on third parties. He presented the party's traditional position: fusion made New York State different. Mahoney argued that the Liberal Party used cross-endorsement to force New York Democrats and Republicans so far to the left that only a conservative fourth party could restore ideological balance. Mahoney also sent documentation of the Conservatives' refusal to align with less respectable third parties, including Kent Courtney's organization.[51]

Conservative leaders hoped to persuade the Goldwater campaign to permit the party to cross-endorse Barry Goldwater in the November election. Having the GOP presidential nominee at the top of the Conservative ticket would help the party attract voters in the general election. It would also demonstrate acceptance by the national GOP, and so bolster the Conservative Party's case that it represented true Republican values. Mahoney worked with top Goldwater aide Dennison Kitchell to develop a way for the candidate to accept the party's endorsement. The party asked for a straightforward acceptance, while the campaign proposed that the candidate say only that he was "favorably disposed to consider" the offer.[52] In the ensuing months, Mahoney continued to send White material supporting the party's legitimacy. Mahoney also argued for his party's importance, given the possibility that the New York GOP might not support Goldwater in the general election.[53] He cited a *Newsday* article that quoted an anonymous state Republican threatening, "Goldwater will have to get his own organization in the state."[54] Mahoney offered the Conservative Party as that organization.

In contrast to the confrontations of the presidential campaign, Conservative leaders viewed congressional and state legislative races as an opportunity to join with members of the state GOP. After all, the party viewed itself as ideologically compatible with most local GOP officeholders. In a memo to local Conservative leaders, Dan Mahoney made clear that "[t]he Party's basic goal for the general election in 1964 will be to have a full line on Row D on every voting machine in New York State."[55] In most cases, Conservatives planned to endorse the Republican candidate. Occasionally, however, Conservatives planned to run an independent candidate rather than endorse an ideologically unacceptable Republican candidate. Mahoney anticipated that a small number of candidates might balk at accepting the Conservative nomination. The party needed to remind these resistant Republicans that, since it intended to run a full slate, a refused endorsement would result in an independent candidate. Mahoney assured local party leaders that this threatened retaliation represented a small part of an overall strategy that relied on extensive cross-endorsements to improve relations with the Republican Party. Mahoney and the Conservative Party completely misjudged the situation. Partisan loyalty proved far more powerful than ideological compatibility. The majority of Republican candidates refused Conservative endorsement, forcing Conservatives to develop a new approach to the year's congressional and legislative races.

The Republican Party blocked cross-endorsement in a number of ways. In some cases, county parties instituted a formal ban. For example, the executive committee of the Rockland County Republican Party unanimously passed a resolution prohibiting GOP candidates from accepting the endorsement of any other party. Representative Katherine St. George, who had initially accepted cross-endorsement, disavowed the Conservative nomination when she learned of the Rockland County ban.[56] In other instances, candidates informally proscribed Conservative cross-endorsement. Long Island's Republican congressmen agreed informally not to accept Conservative endorsement. This group included the Conservative Party's closest congressional ally, Steve Derounian. In most cases, local Republican Party organizations and candidates made no public declaration, but simply refused Conservative Party endorsement. In March, Ted Waterman, the Conservative Party's legislative representative, traveled across the state offering Conservative support to acceptable Republican legislators. To his surprise, he encountered widespread resistance. Legislators often identified the opposition of the county Republican Party as the reason they refused cross-endorsement.[57]

Nelson Rockefeller and the state GOP used the party's county organizations to persuade most Republican candidates to refuse Conservative cross-endorsement. The GOP hoped to isolate and marginalize the new party by denying Conservatives the ability to cross-endorse a large number of Republican candidates. The Conservative Party could, of course, respond by implementing its original plan of running independent candidates in races where the Republican refused its nomination. Challenging the GOP candidate in the majority of races, however, would classify the new party as an anti-Republican organization and doom its potential relationship with the national Republican Party and the Goldwater campaign. An already skeptical Goldwater campaign would never accept an anti-Republican third party. Faced with this predicament, the Conservative Party softened its plans to punish the state GOP by running a full slate of candidates. During the spring, William Miller, a New York congressman also serving as Republican National Committee chairman, persuaded Conservatives to abandon running independent candidates in several congressional and legislative races.[58] In congressional and state legislative races, the Conservative Party endorsed fifty-eight Republican candidates, ran fifty-eight independent candidates, and failed to field a candidate in 132 races. Having fifty-eight cross-endorsed GOP candidates and independent nominees reflected the party's need to project both loyalty and a willingness to impose a price for its rejection.

In the June 2 New York presidential primary, Nelson Rockefeller won the overwhelming number of delegates, but failed to achieve a total victory. Following the strategy outlined in Mahoney's January memo, Goldwater won five New York delegates to Rockefeller's eighty-seven.[59] The campaign's decisive event, Goldwater's victory in the fiercely contested California primary, however, eclipsed the New York results. Rockefeller's loss in the California primary effectively ended his presidential campaign. On June 16, the governor withdrew from the race, and, refusing to back Goldwater, threw his support to a new candidate, Pennsylvania Governor William Scranton.

The New York delegation arrived at the Republican convention in San Francisco committed to opposing the virtually inevitable nomination of Barry Goldwater. In the days preceding the convention, Nelson Rockefeller, Jacob Javits, and New York's other Republican Senator, Kenneth Keating, met with William Scranton and his supporters to formulate a plan to prevent Goldwater's nomination. In addition, New York Republicans continued their public denunciations of the party's likely nominee. In the first of a series of columns for the *New York Post* filed from San Francisco, Javits argued that a Goldwater nomination would realign the two parties along ideological lines, thus threatening the survival of the GOP.[60] As the convention began, members of the state delegation tried to rally anti-Goldwater sentiment, but with little success. On July 14, amidst this discord, Nelson Rockefeller addressed the Republican convention in support of a minority platform plank. Rockefeller's speech focused on the need for the GOP to renounce extremism in all its forms. The combination of message and messenger enraged the convention. The crowd, committed to Goldwater and hostile to Rockefeller, booed and jeered. Rockefeller further provoked the audience by listing the right's excesses during the nomination campaign. By the time Rockefeller finished his speech, any hope that the convention would unify the Republican Party had vanished.[61]

Press reports during the convention speculated that presidential nominee Goldwater might choose New York Congressman William Miller as his running mate. The New York delegation, overwhelmingly opposed to Goldwater, also objected to putting Miller on the ticket. Given the congressman's conservative voting record, many liberal Republicans interpreted Miller's nomination as a repudiation of their wing of the national party.[62] Clif White, Marvin Liebman, and Kieran O'Doherty, representing the Conservative Party at the convention, however, worked for Miller's nomination. Liebman established a headquarters in San Francisco to drum up support for adding Miller to the ticket.[63] One Arizona newspaper went so far as to implausibly conclude that the Conservative Party began the Miller-for-vice-president boom.[64] On July 15, Goldwater chose Miller as his running mate. O'Doherty promptly approached Miller about Conservative cross-endorsement of the presidential ticket. The vice presidential nominee responded that he was "favorably disposed" to accepting it, but warned O'Doherty that he expected Rockefeller's New York Republican Party to oppose the arrangement. The six weeks following the convention fulfilled this prediction.[65]

CLARE BOOTH LUCE

The Republican national convention failed to unify the party behind its presidential nominee. GOP liberals considered Goldwater unacceptable because of his conservative policy positions, his controversial acceptance speech, his choice of running mate, and his supporters' treatment of Rockefeller during the convention. New York Republicans led this revolt. A week after the San Francisco convention, Jacob Javits announced that, while he would not back President Johnson or leave the Republican Party, he could not support the Republican ticket given Goldwater's policy views, particularly on civil rights.[66] Nelson Rockefeller stopped short of this explicit disavowal, but said Goldwater's acceptance speech frightened him.[67] Senator Ken Keating refrained from any direct criticism of Goldwater, but declared he would run an independent campaign in his re-election bid.[68] Within the next several weeks, two New York City GOP congressmen, John Lindsay and Seymour Halpern, also rejected Goldwater, vowing to run independently from the presidential nominee. Former Brooklyn Dodger Jackie Robinson, who campaigned for Rockefeller prior to the convention, called Goldwater a bigot for his vote against the 1964 Civil Rights Act. When Goldwater sent Robinson a somewhat prickly invitation to meet, Robinson responded with a list of the senator's positions and actions that precluded his support.[69] New York Conservatives sought to benefit from the state GOP's disloyalty by making the Goldwater campaign aware of every example of this nonsupport.[70]

The peculiarities of the New York cross-endorsement law and the constitutional system for electing presidents introduced additional complexity in Conservative support for Goldwater. In presidential elections, voters cast their ballots, not for the actual candidates, but for electors who eventually vote for president in the electoral college. This rule meant that Conservatives, rather than endorse Goldwater, needed to endorse the Republican Party's electors pledged to him. In addition, according to a 1947 state law, no party could nominate a candidate without that candidate's approval. Conservatives, therefore, needed the permission of the forty-three Republican electors to endorse Barry Goldwater. Since these electors were chosen by the state organization, the Conservative Party needed the cooperation of Nelson Rockefeller's Republican Party.

In the week after the San Francisco convention, the Conservative Party publicly declared its desire to cross-endorse the state's GOP electors. While officials in the Goldwater campaign remained receptive, the state GOP circulated a confidential memo outlining ways to block the arrangement.[71] On July 29, Dan Mahoney wrote GOP state chairman Fred Young formally requesting the two parties nominate a common slate of electors.[72] Mahoney argued that Conservative endorsement of Republican congressional and state legislative candidates demonstrated the two parties' common ground. He also cited the precedent of Democratic presidential candidates, including Lyndon Johnson in the coming election, accepting Liberal Party endorsement. Chairman Young immediately rejected the proposal, vowing the GOP would never make a political deal with "a political blackmail racket being operated by two self-serving opportunists."[73] To frustrate Conservative intentions, Republicans planned to nominate electors who pledged to refuse the third party's cross-endorsement.

Conservatives, faced with Republican resistance, pursued two plans to force a common slate of electors. First, they prepared a court challenge contending that presidential electors were not candidates for public office in the conventional sense. If electors were not candidates, then the Conservative Party did not need their permission to endorse them. Mahoney contacted William Miller to determine if he and Goldwater would accept Conservative endorsement should the party win this court challenge. On Miller's advice, Mahoney again presented his case for Conservative endorsement to the presidential campaign. This time the chairman focused on Rockefeller's criticisms of Goldwater, characterizing them as acts of disloyalty. Mahoney also promised that the party "would not institute a lawsuit concerning this subject without a prior assurance from Senator Goldwater and Congressman Miller that they would accept our nomination if we won the lawsuit."[74] The party's subsequent pursuit of this lawsuit suggests the campaign responded positively.

As the second method to force a joint slate of electors, the Conservative Party threatened to run a Senate candidate challenging Republican incumbent Ken Keating. This threat took on considerable power once it involved Clare Booth Luce, former congresswoman from Connecticut, former ambassador to Italy, socialite, playwright, and wife of the publisher of *Time*, *Life*, and *Fortune*. While attending the GOP convention to second Barry Goldwater's nomination, Luce denied a rumor that she would run for the Senate on the Conservative Party line, claiming to "know nothing about the New York Conservative Party."[75] In many ways, Luce was an unlikely choice to be the party's Senate nominee. While she and her husband had an apartment in Manhattan, she had little experience with New York State politics. Luce also considered Senator Keating a personal friend and had even recently lent her name to a testimonial dinner in his honor.[76] In the weeks following the convention, however, William Buckley, another friend of Luce, again came to the assistance of the party by speaking to her several times about the situation in New York. He spelled out the failure of the state GOP to support Goldwater, including its refusal of a common slate of electors. Even more critically, Buckley vouched for the respectability of the party, assuring her that it was not anti-Republican. With her friend's counsel, Luce concluded that running for the Senate—or at least publicly considering running—would force the New York GOP to reassess its resistance to cross-endorsed electors. Given the party's reliance on college professors, small businessmen, and "conservatives of the second rank," Luce's involvement represented a major coup for Conservatives.

On August 4, Buckley called Dan Mahoney, recounting his conversations with Luce and explaining her desire to inject herself into the race. That same day, Mahoney issued a press release headlined, "Clare Booth Luce Considers Conservative Party Nomination." This release, and Luce's confirmation of the story, immediately generated intense press coverage. In the *New York Times*, Luce explained that, while she considered Keating a friend and a man of accomplishment, "[h]e has not yet announced his support for the Republican national ticket and I believe the New York electorate is entitled to a Senate candidate unequivocally committed to support that ticket."[77] Over the next few days, Luce continued to say she was thinking about running, but had made no decision. At the same time, she accepted the position of co-chair of Citizens for Goldwater, a decision that intertwined the intraparty conflict of the national GOP and New York's interparty battle.

On August 12, GOP leaders from across the country met in Hershey, Pennsylvania, in search of the party harmony that had proved elusive. The previous day, the two symbols of Republican disunity met when Nelson Rockefeller traveled to Washington, D.C., to speak with Barry Goldwater. At both this private session and the larger meeting the following day, Rockefeller called on Goldwater to address the threat to GOP unity presented by the New York Conservative Party.[78] Speaking privately at the Hershey conference, the governor blamed Conservatives for preventing party unity by running fifty-eight candidates against Republicans in congressional and state legislative races. He did not mention that most of the candidates were running because the GOP blocked Conservative cross-endorsement. Rockefeller contended that Ken Keating and John Lindsay refused to support Goldwater "because they have Conservatives running against them, and they have Democrats running against them, and they are in one Devil of a situation."[79] "I know your problem, Nelson, on that Conservative Party," Goldwater responded, "and we are going to work and see if we can't do something about it. I don't know if we can, maybe we can't."[80] While the conference was conducted behind closed doors, Rockefeller held a press conference at its conclusion. He explained he had urged Goldwater to use his influence with the Conservative Party to end splinter politics and to rally support for all Republican candidates. Rockefeller then identified his principal request. "It is my sincere hope," he said, "due to his [Goldwater's] influence, there will be no Senatorial candidate selected by the Conservative Party to run against Senator Keating."[81]

The Hershey Republican unity conference failed to unite the national GOP or the two New York State parties. Luce told reporters that no Republican, including Goldwater, contacted her and that her interest in running had "intensified."[82] When Dan Mahoney asked Rockefeller, in light of his conference statements urging unity, to relent on the issue of a common slate of electors, the governor failed to respond.[83] On August 18, Senator Keating officially announced he would seek re-election and again refused to support Goldwater. Keating specifically addressed the Conservative Party's potential challenge aimed at persuading him to back Goldwater. "I will not be a party to any deals, and do not intend to trim my sails," he vowed, "to win the backing of any individual or organization that does not support my record."[84]

Following Keating's announcement, the Goldwater campaign and, finally, the candidate himself, urged Luce not to run. The senator made no direct request that Luce withdraw, but appealed to her loyalty, arguing that "Republicans should back Republicans."[85] Luce applied that maxim, however, to reach the opposite conclusion. On August 21, after meeting with Dan Mahoney and Kieran O'Doherty at her apartment, she decided to run. The three drafted an announcement that Henry Luce, upon his arrival home from the office, edited for style. The statement, released on August 23, explained that Luce planned to accept the Conservative Party Senate nomination because she thought it best served the interests of Goldwater in

New York State. She made clear to the GOP how to remove this challenge. "I am still hopeful, as is the Conservative Party state leadership, that unity will be achieved behind the Goldwater-Miller ticket in New York, but it is clear that this has not yet occurred," she said.[86]

Luce's announcement produced front-page news stories the next day and set off a flood of reaction.[87] In a later column devoted to how Luce was pressured to drop out of the race, William Buckley exclaimed, "Oh, how the scorpions struck."[88] Rockefeller's representatives on the Republican National Committee (RNC), George Hinman and Dorothy McHugh, immediately sent a telegram to Dean Burch, formerly of the Goldwater campaign and currently RNC chairman. Their telegram, also released to the press, expressed skepticism that New York Republicans could support Goldwater "when the duly designated co-chairman of the National Goldwater Citizens movement is preparing to run against the regular Republican nominee from New York as a candidate of the so-called Conservative Party."[89] Writing in *The New Republic*, journalist Murray Kempton characterized this threat of total nonsupport as the New York GOP "calling the only mortgage it held on Barry Goldwater."[90] William Miller responded that Hinman and McHugh were mistaken if they thought Goldwater could control the Conservative Party.[91] The issue, however, was not the Conservative Party's behavior, but Luce's. In quick succession, Richard Nixon, Thomas Dewey and Herbert Brownell personally urged her to withdraw. New York Republicans such as Walter Mahoney, Jacob Javits, and Nelson Rockefeller also asked Luce to reverse her decision in the week following her announcement. Dean Burch, in response to the Hinman and McHugh telegram, also urged Luce not to run. Joining this chorus, a *New York Times* editorial explained that "[t]he proper decision is not for Senator Keating to give way but for Mrs. Luce to exercise the traditional womanly prerogative of changing her mind."[92]

In the face of mounting pressure, Luce looked for a way out. She asked William Buckley to replace her as the Conservative Party's Senate nominee. Buckley sent his friend a note declining the offer due to both personal reasons and the belief that his candidacy would fail to pressure the New York GOP. Luce began drafting her withdrawal statement on the back of Buckley's letter.[93] She announced her withdrawal publicly on a public affairs television show that Sunday. Luce withdrew from the race citing two reasons: first, she wanted to concentrate on the Goldwater campaign; second, Luce abandoned her campaign because "certain New York Republican leaders have recently seized upon it as means of shifting the blame for party disunity in the State from themselves to the shoulders of Senator Goldwater and his supporters."[94] Privately, Luce expressed this sentiment more bitingly, telling Conservative Party leaders, "I want the monkey to be on Rockefeller's back."[95] In the short term, however, New York Republicans had succeeded in forcing Luce out of the race. Hinman and McHugh welcomed her decision as "a disavowal by the Goldwater campaign leadership of the destructive tactics of the Conservative Party."[96]

The day following Luce's withdrawal both the New York Republican and Conservative Parties opened their conventions. Clare Booth Luce surprised the Republican delegates by appearing at their convention in a Manhattan hotel. Calling for party unity, she offered Senator Keating a limited endorsement by promising to support the convention's nominee.[97] The convention then nominated Keating by acclamation. Luce's call for party unity enjoyed only limited success at the convention because, except for her presence as his national co-chair, the Republican event contained few overt signs that Barry Goldwater headed the party's ticket. In contrast, the Conservative Party convention in Saratoga Springs displayed a visible commitment to Barry Goldwater. Speakers consistently praised the candidate while standing before a huge photograph of the senator. The event, however, marked the failure of the party's plan to force a common slate of electors. The day before the convention, Conservatives lost their court challenge when a state Supreme Court justice ruled that the party could not endorse Republican electors without their permission. Luce's withdrawal also denied the Conservative Party the high-profile Senate candidate to pressure the state GOP to agree to a common electoral slate. Instead, the party nominated an academic, Iona College history and political science professor, Henry Paolucci. Unlike the GOP convention, Conservatives enthusiastically endorsed Goldwater. The party, however, nominated no presidential electors. Conservatives prepared for the fall campaign unsure of their role in the presidential race.

A VALUABLE DEFEAT

The divisiveness produced by the summer's tumultuous events dominated the fall electoral campaign. The New York GOP never united behind its presidential candidate. Governor Rockefeller made one joint appearance with Barry Goldwater at an Albany rally, where he failed to urge the crowd to vote for the presidential candidate. The party advised its assembly candidates to run campaigns distinct from Goldwater in order to increase their attractiveness.[98] Even Republicans who technically endorsed the national ticket avoided associating with Goldwater. At small campaign events with supporters, Congressman Ogden Reid—who had come out in support of Goldwater—refused to respond to questions about the national ticket.[99] Some New York Republicans went beyond simply distancing themselves from their presidential nominee to working actively against the Goldwater campaign. Nelson Rockefeller's opposition research file on Goldwater found its way to Lyndon Johnson's campaign.[100] When John Lindsay met informally with constituents, an aide held a reproduction of the ballot while the congressman explained how to cast a split vote.

The refusal of most prominent New York Republicans and the state organization to support Goldwater's campaign was not universally popular with the party's rank-and-file. Much of this resentment centered on the only Republican running for statewide office, Ken Keating. The senator was seeking re-election by following the accepted GOP strategy of looking to add enough moderate to liberal downstate voters to his support from upstate Republicans. That approach proved far more challenging, however, because of the GOP presidential nominee. The senator ran a campaign independent of the party's presidential nominee, refraining from any mention of Goldwater or the presidential race in his campaign appearances. Some members of Keating's and Governor Rockefeller's staff even urged him to move beyond silence and speak out actively against Goldwater.[101] Keating's independent campaign, however, had already created animosity within the GOP. When Richard Nixon, who had recently moved to New York City, addressed a Republican rally on Long Island, the crowd booed at every mention of Keating.[102] This animosity among Republicans limited the Keating campaign's ability to distance itself from Goldwater and pursue the electoral strategy that had proven effective for previous statewide GOP candidates.

The Conservative Party, in contrast, continued to search for ways to assist Barry Goldwater's candidacy. The party appealed the court decision that proscribed it from nominating Republican electors without their permission. The State Court of Appeals and the New York Supreme Court, however, refused to overturn the lower court's decision. Denied the ability to cross-endorse Goldwater, the party ran no presidential electors in the general election, leaving the top of its ticket blank. Conservative campaign literature from the last month of the campaign explained how to split a ticket. Unlike John Lindsay's instructions, however, this split ticket produced a vote for Barry Goldwater.[103]

Without a presidential candidate, Senate nominee Henry Paolucci headed the Conservative Party ticket. Paolucci's campaign focused on his Republican opponent's refusal to back Goldwater. His campaign literature advised New Yorkers that "a vote for Keating is a vote to destroy Barry Goldwater and all he stands for."[104] In public appearances, the professor cited Keating's refusal to support the Republican presidential nominee as the reason he entered the race.[105] Still, the potency of any charges by Paolucci's underfunded part-time campaign was limited. Keating safely ignored his Conservative opponent to concentrate on his formidable Democratic adversary, Robert Kennedy.

The most compelling race for Conservatives occurred in Manhattan's Seventeenth Congressional District. The party targeted this seat because the Republican nominee, John Lindsay, had one of the GOP's most liberal voting records in Congress and was thought to be preparing to run for higher office. The party again tapped Kieran O'Doherty as its candidate. O'Doherty took a leave of absence from his law firm to run a full-time, vigorous campaign focused exclusively on broadcasting the failings of the congressman. Like Paolucci, O'Doherty consistently characterized his GOP opponent as a disloyal Republican for failing to support Barry Goldwater. In addition, O'Doherty denounced Lindsay's record in the House, referring to him as a "crypto-Democrat."[106] Unlike other Republican candidates, the congressman actively engaged his Conservative opponent throughout the campaign. Lindsay, in fact, refused to debate his Democratic opponent unless O'Doherty also participated.[107] Lindsay, with a majority Democratic and ideologically liberal district, benefited when attacked from his right. In the three-sided debates, the Democratic nominee charged Lindsay with being a Republican masquerading as a liberal, while O'Doherty claimed the congressman was a liberal masquerading as a Republican.

The Lindsay-O'Doherty confrontation represented an anomaly in the 1964 election. In most congressional and state legislative races, the Conservative Party wanted to cross-endorse the GOP nominee, but an antagonistic Republican Party blocked the endorsement. Conservatives could find only fifty-eight Republican nominees to accept their cross-endorsement. In response, Conservatives ran an equal number of independent nominees, most in races with Democratic incumbents. In the majority of congressional and legislative races, the Conservative Party ran no candidate. The state GOP used the existence of fifty-eight Conservative independent challengers to attack the third party as destructive. The Conservative Party responded by stressing the equal number of Republican nominees it had cross-endorsed. Neither party mentioned the majority of House and legislative races where the Conservatives ran no candidate, usually the result of a GOP nominee's refusing cross-endorsement. The GOP avoided this topic because it undermined its argument that Conservatives were intent on wrecking the Republican Party. Conservatives, on the other hand, failed to mention the subject because it showed that even ideologically compatible Republicans spurned the new party.

In the weeks prior to the November election, the Goldwater campaign realized the extent of the state GOP's lack of help. A confidential campaign report concluded that the New York State GOP "is not lifting a finger" for Goldwater.[108] Clif White responded, more in sadness than in anger, to reports of the state GOP's failure to support Goldwater that "there is no doubt that we must carry the burden of this campaign."[109] This lack of cooperation from state Republicans forced the Goldwater campaign to turn to its most loyal supporters, New York Conservatives. More and more, the campaign relied on Conservative clubs and county organizations. A five-page internal Goldwater campaign memo found that in the midst of the conflict between the New York GOP and the Conservative Party, the third party cooperated with the Goldwater campaign. "The simple truth of the matter is that without the support of the Conservative Party, both past and present, the effectiveness of the Goldwater campaign in New York would be seriously damaged," the memo concluded.[110] In October, the *New York Times* reported that the Goldwater campaign was operating through the New Yorkers for Goldwater & Miller organization and the Conservative Party rather than the state GOP.[111]

As the campaign drew to a close, even casual observers of the political scene recognized that Barry Goldwater would lose the election by a significant margin. With this outcome all but certain, New York Republicans struggled fiercely to disassociate themselves from their presidential nominee, fearing the loss of both houses of the state legislature. Goldwater supporters also reacted to the coming defeat of their candidate. William Buckley's remarks at the Conservative Party's second anniversary dinner in late October mentioned Goldwater only once, and concentrated on the post-election future of conservatism.[112] With victory out of reach, members of the state Goldwater campaign used the final weeks to document the record of GOP betrayal. Leaders of New Yorkers for Goldwater & Miller requested that all regional and county chairmen submit "a statement concerning every Republican Chairman and candidate, by name, noting whether or not they have supported Senator Goldwater and Congressman Miller."[113] Since local Conservative Party leaders often served as county officials of this organization, the request presented many Conservatives with an opportunity to report on the disloyalty of their Republican counterparts. The chairman of the Conservative Party's Columbia County Committee reported a litany of Republican misdeeds, including reports that the local GOP chairman was spotted at the county fair throwing out Goldwater literature rather than distributing it.[114] Goldwater campaign officials unconnected with the Conservative Party shared this negative assessment of the GOP. In Schoharie County, Robert Mickel outlined the failure of the local Republicans to back the candidate and recommended seeking retribution against Rockefeller after the election.[115] As final evidence of this lack of support, no Republican elected official attended Barry Goldwater's rally at Madison Square Garden the week before the election.

Election day confirmed Republican fears as the New York GOP suffered a loss of staggering proportions. In the midst of a national landslide defeat, Barry Goldwater lost every New York county, and the state by over two million votes. Ken Keating ran ahead of Goldwater, but still lost handily to Robert Kennedy. The news for the GOP was even worse in congressional and legislative races. Seven Republican House incumbents lost their seats, giving Democrats a majority of the state's congressional delegation. In addition, the state GOP's worst nightmare was realized when Republicans lost control of both houses of the state legislature. This last development was in some ways the most shocking since the GOP had controlled both the state senate and assembly since the 1930s.

Republican electoral losses were not distributed evenly across the ideological spectrum. The Republican nominees who won had put the most distance between themselves and Barry Goldwater. John Lindsay received over seventy-one percent of the vote and emerged as a favorite for higher office. All seven defeated House members supported Barry Goldwater. In the legislature, Senate Majority Leader and Conservative Party ally Walter Mahoney lost his bid for re-election. Amidst this Democratic rout, Conservative candidates seemed irrelevant. No independent Conservative Party candidate came close to winning election. Kieran O'Doherty, who bested most independent party nominees, still received only five percent of the vote. Cross-endorsed Republican nominees won slightly higher percentages on the Conservative line, but were usually swamped by the electorate's anti-GOP sentiment. In fact, only one cross-endorsed Republican nominee for Congress, Robert McEwen, won his race.

Surviving New York Republicans blamed conservative Republicans for the disastrous election results. Jacob Javits and John Lindsay used the results to demand a purge of conservatives from the national party. The election had already eliminated many of the conservatives in the New York party. Goldwater supporters deciphered the election results very differently, however. National conservatives refused to accept the election as a rejection of their ideology. Rather, they saw winning the GOP nomination as an interim victory on which to build. Most importantly, these conservatives remained active in politics generally and in the Republican Party specifically. As Republicans, they eventually blamed Goldwater's defeat on a number of factors—the aftermath of the Kennedy assassination, hostile press coverage, Nelson Rockefeller's divisive primary campaign, and the refusal of liberal Republicans to unite behind the nominee. New York Conservatives also refused to see the election as a defeat. They argued that Henry Paolucci's two hundred thousand votes represented an improvement for a Conservative statewide candidate. In addition, while the party proved unable to protect its friends, it was able to punish at least its most vulnerable enemies. The Conservative Party helped generate criticism over Ken Keating's lack of support for Goldwater. The resulting controversy damaged the senator's campaign and played a minor role in his defeat.

The 1964 election assisted the Conservative Party in two ways. First, it improved its leverage within the state. Entering the election, Republicans held the governorship, both Senate seats, a majority of the House delegation and both the state senate and assembly. Following the election, they controlled only the governorship and one Senate seat. Murray Kempton wrote that the once powerful New York GOP now "looked like the bleached bones of dead cattle painted by Georgia O'Keefe."[116] A significantly weakened state GOP enhanced the Conservative Party's position. The fact that an ideologically conservative presidential candidate contributed to the GOP's loss of power was an irony that seemed lost on most contemporary observers.

More significantly, the events of 1964 earned the state third party acceptance by the conservative movement and the national GOP. New York

Conservatives succeeded in contrasting themselves favorably with the state GOP. Rockefeller's attacks on the right during the primary campaign, the party's involvement in the stop-Goldwater movement at the convention, its rejection of joint electors, the threat to withhold support for Goldwater if Luce did not withdraw, and the failure of the state's leading Republicans or party organization to work for the candidate in the fall campaign all led many Republicans outside New York to consider the state party disloyal. Two days after the election, Richard Nixon clearly blamed the New York GOP for the loss, calling Nelson Rockefeller a "party divider" and "spoilsport" whose lack of activity had cost Goldwater votes.[117] In contrast, the Conservative Party supported the GOP presidential nominee in any fashion it could. The party worked clandestinely when it had to, in the open when it could. Its commitment convinced many national Republicans that it was not a destructive splinter party, but the political organization in New York State most loyal to the national GOP.

THREE

ATTRACTING NEW CONSERVATIVES

In 1964, the Conservative Party used Barry Goldwater's presidential campaign to differentiate itself from the New York Republican Party. Conservatives displayed a loyalty and commitment to the Republican presidential nominee that contrasted sharply with the state GOP's lack of support, and won them the gratitude of elements of the national GOP. That achievement, however, had come at a less than propitious moment. Staggering losses in the 1964 election called into question the future of the national Republican Party. Some observers predicted the GOP would go the way of the Whig Party if it failed to adjust its course.[1] Liberals in the national party, joined by most of the mainstream media, characterized the election as the country's rejection of conservatism. After all, Goldwater had suffered an overwhelming defeat, and Republican losses in congressional and state races were heaviest for conservative candidates. National conservatives, searching for opportunities to recover from this setback, would never have expected New York State, much less the most liberal location in the state, New York City, to begin their political redemption. But in 1965, state Conservatives used the New York City mayoral campaign to revitalize the political future of their ideology, and to begin to redraw party lines within the state. The Conservative mayoral nominee that year identified a set of issues attractive enough to win over an unexpected group of voters. The Conservative Party built on that achievement the following year as it began collecting the statewide electoral support needed to reshape New York's parties, and eventually, the national parties.

REGROUPING

Following the 1964 election, Republican liberals and moderates wanted the GOP to increase its appeal to young voters, to urban residents, and to minorities. They also moved to purge all vestiges of Goldwater and his ideological compatriots from the party. They started by replacing Goldwater loyalist Dean Burch with the nonideological Ray Bliss as the chairman of the Republican National Committee. New York Republicans, some of the most prominent liberals in the national party, strongly advocated these reforms. Ken Keating, blaming Goldwater's nomination for his unsuccessful re-election bid, urged the GOP to rid itself of conservative officials and ideology.[2] In an article for the Sunday magazine section of the *New York Times* titled "The Road Back for the G.O.P.," Jacob Javits warned that the party would work around the Republican National Committee unless it expelled its pro-Goldwater staff.[3] John Lindsay asserted that the Goldwater campaign left the party "a pile of rubble" and recommended new GOP leaders at all levels as a way to attract young and urban voters.[4]

Goldwater supporters, however, viewed 1964 as a painful first step in the growth of conservatism.[5] Far from being embarrassed by Goldwater's landslide loss, they displayed bumper stickers proclaiming that "27 Million Americans Can't Be Wrong." National conservatives blamed their defeat on a number of alternative explanations: a hostile press, an electorate shaken by the Kennedy assassination, and most of all, the disloyalty of liberal Republicans. Following the election, Barry Goldwater cited the lack of support he received from Republican liberals as evidence of the need for an ideological realignment of the Republican and Democratic Parties.[6] Goldwater and many of his supporters concluded that if the party loyalty of liberal Republicans did not lead them to support conservative GOP nominees, then some sort of realignment was needed. Some of Goldwater's more extreme supporters even wanted to abandon the GOP. In April 1965, radical publisher Kent Courtney used the actions of GOP liberals to attempt to create a national third party. He organized a three-day "Congress of Conservatives" that mixed a strident anti-communism with support for segregation. The congress stopped short of creating a national conservative third party, but resolved to assist and coordinate state conservative third parties in anticipation of a national organization.[7]

As it had since its founding, the New York Conservative Party refused to join with Courtney's third party. The party's goal was not to challenge, but to align with, the national GOP. State Conservative leaders also quickly distanced the party when individual members became involved with Courtney's organization. Donald Serrell, a Long Island attorney and an officer of a local Conservative Party club, attended Courtney's congress in Chicago. When a *Newsday* account of the meeting identified him as a representative of the Conservative Party, Dan Mahoney immediately wrote the paper explaining that Serrell did not represent the party and that New York Conservatives had no affiliation with the congress.[8] The party also continued to reject relationships with other state third parties. Mahoney refused assistance to a new conservative party in Colorado, for example, explaining that only New York's unique circumstances forced conservatives to forsake the GOP.[9]

While New York Conservatives advised their out-of-state ideological compatriots to work with their local GOP, they took a very different course at home. The defeat of many of New York's conservative Republicans in 1964 widened the ideological gap between the two state parties. The New York GOP emerged from the election more liberal, and more convinced of the electoral damage caused by conservatism.[10] Conservatives, seeing a state GOP even less hospitable to their views, vowed to oppose Republicans at every opportunity. Party leaders considered their state conflict a vital part of the national struggle over the GOP's future. In December 1964, Dan Mahoney rallied party members: "The critical political struggle to consolidate the gains we have achieved will take place within the national Republican Party. By continuing its battle against the renegade leadership of the New York Republican Party, the Conservative Party will play a crucial role in this battle," he wrote.[11]

Initially, the conflict between New York Conservatives and Republicans focused on the organization and actions of the state legislature. Republicans had lost control of both the assembly and the senate in the 1964 landslide, although Democrats enjoyed only slim majorities in both houses. When the Democratic Party failed to agree on its legislative leadership, Democrats and Republicans worked together to select the leaders for the assembly and the state senate. Conservatives, suspecting a deal between Governor Rockefeller and Democratic New York City mayor Robert Wagner, viewed that bipartisan alliance as additional evidence of the state GOP's move to the left. Conservatives also criticized Rockefeller for proposed spending and tax increases in his state budget. The party's rebuttal to Rockefeller's state of the state address scolded the governor for adopting the Democratic agenda and "readying New York State for junior partnership in President Johnson's Great Society."[12] Dan Mahoney wrote Rockefeller a tongue-in-cheek letter asking him to proclaim a "Greater Citizen Participation Day" since the governor's budget required New Yorkers to participate more fully as taxpayers. The governor's staff understandably ignored Mahoney's sarcastic letter.[13]

Conservative leaders also prepared for the year's upcoming electoral campaigns. New York scheduled special elections for the state legislature in 1965 as the final stage of a court-ordered redistricting plan. These elections used the recently redrawn legislative districts and elected members to a one-year term, allowing a return to the normal election cycle in 1966. Republican leaders considered the special election a tremendous opportunity to recover from their recent defeat. They blamed the defeat of candidates for the state senate and assembly in 1964 on the man at the top of the ticket, Barry Goldwater. Republican leaders believed the party, freed from running with Goldwater, could recapture its traditional control of both houses. Conservatives also saw the election as an important opportunity. They hoped to exploit Republican eagerness to regain legislative control to persuade more GOP candidates to accept cross-endorsement. Conservatives believed that Republicans, rather than run against independent Conservative nominees who could siphon off traditional GOP votes, would recognize the wisdom of fusion.

Conservatives viewed the year's other major political campaign, New York City's mayoral election, with less urgency. Everyone considered Mayor Robert Wagner a prohibitive favorite to win re-election. Wagner, a Democrat in an overwhelmingly Democratic city, also enjoyed Liberal Party support, a nearly unbeatable combination. New York City Republicans hoped to identify a candidate to run a fusion campaign against Wagner. Republicans used a variety of fusion strategies to reach out to voters beyond their party, a sensible response to a city as overwhelmingly Democratic as New York. Some fusion campaigns involved two or more of New York's traditional third parties cross-endorsing a candidate. Others depended on a paper party created for a specific election. In the 1961 New York City mayoral race, for example, Republican nominee Louis Lefkowitz also ran with the endorsements of the just-created Civic Action and Non-Partisan Parties. Fusion also described campaigns in which a candidate attracted the votes of members of another party. Jacob Javits used that definition when he called for a "citizens' fusion movement" of individual Democrats, Liberals and independents to defeat Wagner.[14]

In 1965, speculation centered on Javits or John Lindsay as potential candidates to lead a fusion campaign to beat Wagner. Both men expressed interest, conditioned on an early Republican endorsement and a commitment of financial support. Governor Rockefeller, however, balked at this timetable, and Javits and Lindsay withdrew from consideration for the mayoral nomination. Republican leaders began searching for a lesser-known candidate who could still attract the city's overwhelming majority of non-Republican voters. The Conservative Party, always opposed to the GOP aligning with parties or individuals to the left of the political spectrum, needed to find a candidate for its first New York City mayoral campaign.

"BUCKLEY FOR MAYOR?"

In the early spring of 1965, the New York City mayoral race seemed incapable of generating public interest or altering the political landscape. As a reasonably popular incumbent and the likely Democratic and Liberal Party nominee, Mayor Robert Wagner was the odds-on favorite. In addition, the Republican Party was unprepared to mount a serious challenge to the mayor. Already outnumbered in registration in New York City, the GOP faced a choice between little known-Republican candidates and several Democratic hopefuls whose selection would only confirm the party's infirmity. Finally, the Conservative Party faced an election with no prominent candidates on the horizon in a city renowned for its liberal tradition. A lackluster campaign followed by the predictable re-election of a Democratic incumbent seemed imminent.

Two decisions by political veterans, however, transformed the mayoral race. On May 4, Nelson Rockefeller announced plans to seek a third term as governor the following year. The announcement delayed any ambitious Republican's chance at the state house for another five years. At the same time, New York's two senators, Jacob Javits and Robert Kennedy, seemed secure in their offices. Denied these opportunities for advancement, John Lindsay re-evaluated his decision not to run for mayor. On May 13, the Republican congressman declared he would seek his party's nomination for City Hall. At the announcement, Lindsay echoed the national themes of his fellow liberal Republicans, declaring his campaign would spark a revival of the GOP that would begin in America's cities.[15] Shortly after Lindsay announced his candidacy, Robert Wagner made the second decision that changed the nature of the race. Citing family responsibilities following his wife's death, Wagner decided not to seek re-election. The mayor's retirement reshuffled the political situation of three parties. Unable to renominate their incumbent, Democrats scrambled to find an alternative among candidates who lacked Wagner's public support. The Democratic predicament, however, brightened the political prospects of the Republican Party and its all-but-official nominee, John Lindsay. Finally, Wagner's retirement left the Liberal Party without a candidate. While the party traditionally backed the Democratic nominee, its leaders were unenthusiastic about that party's current contenders.

The Conservative Party opposed John Lindsay on an almost visceral level. Lindsay's liberal views on issues such as social welfare, civil liberties, and foreign affairs made the congressman the type of Republican who would have no place in an ideological conservative GOP. Additionally, his decision, in 1958, to seek the GOP nomination in Manhattan's "Silk Stocking" district helped push Republican Congressman Frederic Courdert, an ideological conservative, into an early retirement. Lindsay's record in Congress, especially his opposition to the House Un-American Activities Committee, and his refusal to support Goldwater in 1964 further increased Conservative enmity. In 1964, the party devoted a disproportionate amount of time and energy to Kieran O'Doherty's unsuccessful challenge of Lindsay's re-election to Congress. Even on the night of this defeat, however, O'Doherty assured the crowd at Conservative headquarters that the party remained dedicated to "the prevention of any bid by Lindsay for higher office."[16] The more local and national press attention focused on the mayor's future prospects, the more Conservatives searched for ways to frustrate Lindsay's ambitions. With this history, Dan Mahoney surprised no one when he appeared on a public affairs television show in late May of 1965 and promised that the party would oppose Lindsay in the mayoral race.[17] Since Conservative opposition threatened to deny Lindsay a portion of his already small Republican base, the story still made front-page news.[18]

The set of circumstances that delivered the Conservative Party its mayoral candidate began with a joke headline. Bill Buckley devoted his column in the June 15 issue of *National Review* to a list of policy recommendations for any potential mayoral candidate. The ideas, typical of Buckley's love of the provocative, ranged from the decriminalization of narcotics to permitting anyone without a police record to operate any car as a taxi.[19] Buckley chose "Mayor, Anyone?" as the title of his column, and his sister Priscilla, an editor at *National Review*, added the headline "Buckley for Mayor?" to the magazine's front cover. This question prompted Dan Mahoney to approach Buckley about accepting the Conservative nomination. Buckley, unable to interest *National Review* publisher William Rusher in accepting, decided to run.

Why did William Buckley run for mayor? First, while never involved in day-to-day operations, Buckley believed in the Conservative Party's goals, including an ideological realignment of the two major parties. Buckley considered assisting the party so important that he characterized his campaign as a civic obligation similar to jury duty.[20] Second, a mayoral race fit the other demands of Buckley's life. He insisted, as a condition of accepting the nomination, that the race not compromise his work as magazine editor and syndicated newspaper columnist. A campaign for a statewide office, such as governor or senator, could not have satisfied this condition. Third, Buckley believed New York City faced a number of serious problems the two major parties ignored because they appealed to voters only as members of ethnic, religious, or economic blocs. Running for mayor allowed Buckley to focus on these problems and their solutions. Fourth, Buckley wanted an opportunity to recover from recent public controversy. On April 4, he had addressed the New York City Police Department's Holy Name Society, an organization of Catholic police officers. Buckley cited recent violence against civil rights workers in Alabama to illustrate current challenges for law enforcement, and criticized the press for denouncing police so quickly. The speech set off a firestorm in the press and political world that cast Buckley as a racist and supporter of police violence. Jackie Robinson condemned Buckley's speech and called for an investigation of John Birch Society members in the police department.[21] Believing the attacks against him unjust, Buckley saw the mayoral race as a chance to set the record straight. Finally, and most importantly, there was John Lindsay.

According to his friend Kieran O'Doherty, Bill Buckley held a "special animus" for John Lindsay.[22] Part of this animus may have emanated from their similarities. Along with sharing such physical characteristics as age, height, and weight, both men were Yale-educated, financially comfortable members of Manhattan society. There was also a personal connection. Bill

Buckley's brother James had become friends at Yale with John Lindsay's twin brother, David. These connections, however, only intensified Buckley's antipathy towards Lindsay. Buckley disagreed with the congressman on virtually every public policy issue of the day. These policy differences were even more divisive because John Lindsay was a Republican. Since any Lindsay electoral victory strengthened the liberal wing of the GOP, Buckley considered Lindsay's career a threat to the future health of the Republican Party. He also regarded Lindsay as a disloyal Republican. As a friend and supporter of Barry Goldwater, Buckley saw Lindsay's refusal to support the senator in 1964 as a personal betrayal. Finally, Buckley considered Lindsay something of a fraud, enjoying an overblown national reputation due to his good looks and a flattering press corps. He wanted to run for mayor to expose the gap between Lindsay and this unwarranted public image.

Buckley announced his candidacy on June 24 at a news conference that set the tone for the campaign. First, the candidate emphasized his principal theme by criticizing John Lindsay as unconnected to the tradition and philosophy of the national Republican Party. He then displayed his propensity to make news. When asked if he had a chance of winning, Buckley said no. When asked if he wanted to be mayor, he replied that he had never considered it. And when a reporter asked, "How many votes do you expect to get, conservatively speaking?," Buckley retorted, "Conservatively speaking, one."[23] Buckley's candidacy precipitated the final element in the transformation of the mayoral race. With a prominent conservative, pro-Goldwater candidate entering the race, the Liberal Party decided to back an alternative vision of the Republican Party. At the direction of Liberal leaders, most importantly Alex Rose, the party endorsed John Lindsay.

A SOCIAL CONSERVATIVE

As the summer of 1965 began, what initially promised to be a lackluster campaign run along traditional political lines with a predictable result had become something very different. While the Democratic Party would not select its mayoral nominee until its September primary, John Lindsay and Bill Buckley spent the summer campaigning for the general election. Lindsay chose to run an independent campaign despite the overwhelming support of both the state and national GOP. Governor Rockefeller and newly elected Republican National Chairman Bliss had urged the congressman to run. State Republican leaders were especially eager to help the GOP mayoral candidate in the 1965 race because of the special legislative elections also being held. Whether or not Lindsay won, a strong showing by the candidate would assist Republican legislative candidates in New York City. Rockefeller and Bliss, as well as Republicans across the country, offered assistance to the Lindsay campaign. Lindsay, however, declined virtually all offers of aid from fellow Republicans, including any potential help from former President

Eisenhower. Lindsay wanted no assistance from the national Republican Party or individuals he considered national Republicans.[24] This somewhat vague definition allowed him to refuse assistance from Nelson Rockefeller while accepting help from Senator Javits, a more popular figure in New York City. In actuality, Lindsay refused only Rockefeller's offer to campaign for him; he privately accepted a one hundred thousand dollar contribution from the governor.[25]

Lindsay declined GOP assistance because he planned to distance himself from the Republican Party. Lindsay portrayed himself as a fusion candidate and structured his campaign to obscure his Republican affiliation. He created campaign storefronts across the city to allow him to assemble a grassroots organization independent of the Republican Party. Lindsay also created an additional party for the election, the Independent Citizens Party, to attract New Yorkers uncomfortable voting for him on either the Republican or Liberal lines. Lindsay's choice of running mates further demonstrated his commitment to fusion. The congressman chose Timothy Costello, a Liberal, to run for City Council president and Milton Mollen, a Democrat, for controller. Lindsay also requested that the county GOP nominate a Democratic candidate in races where there was no properly liberal Republican. In addition, the congressman asked all GOP candidates in New York City to refuse Conservative cross-endorsement.

Lindsay took great pains throughout his campaign to present himself as the fusion candidate, not the Republican nominee. When asked if he was running as a Liberal or a Republican, the candidate consistently responded that he was running as Lindsay.[26] His campaign material also neglected to mention the Republican Party. Lindsay's success at obscuring his party affiliation so infuriated the Democrats that they eventually took out a full-page advertisement in the *New York Times* with the headline, "John Lindsay is a Republican. (No matter how he tries to hide it.)"[27] The advertisement used a series of quotations to demonstrate that, despite his current silence, the Republican nominee had a history of saying complimentary things about his own party.

If John Lindsay refused to say the words "Republican Party," Bill Buckley seemed to repeat them constantly. Buckley consistently attacked Lindsay for not belonging in the GOP. For example, he condemned Lindsay on these grounds at the National Press Club. "John Lindsay's voting record, and his general political pronouncements, put him left of center of the Democratic Party," he explained. "As such, he is an embarrassment to the two-party system."[28] Throughout the campaign, Buckley characterized Lindsay as an illegitimate Republican who did not deserve the support of party members. Buckley frequently cited Lindsay's alliance with the Liberal Party as evidence of the congressman's disloyalty. The campaign often referred to a statement Lindsay reportedly made when he attempted to secure Liberal cross-endorsement. "Under no circumstances would I use the office of mayor to promote the interests of the Republican Party," Lindsay allegedly assured Liberal leaders.[29] Buckley's rejection of Lindsay as a member of the GOP was not a campaign ploy. When a personal friend of Buckley's suggested that Lindsay might move to the ideological center once in office, the candidate disabused him of the notion. "It is my judgment that John Lindsay will do as much harm to the Republican Party if he is elected and becomes powerful, as anyone who has threatened the Party's role as defender of the tablets in recent history," he wrote in an impassioned letter. He concluded with the promise that "[i]f the Republican Party is transformed in his image, I shall give you the Republican Party, and go elsewhere."[30]

Buckley's attacks on Lindsay's Republican credentials alarmed the Lindsay campaign. In October, an internal Lindsay campaign memo tried to identify the motives for Buckley's assaults on their candidate. Its conclusion matched the Conservative candidate's public statements, that Buckley wanted to stop Lindsay's career in order "*to eliminate from major elective office a moderate Republican* who would, if elected, become a threat, *within the Republican Party*, to the Goldwater extremists."[31] The candidate's anti-Lindsay focus also created controversy within his campaign. Dan Mahoney criticized a proposed Buckley fundraising letter for its strong anti-Lindsay orientation. He feared that Lindsay could exploit the negative approach to spur a "liberal backlash."[32] Others in the campaign, however, wanted to step up the attacks. William Rusher, who shared Buckley's "special animus" toward Lindsay, argued for increasing the pressure in order to destroy the congressman's future in the Republican Party. At one point, Rusher urged Buckley to force Lindsay to announce his preference for the presidency in 1968 as a way of "widening the area of his already-damaging apostasy."[33]

In conjunction with attacking John Lindsay's Republican credentials, Buckley presented himself as in the mainstream of politics and the Republican Party. Barry Goldwater's presidential campaign the previous year made the GOP more hospitable to ideological conservatives like Buckley. Buckley also took concrete steps to emphasize his place in the national GOP. He created an organization distinct from the Conservative Party called "Republicans for Buckley" to attract Republicans reluctant to vote for him on the Conservative line. The group, headed by Clare Booth Luce, cast Buckley as the "Real Republican" who was running on Row D.[34] Lindsay, a fusion candidate, could not counter that he was the "Real Republican" and continue to obscure his party affiliation. Lindsay's nonpartisan campaign won him more votes than it cost him, but some of the support he lost was from Republicans who voted Conservative for the first time.

Unlike in previous races, the Conservative Party did not run Buckley's mayoral campaign. Buckley, wanting a more effective organization than the party could supply, assembled his own staff. He chose his older brother James as his campaign manager, charging him to provide protection from the "extreme zeal of party brethren."[35] The candidate brought on Marvin

Liebman to raise money independently of party channels, often using lists of contributions to the 1964 Goldwater campaign. Buckley also hired a researcher to help him write his speeches. Finally, the candidate used members of the *National Review* staff to fill out his campaign organization. At times, Buckley's independence from the Conservative Party created discord. When the Buckley campaign proposed literature that neglected to mention the Conservative Party, Dan Mahoney rejected the proposal.[36] Party leaders also resisted the Buckley campaign's plan to run on an additional ballot line with perennial candidate Vito Battista. Discussion of this proposal degenerated into a heated argument between campaign staff and party officials.[37] In the end, Conservatives successfully argued that the move would draw votes away from the party's line, and Buckley remained a one-party candidate.

The Conservative Party also bristled at aspects of Buckley's public style. Part of the candidate's appeal was his ability to be clever and provocative. His comments, however, at times appeared flippant. Buckley's infamous initial press conference confirmed Conservative Party concerns. Fearful that the event's tone would cost the party votes, Dan Mahoney tried unsuccessfully to get the candidate to issue a public statement that he was in the race to win. Buckley eventually assured party officials of his seriousness in a confidential memorandum. Buckley admitted that while he continued to believe he would not win, he now realized that the truth "is often a subversive distraction in politics."[38] Buckley further explained that he considered the race of critical importance because the future hopes of the national GOP depended on the fortunes of the Conservative Party. Clare Booth Luce shared this concern about Buckley, and wrote Barry Goldwater that she believed Buckley could be more serious.[39] The senator passed the advice on to the candidate, adding, "Why not really tie into the whole Lindsay-Javits-Rocky situation and let's find out where our party is really positioned?"[40] Buckley again promised to be a more solemn candidate.[41]

Most national conservatives supported Buckley's third-party candidacy. At an early stage of the campaign, Barry Goldwater spoke for many in the conservative movement when he wrote a personal friend explaining that Lindsay "represents no more a Republican candidate to me than Mayor Wagner."[42] Buckley transformed this national anti-Lindsay sentiment into financial support for his campaign. In 1964, Goldwater's campaign relied on an unprecedented number of small donations. Following the election, conservative fundraisers—most prominently Richard Viguerie—used the campaign's donor list to raise funds for conservative causes and candidates over the next two decades.[43] When Buckley entered the race, he tapped Marvin Liebman as the campaign's fundraiser. With the help of ten wealthy conservatives, including Jeremiah Millbank, who had helped bankroll *National Review*, Buckley immediately raised ten thousand dollars. Liebman used this money to purchase Viguerie's mailing lists and to contact tens of thousands of conservative contributors as part of a national direct-mail campaign.[44]

The letters to potential out-of-state donors cast the election as a struggle for the national Republican Party. They warned that the New York GOP wanted to overturn recent conservative gains, and predicted that, if John Lindsay was elected mayor, "his brand of 'Republicanism' is apt to control the next presidential convention and spell an end to meaningful opposition."[45] Some conservatives required additional convincing. Arthur Nielsen, founder of the company that provides viewer ratings of television programs, asked why a Republican from Chicago should fund a New York third party.[46] The campaign responded with the state's history of fusion and the warning that a Mayor Lindsay would define the future of the national GOP. Nielsen sent the Buckley campaign a check for five hundred dollars.[47] With message and organization, the Buckley campaign raised over two hundred fifty thousand dollars at a time when the party's annual budget, including all congressional and legislative races, was under one hundred thousand dollars. Much of this money came from outside New York.[48]

Buckley's celebrity, fundraising ability, and propensity for the provocative assured a high-profile campaign. The focus of his campaign, however, proved most significant for the party's history. Buckley continued to campaign on traditional conservative positions such as the dangers of centralized government and the need to combat communism in all its forms. Along with these subjects, however, Buckley introduced what eventually became known collectively as social issues. In part, these issues reflected a mayoral candidate's natural focus on local issues. Mostly, however, the new focus reflected Buckley's belief that social issues were at the heart of a burgeoning urban crisis. On the campaign trail, Buckley identified crime as New York City's primary problem, and advocated policies to promote law and order. Buckley favored hiring additional police, stiffening criminal sentences, providing financial compensation for victims, informers, and witnesses, and blocking a proposed Police Civilian Review Board. The candidate considered education the second most important issue. Buckley favored neighborhood schools over any integration policies, such as busing. He also favored decentralizing school administration and increasing the disciplinary authority of educators and administrators. Buckley also proposed fundamental shifts in a number of other policy areas, including more stringent regulations on welfare recipients.

Buckley's policy proposals—restoring law and order, protecting neighborhood schools, reforming welfare—all involved the issue of race. Buckley assiduously avoided casting these problems or his solutions in racial terms during the campaign. Instead, he consistently emphasized that his conservative philosophy was at the heart of all these positions.[49] While Buckley's solution to these social problems did correspond with his conservative philosophy, the reality was more complicated than the candidate portrayed. Riots by African-American residents of Harlem and Rochester in the summer of 1964, along with a rising crime rate, helped change the political implications of race.

Social welfare programs that had been generally popular were becoming more controversial as they were also increasingly seen through the prism of race. Buckley's conservative positions, including his advocacy of law and order and welfare reform, reflected his conservative philosophy and tapped into the growing disenchantment with liberalism. Not everyone was convinced, however. Editorial boards and liberal Republicans denounced the candidate as a racist, and Buckley spent the final stage of the campaign defending his reputation and his policy positions.

WINNING NEW SUPPORT

Bill Buckley was the Conservative Party's most prominent, but not its only, candidate. As 1965 began, Conservative leaders expected Republican legislative candidates to be far more amenable to cross-endorsement. The state GOP, however, remained unwilling to allow an alliance with Conservatives. Just as in 1964, Republican nominees overwhelmingly rejected Conservative cross-endorsement. The Conservative Party response to this rejection, however, changed dramatically. In 1964, in order to encourage acceptance by Barry Goldwater's presidential campaign, Conservatives minimized conflict with state Republicans. When Conservative offers of endorsement were rebuffed by Republican nominees, the party usually chose to leave the line blank. As a result, the party ran no candidate in the majority of races in 1964. In 1965, strengthened by the inroads it had made with the national GOP, the party could afford to confront state Republicans. When GOP candidates turned down cross-endorsement, Conservatives usually fielded an independent party nominee in the general election. In 1965, the Conservative Party ran independent nominees in fifty-five percent of the legislative races. It ran no candidate in thirty-one percent of the races, and cross-endorsed the Republican nominee in a mere thirteen percent of the races. Party leaders believed that they needed to run independent challengers to deny Republicans control of the legislature in order to eventually win the GOP's acceptance. This shift in strategy set up the first true test of Conservative electoral strength on the legislative level.

New York's City's mayoral race, however, remained the year's major story. Bill Buckley's position on social issues distinguished his campaign from those of his opponents. John Lindsay and Abraham Beame, winner of the Democratic Party's September primary, shied away from these controversial issues. In contrast, Buckley, motivated by his convictions, stressed them incessantly. The candidate paid a price for his positions, however, finding himself vilified at various times as a fascist, a racist, and a fool. His positions, however, also captured emerging public sentiment. Working- and middle-class New Yorkers, who saw crime and taxes rising, and schools and other municipal services declining, found Buckley a welcome addition to the campaign. These voters of Irish, Italian, or other European descent from outside Manhattan were lifelong Democrats. Previously, Conservative candidates attracted Republican voters dissatisfied with their treatment by the GOP. Buckley's campaign represented an important breakthrough for the party. He attracted the interest of these Democratic voters not with his charges that Lindsay was a disloyal Republican, but by stressing the social issues—crime, welfare, schools—that the other campaigns avoided. Both in this campaign and in the future, these voters proved significant. A recent study of the Lindsay administration concluded that the positive response to Buckley's positions proved "the existence of a 'silent majority' more than four years before the term was used by President Richard Nixon."[50]

This mixture of style, substance, and financial support made Buckley a real factor in the mayoral race. He also benefited from his adept television performances. With New York City's newspapers on strike in September, television, especially the televised candidate debates, gained influence. Buckley's aggressive and droll style in these debates further increased his popularity. Looking back on the campaign, Kieran O'Doherty, Buckley's press secretary, estimated that the newspaper strike was his candidate's biggest break.[51] By October, the Conservative candidate exceeded twenty percent in polls. That much support in a close race made Buckley a tempting target, especially given his controversial policy proposals.

The Lindsay campaign, which had been ignoring Buckley, changed its overall strategy and began running against him. John Lindsay used his attacks on Buckley to demonstrate his liberal credentials and lure away supporters of Democratic nominee Abraham Beame. The Lindsay campaign charged Buckley and his party with being extremists outside the legitimate political spectrum. Jacob Javits called Buckley a member of the radical right whose election threatened the future of New York City and State.[52] Likewise, Lindsay warned any Republican considering supporting Buckley that "he is not joining a conservative cause; he is joining a radical cause, an extremist penetration."[53] The campaign assailed Buckley's proposals on social issues as a racist agenda, warning that Buckley was fomenting racial tension in a city that might explode. Coming the year after the Harlem and Rochester disturbances and just months after the Watts riot, this accusation carried great weight. Buckley denied that either he or his policies were racist. The campaign even purchased fifteen minutes of New York City's expensive television time to rebut the accusations. Dan Mahoney opened the broadcast by calling the charges against Buckley unjust. He continued his argument through a series of rhetorical questions to the television audience. "Are those New Yorkers who believe in neighborhood schools racists? Are those New Yorkers who support the police hate mongers?" he asked.[54]

Republicans also used Buckley's real and supposed allies in an attempt to label him an extremist. Most often these charges concerned general links to the John Birch Society. In these cases, Buckley responded effectively by denouncing the society. When a reporter raised the issue on a public affairs television show, Buckley explained that "the lunatic pronouncements of Robert Welch have, in my judgment, made a defense of the John Birch Society impossible."[55] Republicans also tried to link Buckley to Kent Courtney and his Conservative Society of America. Courtney had sent a letter to conservatives across the country using the New York City mayoral race as a recruiting and fundraising device for his far-right organization.[56] Courtney focused on what he called Lindsay's pro-communist voting record in Congress, and misrepresented his society as being allied with New York Conservatives in creating a national third party. He also used the national letter to sell copies of a pamphlet titled "Beware of Lindsay."[57] Within a week, the letter and pamphlet created a controversy for Buckley in New York. To defuse the situation, Buckley publicly denounced Courtney. According to a front-page story in the *New York Times*, he dismissed the letter and its author with the assessment "Courtney's a kook."[58]

New York Republicans also linked Buckley to Barry Goldwater. While Buckley considered Goldwater a responsible conservative, he knew many New Yorkers did not share this judgment in 1965. Accordingly, Buckley resisted public use of the senator's support. In the first week of October, Goldwater traveled to New York City to meet Buckley and his brother and campaign manager, James, for lunch.[59] Goldwater explained to the brothers that he felt no party loyalty toward Lindsay. James Buckley, seizing this opportunity, quickly drafted a statement of support for his brother's candidacy. Goldwater immediately signed it. The Buckley campaign, however, never released the endorsement from the nation's leading conservative. The candidate wrote Goldwater saying that the decision stemmed from the fear that the endorsement would invite comparison with the senator's 1964 vote in New York City, a level he felt he could not achieve.[60] More likely, Buckley recognized that the Arizonan could become an issue in the election. During the last month of the campaign, Lindsay consistently stressed Buckley's link to Goldwater, hoping to tie the Conservative nominee to the public's rejection of Goldwater the previous year. Buckley denied Lindsay's charges that he was acting as an agent of Barry Goldwater, asserting that he was a friend of the senator, but received no help from him.[61] The statement skirted the truth, given that Goldwater provided the campaign his advice and his endorsement.

The Lindsay campaign also attacked Buckley because of his supporters. On September 9, the major story in the *New York World Telegram and Sun* quoted an anonymous source from the Lindsay camp alleging that the congressman's campaign was the victim of "vicious right-wing hate tactics."[62] The rest of the city's papers soon picked up the story. The specific charges involved roughed-up volunteers, slashed telephone lines, smashed storefront windows, and threats against the candidate. The source claimed the campaign had evidence linking these activities to the Conservative Party. Buckley and Conservative Party officials denied any involvement. The candidate attributed those crimes to "crackpots," adding that Lindsay should fear not crackpots but rather rational and intelligent men.[63] Skeptical that these incidents actually occurred, the Conservative Party responded to subsequent allegations by contacting the police to see if a crime had been reported.[64] An interview of a key Lindsay aide, published decades later, seems to confirm, at least partly, the Conservative contention that the congressman's campaign manufactured this controversy.[65] Beyond dispute, however, is that John Lindsay encountered negative, even ugly, public receptions when he campaigned outside Manhattan. Crowds booed and jeered the candidate, sometimes using racial epithets. The hostile crowds, while not organized by the Buckley campaign or his party, usually supported the Conservative nominee and reflected the racially charged atmosphere of the time. As a result, by the end of the campaign, Buckley more frequently faced the charge of racist than extremist.

A final Republican criticism of Buckley provided one of the campaign's most curious episodes. Timothy Costello, Republican nominee for city council president, seemed to have nothing in common with the Conservative nominee save Catholicism. On October 15, Costello addressed the student and faculty of Fordham University, his alma mater. Costello criticized Buckley not only as a threat to the future of New York City, but also as a danger to the Catholic Church. He argued that Buckley's policy positions—such as rejecting Lyndon Johnson's War on Poverty—put him into direct conflict with the history and teachings of the church.[66] Costello called a vote for Buckley anti-Catholic and asked all Catholics to disavow the Conservative. Two days later, Buckley announced that he would not make religion an issue in the campaign. "If I am a bad Catholic, I shall be punished by someone I fear far more than the New York Catholic voter," he explained.[67] He also filed a complaint with the Fair Campaign Practices Committee charging the Lindsay campaign with a "deliberate and continuing strategy to exploit fears and prejudices."[68] The complaint claimed that Costello injected religion into the campaign while Lindsay injected the issue of race. Buckley also asserted that the Lindsay campaign manufactured the allegations of vandalism by Buckley supporters.[69] In its response to the committee, the Lindsay campaign argued that Buckley's charges were untrue and "clearly intended to camouflage Mr. Buckley's own questionable tactics."[70] As evidence, Lindsay campaign manager Robert Price provided a large sampling of hostile press accounts concerning both Buckley's statements and the unfriendly public reaction his candidate often received. Price also linked the Buckley campaign to Kent Courtney and his anti-Lindsay pamphlet. In light of this conflicting evidence, the committee took no action on the complaint.

A FUSION MAYOR

On November 2, John Lindsay, with 43 percent of the vote, narrowly defeated Abraham Beame to become mayor of New York City. The last-minute flood of criticism and traditional reluctance to vote for third-party candidates in close elections reduced Buckley's support from levels predicted by earlier polls. He won 12.9 percent of the vote, with his highest percentages in Queens and Staten Island, a significant improvement on all previous Conservative efforts. The final numbers came as no surprise to the candidate. Along with his brother and campaign manager, James, his fundraiser Marvin Liebman, and two other campaign staffers, the candidate had wagered fifty dollars on his vote total. Buckley won the pool, forecasting he would receive 340,000 votes, about twelve hundred fewer than his final total.[71]

Lindsay's election made him a political star of the first magnitude. Most commentators praised Lindsay for his campaign and predicted a bright political future. In an editorial titled "Lindsay's Astounding Victory," the *New York Times* congratulated the candidate for his "vindication of high principle."[72] Many in the press drew a comparison between Lindsay's election and Republican fortunes the year before. A *Newsweek* article explained that only the most die-hard right-wingers denied that Lindsay offered the GOP a road back from the Goldwater debacle of 1964.[73] Exultant over the victory of one of their own, the liberal Republican Ripon Society concluded that the GOP could hope to win future elections only by following John Lindsay's example.[74] Most initial reaction judged Buckley's campaign a failure. Many in the press compared his effort to Lawrence Gerosa's third-party candidacy in the 1961 New York City mayoral campaign. Gerosa, a veteran of the Wagner administration, challenged the incumbent mayor by running on the Independent Party and Citizen Party lines in the general election, winning 13 percent of the vote. A front page *New York Times* article speculated that Buckley merely inherited the Gerosa vote.[75] A *Life* magazine editorial mocked Buckley because, for all his "cocksure television razzle-dazzle, he polled only a few more votes than a lackluster conservative [Gerosa]."[76]

Critics focused on Buckley's inability to prevent Lindsay's election as a central failure. Some Buckley supporters also shared this assessment. Interviewed years later, Kieran O'Doherty remembered that with Lindsay's election, "I felt I had ashes in my mouth."[77] Even Barry Goldwater humorously acknowledged this failure at a dinner in honor of *National Review's* tenth anniversary. "As a political kingmaker, you're a Wrong-Way Corrigan," he teased Buckley.[78] Buckley and the party responded when some observers went an additional step, concluding that his campaign helped Lindsay win. The Conservative candidate's popularity with Democratic voters made this charge plausible. Pundits critical of Buckley noted the poetic justice. Columnist Joseph Alsop wrote that John Lindsay should issue a statement thanking Buckley for helping him to be elected.[79] An account of the 1965 campaign sympathetic to Lindsay characterized Buckley's draw of Democratic votes as a "delicious irony."[80] Conservatives denied they helped elect the candidate they had sworn to stop. Both Buckley's account of the campaign and Dan Mahoney's history of the party argued in detail that Lindsay would have won regardless of whether Buckley ran.[81]

Conservatives missed, however, the significance of the campaign's principal achievement. Bill Buckley—a patrician, intellectual candidate from Manhattan with a proclivity for obscure words and a disdain for street-corner campaigning—attracted the votes of working and middle-class ethnic white Democrats from the outer boroughs. By supporting Buckley, these voters demonstrated a skepticism toward the charges that dominated the final weeks prior to the election. The Lindsay campaign attacked Buckley by charging that his position on social issues revealed racial prejudice and a failure to live up to his Catholic faith. New Yorkers who voted for Buckley rejected these links. Sensitive to the charge that they helped elect John Lindsay, however, Conservatives de-emphasized the size and significance of this Democratic support. In addition, since Buckley won these Democratic votes largely on the basis of his controversial positions on crime, race, and busing, many critics characterized this support as a "white backlash" undeserving of respect. But these Buckley voters—both who they were and the issues they cared about—proved consequential to state and national politics. In subsequent years, Richard Nixon courted these Democratic voters by calling them the country's silent majority. By the 1980s, they became the "Reagan Democrats" who helped bring conservatism to power. In 1965, however, mainstream critics dismissed the group as illegitimate, and Conservatives refused to trumpet their support.

Conservatives stressed a more obvious achievement in the immediate aftermath of the 1965 election. In the special election of state legislators, the Republican Party won back control of only one chamber, the state senate. Democrats retained a majority in the assembly. Conservative leaders boasted that their party's independent nominees denied the GOP this prize. In eleven races won by Democratic assembly candidates, the votes received by the Conservative nominee exceeded the Democrat's margin of victory. In other words, if the Conservative Party had cross-endorsed the Republican candidate in those races, that Republican candidate would have won. In addition, if those eleven Republican assembly nominees had won, the GOP would have regained control of the assembly. For the first time, Conservatives succeeded in imposing an electoral punishment on the state GOP. An overall increase in public support for Conservative nominees permitted this accomplishment. Conservative legislative candidates attracted an average of 5.8 percent of the vote, almost two and one-half times better than the comparable 1964 average. While still a small percentage, these votes affected the outcome of competitive races. The party credited this increased support to the experience from having run candidates the previous year and the energy generated by running so many independent nominees. The New York City mayoral campaign also played a part. The interest of the national press and upstate newspapers brought Buckley's campaign to all residents of New York State. For many, it represented their first exposure to a Conservative Party candidate. Buckley's controversial policy proposals attracted some upstate New Yorkers in the same way they attracted residents of Queens and Brooklyn. Support for the party's most prominent nominee translated into increased support for local Conservative candidates.

CONSEQUENCES

The 1965 New York City mayoral election transformed William Buckley from a leader of the conservative movement to a national celebrity. In 1966, largely because of his performance in the previous year's debates, William F. Buckley began moderating the television show *Firing Line*. Broadcast initially on a local New York City commercial station, it soon moved to public television with a national audience. Buckley's mixture of erudition, humor, and invective produced a blend of serious discussion and rhetorical fireworks that won viewers across the political spectrum.[82] As a national celebrity, Buckley dominated the public's perception of the Conservative Party. Commentators often erroneously credited him with overseeing the party's operational management. In reality, Buckley devoted his time to editing a magazine, writing a syndicated newspaper column, and hosting a weekly television show. Dan Mahoney and other Conservative leaders, however, usually chose not to correct this misperception. Buckley's fame brought the party press attention, increased fundraising potential, and prominence among national conservatives.

The party struggled to identify an electoral strategy that would produce change in the state GOP. All Conservatives agreed that the party should oppose liberal Republican candidates. The party divided, however, over how to respond when ideologically acceptable Republicans refused Conservative endorsement, usually at the request of the local GOP organization. The policy dispute intensified as the Conservative Party's strength, and therefore its ability to punish the GOP, grew. Donald Devine, a graduate student at Syracuse University and a national director of YAF, publicly criticized the party on this issue. In YAF's monthly magazine, Devine reproached party leaders for fielding independent candidates when ideologically acceptable Republicans declined cross-endorsement. He cited several examples of Republicans whose careers were derailed by what he viewed as unnecessary Conservative opposition. Devine accused Conservatives of now wanting to replace, not reform, the state GOP. "The Conservative Party has turned its emphasis from *conservative* to *party*," he argued.[83] Earlier in the year, Neal Freeman, a *National Review* staff member, wrote Bill Buckley making the same argument. He also believed the Conservative Party's strategy would only defeat ideologically conservative Republicans and "de-conservatize" the GOP.[84] Dan Mahoney countered this argument with his own article in YAF's magazine. Mahoney contended that Conservatives had no desire to become the state's second party, and blamed the state's liberal GOP leaders for pressuring its candidates to reject Conservative endorsement. He reiterated the party's commitment to a "full-line" policy in all but the most exceptional circumstances. Mahoney concluded by calling on GOP candidates to accept Conservative endorsement when it was offered.[85]

Conservative Party endorsement of Republican candidates split the party between those comfortable with the political compromise inherent in cross-endorsement and those inspired by a belief in unadulterated conservatism. Some prominent activists, such as Devine and Freeman, with ties to ideologically conservative politicians favored a conciliatory approach to the GOP. Other party members, active at the grassroots level, supported a confrontational approach. These local members already believed the party was too willing to make deals that sacrificed conservative principles for short-term political gain. Mahoney and other state party leaders continually negotiated compromises between these two opposing factions. The issue of when to cross-endorse Republicans, when to run independent nominees, and when not to field a candidate remained a consistent source of tension within the Conservative Party. Despite Mahoney's contention that the party diverged from its "full-line" approach only under "exceptional circumstances," the party routinely compromised on this point. Conservatives did not field a candidate in over 31 percent of races in the 1965 election and again failed to do so in 26 percent of races in 1966. Arguing for the necessity of a "full line" while abandoning this policy in one-quarter to one-third of all races demonstrated the party's struggle to find an acceptable compromise.

John Lindsay's election as mayor of New York City and continuing commitment to fusion also introduced internal pressures into the New York City GOP. The initial clash took place in Queens, where the leader of the county GOP, George Archinal, reportedly barred members of the administration from speaking at his Queens Republican clubs. While denying the specific charge, Archinal blamed the administration's refusal to distribute patronage positions for creating discord and crippling his ability to build the party organization. Other disputes extended beyond mere patronage, however. Republicans in Queens, as well as in the Bronx, Staten Island, and parts of Brooklyn, were more conservative than the mayor. Many of these Republicans voted for Buckley in 1965. They also had a different background and approach to politics. Local GOP organizations were staffed by traditional clubhouse politicians who placed a high premium on party loyalty. They were bewildered and frustrated by a nonpartisan mayor who filled his administration with an enthusiastic staff long on academic credentials but short on political experience. The local politicians often dismissed these newcomers as inexperienced and arrogant. For their part, Lindsay and his representatives considered these local party members as Republicans of the past, in terms of both their approach to politics and the conservatism they espoused.

By the following year, GOP discontent with the mayor spread to the Bronx. While the borough was heavily Democratic, the ideologically conservative county GOP maintained a disciplined organization. Paul Fino, both a congressman and head of the Bronx Republican Party, led this mutiny against the mayor. As with Archinal from the Queens GOP, a traditional power struggle accounted for some of the animosity between the two politicians. Fino felt slighted by a Republican administration more willing to appoint members of the Liberal Party. For his part, Lindsay unsuccessfully attempted to replace Fino loyalists with his own troops in the local party organization. Fino dramatized the controversy by erecting a billboard on the Bronx end of a bridge connecting the borough to Manhattan. Poking fun at the mayor's nickname for New York, the sign declared "Fun City Line Ends Here. Republicans of Bronx County want no fun riots, no fun taxes, no fun crimes, no fun mayor."[86] Fino backed up these words by successfully fending off the mayor's attempts to reduce his control of the county GOP.

This political squabble also contained an ideological component. Lindsay's liberalism alienated Bronx Republicans who believed the mayor focused on race relations and social welfare programs rather than their concerns of crime, taxes, and the delivery of basic city services. This ideological division drew the Conservative Party into the GOP battle. The party had cross-endorsed Fino in his successful 1966 re-election bid for Congress. By 1967, the Bronx Conservative Party aggressively backed Fino and his organization in their quarrel with county Republicans, even taking advertisements in local newspapers calling for his re-election as the leader of the county GOP.[87] Fino clarified his allegiances in a rebuttal to a *New York Times* editorial that characterized Lindsay's supporters as "bright young men." The congressman countered: "Let me assure you that I am not worried about the young people of our city—the last time I saw them active politically they were wearing Buckley buttons."[88] By the spring of 1967, Fino's opponents in the county GOP formed an organization to work for a progressive Bronx Republican Party instead of one that was "cozy" with the Conservative Party.[89] Although Conservatives did not create the dispute in the Bronx, they benefited when the GOP quarreled along ideological lines.

Conservative success in the 1965 New York City mayoral race failed to significantly alter the party's relationship with the state GOP, however. In elections across the state in 1966, New York Republican politicians continued to shun both the Conservative Party and even the label of conservative. A high-profile battle for a Republican congressional nomination on Long Island demonstrated this dynamic. In the party's 1964 debacle, Steven Derounian lost his traditionally Republican seat in Nassau County. An ideological conservative, Derounian had hosted the Conservative Party's controversial Washington, D.C., meeting with most of the state's Republican congressional delegation. Derounian's opponent in the 1966 Republican primary, Long Island attorney and future head of the Central Intelligence Agency,

William J. Casey, shared his conservative viewpoint. This face-off between two ideological conservatives became, according to *National Review*, "one of the strangest contests in history."[90]

Chastened by his 1964 defeat, Derounian emerged two years later as a transformed candidate emphasizing his support of progressive causes and consistently denouncing far-right extremists. Casey's conversion was even more dramatic. His self-financed campaign positioned him as a forward-thinking Republican with a better chance in the general election.[91] Conservatives such as Barry Goldwater and William Buckley expressed surprise at how the candidate presented himself. Buckley, who had a long personal relationship with Casey, devoted a column to his belief that the lawyer was a conservative.[92] Casey responded by accusing conservatives of trying to sabotage his campaign with their public embrace. He wrote Jacob Javits, a supporter, "I hope Goldwater and Buckley, in moving for Derounian and against me, do me as much good as they did Lindsay last fall."[93] Eventually, each candidate worked to define his opponent as a conservative. Derounian held a series of news conferences to announce new examples of Casey's conservatism. Casey retaliated by publicizing Derounian's ties to the Conservative Party as evidence of the former congressman's true beliefs.[94] Derounian's response that he never accepted third-party endorsement, while technically true, obscured his past relationship with the party. On June 28, Steven Derounian handily defeated Bill Casey in the Republican primary. Some Conservatives, in light of Casey's extreme ideological apostasy, claimed victory.[95] In reality, the campaign's significance eclipsed its outcome. Derounian and Casey, both with solid conservative credentials, campaigned by running away from that ideology. The Conservative Party still had much work to do with New York Republicans.

A disagreement among supporters of Nelson Rockefeller further demonstrated the controversial image of conservatism in the state GOP. On April 24, a front-page story in the *New York Times* reported that former Congressman William Miller offered to assist Rockefeller in his re-election campaign.[96] Since Miller was Barry Goldwater's running mate in 1964, his offer seemed to promise an end to the party's divisions opened by the 1964 presidential campaign. Rockefeller responded positively, if somewhat cautiously, to Miller's overture. His instinct toward caution proved sound. Almost immediately, Jackie Robinson publicly called on the governor to reject Miller's assistance. Robinson viewed the former congressman as part of the GOP's abandonment of blacks in the 1964 campaign. He told the press that with Miller in the governor's re-election campaign, "There's no room for me."[97] Robinson, as Rockefeller's most prominent longtime African-American supporter, represented the governor's hope to expand the Republican Party's standing within minority communities. After meeting with Robinson, the governor rejected Miller's assistance, asserting that his seemingly clear acceptance had been misinterpreted. This brief skirmish demonstrated the tension developing within the GOP's ideological coalition. Robinson and many other black Republicans saw the Goldwater-Miller campaign as unacceptably conservative and opposed a GOP that included advocates of this ideology. Forced to choose, Rockefeller never hesitated, selecting the constituency he saw as the future of the Republican Party.

A CONSERVATIVE REFERENDUM

As 1966 began, political observers focused on the state's most important race, the gubernatorial campaign. The Liberal Party balked at cross-endorsing the Democratic gubernatorial nominee, and decided to run an independent nominee, former Congressman Franklin D. Roosevelt Jr. This decision, in part, was a reaction to the Conservative Party's growing electoral strength. New York election law stipulated that state ballots list parties according to their gubernatorial candidates' order of finish. Each gubernatorial election, therefore, determined the ballot order of every party for the next four years. Nelson Rockefeller's victory in 1962 meant GOP candidates enjoyed Row A for four years. Many politicians believed that an enhanced ballot position increased both intentional and inadvertent votes. Liberals, as the most prominent alternative to the two major parties, traditionally secured Row C. A growing Conservative Party vote threatened liberal retention of that row on the ballot. Running an independent campaign with the most famous name in American politics improved the party's chances of winning more votes than the Conservatives. Conservatives had no presidential sons to whom they could offer their nomination. Although the party briefly flirted with nominating William Rickenbacker, the son of famed World War I flying ace Eddie Rickenbacker, it reverted to past form and nominated a little-known academic and political neophyte. Paul Adams served as dean and taught political science at Roberts Wesleyan College outside Rochester. A registered Republican, Adams supported the Conservative Party and its ideological principles. An articulate speaker, he presented a reassuring figure with his calm and reasoned manner. Still, the professor, with no experience or name recognition, seemed politically overmatched by Franklin D. Roosevelt Jr.

The year's congressional and state legislative elections presented the Republican Party with another opportunity to recoup its 1964 losses. In congressional races, the party concentrated on winning back at least some of the seven House seats lost in that earlier election. For the most part, the year repeated the pattern of recent elections with Republican candidates rejecting Conservative Party attempts to cross-endorse. A short-lived break from this policy surfaced in the suburbs of New York City, however, when Suffolk County's Republican chairman briefly allowed individual GOP candidates to accept or reject Conservative endorsement. Several Republican nominees, including Congressman James Grover, accepted this offer of Conservative support. In the face of pressure from the state Republican organization, the county GOP reversed course again, requiring Conservative endorsement of all Republican nominees as a precondition to any GOP candidate's accepting cross-endorsement. Having already endorsed one Democratic assembly candidate, the Conservative Party rejected this demand. Again denied the opportunity to cross-endorse a Republican, Conservatives ran an independent candidate against Grover.

A similar situation in neighboring Nassau County produced an electoral version of a shotgun wedding between the two parties. The Conservative Party offered its endorsement to Thomas Brennan, the Republican congressional candidate. Brennan accepted the endorsement in spite of the county Republican Party's hostility toward Conservatives. The county GOP reportedly threatened to replace Brennan as its nominee, leaving him to run only on the Conservative Party line.[98] Brennan relented, and rejected the Conservative nomination. The candidate, however, had signed an affidavit accepting the Conservative endorsement, and the party filed suit to force him to accept it. A lower court ruled in favor of Brennan, but a state appeals court reversed the decision and required the candidate to accept the Conservative nomination. The suit demonstrated both the Conservative Party's overwhelming desire to align with the GOP and the Republican Party's determination to prevent this alliance.

In elections for the state legislature, the Republican Party again hoped to retake control of the assembly it had lost in 1964. Conservative Party headquarters urged local party leaders to remind Republicans that Conservative candidates proved costly in the 1965 election. The headquarters memo reassured local party leaders that "there is little hope of Republicans gaining control of the Assembly in absence of our support."[99] Despite this incentive, Republican candidates still rejected Conservative support. The Conservative Party's legislative liaison, Ted Waterman, continued to encounter GOP candidates who wanted to accept Conservative cross-endorsement, but were prevented from doing so by their county GOP organization.[100] As a result, the pattern of the previous year's election remained virtually unchanged. In 1966, Conservatives cross-endorsed only 20 percent of Republican legislative and congressional candidates while running an independent nominee in 52 percent of these races.

The political isolation imposed on the Conservative Party by Nelson Rockefeller and the New York GOP proved beneficial, however, in the year's most consequential campaign. Surprisingly, this critical election concerned a referendum, a political instrument that traditionally met with public apathy. This referendum, although it concerned only New York City, became the most controversial and closely watched contest in the state. More importantly, it allowed the Conservative Party to reinforce the themes articulated in the Buckley campaign that attracted Democratic converts.

Soon after assuming office, John Lindsay made good on a campaign promise to change the composition of the city's police review board. In May of 1966, citing the lack of confidence many New Yorkers had in their police force, he issued an executive order creating a civilian majority on the board. The Conservative Party immediately criticized the new board as endangering the safety of New Yorkers and drafted a referendum to nullify the mayor's executive order. The Patrolmen's Benevolent Association (PBA), an organization vehemently opposed to a Civilian Review Board, also planned to initiate a referendum. Given the PBA's far greater financial resources, party leaders considered supporting the association's initiative rather than sponsoring their own referendum. Two considerations, however, persuaded Conservatives to pursue an independent course. First, the party feared that the PBA's proposed referendum was vulnerable to a court challenge because its language was too specific for a city charter amendment. Conservative leaders believed that their more generally worded referendum offered protection from this type of challenge. Second, the Buckley campaign proved that opposing the Civilian Review Board was politically popular. During a statewide election year, the lure of such a popular issue proved too great to pass up. In June, after meeting with the PBA, the party decided to pursue a referendum of its own. The Conservative Party needed to gather signatures from thirty thousand New Yorkers by July 7, and an additional fifteen thousand by September 8, to get its referendum on New York's ballot.

Conservative leaders asked James Leff, who had overseen the party's 1962 petition campaign, to head this review board effort. Leff agreed to sign on, provided the party raised the twenty-five thousand dollars he believed was needed. To obtain this money, Conservatives enlisted conservative fundraiser Marvin Liebman. Liebman identified three ways to raise the needed money, all possible as a result of the Buckley mayoral campaign. First, he wanted use of the roughly eight thousand dollars left over from Buckley's run. Second, he wanted the party to host a small gathering of large donors identified the previous year. Finally, Liebman planned a mailing to the roughly nine thousand five hundred small contributors to Bill Buckley's campaign.[101] The fundraiser's appeals emphasized the growing tension within the GOP's broad ideological coalition. He wrote James Buckley, who had managed his brother's mayoral run, asking for use of the campaign's residual funds. His letter promised that "[i]f the vote goes against a review board, it will add to the damage to the 'moderate' Republican image of Lindsay and his colleagues."[102] To host the small gathering of conservative donors, Liebman turned to the dependable Jeremiah Milbank. Liebman reminded the financier that Buckley's mayoral campaign tarnished both Lindsay and moderate Republicanism. "We now have the opportunity," he reported, "to continue the attack through the issue of the Civilian Review Board."[103] For the fundraising letter aimed at contributors to the Buckley campaign, Liebman recruited Charles Edison. On June 22, the Conservative Party sent Edison's letter to all contributors to Bill Buckley's 1965 campaign. It praised Bill Buckley for predicting "the inadequacies and potential dangers of 'liberal' Republicanism" and called the review board referendum "a major opportunity to consolidate this accomplishment."[104]

Liebman's three-pronged fundraising strategy raised the money needed for the Conservative Party to begin its referendum campaign. In accordance with election law, the party established a separate petition organization, the Committee on Public Safety, better known by its apt acronym, COPS. While COPS had a separate headquarters, it was run by party leaders and staffed by party members. The organization turned to Conservative Party volunteers to do most of the basic work of gathering signatures. On June 22, the committee sent a petition to every Conservative Party member in the five boroughs. The cover letter, signed by Bill Buckley, laid out the necessarily rushed procedure for collecting petition signatures. Because petitions had to be filed by July 7, Buckley's letter instructed Conservatives to gather twenty-five petition signatures and bring them personally to the organization's headquarters by July 1. Explaining the urgency of the situation, Buckley called the party's effort "the most vital political action program New York conservatives have undertaken in years."[105] The letter had the desired effect. Party members gathered signatures in their neighborhoods and brought them to committee headquarters. On July 7, the party filed just over forty thousand petition signatures with the New York City clerk. The second requirement to place a referendum on the ballot, an additional fifteen thousand signatures by September 8, offered less of a challenge, and the party had little trouble collecting those signatures. By then, however, the battlefield had shifted to the courts.

After Conservatives filed the first batch of petition signatures, New York City Clerk Herman Katz ruled the petition invalid on two grounds: Katz held that the party's referendum was not in the proper form for a charter amendment and that eighteen thousand of its initial batch of signatures were invalid. James Leff persuaded the courts to reverse Katz's ruling concerning the form of the referendum and to institute a procedure to allow the party to revalidate the disputed signatures. This revalidation process seemed to ensure the party's referendum a place on the ballot. Conservative chairman Dan Mahoney, however, directed Jim Leff to temporarily cease submitting signatures for revalidation. Mahoney believed the party should abandon its referendum. The PBA referendum had survived its own legal challenges and secured a place on the November ballot. The Conservative Party referendum seemed redundant and likely to further confuse an already complex issue. Withdrawing the party's referendum was not without its risks, however. That decision might alienate the party's rank and file who had worked so hard gathering petition signatures. Additionally, it jeopardized any political windfall from being closely identified with a popular issue.

The party held a series of meetings throughout September, sometimes with PBA representatives, sometimes just with Conservative officials, to consider its options. On September 28, the party finally decided to withdraw its petition. The following morning, Leff informed the court that the Conservative

Party would not move to revalidate any signatures beyond the current level of 29,985, just fifteen short of the required number. Lawyers for the Lindsay administration reacted by also reversing their approach. They now argued that the signature requirement had actually been met and that the referendum must appear on the November ballot. The party concluded that the Lindsay administration aimed to confuse voters by forcing two referendums onto the ballot. Leff returned to court. On October 25, after two lower courts divided on the question, the Court of Appeals handed the Conservative Party a victory and allowed it to withdraw its referendum.

As this legal battle worked its way through the courts, a high-profile and at times bitter political campaign over the remaining referendum captured the attention of New Yorkers. Without its own referendum, the Conservative Party threw its support behind the PBA's version. The PBA, however, sought to distance itself from the Conservative Party. Reacting to a private poll that indicated the party could be a liability to its referendum campaign, the PBA attempted to limit its public connection with Conservatives.[106] When the press revealed that PBA representatives consulted with Conservative leaders when the party withdrew its petition, the association played down any connection. A PBA spokesman told reporters, "The Conservative Party happens to be working the same side of the street—that's all."[107] When the party stamped its name on pro-referendum literature, the PBA warned it to stop.[108]

Advocates of the Civilian Review Board tried to undermine support for the referendum by attributing it to the "radical right." The organization created to oppose the referendum, the Federated Association for Impartial Review, or FAIR, embraced this strategy. Representatives of FAIR reportedly delighted in the Conservative Party's participation because it made this strategy easier. In an interview with a *New York Times* reporter, a leader of FAIR predicted that "[b]efore this campaign is over, people will feel ashamed to do anything but vote against the referendum." "It'll be like the Goldwater thing all over again," he added.[109] On the day after the Conservative Party and the PBA filed their petitions, John Lindsay warned of the "highly organized, militant, right-wing groups" opposed to the board.[110] While the mayor did not name any of these groups, he urged New Yorkers to frustrate them by supporting the board. By the fall, the charges became more frequent and more explicit. At one news conference, Lindsay displayed and denounced racist literature from the National Renaissance Party, a neo-Nazi group that approved of the referendum. Press releases from FAIR routinely linked the Conservative Party and the PBA to these extreme groups on the right. A FAIR pamphlet further escalated the controversy. The pamphlet listed the major participants on each side of the political struggle. The column of review board advocates included Mayor Lindsay, Senators Javits and Kennedy, Governor Nelson Rockefeller, Democratic gubernatorial nominee and New York City Council

President Frank O'Connor, and Liberal gubernatorial nominee Franklin D. Roosevelt Jr. Also listed were newspapers such as the *New York Times*, *New York Post*, and *New York World Journal Tribune*, and religious and political organizations such as the Catholic Interracial Council, the American Jewish Committee, the Protestant Council, and Americans for Democratic Action. Opposed to this collection of the city's establishment elite were five groups and one named individual: the Conservative Party, the PBA, the John Birch Society, the National Renaissance Party, the American Nazi Party, and its leader, George Lincoln Rockwell. Following this rather lopsided comparison, the pamphlet asked, "Which Side Are You On?"[111]

The Conservative Party responded immediately. Kieran O'Doherty, that year's lieutenant governor nominee, called the pamphlet "the most vicious, dirty, low smear ever conducted by a political organization in New York."[112] Conservatives contended that, while the Birch Society and various Nazi groups approved of the referendum, those organizations had no role in the campaign. They accused opponents of the referendum of focusing on extremists to bolster the "radical right" charge. The party filed a complaint with the Fair Campaign Practices Committee, a political watchdog group, accusing FAIR of practicing guilt by association. The *Daily News*, the only paper in the city supporting the referendum, ran an editorial seconding the complaint.[113] These objections, however, produced little in the way of results. Ten days before the election, Senators Kennedy and Javits held a news conference to publicize a report charging that the John Birch Society was central to the anti-review board effort. To counter these attacks, *National Review* routinely ran articles on the review board, including an interview with Dan Mahoney on the issue. Mahoney argued that a review board would destroy the morale and effectiveness of the police force at a time when it was critically needed.[114] Buckley also devoted an installment of his new television show, "Firing Line," to the referendum campaign. In a surprisingly civil debate with labor leader and review board supporter Theodore Kheel, Buckley argued for the need to protect the police from unjust criticism.[115] Across the city and even beyond, the party's candidates for office consistently emphasized the review board issue in their campaigns.

FAIR's harshly negative campaign may have actually helped the Conservative Party. Some Conservatives feared that the party's decision to withdraw its own referendum cost them visibility and a significant political advantage. The "radical right" charge, however, guaranteed that the Conservative Party and the referendum remained linked in the public's mind. The press covered charges that the party was part of a right-wing alliance, and the party's rebuttals. It resulted, literally, in publicity the party could not have bought. Throughout the fall, Conservative Party candidates stressed the importance of law and order when campaigning for the referendum. As in Buckley's mayoral campaign, this theme proved immensely popular.

TWIN VICTORIES

The gubernatorial race dominated politics in the rest of the state. Conservative Party nominee Paul Adams combined an aggressive campaign with the low-key, affable manner befitting his years in academia. Reporting in the *New York Times*, Terence Smith wrote that the candidate "gives a political speech as if it was a lecture on early American history."[116] This style belied a campaign aggressively critical of Nelson Rockefeller. Adams' slogan—"I've had enough"—crystallized dissatisfaction with the governor's record. Principally concerned with the growth in state spending, the candidate proposed a 5 percent across-the-board spending cut. Adams also consistently opposed the civilian review board. In fact, Adams stumped so heavily for the referendum that columnists Rowland Evans and Robert Novak wrote that the college professor was basing his entire campaign on the issue.[117] While that was an exaggeration, Adams, as well as the party's congressional and legislative candidates, seldom passed up an opportunity to stress their individual and their party's support for the referendum.

Throughout 1966, the Rockefeller campaign monitored and reacted to the Conservative threat. The campaign, viewing this challenge as more serious than it had been in 1962, responded more aggressively. In February, Lieutenant Governor Malcolm Wilson prepared a memo on the "Conservative Party Problem."[118] As part of its solution, the governor's campaign resurrected lectures Thomas Dewey had delivered at Princeton University more than a decade and a half earlier on the dangers of splinter parties. In 1966, Doubleday published the lectures along with an introduction by Rockefeller advisor John Wells that vouched for their continued relevance.[119] Rockefeller also assigned surrogates to woo Conservative voters. In August, the governor's campaign sent Richard Nixon to Syracuse with this assignment.[120] By the fall, the campaign used Dewey and Malcolm Wilson for this same job.[121] Rockefeller staff rejected using William Miller to try to win back Conservative voters, however, lest the campaign acquire a "Goldwater patina."[122]

On election day, New York State voters re-elected most incumbents, keeping the fortunes of both major parties largely unchanged. In the gubernatorial race, Nelson Rockefeller won re-election, easily defeating Democrat Frank O'Connor. While the governor's margin of victory was comfortable, his percentage of the vote declined to 45 percent. This drop resulted from the number of votes received by the Liberal and Conservative candidates. Together, Franklin D. Roosevelt Jr. and Paul Adams won over one million votes. Adams's share of this total represented a high-water mark for a Conservative candidate and demonstrated the party's increasing statewide presence. A *New York Times* editorial grumbled that "Conservative strength in election after election indicates a disturbing right-wing tide within the Empire State, which has long been a citadel of political reform."[123] Elections in the House and the state legislature also returned most incumbents to office. Most importantly, the GOP failed to win back any of the seven state assembly seats it had lost in 1964. All of the Democratic freshmen in those races won re-election by comfortable margins and the party retained control of the assembly.

Despite the fact that the results seemed to endorse the status quo, the Conservative Party made important progress in the election. First, the Conservative Party imposed a significant political price on Republicans by assisting in the GOP's failure to regain control of the assembly. In 1965, the state GOP continued to insist that Republican nominees refuse Conservative cross-endorsement. The following year, however, Conservatives responded by fielding candidates against even ideologically compatible Republican nominees. Because Conservative Party legislative candidates increased their average percentage of the vote to 6.8 percent, they siphoned off enough traditionally Republican votes to affect the outcome in numerous races. Republican candidates often lost by fewer votes than the Conservative nominee received. These Republican losses prevented the party from regaining control of the assembly. From its inception, the Conservative Party recognized that it would not be able to change the state GOP if it could not impose an electoral cost when defied. In 1966, the party was able to do this on a statewide basis for the first time.

Second, the party benefited from New York City voters overturning the Civilian Review Board by an almost two-to-one margin. The referendum lost narrowly in Manhattan, but piled up large majorities in all other boroughs. Virtually every prominent Republican and Democrat opposed the referendum, characterizing it as so extreme as to be outside the political mainstream. An overwhelming majority of New York voters, however, supported the measure as part of a necessary effort to restore law and order. Because Conservatives stood alone in their support of this popular issue, they shared in the referendum's victory.

A final achievement took several weeks to emerge. On November 23, the Liberal Party placed an advertisement in the *New York Times* touting its success in the recent election. Besting the Conservative Party by twelve thousand votes, the party emphasized the significance of its nominee's finishing third in the gubernatorial race. "Had we lost Column 'C' to the Conservative Party," the Liberal advertisement explained, "it would have been a blow to liberal-minded people throughout the nation and front-page news everywhere."[124] The party's predictions came back to haunt it when a recount showed that Adams had actually beaten Roosevelt by some seven thousand votes. The Conservative Party exulted over the turn of events, calling the winning of Row C a culmination of "five years of hard won achievement."[125] While Row C's electoral benefits were likely overblown, securing this line on the ballot did prove helpful for the party. The party's third-place finish, and the publicity windfall resulting from an entertaining political story, gave Conservatives an increased measure of respectability. Many liberal Republicans justified their hostility toward Conservatives by charging the party was outside the political mainstream. Securing Row C made Conservatives appear less extreme and more like just another minor party.

Many leading New York Republicans were unimpressed with Conservative achievements in the election. Several of these GOP politicians dismissed the Conservatives' winning Row C as a one-time consequence of the Civilian Review Board referendum. They argued that Conservatives won Row C only because the referendum inflated their vote in New York City. Republicans predicted the Conservative Party would be unable to retain its current level of support in future elections. Appearing on television shortly after the recount re-awarded Row C, Javits dismissed Conservative electoral strength as a merely temporary reflection of voter displeasure over the referendum.[126] The *New York Times* quoted an anonymous state Republican official predicting that any member of the GOP who identified with the Conservatives "would sign his own death warrant in New York."[127]

While Republicans and their supporters looked to explain away Conservative achievements, the reality was that the third party had made significant gains. Winning Row C meant the party could not be as easily marginalized as it had been during its early years. The party's role in the Civilian Review Board referendum proved even more important. Even though only New York City residents voted on it, the measure influenced a wider region. Most clearly, the surrounding suburbs followed the campaign in numerous newspaper and television accounts. Partly as a result of the referendum's popularity, the party's candidates made tremendous gains in the four counties surrounding New York City. For example, Paul Adams captured 15 percent of the vote in Long Island's Suffolk County. Its opposition to the civilian review board distinguished the Conservative Party from the state's other parties, and created common ground with many New Yorkers for the first time. On a broader level, the referendum's approval challenged New York's ideological image. Conventional wisdom considered New York a liberal state principally because New York City was so liberal. Now the city's electorate overwhelmingly rejected a liberal cause supported by most political leaders.[128]

The elections of 1965 and 1966 forced politicians within and outside the state to reassess the relative electoral strength of liberal and conservative policies in New York. The referendum victory, like Buckley's surprisingly strong showing the previous year, demonstrated the widespread popularity of conservative positions on social issues. Conservatives did not abandon their traditional belief in anti-communism or smaller government. The 1965 Buckley mayoral campaign and the 1966 Civilian Review Board referendum, however, taught them the power of advocating welfare reform, supporting neighborhood schools, and above all, restoring law and order. The potency of these issues, and the voters they attracted, ethnic blue-collar whites, made a more conservative state GOP seem possible. Even more importantly, these same issues and voters soon attracted the attention of national Republicans.

FOUR

THE BEGINNINGS OF CHANGE

The achievements of the New York Conservatives in 1965 and 1966 demonstrated the rising popularity of the party and of conservatism in general. These displays of Conservative electoral strength persuaded elements of the state GOP to shift their approach and cooperate with the third party. The state's more prominent and more liberal Republican politicians, however, continued to reject any alliance with the Conservative Party. Richard Nixon resolved the political stalemate. First as the Republican presidential nominee and then as president, Nixon demonstrated a willingness to align with New York Conservatives. The Conservative Party began to use its growing strength to reshape New York's political landscape, a fact made clear to liberal Republicans when one of their stars suffered an electoral defeat.

LOOKING AHEAD

In 1967, a 54-year-old Wall Street lawyer and Manhattan resident began campaigning for the Republican presidential nomination in earnest. The fact that no one thought of Richard Nixon as a New York Republican demonstrated the former vice president's lack of local ties or connection to the state party. Nixon had moved to New York City following his bitter defeat in the 1962 California gubernatorial race. He maintained a low public profile and played no role in the New York Republican Party. Even Nixon considered himself "in political terms a man without a country" during this time.[1] None of the state's leading Republicans supported Nixon's initial campaign for the presidency. Nelson Rockefeller claimed to back Michigan Governor George Romney, even allowing several key aides to join Romney's campaign. Many supporters and detractors considered Rockefeller's support of Romney to be a ploy and predicted that the governor, a declared noncandidate, would end up running himself. Jacob Javits also supported Romney, but tempered this support with a personal agenda. In a private meeting with leaders of the Ripon Society, Javits advised the Republican liberals that he planned to launch an "ideological bid" for the presidency to ensure greater attention for his policy proposals.[2] John Lindsay preferred Illinois Senator Charles Percy, an ideological choice similar to Romney. These three leading New York Republicans managed to turn this near-agreement into a political feud through much of 1967. Javits and Rockefeller quarreled about who would lead the state convention delegation as New York's favorite son. Lindsay and Rockefeller bickered when the mayor announced he supported Rockefeller for president. Given his noncandidacy, the governor considered this a hostile act intended to expose him to criticism and promote a Lindsay candidacy. The three Republicans all agreed, however, on Richard Nixon's unacceptability. They denounced the former vice president as an ideological conservative and completely discounted his tenuous New York connections.

New York Conservatives viewed the presidential race very differently. They rejected both Romney and Percy, stalwarts of liberal republicanism, as ideologically unacceptable. With Barry Goldwater no longer a viable candidate, most New York Conservatives gravitated toward recently elected California governor Ronald Reagan. In the party's newsletter, Kieran O'Doherty wrote that Reagan was a serious Republican candidate who consistently dazzled party regulars with his charisma.[3] Dan Mahoney advised Conservatives "to provide maximum support to Reagan at every stage of the pre-convention effort."[4] In the fall of 1967, the party began courting Reagan by hosting a speaking tour by the governor's daughter, Maureen.[5] Conservatives favored Ronald Reagan, but the governor was in his first year of elective office and had yet to clarify his political ambitions. In contrast, an experienced Richard Nixon was putting together a presidential campaign from within New York State. While Conservatives regarded the former vice president as more acceptable than liberals such as Javits or Lindsay, they never considered him an ideological comrade. Party leaders cited Nixon's "Treaty of Fifth Avenue" with Rockefeller as evidence that he had few bedrock principles besides political expediency. Conservatives were also alarmed by a much more recent incident where Nixon seemed to smear the party.

During the 1965 New York City mayoral campaign, an Evans and Novak column reported that Nixon had characterized the "Buckleyites" as a threat to the Republican Party even more menacing than the Birchers. The comment so enraged *National Review* publisher William Rusher that he began a crusade to force Nixon to confirm or deny the report. Rusher sent several letters to the former vice president, all of which went unanswered. Rusher related the incident on television and used *National Review* to keep the issue before its conservative readers.[6] In the spring of 1966, newly hired Nixon aide Patrick Buchanan finally responded. Buchanan, in what he later characterized as a "tortured letter," claimed Nixon had been misunderstood.[7] His version of events, however, bore no resemblance to the original newspaper report. Buchanan maintained that, when questioned about the Buckley campaign and the John Birch Society, "Mr. Nixon invariably replied that Mr. Buckley, by his repudiation of the Birch Society in his magazine and syndicated column, had therefore made himself a much stronger candidate and a greater threat to the Republican candidate, Representative Lindsay."[8] Privately, Buckley expressed a lack of surprise at this response, although he noted its inconsistencies with previous accounts.[9] In May 1966, *National Review* published Buchanan's letter, and an editorial that expressed a belief in Mr. Nixon's explanation while managing to convey the opposite impression.[10]

Nixon went to great lengths to deny his derogatory comment about Buckley because he needed conservative support in his quest for the presidency. In the months prior to the official campaign, Nixon made a sustained effort to woo Republican conservatives. Hiring Buchanan represented a successful first step. Even the critical Rusher applauded the move, noting that, "[u]nder Buchanan's careful tutelage, Nixon made no more serious blunders in dealing with 'the Buckleyites.' "[11] The former vice president also personally courted Buckley, a recognition of the editor's status in the conservative movement. On a Sunday afternoon in January 1967, Nixon invited Buckley, Rusher, and several other prominent conservatives to his New York City apartment. For three hours, he expounded on domestic politics and foreign affairs. The performance was impressive enough to win Buckley, if not a more skeptical Rusher, to his side.

Nixon, of course, needed more than just conservative support to secure his party's presidential nomination. He wanted to present a moderate image that allowed all types of Republicans to endorse him. As part of this effort, the candidate also looked to secure at least the partial backing of the New York State delegation to the Republican convention. The delegation's support depended on the support, or at least the acquiescence, of the state's major Republicans. Nixon solicited Jacob Javits's opinion on foreign affairs and talked publicly about John Lindsay's strengths as a vice presidential candidate. Nixon also capitalized on the fact that Jacob Javits needed him as much as he needed Javits. The senator wanted to bolster his Republican credentials because he now faced a potential primary challenge.

In 1967, the New York legislature overhauled the state's nominating system. Under the new system, each party's state committee designated a candidate for statewide office. The new system also permitted any candidate who received 25 percent of the committee vote to challenge the designee in a party primary. In addition, any member of a party could force a primary by gathering ten thousand petition signatures with at least five hundred from each county. Rockefeller, who had blocked earlier attempts to reform the state's nominating system, now expressed concern that the legislation did not go far enough to establish a true direct primary. The governor set aside these reservations, however, and signed the bill. At first glance, this legislation seemed to address one of the major Conservative complaints about the state's politics. The Conservative Party cited the exclusive use of party conventions to nominate statewide candidates as one of the undemocratic methods used to unfairly marginalize conservative Republicans. The new nominating system seemed to promise relief from this problem. In reality, however, this revision failed to revolutionize the state's politics. Republican legislators enacted a measure that allowed parties to retain at least some control. Primaries occurred only when a challenger gained the support of a significant number of party officials or successfully completed a petition campaign. Additionally, Nelson Rockefeller remained in control of the state GOP through a combination of his gubernatorial powers, his willingness to use his great personal wealth, and the loyalty of most county and local party officials. These realities all created significant barriers to unwanted primaries and allowed party organizations to retain much of their power.

Concerned about even the limited possibility of a party primary, Senator Javits worked to bolster his support among upstate Republican voters and officials. A staff member reported that local party officials in four upstate counties knew of "small but vocal and dedicated groups of conservatives that were cause for concern."[12] The chairman of the Chemung County GOP warned him that Buckley or an upstate candidate could represent a real challenge in the primary. John Wells, an advisor to Javits as well as to Nelson Rockefeller, sent the senator an analysis concluding that he could lose a primary. At the same time Javits needed to shore up his party credentials, Richard Nixon wanted to increase his connection with the state GOP to strengthen his campaign in New York. In a single solution to these two problems, Nixon agreed to appear at a Javits fundraising dinner in December.[13] The first appearance of the former vice president at a state party function helped Javits with his Republican problem and Nixon with his New York problem. During this very successful event, Nixon explained that he hoped his appearance would discourage a primary challenge to Javits.[14] Javits maintained his support for Romney in the presidential race, but assured the crowd that Nixon would make an acceptable nominee. Given the senator's antagonism toward the party's presidential nominee in 1964, this statement represented something of a triumph for Nixon. The Conservative Party viewed Nixon's support of Javits as evidence of his unreliability and threatened to impose a political price. Kieran O'Doherty reminded Nixon that "[t]he Conservative Party at this time is not committed to the support of any individual for the Republican nomination for President."[15]

The new nominating system potentially offered Conservatives another way to impose an electoral cost on Republican liberals. The idea seemed especially tempting in the case of Jacob Javits. While a proven vote-getter in general elections, Javits's liberal record made him vulnerable in a party primary. A promising young political advisor provided statistical validation. In March, Bronx Republican congressman Paul Fino's administrative assistant, Kevin Phillips, sent William Buckley his recent study of New York City voting patterns. Phillips concluded that Javits was vulnerable in a

Republican primary given the state's growing conservative sentiment, and urged Buckley to run.[16] The party's efforts over the last several years had both revealed and enhanced the "state's growing conservative sentiment." Phillips cautioned Buckley, however, that his analysis and his advice were "completely unofficial." As a young aide to a New York Republican congressman, party loyalty mattered and he could not publicly work against the re-election of New York's Republican senator. By 1968, Phillips used this voting study as the basis for a manuscript which garnered him jobs first with Nixon's campaign and then the White House. The success of the subsequent book, *The Emerging Republican Majority*, allowed Phillips to leave the White House to become a writer and political commentator.

Throughout 1967, press reports speculated that a high-profile, ideologically conservative candidate like Buckley could present Javits with a difficult primary challenge. Even a newsletter published by *National Review* floated the idea of a Buckley candidacy.[17] In March, Dan Mahoney approached Buckley with the promise of Conservative Party support in a GOP primary. Buckley, believing he would lose a Republican primary and then be obliged to support Javits in the general election, declined to run.[18] He also feared the potential impact of a campaign on his reputation and career. Because Jacob Javits was Jewish, the editor risked being linked to the anti-Semitic portions of the far right from which he had worked to disassociate himself and the conservative movement. This linkage could, in turn, endanger his status as a television host and syndicated columnist.[19] In addition, Buckley was more interested in waiting until 1970 to challenge New York's other senator, Robert F. Kennedy. When a friend raised this possibility, Buckley equivocated, but promised that if Kennedy "is as menacing as he is now, it will certainly be the moment to try."[20]

Buckley allowed the party to keep his refusal to challenge Javits private. He wrote Mahoney that if the party found it "tactically useful," it could float his name as a potential candidate. Buckley warned the chairman, however, that he would have to make his intentions known if a draft movement materialized. He felt publicly rejecting a draft "would leave me looking selfish and petulant if I backed out at the last minute."[21] Mahoney agreed. "In the event we do mention your name from time to time in connection with the Javits race, I will make sure that it is not done in such a way as to get a serious 'Buckley for Senator' drive underway that might cause you embarrassment," he assured Buckley.[22] Reluctant to abandon the possibility of a celebrity nominee, Mahoney also gently reminded Buckley that he still had several months to become a state resident should he wish to qualify for the race.

By September, despite Dan Mahoney's promise, a movement to draft Buckley started. Several Conservatives in Queens formed the "Citizens Committee for the Election of William F. Buckley as U.S. Senator." The committee leaders acknowledged that Buckley did not support their effort, but found encouraging Buckley's refusal to declare he would not be a candidate.[23] Buckley immediately went public with his true plans, informing the Citizens Committee and the press that he would not challenge Jacob Javits.[24] The committee, faced with this public rejection, disbanded, albeit with some of the hurt feelings that Buckley feared.

ANOTHER BUCKLEY

By 1968, a number of local Republican organizations began to cooperate with the Conservative Party. This movement was most pronounced in the New York City suburbs where Conservative candidates had demonstrated significant appeal to voters. In Long Island's Nassau and Suffolk counties, leaders of the two parties began to meet jointly to determine which cross-endorsed candidates to run in upcoming elections. In Rochester's Monroe County, local representatives of the two parties also began to cooperate on a limited basis.[25] In Albany, State Senate Majority Leader Earl Brydges added Conservative Rosemary Gunning to his legislative staff. Gunning, who had run for New York City council president with William Buckley in 1965, served as the party's liaison with sympathetic Republican legislators. The party's enhanced role in Albany helped to win state senate approval of state financial assistance for parochial schools, something that had long been a part of the Conservative platform. The party's enhanced influence with the Republican majority helped pass the bill. The state GOP organization, however, opposed this new cooperation with the Conservative Party and continued to refuse any interparty alliance. The state's leading Republicans, Nelson Rockefeller and Jacob Javits, viewed any alliance with Conservatives as politically unwise. Running for a third Senate term in 1968, Javits planned a campaign that advocated liberal policies and spurned any connection with the Conservative Party.

As 1968 began, the Conservative Party, convinced that Jacob Javits was vulnerable with an electorate limited to GOP members, planned to sponsor a candidate in the Republican primary. New York's new nomination laws prohibited any registered Conservatives entering the Republican primary without GOP approval. Conservatives, convinced that the state GOP organization would not approve a Conservative candidate, searched for a member of the GOP willing to challenge Javits. Party leaders approached Henry J. Taylor about running, but the former ambassador and columnist declined.[26] The *New York Times*, quoting anonymous Republican sources, reported that former Congressmen William Miller and Steven Derounian also turned down Conservative Party offers.[27] Press reports speculated—as they had since 1965—that the Conservative Party would turn to William Buckley, who remained a registered Republican. The state YAF even took out a tongue-in-cheek classified advertisement in the *New York Times* to fill this position. Requesting a "Legitimate Republican to oppose Senator

Javits in a primary race," the notice promised YAF support to the winning applicant.[28] Like the Conservative Party efforts, however, this search proved fruitless. Jacob Javits's formidable political arsenal certainly discouraged Republican primary challengers. Javits was unparalleled among statewide Republican candidates in attracting popular support and winning elections. More importantly, Nelson Rockefeller placed the state party and his financial connections at the senator's disposal. As a result, any prospective Republican challenger faced long odds and the likelihood of political retribution.

Without a candidate for the primary, Conservatives shifted their attention to finding a nominee to run in the general election. In late February, again at the behest of Dan Mahoney, William Buckley called his older brother James offering Conservative support for a Senate campaign. James Buckley ran the family's oil and mining consulting firm, the Catawba Corporation, based in New York City. His political experience consisted of managing his brother's 1965 mayoral campaign. Mahoney pressed the party's case to the reluctant businessman. When James Buckley expressed doubts about the race because of his lack of experience and the potential impact on the family business, Mahoney assured him that the extremely long odds of winning meant the race only required a minimal time commitment.[29] With this understanding, Buckley agreed to become a candidate, and, on April 2, 1968, the Conservative Party formally designated him its Senate nominee. Calling his campaign "not quite quixotic," the candidate promised to speak out for true Republican principles.[30] These principles included the resumption of bombing if North Vietnam failed to demonstrate good faith in the peace talks. In keeping with a long-standing Conservative position, Buckley also advocated shifting power from the federal government to the state and local level. The candidate also emphasized issues that had become important to the party more recently, including the need to restore law and order to the country. When students seized control of several buildings at Columbia University later that month, Buckley easily integrated this controversy into his speeches about the issue.

As the Conservative Party prepared for a Senate campaign, Jacob Javits, spared a potentially difficult primary, looked to strengthen his position in the general election. The senator weighed running with the Liberal Party endorsement, something no statewide Republican candidate had ever done. Javits's staff contacted several upstate Republican county chairmen to gauge reaction to this cross-endorsement. In a typical response, Monroe County GOP chairman Richard Rosenbaum, future chairman of the state party in the 1970s, saw little advantage in his county from Javits's accepting the Liberal nomination. Rather, Rosenbaum feared that it might have a negative impact on local Republican candidates.[31] Javits, nonetheless, decided to pursue the Liberal Party nomination. On April 1, Liberals designated Javits as their Senate nominee, and Liberal Party activist Murray Baron promptly pledged to force a primary. With a Liberal primary looming, state GOP chairman

Charles Schoeneck asked Javits not to campaign publicly for the Liberal nomination because of its potential negative impact upstate.[32] Javits ran a nearly invisible campaign, relying on mailings to Liberal voters that focused on a common foe: the Conservative Party. In one letter, Javits identified himself as the primary target in a bitter war being waged by Conservatives and appealed to Liberals for help.[33] This approach worked; Javits easily won the Liberal party primary.

Armed with this cross-endorsement, the senator prepared for a general election campaign in which he courted Democrats, Liberals, and independents and denounced Conservatives. Richard Aurelio, the senator's campaign manager, judged Conservatives unrelentingly hostile to his candidate and incapable of being won over. He advised Javits to appeal to Democrats and Liberals by advertising his antagonistic relationship with Conservatives.[34] Following this advice, Javits told the *New York Times* that he expected Conservative opposition in the campaign and predicted that "there will be no quarter given or asked."[35] Jacob Javits' electoral strategy, accepting Liberal cross-endorsement and denouncing Conservative support, differed from that of most New York State Republicans. In 1968, more Republicans moved closer to the Conservative Party than to the Liberal Party. In the 1968 legislative and congressional races, Conservatives cross-endorsed Republican candidates in 38.7 percent of the races, up from 19.8 percent in 1966. Not surprisingly, this cooperative spirit was strongest in the suburban counties on Long Island. In Nassau County, Conservatives endorsed most Republican candidates in exchange for the GOP's backing a Conservative congressional nominee, Mason Hampton, and an assembly nominee, Charles Jerabek. The Ripon Society condemned the arrangement as blackmail by a third party while Conservatives applauded it as a sensible reaction to their increased political influence.[36] This electoral alliance on Long Island stood in stark contrast with Senator Javits's campaign of public hostility aimed at the Conservative Party. The New York GOP stood at a crossroads in terms of its relationship with state Conservatives.

NIXON

At the onset of 1968, Conservative leaders preferred California Governor Ronald Reagan for president, but were prepared to accept Richard Nixon, the front runner for the GOP nomination. If, however, Michigan Governor George Romney, Illinois Senator Charles Percy or—as always—Nelson Rockefeller won the GOP nomination, the party planned to nominate another candidate.[37] Conservative Party officials publicly and consistently criticized the governor during the early months of 1968. As they had in 1964, Conservatives also worked behind the scenes to frustrate Rockefeller's national ambitions. In March, Dan Mahoney contacted a select number of national conservative leaders and writers concerning the presidential race. He sent the group a voting analysis showing that Rockefeller's gubernatorial victories failed to provide coattails to other Republican candidates on the ballot. Mahoney explained that the study "should be useful ammunition against the Rockefeller contention that a Rockefeller presidential candidacy would sweep Republicans into local offices throughout the nation."[38] Following this limited distribution, the Conservative Party mailed this study to seven thousand eight hundred GOP officials across the country. The analysis prompted several articles critical of the governor in conservative publications.[39]

Conservatives also confronted a third-party presidential campaign when Alabama governor George Wallace began his independent bid for the presidency. Although he was seemingly an ideological ally, Conservative leaders opposed Wallace's candidacy for three reasons. First, Conservative leaders suspected that Wallace was not a true conservative, but a populist who embraced a free-spending federal government. Second, while party leaders shared the Governor's position on some racial issues, such as opposition to school busing, they shrank from his rhetoric and the visceral reaction he often generated. Third, and most importantly, Conservatives were committed to creating a Republican Party that advocated conservative policy positions. The party's support of a Democratic governor would work against its goal of an ideological realignment of the major parties. It would also jeopardize the acceptance Conservatives had won from national and state Republicans. Dan Mahoney, therefore, cautioned members of the party against supporting the governor in the coming campaign.[40] Privately, Conservative leaders estimated that 10 percent of the state executive committee, and a slightly higher percentage of the rank and file, favored Wallace.[41] These dissenters carried their case to the Conservative Party convention in September but never were strong enough to deliver the nomination to the Alabama governor. Unhappy Wallace backers complained that Dan Mahoney and other party leaders bullied them during the convention to ensure support of the Republican nominee.[42] Some dissidents joined the Courage Party, Wallace's organization in New York State, while others continued to distribute Wallace literature at local Conservative headquarters.[43]

In early 1968, New York Republicans remained loyal to Nelson Rockefeller's potential candidacy. In March, however, Rockefeller surprised observers, and his supporters, when he declared he would not run for president. Less than a month and a half later, after Richard Nixon progressed from the party's leading candidate to its likely nominee, Rockefeller again reversed course by announcing he would seek the Republican presidential nomination. When the governor finally entered the race on the last day of April, the electoral calendar allowed for few options beyond a last-minute appeal to the party's convention delegates. The governor's late-starting effort failed, and Richard Nixon won the Republican presidential nomination on the convention's first ballot. The convention's major controversy concerned the vice-presidential nomination. Nixon surprised his party by choosing little-known Maryland governor Spiro Agnew as his running mate. New York Republicans, resigned to a ticket headed by Nixon, rebelled at the addition of the controversial Agnew. Congressman Charles Goodell helped launch a convention rebellion against the Agnew nomination.[44] This group asked John Lindsay, as a proponent of liberal republicanism, to become an alternate vice presidential choice. Lindsay rejected their appeal. Instead, he addressed the convention to second Agnew's nomination, ending the mutiny. The convention overwhelmingly nominated Spiro Agnew.

The Conservative Party approached Richard Nixon about the issue of cross-endorsement prior to the Republican convention. In July, Jeremiah Milbank submitted a memo to the Nixon camp on behalf of the party.[45] It urged the candidate not to permit a repeat of 1964 when the state GOP blocked Conservative cross-endorsement of Barry Goldwater. It also emphasized how the state's unique political structure fostered a tradition of third parties, and warned that the party's increasing electoral strength meant Nixon needed its cross-endorsement. While party leaders made this case privately to the Nixon campaign, Senate nominee James Buckley presented the case to the public. In the rally officially opening his campaign, Buckley announced the party's desire to back Nixon and argued that recent achievements demonstrated Conservatives deserved to be able to do so.[46] Buckley's public support of cross-endorsement prompted warnings from Jacob Javits's staff.[47] John Wells advised the senator that Nixon's name on the Conservative line would deliver votes for Buckley in November. Wells recommended that Javits ask Rockefeller and the state GOP to prohibit electors from accepting Conservative cross-endorsement."[48] Javits made this case to the governor, and Rockefeller agreed to oppose any cross-endorsement to protect the senator's re-election prospects. At the governor's suggestion, Javits also sent copies of Wells's analysis to the state GOP chairman. His forwarding memo explained that "this issue is most important in terms of my own candidacy as well as the future of the party."[49] Javits also spoke out publicly against such an alliance. In a television interview, the senator said that, if the GOP allowed cross-endorsement, it "would compromise itself, its soul, and its principles."[50]

Both New York parties looked toward an August 21 meeting between Nixon and Rockefeller to resolve this issue. John Wells sent Rockefeller a memo warning "that the Republican Party in New York State, as a matter of preservation, can in no circumstances allow its candidates for the Electoral College to run on the Conservative Party line."[51] The governor's notes indicated he planned to use this memo as the basis for the meeting.[52] In the weeks prior to the Nixon-Rockefeller meeting, Conservatives publicly argued for joint electors. Behind the scenes, the party also approached the Nixon camp in an effort to reach an understanding. When Nixon aides agreed to discuss the issue following the meeting with Rockefeller, the party leaked the information to the press.[53] The day prior to the Nixon-Rockefeller meeting, Conservatives tried to increase the pressure on its participants. Dan Mahoney announced that the party's executive committee had voted to nominate an independent slate of Nixon electors if denied the opportunity to cross-endorse the Republican slate.[54] Although these electors would also be pledged to Nixon, their vote total would remain separate from the votes received by the GOP slate of electors, and so would not help the candidate carry the state.

On August 21, 1968, Richard Nixon and Nelson Rockefeller met in the former vice president's Manhattan apartment. Jacob Javits joined the meeting to help defend his re-election prospects. Using the Wells memo as his guide, Rockefeller argued against cross-endorsement.[55] The governor's notes from the meeting documented that the group discussed the elector issue early in the session.[56] Following the meeting, aides of Rockefeller and Javits told the press that Nixon made no commitment on cross-endorsement.[57] Nixon and Rockefeller also issued a formal statement announcing the governor would head a committee to promote Nixon as well as all other Republican candidates in New York State. The statement made no mention of joint electors.[58]

State Republicans interpreted Nixon's silence as agreement, or at least acquiescence, in blocking cross-endorsement. Nixon, however, dispatched John Mitchell, his campaign manager and a former Wall Street lawyer, to pursue a possible agreement with Conservatives. Mitchell approached William Buckley to serve as the contact between the campaign and the party.[59] On August 27, Buckley, in Chicago to appear with Gore Vidal as a television commentator on the Democratic convention, flew to New York for a morning meeting with Mitchell and Conservative Party leaders.[60] At this meeting, Mitchell expressed Nixon's willingness to be endorsed by the Conservative Party. He also explained that while the Nixon campaign would not publicly call for cross-endorsement, it would work with the Conservative Party on the problem. Dan Mahoney, looking to help the campaign defuse Republican opposition, prepared a memo refuting New York GOP claims that local Conservative candidates precluded cooperation between the two parties. Mahoney described a party that loyally supported GOP candidates and fielded opposition only in the most extreme circumstances. The chairman also wrote the members of the Republican state committee, responsible for selecting the party's electors, asking them to support cross-endorsement. Citing Nixon's desire for such an arrangement, he called on committee members to defy their state leaders and support their presidential nominee on this issue.[61] Finally, Mahoney informed the press of his letter to Republican state committee members and of Nixon's desire for cross-endorsement. Mitchell offered no protest to the story, saying only that Nixon sought the support of all voters who agreed with his principles, and that the two state parties needed to reach an agreement on joint electors.[62] Mitchell's response indicated that, while the Nixon campaign expected the Conservative Party to win Republican acceptance of cross-endorsement, its only expenditure of political capital would be the candidate's privately expressed willingness to accept cross-endorsement.

Republican resistance intensified as soon as the outline of the alliance between Nixon and the Conservative Party emerged. Lindsay, Javits, and Rockefeller issued complementary statements pledging to block any agreement between the Republican and Conservative Parties. The three leading members of the state GOP cited the damage such an alliance would cause to the New York Republican Party and the Nixon campaign. Their opposition forced the Nixon camp to revise its account of recent events. Abandoning the ambiguity of his earlier comments, Mitchell denied that he conveyed Nixon's desire for cross-endorsement to the Conservative Party. Bolstered by this denial, GOP chairman Schoeneck took his case to the party's state committee members. In a letter he released to the press, Schoeneck used Mitchell's revised statement to call on committee members to reject joint electors. For its part, the Conservative Party insisted that Mitchell had expressed Nixon's desire for the Conservative cross-endorsement but that the state GOP had bullied a denial out of the Nixon campaign. An anonymous Nixon aide summed up the confusing negotiations over joint electors as "a pretty delicate thing and the candidate had been caught unfairly in the middle."[63]

Conservatives had hoped to use Nixon's acceptance of cross-endorsement to persuade the Republican state committee to support joint electors. With Nixon's acceptance publicly rescinded, however, the party had little chance of winning the committee's approval. A *New York Times* editorial advised the state committee to reject joint electors. "The spectacle of the G.O.P. voluntarily allying itself with the right-wing Conservatives would permanently alienate the great body of independent voters," it warned.[64] Conservatives, nonetheless, refused to abandon their strategy. On the day before the Republican state committee met in New York City, Dan Mahoney asked to address the meeting. The state GOP ignored the request.[65] Unable to gain access to the meeting, Dan Mahoney and Kieran O'Doherty literally lobbied members of the Republican state committee. True to the word's original meaning, Mahoney and O'Doherty stood in the Hotel Roosevelt lobby and tried to convince incoming committee members of the justice of their case. This last-ditch effort produced nothing of consequence, however. The committee rejected on a voice vote a proposal for joint electors. For good measure, it approved a resolution stating that the committee nominated electors with the understanding that they would not accept any cross-endorsements, and that any elector who accepted cross-endorsement would be disqualified as the Republican nominee. The *New York Times* editorial board praised the committee for displaying "high moral courage."[66] The state GOP, despite recent changes in the political landscape, maintained its policy of noncooperation with the Conservative Party. Republicans outside the state considered the controversy another demonstration of the disloyalty of the New York GOP.[67]

Just as it had in 1964, the New York GOP prevented the Conservative Party from cross-endorsing the Republican presidential nominee. Rebuffed, Conservatives could only run an independent slate of electors that would harm Nixon's chances or run no electors. John Mitchell resumed talks with the Conservative Party in order to prevent an independent slate. Dan Mahoney made their agreement public—at least in part—at the Conservative Party state committee meeting on September 8. Mahoney read a letter from Richard Nixon to the party. Nixon's letter asked Conservatives not to nominate a slate of independent electors since it would split his vote in the state. In addition, the presidential nominee asked for Conservative Party support. "I welcome the support of the Conservative Party, which I regard as a responsible political organization, and solicit the support of its members in the forthcoming political campaign," he wrote.[68] The normally unsympathetic *New York Times* characterized the candidate's statement as "the sort of recognition that the Conservatives have been seeking."[69] Nixon's declaration demonstrated the growing legitimacy of the Conservative Party. Four years earlier, Barry Goldwater, a far more ideologically harmonious candidate, offered the party no such public endorsement. By 1968, however, the party was respectable and influential enough to warrant such a statement from the Republican presidential nominee.

In early October, an additional concession from the Nixon camp created a controversy. According to press reports, GOP vice-presidential nominee Spiro Agnew planned to attend the Conservative Party anniversary dinner honoring Senate nominee James Buckley. Nelson Rockefeller sent Richard Nixon a telegram protesting this news. The governor's telegram threatened that Agnew's appearance "would not only undercut Republican candidates throughout the state; it would seriously undermine the appeal you have made for unified support of the Republican ticket from top to bottom."[70] Agnew's plans so incensed Rockefeller that he reportedly intended to release the telegram publicly until dissuaded by state chairman Schoeneck.[71] Unlike Barry Goldwater in his reaction to the controversial Clare Booth Luce candidacy four years before, Nixon did not accede to the state GOP's demands. Both the presidential candidate and the Conservative Party were stronger than in 1964 and could pursue a relationship despite the protests of New York Republicans. The campaign, however, downplayed the significance of Agnew's planned appearance. The vice-presidential nominee explained that he did not support Buckley's campaign and would vote for Senator Javits if he lived in New York.[72] Nixon aides characterized Agnew's appearance as a "drop-by." Conservative leaders also downplayed the event's significance in an effort to defuse the controversy. This effort included trying to convince a skeptical press corps that, while Agnew's appearance was arranged at the talks where the party agreed to forgo independent electors, there was no connection.

On the afternoon of October 14, just hours before the Conservative dinner, Jacob Javits warned a lunch-time rally on Wall Street of the danger presented by the Conservative Party. Javits charged that Conservatives wanted to ruin the GOP "and to fashion the broken remnant of the Party it has destroyed in its backward-looking image."[73] His condemnation of the Conservative Party was undermined, however, by numerous hecklers wearing Buckley buttons. That evening, seven hundred Conservatives filled the ballroom at the Waldorf-Astoria Hotel to hear Spiro Agnew. Although he arrived a full hour behind schedule, Agnew spoke to the attendees for over twenty minutes. He carefully avoided any mention of state politics, and limited his remarks to criticizing Yippies as promoters of social unrest.[74] The party faithful—a much larger crowd due to Agnew's drawing power—cheered the speech, often interrupting to chant, "We want Agnew."[75] The crowd reacted as much to the presence of the messenger as to the message. Conservatives knew that, while Agnew's remarks failed to address New York politics, his appearance signaled their acceptance by the national Republican Party.

AN IMPRESSIVE PERFORMANCE

Robert F. Kennedy's assassination in June 1968 left one of New York's Senate seats vacant. The job of appointing a successor to serve out the two years remaining in Kennedy's term fell to the governor. Rockefeller's failure to name anyone for several months prompted speculation that he did not wish to jeopardize his presidential ambitions by disappointing any state Republicans with a selection.[76] John Lindsay, initially, appeared the leading prospect, given his political appeal, especially with Kennedy's former supporters. Lindsay's selection was undermined by his lack of rapport with the governor, however. Rockefeller announced that he would not support Lindsay unless the mayor asked for the job, and Lindsay countered he would consider the job if offered, but would not ask for it. Following the GOP national convention, Rockefeller narrowed the list of potential choices to two Republican congressmen: Ogden Reid from Westchester and Charles Goodell from Jamestown. In September, the governor finally chose Goodell, preferring the congressman's moderate-to-conservative image over that of the more liberal Reid. Rockefeller chose Goodell, in part, to reassure those Republicans upset by Javits's acceptance of the Liberal nomination. The *New York Times* editorial page criticized Rockefeller for a lack of courage in the face of pressure from the Conservative Party.[77] In later years, Goodell contended that this depiction of him as a conservative House member failed to recognize his ideological shift to the left during the previous two years.[78] Whether it began in the House as he contended or in the Senate as his critics charged, Goodell's transformation surprised most Republicans, including Governor Rockefeller.

Voters, however, were more focused on the campaign for New York's other Senate seat. James Buckley's campaign benefited from both his connections to, and differences from, his more famous brother. Bill Buckley's celebrity ensured that the family name was well-known throughout the state, and the editor appeared frequently at political events for his brother. James Buckley, however, cut a figure on the campaign trail very different from that of his younger brother. Quieter and more easy-going, he combined a conservative ideology and a manner that was neither provocative nor controversial. An internal Javits campaign staff memo acknowledged that James possessed none of his brother's distracting traits. "He is intelligent but not abrasive or arrogant in the manner of his brother Bill," it complained.[79] While the Buckley campaign benefited from a high-profile candidate, it also suffered from the party's historical weakness, a lack of funds. In March, Marvin Liebman proposed raising money from contributors to Bill Buckley's 1965 mayoral run.[80] The campaign's earlier attempts to raise money nationally from these previous contributors and other conservatives had produced limited results.[81] An August mailing of 150,000 letters raised only $17,000.[82] By the fall, funds were so tight that the candidate wrote a member of his campaign committee explaining that only an immediate infusion of cash would allow the purchase of bumper stickers, leaflets and other campaign materials.[83] Buckley's campaign raised a total of $160,000, far more than past Conservative efforts, but only about 10 percent of Javits's total. This financial disparity between the two campaigns precluded Buckley from ever seriously threatening to overtake Javits.

While Buckley could not match Javits's fundraising accomplishments, he nonetheless waged a lively campaign. The Conservative candidate criticized Javits's congressional record, especially his support of President Lyndon Johnson's Great Society. He also consistently questioned the senator's standing as a Republican. He focused on Javits's Liberal nomination as evidence the senator was "a mini-Republican and a maxi-Liberal."[84] Additionally, Buckley returned again and again to Javits's performance during the presidential race, specifically his role in blocking joint electors. In a televised debate, Buckley accused the senator of sacrificing party loyalty to further his own re-election campaign.[85] Citing Javits's disloyalty to the GOP, he created "Republicans for Buckley."[86] Headed by Clare Booth Luce and William Rusher, the organization targeted upstate GOP voters, arguing that Buckley, and not Javits, reflected authentic Republican values.[87] This shift in geographical focus demonstrated that the party looked to expand its support beyond its traditional base in and around New York City. "Republicans for Buckley" purchased a series of advertisements in upstate newspapers contrasting Buckley's enthusiastic backing of Richard Nixon with Javits's tepid support. Picturing Nixon and Buckley with the headline "They Stand Together," the ads paired Buckley's statement endorsing Nixon and Agnew with Nixon's statement welcoming

Conservative Party support.[88] While clearly promoting Buckley and Nixon, the ads also sought to punish Javits. Kieran O'Doherty wrote William Rusher after the election expressing disappointment that the campaign could not afford to purchase more newspaper space. "I relished doing this job on Javits," he admitted.[89]

While Conservatives embraced Richard Nixon's campaign, they faced a more delicate task with George Wallace's candidacy. The party needed to support Nixon without alienating the state's Wallace voters. James Buckley, in particular, hoped to win votes from many Wallace supporters. Throughout the campaign, Buckley consistently supported Nixon and reached out to Wallace's supporters. He refused to criticize the Democratic governor, and consistently emphasized a common concern about the rising level of civil disorder in the country. When a television interviewer asked if New Yorkers wearing Wallace and Buckley buttons embarrassed him, Buckley responded that he backed Nixon for president but "respect[ed] the views of those who are supporting Mr. Wallace."[90]

Jacob Javits took a similarly cautious approach to Richard Nixon. Unlike most state GOP candidates, Javits wanted to appeal to New York Democrats, Liberals, and independents, many of whom were hostile toward, or at least suspicious of, Nixon. His Liberal Party nomination, in particular, forced the senator to distance himself from Nixon. At a rally in New York City's garment district, Liberal Party organizers harshly criticized Nixon before introducing Javits as "a Republican, who's not a Republican."[91] The Liberal Party also ran newspaper advertisements featuring pictures of its presidential nominee, Hubert Humphrey, and its Senate nominees, including Javits. This ad created a minor controversy, with several upstate Republican chairmen publicly criticizing the senator.[92] Javits responded with his own newspaper advertisement asking voters to join him in voting for Nixon. The ad revealed some of the political and institutional constraints on the senator, however, in its failure to mention either Nixon's political party or his running mate.[93]

Javits followed Richard Aurelio's advice in courting non-Republican voters, and consistently criticized the Conservative Party. Hoping to deny free publicity to his lesser-known opponent, the senator's criticism never referred specifically to Buckley. He concentrated, instead, on accusing the Conservative Party of trying to destroy the GOP. In September, Javits's staff studied the Conservative platform and concluded that the document was far more negative in tone than the national Republican platform.[94] Late in the campaign, the senator also linked the Conservative Party, and by association Buckley, to George Wallace. Javits characterized the Alabama governor and Conservative Party as spoilers and called on voters to reject both at the polls.[95]

In congressional and legislative races, the Republican Party again hoped to recapture some of the seats lost in the 1964 election. The race in Nassau County's Fifth Congressional District drew the most attention. Mason Hampton, a Conservative candidate endorsed by the GOP, faced a nationally-known Democratic opponent, Allard Lowenstein. Press coverage focused on the enormous ideological gulf separating the two candidates. Behind the scenes, however, the campaign exposed some difficulties with Republican-Conservative cooperation. James Griffin, the Conservative Party's executive director and James Buckley's campaign manager, sent Hampton a telegram suggesting the candidate publicly criticize Jacob Javits. Hampton declined, fearing such an attack would hurt his local Republicans allies. He assured Griffin that he backed Buckley, but refused to "publicly kick Senator Javits in the shins to give emotional gratification to a few Conservatives who are so obsessed by the need for denunciations as to overlook our mission."[96] Griffin reminded him that Conservatives created their party to oppose Jacob Javits. "I must count myself, as Jim Buckley's campaign manager, among the conservatives who would get emotional gratification from seeing you publicly kick Senator Javits in the shins," he added.[97] As a cross-endorsed candidate, however, Hampton refused to criticize a Republican nominee.

On November 5, many New Yorkers split their votes among the four state parties fielding candidates. In the presidential election, Nixon lost the state handily to Humphrey but won a close national race. State Republicans argued that Nixon's relationship with the Conservative Party, especially Agnew's attendance at the party's dinner, cost the former vice president the state. "To play footsie with the Conservatives as Nixon did is suicidal in a statewide election," one GOP official, quoted anonymously, charged.[98] Conservatives countered that Nixon lost New York because the state GOP had once again acted disloyally and sabotaged the presidential campaign. They contended that Nixon would have carried the state if the New York GOP had allowed him to run on the Conservative line.

Senate election results also inspired conflicting interpretations. Since Jacob Javits easily defeated his ineffectual Democratic opponent, Paul O'Dwyer, Republicans pointed to the senator's margin of victory as evidence of the vitality of liberal republicanism. Conservatives, meanwhile, focused on James Buckley's surpassing all previous third-party efforts, winning over one million votes, about 17 percent of the total vote. In Long Island's two counties, Buckley even finished second, running ahead of O'Dwyer. This growth in support came from the source identified in the 1965 and 1966 elections, specifically traditional Democrats attracted by the party's tough stands on social issues. The Conservative Party later estimated that between 40 percent and 50 percent of Buckley's support came from Democrats.[99] At a celebratory election night rally, the candidate characterized his address to the enthusiastic crowd as a victory statement. "The vote we got tonight will be the most carefully weighed of any gotten in New York State," he promised.[100]

In congressional races, Republicans failed to increase their seats in the state delegation. Voters again sent twenty-six Democrats and fifteen

Republicans to the House, although the two major parties traded control of several individual seats. Overall, Conservative Party congressional and legislative candidates continued to improve their showing, attracting 7.3 percent of the vote in their races. The party suffered a disappointment on Long Island, however, when Mason Hampton lost his race to Allard Lowenstein. More importantly, however, Republicans regained control of the assembly they had lost four years earlier. The Republican majority rested on a narrow margin, with the new assembly consisting of seventy-seven Republicans and seventy-three Democrats. The Conservative Party took credit for this victory because of its increased cooperation with some Republican county organizations. The Conservative Party cross-endorsed thirty-six victorious GOP assembly candidates because of this increased cooperation. In nine of those races, the Republican candidate won only as a result of votes received on the Conservative line. Conservatives claimed that without their cross-endorsement these nominees would have lost their races, and the GOP would have fallen short of retaking the assembly. In addition, Conservatives elected their first party members to the assembly. Rosemary Gunning of Queens and Charles Jerabek of Nassau County, Conservatives cross-endorsed by the GOP, won their respective races. In 1966, Republican had overwhelmingly refused Conservative cross-endorsement and failed to retake the assembly. Two years later, a number of Republicans adopted a policy of cooperation and accepted Conservative cross-endorsement. The resulting Republican takeover of the state assembly seemed to validate the wisdom of this new alliance.

DRAWING BLOOD

The 1968 election results gave the Conservative Party two new avenues to political power. At the state level, the party enjoyed more influence in the legislature. It looked to newly-elected Conservative assemblymen Charles Jerabek and Rosemary Gunning to promote its legislative agenda in Albany. Both secured seats on the Ways and Means Committee, maximizing their ability to influence the state budget. Conservatives also knew that the GOP's slim majority in the assembly presented them with their greatest opportunity. The GOP's margin was so slight that any defections by Republican legislators—including those who owed their seats to cross-endorsement—doomed any piece of legislation. Conservatives, eager to capitalize on their new power, provided an analysis of the state budget to all endorsed legislators in order to spur spending cuts.[101] By the end of the legislative session, the party boasted of its crucial role in imposing cuts in the state's welfare and medicaid programs, as well as in the creation of a fiscal review commission.[102] Some Republicans, however, resisted the greater Conservative role in governing. In the months following the 1968 election, a number of Republican legislators, how many is unclear, explored legislation banning cross-endorsement.

Nationally-syndicated columnists Rowland Evans and Robert Novak touted this legislation as the only way to rescue the state GOP from Conservative control.[103] Governor Rockefeller again took no stand on the legislation, an approach that backers of the ban interpreted as support. In order to pass, however, the bill needed votes from Democrats willing to antagonize the Liberal Party and Republicans willing to do the same to the Conservative Party. With an evenly divided assembly, Republican legislative leaders recognized their dependence on Conservative-endorsed members and refused to back such hostile legislation. The bill died quietly in the legislature.

The 1968 election also provided increased Conservative influence at the national level by virtue of the party's relationship with the Nixon administration. While New York Republicans argued that Nixon's dealings with the Conservative Party cost him the state, the new administration refused to sever contact with the third party. Dan Mahoney was reportedly "on excellent terms with top people in the Nixon camp."[104] Indeed, John Mitchell offered Mahoney an open invitation to meet with him to offer appointment recommendations.[105] Some state Republicans expressed concern about Mitchell's role in the new administration given his past dealings with the Conservative Party.[106] Mitchell, nonetheless, became the new attorney general. Bill Buckley also enjoyed unparalleled access to the White House. Partly as a result of Buckley's personal friendship with the new head of the United States Information Agency (USIA), Frank Shakespeare, Nixon appointed Buckley to the board of directors of the USIA. Buckley also enjoyed a personal relationship with the administration's national security advisor, Henry Kissinger. The former advisor to Nelson Rockefeller routinely invited Buckley to meet with him in Washington. On some of these trips, Buckley also met with President Nixon to discuss politics and policy. As they had in the campaign, Nixon and Kissinger sought out Buckley with an eye to winning conservative support. Similarly, Buckley's relationship with the new administration provided the Conservative Party with a strong link to the White House. G. Gordon Liddy provided another connection between the Conservative Party and the Nixon White House. In 1968, Liddy, then the assistant district attorney in Dutchess County, prepared to run for an open congressional seat. Hoping to raise his profile in a Republican primary against Hamilton Fish, the fourth generaton of a local political dynasty, Liddy approached the local Conservative Party to secure its nomination.[107] His hawkish view on Vietnam and tough law-and-order record as a prosecutor impressed Conservatives. Liddy also pledged that if he lost the GOP primary, he would not campaign for Fish in the general election. Despite the Conservative endorsement, Liddy still lost to Fish in a close Republican primary. The district attorney, however, used his Conservative nomination to further his career. He explained to local GOP officials that unless he was convinced of their goodwill, he would actively campaign on the Conservative line in the general election. To protect the Republican nominee, local GOP officials displayed their goodwill by introducing Liddy to national Republican leaders. Liddy soon endorsed Fish, but kept his pledge to Conservatives and did not actively campaign for him. Local Conservatives initially misread the situation, believing that Republicans had threatened the district attorney into submission. They re-evaluated the likely method of persuasion when Liddy received a plum job from the new Nixon White House.[108]

Richard Nixon began his new administration with cordial, if not close, relations with most leading New York Republicans. Speculation in the state focused on Rockefeller as secretary of state or defense, but Nixon reportedly offered the governor only the post of United Nations representative. Rockefeller expressed no interest in this lesser position.[109] Despite this inauspicious beginning, Nixon and Rockefeller developed an effective working relationship, bolstered by almost monthly meetings. John Lindsay met repeatedly with members of the new cabinet in order to secure federal government aid for New York City. Other New York Republicans, however, were more critical of the new administration. Writing in *Look* magazine, Congressman Ogden Reid doubted that the president would make the hard decisions necessary to end the war, halt the arms race, and help the nation's cities.[110]

As Conservatives and Republicans adjusted to life with Richard Nixon in the White House, the New York City mayoral election dominated the year's politics. At a City Hall ceremony on March 18, Lindsay formally announced he would seek a second term. The event marked the final time liberal republicanism stood atop New York State politics. The GOP controlled both houses of the state legislature, and Republicans served as governor, lieutenant governor, attorney general, and as both of the state's senators. For the ceremony, Lindsay mustered all of the state's leading liberal Republicans, including Governor Rockefeller, Senators Javits and Goodell, former Governor Tom Dewey, and former U.S. Attorney General Herbert Brownell. Longtime financial backers of the GOP, such as financier John Hay Whitney and New York Stock Exchange Chairman Gustave Levy, also attended. For good measure, Fiorello LaGuardia's widow—representing Republican fusion—also graced the ceremony. Lindsay praised this collection of party heavyweights for making "progressive Republicanism synonymous with winning Republicanism." Turning to the upcoming campaign, he accused forces within the GOP of working with the Conservative Party to destroy this kind of republicanism. "If Republicans permit themselves to be captured by the Conservative Party," the mayor warned, "it will ruin our party as an effective political force in this city and state . . . perhaps for decades to come."[111] As Javits had the year before, Lindsay centered his re-election campaign on hostility to the Conservative Party.

John Lindsay's confident entrance into the 1969 campaign belied the presence of significant obstacles to his re-election. Lindsay faced widespread criticism over the performance of his first administration. During his term, the city endured seven major strikes by municipal unions, including actions by transit workers, sanitation workers, and two by city teachers. Campus demonstrations, most prominently at Columbia University, and rising crime rates combined to create a sense of anarchy and anxiety among the city's residents. Finally, doubts remained over the city's ability to deliver basic services, such as snow removal. New Yorkers perceived a decline in the city's quality of life.

A potential Republican primary compounded Lindsay's difficulties. In 1965, Lindsay secured both the GOP and Liberal nominations without a primary. Given William Buckley's popularity with Republicans in the general election, however, Lindsay may not have won a majority of GOP votes if there had been a Republican primary. Since 1965, GOP support for Lindsay, especially in the Bronx, Queens, and Staten Island, had eroded. Significant GOP opposition to a second Lindsay term increased the probability of New York City's first GOP mayoral primary since 1941. The Lindsay camp understood the risk of a primary. An internal poll found that 53 percent of New York City Republicans did not favor a second term for the mayor, with almost all of these "very definite" in their opposition.[112] Given this hostility, Lindsay's campaign manager, Richard Aurelio, advised Lindsay to make only a minimal effort in a Republican primary, and conserve resources for running on the Liberal line in the general election. Lindsay's chief financial contributors, men like Levy and Whitney, opposed this strategy. They had devoted their lives to liberal republicanism, and refused to abandon the cause now. They prevailed on Lindsay to make a full effort to win the Republican primary.[113] Lindsay's decision to invite the roster of liberal GOP stars to his announcement ceremony began his campaign to win the approval of his fellow Republicans.

The Conservative Party also understood Lindsay's vulnerability in a Republican primary. Back in January of 1968, Kevin Phillips, at the time still an aide in Paul Fino's congressional office, prepared a voting analysis outlining the mayor's problems with GOP voters. "If John Lindsay is challenged in the 1969 Republican primary," Phillips concluded, "he will be defeated without the intervention of a party administration in Albany or Washington desirous of preventing bloodshed."[114] The congressional aide sent the analysis to William Buckley, who forwarded it to Dan Mahoney. Conservatives prepared to mount a primary challenge to exploit the mayor's weakness within the GOP. In December 1968, Kieran O'Doherty announced the Conservative Party's intentions by publicly promising party support for a primary challenge.[115] The party planned to help the challenger by distributing literature, contacting potential voters, providing campaign advice, fundraising, and circulating petitions. Most importantly, the party planned to use its endorsement to influence sympathetic Republicans.

While Conservatives wanted to encourage a GOP mayoral primary challenge, they still needed to find a candidate. Conservatives were unwilling to support Brooklyn assemblyman Vito Battista's candidacy for the

Republican mayoral nomination. They shared Battista's anti-tax views, but bristled at his colorful antics, such as dramatizing the impact of high taxes by strolling Wall Street wearing a barrel and suspenders. Battista also alienated Conservatives by criticizing Bill Buckley in the 1965 mayoral race as an extremist lacking any rapport with New Yorkers.[116] Conservative Party leaders preferred Staten Island Republican state senator John Marchi as their candidate. Marchi, an ideological conservative, was first elected to the state senate in 1956. In Albany, he focused on the mechanics of legislation and chaired the committee that oversaw New York City's affairs. Marchi, nicknamed "the Perry Como of politics," also had the quiet personal style the Conservatives courted.[117] Marchi seemed an unlikely choice to challenge an incumbent Republican mayor. Angered at Lindsay's tenure as mayor and bolstered by Conservative support, however, Marchi entered the race. At a time when party organizations still imposed discipline on its politicians, Rockefeller's failure to protect Lindsay by keeping Marchi out of the race raised eyebrows. The governor contended that he tried, unsuccessfully, to keep Marchi out of the Republican primary.[118] Others speculated that the personal animosity between Rockefeller and Lindsay tempered the governor's effort to restrain Marchi. Few believed that Rockefeller used all his resources as governor of New York, head of the state GOP, and a member of one of the country's wealthiest families to prevent Marchi's run.

Conservative leaders immediately embraced Marchi's candidacy. They faced two problems with the Marchi campaign, however. First, their candidate was virtually unknown outside his home borough of Staten Island, the city's smallest in population. Conservatives started to aggressively raise money to overcome his obscurity. William Rusher contacted prominent Republicans, explaining that only money could boost Marchi's name recognition.[119] Dan Mahoney, now on the board of directors of the American Conservative Union, appealed to his fellow board members. He explained that an immediate infusion of money would "put John Lindsay out of the political business."[120] Using Lindsay's presumed presidential ambitions to cast the election in national terms, the Marchi campaign successfully raised money outside New York.[121] Marchi raised approximately $160,000 for the primary, less than Lindsay raised, but enough to finance a viable campaign.

Second, Conservatives confronted the challenge to Marchi presented by Battista's candidacy. They feared Battista would compete with Marchi for the anti-Lindsay vote, even within the Conservative Party. While Conservative leaders backed Marchi, some party members preferred the fiery Brooklyn assemblyman. Conservative leaders crushed the grassroots opposition to their candidate just as they had in the presidential race the previous year. Following a rancorous showdown, the party's executive committee voted to endorse Marchi. Party leaders then moved to persuade Battista to abandon his campaign altogether. After several weeks of negotiation, Mahoney brokered a deal between the Republican candidates. On May 13, the two politicians held a news conference announcing they had joined forces. Battista ended his mayoral campaign and joined Marchi's ticket as the nominee for controller. The men, now running mates, downplayed their earlier animosity and pledged a united campaign against Lindsay.

John Lindsay also used the spring of 1969 to strengthen his candidacy. Lindsay's financial backers and his national celebrity allowed him to raise about three times as much money as Marchi. The mayor secured the Liberal Party nomination as he had in 1965. In addition, much of the state GOP supported Lindsay's campaign for the Republican nomination. Republican legislators briefly considered switching the primary from June until September to allow the mayor more time to regain his political popularity. New York's two senators, Jacob Javits and Charles Goodell, aggressively campaigned for Lindsay. Twenty-four Republican senators endorsed the mayor, although several of these withdrew their endorsement when they learned that Lindsay was in a contested Republican primary.[122] Governor Rockefeller, while personally backing Lindsay, did not become involved in the campaign. A *New York Times* editorial called his passive approach "a setback not only for the mayor, but for the cause of progressive Republicanism as well."[123]

The Nixon administration tried a similar strategy of noninvolvement in the primary campaign. In April, presidential advisor Daniel Patrick Moynihan warned Nixon that Lindsay was in "awful trouble" in the Republican primary. He asked if a special effort should be made to expedite money from federal programs to New York City to help the mayor.[124] Lindsay's display of party loyalty in seconding Agnew's nomination at the Miami Beach convention, however, earned him no consideration. John Ehrlichman decided that "no overt action should be taken by the White House."[125] Lindsay, unaware of this policy, asked that cabinet members expedite federal grants headed to New York City so they would arrive before the primary. The White House directed cabinet secretaries to deny Lindsay's request.[126] In an administrative foul-up, however, two departments, Housing and Urban Development and Health, Education, and Welfare, approved and delivered the requested grants without contacting the White House. As a result, some observers mistakenly assumed the White House backed the mayor in the primary.[127]

The Lindsay campaign, along with a general defense of the mayor's performance in office, made two principal appeals to Republican primary voters. First, the mayor presented himself as the only Republican who could win the general election. Given the Democratic Party's four-to-one registration advantage in New York City, any Republican needed to reach far beyond his own party to be a viable candidate. Lindsay argued that only his brand of liberal republicanism could attract Democrats, Liberals, and independents.[128] Second, Lindsay stressed the threat to the GOP represented by John Marchi's candidacy. The mayor first articulated this theme at his campaign kick-off when he asserted that progressive republicanism was under attack. When Marchi and Battista joined forces, Lindsay criticized the arrangement as proof that his opponents would do anything to gain control of the GOP. Throughout the campaign, he equated the Marchi challenge with a Conservative take-over of the GOP. He increased the volume of his attacks when the Conservative presence became more visible in the Marchi campaign in the weeks preceding the primary. During a televised June debate, the mayor even dismissed Marchi as a tool of the Conservative Party.

As the primary campaign drew to a close, strategist Richard Aurelio gently warned the Lindsay campaign "that in view of the strong anti-Lindsay feeling we have encountered in certain areas outside of Manhattan, there is clearly the potential for defeat in this primary."[129] The weekend prior to the election, Conservatives focused on increasing voter turnout. Throughout the Bronx, Queens, and Staten Island, party members made telephone calls, rang doorbells, and handed out literature in an effort to get Marchi supporters to the polls. The strategy worked. On June 17, Republican voters chose John Marchi as their mayoral candidate. Lindsay won Manhattan, but lost in the city's four other boroughs. While the vote was close—a difference of 5,000 votes out of 220,000 cast—the significance was clear. An unknown, underfinanced, charismatically challenged conservative candidate defeated one of the country's leading liberal Republicans in a party primary. The Conservative Party had claimed its first notable victim and had begun to reshape the ideological make-up of the state GOP.

A MAYOR WITHOUT A PARTY

On the night GOP voters rejected him, John Lindsay promised to continue his re-election campaign as the Liberal Party's nominee. He called the vote a defeat for the Republican Party, and decried that the GOP was now controlled by "a band of ultra-right men—in concert with the Conservative Party—who will destroy the party unless they are repudiated."[130] The mayor's supporters shared this assessment of the primary. The *New York Times* editorial board called the result "a tragedy for the Republican Party."[131] It also maintained that, given Marchi's negligible prospects in the general election, "[t]he conservative forces who support him may now own the party, but, with his defeat, they will own only ashes." Predictably, Conservatives viewed the outcome differently. At Marchi campaign headquarters, Bill Buckley explained the result to an exuberant crowd. "Here's what happened—a great and historical event—the recapture of the Republican Party by people whose identification with the Republican Party makes sense nationally," he said.[132] In a letter to Buckley concerning the primary, Barry Goldwater added an exultant postscript, "Ain't it great!"[133] The White House joined in this response. Early on election night, anticipating a Lindsay victory, Richard Nixon instructed H. R. Haldeman to send the mayor a congratulatory telegram. Lindsay's defeat surprised, and, in Haldeman's estimation, pleased Nixon.[134] Over the next few days, Patrick Buchanan, now a presidential speechwriter, analyzed the primary and advised Nixon that it was "a *permanent* blow to the Dewey-Rockefeller, Eastern Liberal Establishment coalition." Buchanan, in a somewhat overheated historical comparison, wrote the president, "The Bastille has fallen."[135]

John Lindsay's loss had important consequences for the GOP, but despite Pat Buchanan's claim, the Bastille had not fallen. Liberal Republicans did not simply capitulate with the defeat of their standard bearer. In the general election, Lindsay, running as the Liberal Party candidate, and John Marchi embraced their roles as representatives of the liberal and conservative wings of the GOP, respectively. On one side, a handsome, charismatic mayor stood as a national leader of progressive Republicans. He did so, however, without the GOP nomination. On the other side, a little-known and ideologically conservative state legislator stood, advocating a law-and-order platform. New York Republicans were forced to choose.

Prior to the primary, Senator Charles Goodell pledged to support John Lindsay even if he lost the Republican primary. New York's senior senator, Jacob Javits, quickly joined Goodell in backing the mayor. Javits answered challenges to his party loyalty by citing Marchi's ties to the Conservative Party, an organization he accused of seeking to damage the GOP.[136] When Manhattan GOP Chairman Vince Albano continued to back Lindsay publicly, conservative Republicans sued to prevent party money from being used for the Liberal Party nominee. They prevailed when a State Supreme Court judge limited Republican help to Lindsay.

During the primary campaign, Nelson Rockefeller announced he would support the choice of Republican voters. When the governor remained silent following Marchi's win, however, critics charged Rockefeller with abandoning this pledge. The week after the primary election, John Wells outlined the governor's three options—supporting Marchi, supporting Lindsay, or straddling the choice. Wells recommended that Rockefeller back Marchi. He explained that choosing either of the other options would jeopardize the support of small "c" and capital "C" conservatives. His memo highlighted the danger of losing this goodwill. "The repercussions will undoubtedly be felt next year," Wells explained, "and they will hurt his [Rockefeller's] chances of nomination and be fatal to his chances of election."[137] In reply, the governor thanked Wells, saying he "followed very closely the course you suggested."[138] A week after the primary, Rockefeller endorsed John Marchi. Limiting his commitment, however, the governor added that he would not campaign personally in the municipal election. Even with this limitation, the significance of the endorsement was clear. Nelson Rockefeller had sided with conservative Republicans and Conservatives in their struggle against liberal republicanism.

New York City's Republican primary also forced national party leaders into the state GOP conflict. Shortly after the primary, Vice President Agnew and Rogers Morton, chairman of the Republican National Committee, endorsed Marchi. Richard Nixon, initially silent, also announced his support for Marchi, but, like Rockefeller, barred any campaigning. Behind the scenes, Nixon also froze all discretionary federal aid to New York City lest it be viewed as an endorsement of Lindsay.[139] The White House informed all departments and independent agencies that, despite the mayor's request for federal money, "there are to be no actions regarding the City of New York during the course of the campaign."[140] The White House was more successful in enforcing this ban during the general campaign than it had been during the primary. When an official at the Department of Housing and Urban Development publicly praised New York City's implementation of the Model Cities Program, the White House scolded the department's political coordinator for failing to follow its directive.[141]

Other national conservatives also rallied, within limits, to the Marchi campaign. Barry Goldwater contacted Bill Buckley to see if a public endorsement would help the candidate.[142] William Rusher and Dan Mahoney doubted Goldwater's endorsement would produce additional votes for Marchi, but Rusher suggested an alternate way for the senator to help. Rusher and many other Conservatives feared that Lindsay might still have a future with the GOP. "It behooves us, therefore," he explained, "to make 1969 as costly as possible for Lindsay, in terms of future Republican nominations at the state level and especially at the national level."[143] Rusher asked Goldwater to submit a statement to the *Congressional Record* that proclaimed that, by virtue of remaining in the mayoral race after losing the GOP primary, John Lindsay had forfeited all future claims to running as a Republican. Goldwater, however, equivocated at taking the lead in this attack, suggesting that someone else initiate the statement. Rusher turned to Representative John Ashbrook of Ohio. As head of the American Conservative Union, Ashbrook was a favorite of conservatives across the country. Rusher sent Ashbrook two drafts of the anti-Lindsay statement, assuring him that "either of these statements will do John Lindsay grave damage."[144] Like Goldwater, however, Ashbrook declined to take the lead and Conservatives abandoned the effort. Still, party leaders continued to view the 1969 mayoral election as an opportunity to end John Lindsay's career as a Republican. Marchi's win in the GOP primary was only the first step in this strategy. Conservatives planned to finish the job in the general election.

John Lindsay's defeat in GOP primary freed him to refocus his campaign along more liberal lines. Initially, the mayor announced he planned to form an urban party, while aides spoke of a new politics based on issues rather than parties.[145] The reality turned out far more prosaic. The candidate courted the vast majority of New York City voters who were not Republicans. Mario Procaccino, the Democratic nominee, provided invaluable, if unintentional, assistance. Procaccino was a conservative Democrat already unpopular with many in his party. He compounded his difficulties by running an ineffectual campaign that failed to unite his party. Lindsay encouraged further defections by backing Liberal and Democratic candidates in municipal races. By the end of the race, Procaccino, frustrated by the blurring of party lines, took out a newspaper advertisement that screamed, "I'm talking to you, my fellow Democrats: Vote for a Republican—and you'll get a Republican."[146]

In 1969, any of the varied problems confronting New York City could have dominated the mayoral race. As election day approached, however, John Lindsay made a less than obvious issue, his opposition to the Vietnam War, central to his campaign. The mayor argued that the war was relevant to the mayoral race because it diverted federal money from the nation's cities.[147] On October 15, Lindsay participated in the New York City portion of the national anti-war moratorium. In sympathy with the protest, the mayor ordered all of the city's flags to be flown at half-staff. Lindsay then visited ten anti-war rallies throughout the city in twelve hours. With the exception of Senator Charles Goodell, Lindsay was often the only Republican at these events. Lindsay's focus on the Vietnam War helped his campaign in two significant ways. First, the mayor placed himself on the same side as the vast majority of Democrats, Liberals, and independents regarding the nation's most visible public policy issue. Second, Lindsay's anti-war efforts saved him from having to defend his record as mayor. The campaign's new focus, however, angered the Nixon administration. The evening of the moratorium, Richard Nixon called H. R. Haldeman at home concerned about the actions of Charles Goodell and John Lindsay that day.[148] Two days later, White House aide Harry Dent began arrangements for an anonymous advertisement critical of Lindsay's anti-war actions to appear in New York City newspapers.[149] Reflecting the administration's new animosity, Vice President Agnew and Lindsay traded hostile words at the annual Al Smith dinner. Nixon monitored the mayoral race looking for a way to intervene and to help defeat John Lindsay. When a newspaper poll showed Marchi trailing badly, the president expressed frustration at being unable to intercede effectively.[150] Nixon would have to wait until the following year for an opportunity to intervene effectively in New York politics.

On November 4, New York City residents re-elected John Lindsay as their mayor. While failing to win a majority, Lindsay comfortably defeated Mario Procaccino with Marchi a distant third. The Conservative Party badly miscalculated its chances in the general election. It overestimated the value of the GOP nomination in New York City in attracting votes and raising money. Lindsay, even without the nomination of either major party, raised 60 percent of the money in the race. Marchi's financial disadvantage limited his campaign's effectiveness, just as the same problem hurt Jim Buckley's Senate run in 1968. The party also overestimated John Marchi's potential as a candidate. Marchi, who took an extended European vacation after winning the Republican primary, could not ignite a crowd, much less the city. He picked up little additional support when the electorate expanded beyond Republican voters.

The election, however, represented a significant achievement for Conservatives. First, the party showed that, even in the supposed capital of liberalism, most Republicans favored ideologically conservative nominees. It demonstrated that most Republicans agreed with the Conservative goal of an ideologically conservative GOP. Second, the election mortally wounded John Lindsay as a member of the Republican Party. Conservatives carefully framed their campaign to impose that price on Lindsay. The mayor, with no other options, focused exclusively on Democratic and Liberal voters. John Lindsay did not formally leave the Republican Party until 1971, but the process began with the 1969 GOP mayoral primary. Finally, and most significantly, the election brought the Nixon administration into the state battle on the side of Conservatives. In 1969, the White House failed in its attempt to defeat a liberal critic, although it had started the process of pushing him out of the GOP. It would prove even more successful the following year.

FIVE

A CONSERVATIVE SENATOR

"We got that son of a bitch."

—Spiro Agnew on the electoral defeat of
Charles Goodell, November 3, 1970

The vice president's impassioned reaction to the defeat of a fellow Republican demonstrated just how vigorously the Nixon White House engaged in the political battles of New York State. Convinced in 1968 and 1969 of the merit of siding with New York Conservatives in their struggle against state Republicans, the White House acted on that conviction with a vengeance in 1970. This intervention by the Nixon White House came in response to a number of recent events. In 1964, the Conservative Party, through its commitment to the Republican presidential nominee, began to win acceptance among national Republicans. The 1965 and 1966 elections revealed the popularity of Conservative positions on social issues, especially among significant numbers of traditional Democrats. The state GOP's blocking of Conservative cross-endorsement in the 1968 presidential election exposed the limits of the New York Republicans' loyalty to their party. Legislative elections that same year demonstrated the potential rewards of a Republican-Conservative interparty alliance. Finally, in 1969, John Lindsay failed to win the Republican New York City mayoral primary and became a vocal critic of the Vietnam War. To Richard Nixon and his advisors, these events demonstrated both the increased willingness of New Yorkers to favor a more conservative version of the GOP and the troublesome nature of many liberal Republicans. These events helped persuade President Nixon to support the Conservative Party when an opportunity arose in 1970.

NEW YORK'S NEW SENATOR

Upon his appointment in 1968 to fill the Senate seat of assassinated Robert F. Kennedy, Charles Goodell faced a variety of political challenges. First, as an appointed senator, Goodell had never campaigned outside his congressional district on the western edge of the state. He never assembled the network of supporters, party allies, and contributors successful candidates acquire in the course of getting elected. Second, most New Yorkers knew next to nothing about him. While his career in Congress included a prominent role in the party rebellion that made Gerald Ford the House minority leader in 1965, Goodell's Washington career never translated into prominence back in New York. Third, Goodell's new constituency, the residents of New York State, appeared dramatically different from the residents of his former congressional district. Goodell easily won re-election to the House for over a decade with a moderately conservative record. The congressman's remote district, however, shared few characteristics or problems with the state's metropolitan areas. As a senator, he needed to determine how to best serve his new constituency. Finally, Goodell faced a demanding schedule in which to overcome these challenges. Appointed in the fall of 1968, he faced election in 1970, with a potential primary in the spring of that year.[1] This schedule demanded that Goodell quickly establish his reputation as a senator, raise his visibility with New Yorkers, and assemble the network of support needed to run a successful statewide campaign.

Charles Goodell frequently joked that when he received his Senate appointment in Albany and asked, "How do I get back to Washington?," the reply was, "Go to New York City and turn left."[2] Confronted with an array of political challenges, Goodell adopted the political advice embedded in this joke. The new senator turned left by adopting an array of liberal policy positions. Unfortunately for Goodell, the liberal Republican approach for statewide office holders was not as effective as it once had been. Conservatism's rise in popularity and the subsequent ideological polarization of the GOP complicated the lives of liberal Republicans. John Lindsay's 1969 defeat in the Republican mayoral primary was evidence of this new reality. Facing a changing political landscape, Goodell found his ideological transformation imposed unexpected costs. Shortly after being appointed in the midst of the 1968 campaign, the senator made news by criticizing his party's presidential nominee, Richard Nixon, for his silence on civil rights, for his support of the anti-ballistic missile, and for his views on the Vietnam War. These criticisms enraged many state Republicans who viewed the new senator as disloyal to his party and did not hesitate to express this displeasure. Nonetheless, Goodell continued to press his case. Following Nixon's election, the new senator called on the president-elect to focus on minorities, young people, and urban residents, the constituencies he had neglected in the campaign. In December 1968, Governor Rockefeller sent

Goodell a letter he had received from a "prominent Republican business leader" who took issue with a recent speech by the senator criticizing the president-elect. When the governor suggested a meeting to discuss the letter, Goodell consented, but assured Rockefeller there was no cause for concern because the speech in question had gone fine.[3]

Relations between Goodell and state Republicans continued to deteriorate in 1969 because Richard Nixon's presence in the White House made Goodell's anti-war stance seem anti-Republican. The senator also canceled a number of appearances at state party functions to travel to Biafra, an African country suffering a devastating famine. As a politician yet to establish a personal relationship with many party officials across the state, Goodell's decision prompted criticism, including a private warning from Rockefeller.[4] In the New York City mayoral race, Goodell announced prior to the GOP primary that he would back John Lindsay no matter the outcome. While other Republicans, most prominently Jacob Javits, also endorsed Lindsay, Goodell's near probationary status made his backing the mayor more controversial. The chairman of the Fulton County GOP, for example, wrote the senator asking if he considered himself a Liberal or a Republican.[5] Throughout the summer of 1969, dissatisfaction with the new senator grew. Goodell's staff warned the senator that his ideological opponents within the GOP, with Conservative Party assistance, were working to encourage and broadcast this frustration. They advised Goodell to reassure the governor that he was still acceptable to the vast majority of the party, despite mounting evidence to the contrary.[6] The senator responded with a concerted effort over the summer to woo New York Republican officials, traveling throughout upstate New York talking with local GOP chairmen. A primary challenge seemed likely, however, given how members of the GOP state committee lashed out at Goodell during a September meeting. State chairman Charles Lanigan, unable to contain this mutiny, could only urge the committee to turn to more pressing problems.

While Goodell labored to repair relations with Republicans, he also continued to advocate liberal policy initiatives. On September 25, Goodell introduced a Senate bill calling for the withdrawal of all American troops from Vietnam by the end of 1970. Goodell's proposal made him something of a celebrity and a popular speaker on college campuses across the country. The senator's challenge to the foreign policy of his own party's president inspired comparisons to Eugene McCarthy's role in ending Lyndon Johnson's presidency. Critics also cited Goodell's ideological transformation, calling him an "Instant Liberal" or "Changeable Charlie." The senator rejected this criticism, insisting he had gradually shifted while a member of the House.[7] Goodell embraced the "liberal" label, but objected to being characterized as an "instant" one.

Predictably, Goodell's introduction of the anti-war legislation intensified his problems with the New York GOP. Governor Rockefeller, reflecting a traditional liberal support of Cold War foreign policy, immediately condemned Goodell's bill as "ill-advised."[8] Other state Republicans were less restrained. The Montgomery County GOP chairman wrote Goodell, accusing him of joining a movement "intended to embarrass and degrade this nation."[9] A poll of GOP committeemen found seventy-three of the eighty-four Republican respondents opposed to Goodell's stand on Vietnam.[10] Dan Mahoney captured the intensity of this reaction. In a reference to Goodell's appointive status, Mahoney joked that the senator began with a constituency of one and had eroded his base.[11] Richard Nixon offered no public condemnation of the senator. Some observers, however, speculated that the president's consistent mispronouncing of Goodell's name at a news conference was evidence of a certain amount of animosity.[12]

In November, Republican state senator Edward Speno, an ideological conservative from Long Island's Nassau County, announced he would seek his party's Senate nomination. While the legislator attributed his challenge to Goodell's appointive status, press accounts reported that Speno acted because of Goodell's anti-war legislation.[13] John Marchi, just days after losing the New York City mayoral race, also expressed a cautious interest in the Senate race. Far bolder by the end of the month, Marchi boasted he could defeat Goodell in a Republican primary and launched an undeclared campaign.[14] The state senator wrote all GOP county chairmen making the case for replacing Goodell and asking the state party to examine alternatives to the senator. Marchi grounded his challenge to Goodell on the senator's anti-war legislation, condemning it as part of a "highly irresponsible approach to the conduct of American foreign policy."[15]

Charles Goodell would have likely faced a serious challenge for the GOP nomination in a state with an open primary system. But because New York's political parties designated statewide candidates at their conventions, Nelson Rockefeller could, if he chose, offer some protection to the new senator. Rockefeller would have preferred getting rid of Goodell, but decided against a bruising primary campaign that would have deepened Republican divisions and threatened his own re-election.[16] The governor, who had recently criticized the senator's anti-war legislation, strained credibility by now calling Goodell "the brightest ablest man that I know on the political scene."[17] Rockefeller and state GOP chairman Lanigan also prevailed on county chairmen to refrain from publicly backing any challenger. On December 9, in a closed-door meeting with the party's county leaders, Rockefeller instructed them to get in line behind Goodell. When the meeting ended, the county leaders unanimously supported the GOP senator. Rockefeller and other state Republican leaders, especially Lieutenant Governor Malcolm Wilson, also warned John Marchi that challenging Goodell would divide New York Republicans and hurt the party.[18] Marchi responded to the call for party loyalty and announced he would not seek the GOP Senate nomination. Edward Speno refused to be warned off, but his campaign for the Republican nomination failed to win the support of even his local party and quickly died.

Although state Republican leaders were unwilling to defy Nelson Rockefeller, they remained unhappy with Goodell. Shortly before Goodell officially declared his candidacy for the Republican Senate nomination, his staff notified GOP county chairmen privately of the forthcoming announcement. The negative responses from the GOP county chairmen highlighted the forced nature of his Republican support. One GOP chairman recommended Goodell restrict his candidacy to the Liberal Party ticket, while another suggested the senator not run for the Senate, but get a haircut instead.[19] Goodell's official announcement, in which he called for a swift U.S. withdrawal from Vietnam and criticized the Nixon administration on several policy fronts, further enraged the party.[20] Many fellow Republicans booed him when he addressed the GOP convention in Rochester. Facing only token opposition, however, the senator had no problems securing the nomination. The convention designated Goodell as the GOP Senate nominee on a voice vote. There would be no Republican senate primary.

THE CONSERVATIVE OPPOSITION

Conservative Party leaders realized Charles Goodell's vulnerability presented them with a unique electoral opportunity. In the fall of 1969, Dan Mahoney and political consultant F. Clifton White advised William Buckley that he could actually win in 1970.[21] White further tempted the editor with the possibility of then using a Senate seat to make a challenge for the presidency in 1972. Although intrigued, Buckley declined the offer. The party then approached its most recent Senate nominee, James Buckley. Comfortable out of the public spotlight, Buckley initially saw no reason to repeat his 1968 campaign, but reconsidered after concluding that Charles Goodell's liberal conversion alienated many New Yorkers.[22] Buckley resolved, however, to run only if he could win. Eager to convince the reluctant Buckley, Conservative leaders provided Clif White with fifteen thousand dollars to conduct a poll on Buckley's viability. The party, facing a state filing deadline and an undecided candidate, nominated Buckley with the understanding that he would withdraw if the poll failed to produce encouraging results. The results, however, reflected the party's recent success in winning converts to its cause. The poll showed that 23.8 percent of New Yorkers considered themselves ideologically conservative, with an additional 32.6 percent characterizing themselves as moderate.[23] As important, it also found that one-quarter of New Yorkers favored James Buckley's candidacy, one-quarter opposed it, and the rest of that state's electorate was undecided. White reported these numbers to Buckley, concluding, "We can win."[24] Reassured, Buckley declared for the United States Senate.

Buckley quickly began assembling a campaign organization. The campaign attracted an experienced staff. Clif White, a highly respected figure in conservative circles credited with securing the presidential nomination for Goldwater, signed on as campaign manager. William Rusher helped recruit David Jones, a veteran of several national conservative organizations, as White's number-two man. Arnold Steinberg, editor of YAF's magazine, became press secretary. The campaign also named Leon Weil, a Wall Street broker, to chair its finance committee. Two characteristics of the campaign's fundraising arm were noteworthy. First, its ambitions and accomplishments were unprecedented in Conservative Party history. In May, an internal party memo estimated that the campaign required a minimum of one million dollars, characterizing these needs as "substantial, but not prohibitive."[25] This pronouncement represented extreme confidence, given the party's history of shoestring campaigns. A second significant characteristic of the campaign's fundraising was its independence from the Conservative Party. All other candidates, including the party's gubernatorial nominee, relied on a common pool of money raised and distributed by state headquarters. Buckley received a forty-four-thousand-dollar contribution from the state party, only about 2 percent of his campaign funds. The campaign's own fundraising operation raised the remaining 98 percent.

Separating Buckley's fundraising operation from the Conservative Party reflected the campaign's overall strategy. Dan Mahoney and other state party leaders recognized that Buckley—and so the party—needed a strategy to win a statewide election. To win a three-way race, Buckley needed to double his 1968 total of 1.1 million votes. The campaign planned to enhance its electoral totals by retaining Conservative support and adding disaffected Republicans and Democrats. The Buckley campaign established an independence from the Conservative Party to appeal to these voters. Rather than a strain between the campaign and the party, this distance reflected a shared belief that a degree of independence offered the best chance to capitalize on this unique opportunity for victory. Behind the scenes, the lines of communication between the party and the Buckley organization remained strong. Dan Mahoney, for example, served as one of the campaign's inner-circle advisors for the duration of the campaign.

Another way to attract needed Democratic and Republican voters was to secure a ballot line in addition to the party's Row C. By running on another line, Buckley hoped to attract non-party members reluctant to cast a vote on the Conservative line. Dan Mahoney supported the tactic but worried about antagonizing party loyalists. On June 25, the chairman introduced the idea at a Conservative executive committee meeting, explaining that both major party candidates would have an additional line for the same purpose.[26] Committee members agreed to the strategy on the condition that Buckley would not campaign actively for votes on another line. Mahoney also approached the Buckley campaign about a proposal by

Arnold Steinberg, the campaign press secretary, to refer to Buckley as the "conservative Republican" candidate. He understood that Steinberg, and others in the campaign, hoped to portray Buckley as a Republican who was ideologically conservative. This degree of independence crossed a line, however, and Mahoney demanded that Buckley be referred to as the Conservative candidate. "It would be a pointless affront to the Conservative Party, to describe him in any other way," he added.[27]

Buckley responded personally to Mahoney in order "to allay any fear that others may have that I may be trying to sever the umbilical cord between my campaign and the Conservative Party."[28] He pledged that the independent line would serve only as a convenience to allow GOP committeemen to work for the campaign. Throughout the campaign, Buckley took steps to demonstrate his loyalty. He consistently complimented his Conservative running mates, especially the party's gubernatorial nominee, Paul Adams. At Mahoney's suggestion, Buckley also hosted a dinner for all of the party's statewide candidates. These reassuring gestures were limited, however, by countervailing pressures on the campaign. As the campaign's pollster recognized, "Conservatives have no where else to go."[29] To attract the large number of New Yorkers who were, at best, ambivalent about the Conservative Party, the campaign's newspaper and television advertisements failed to mention Buckley's party.[30] Some Conservatives objected to the campaign's distance from the party. In August, the Erie County Conservative Party complained to the Buckley camp about its brochures and flyers. The county chairman blamed the literature's failure to mention either the party's name or Row C for causing "significant consternation" among Erie County Conservatives.[31] Local leaders in Marcellus confronted Buckley at a party picnic about being excluded from the campaign.[32] Other upstate party leaders became so frustrated by the campaign's independence that they suggested questions to reporters intended to embarrass Buckley on the subject.[33]

Despite these incidents, discontent within the party never grew into a widespread rebellion that threatened the campaign. Dan Mahoney managed to maintain unity. As an advisor to the Buckley campaign, Mahoney made sure the candidate offered enough reassuring words and actions to keep party members committed to his candidacy. As party chairman, Mahoney also defused potential local revolts against Buckley. Having led the party for almost a decade, Mahoney had become accomplished at subduing flare-ups of rank-and-file opposition to cooperation with the GOP. The chairman now applied these skills to keep the party committed to its most competitive statewide candidate ever.

Buckley downplayed his Conservative affiliation and cast himself as the only true Republican in the race. The candidate contended that his conservative approach, and not Senator Goodell's liberal views, belonged in the Republican Party. Buckley also displayed his loyalty to the GOP by pledging to vote with Republicans to organize the Senate. His appeal to Republicans along ideological lines benefited from divisions the 1969 New York City mayoral race had created in the state party. John Marchi immediately endorsed Buckley's third-party candidacy and called on other Republicans to join him.[34] In June, five Republican House members attended a reception for Buckley in Washington, D.C., and Representative Martin McKneally, the reception's organizer, endorsed him shortly afterward.[35] Numerous Republican elected officials, as well as some county organizations, also backed Buckley. By the end of the summer, Buckley was practically the de facto GOP nominee in parts of the state. He often spoke at local Republican functions, and when he traveled to Goodell's home of Jamestown, GOP officials turned out to meet him. Kevin Phillips, now a syndicated columnist, wrote that in New York City's suburbs and upstate, Republican officials openly backed Buckley. Phillips reported that local polls showing unprecedented popular support for the third-party candidate propelled this shift.[36]

Buckley's conservative views and support for President Nixon won him support from the national Republican Party. Some of these GOP politicians had backed previous Conservative efforts. Barry Goldwater sent Bill Buckley a check for his brother's campaign and a potentially damaging report on Goodell's opposition to anti-pornography legislation.[37] Ready to do more damage to the campaign of his Senate colleague, Goldwater inquired "if there is anything that comes to your mind that I might do that could put the shaft to you know who."[38] The Buckley campaign also attracted national Republicans new to the party's cause. Congressman George H. W. Bush, a Senate candidate in Texas, sent a campaign contribution to Bill Buckley to pass along to his brother. Bill advised James that, while the contribution should not be made public, "I don't suppose it would be any break of confidence to mention the fact here and there, when it might do the most good."[39] When William Buckley encountered Senator John Tower at a political function over the summer, Tower, the head of the Republican Senate Campaign Committee, asked if there was anything "extra-official" he could do for Buckley's brother. Buckley followed up with a letter explaining that his brother needed to be financially competitive with Goodell. "The less money CG [Goodell] gets, the less Jim needs. Enough said?" he explained.[40] By the fall, the Senate Campaign Committee's lack of support for Goodell became a matter of controversy, with Senator Tower repeatedly denying Goodell's liberalism and lack of support for the president played a factor in his decision-making.

The Buckley campaign also needed to reach beyond the Conservative and Republican parties to attract Democrats. An event in the spring of 1970 brought to light the number of disaffected conservative Democrats who were potential Buckley supporters. On May 8, approximately two hundred construction workers, many from the site where the World Trade Center was being built, marched to Wall Street to confront a group of anti-war demonstrators. The construction workers attacked the student demonstrators, sometimes using their metal tools in the assaults. The workers marched on to City Hall, where they protested John Lindsay's strong anti-war stand with shouts of "Send Lindsay to Moscow" and signs reading "Lindsay is a faggot." The workers also demanded the American flag, at half-staff to commemorate the student deaths at Kent State earlier that week, be fully raised. Meeting police resistance, they stormed City Hall and raised the flag themselves. When students at nearby Pace College protested these actions, the workers entered the college buildings, beating up students and damaging property. The altercation ended with over seventy people, almost all anti-war demonstrators, injured. Over the next several weeks, construction workers staged several additional pro-war demonstrations in lower Manhattan. At these subsequent, and generally peaceful, rallies, protesters invariably supported President Nixon and attacked Mayor Lindsay. In the last demonstration, held on May 20, construction workers led a crowd of one hundred fifty thousand to a rally outside City Hall.

While the demonstrations by construction workers lasted less than two weeks, they dominated the year as a political symbol. Almost immediately, the public adopted a single word, *hardhats*, to capture the workers, their demonstrations, and their grievances. The term served as shorthand for the far larger group of working-class ethnic whites who objected to the anti-war movement, the counterculture, and the increasingly northern focus of the civil rights movement. These traditional Democrats were becoming alienated from their party and open to appeals from candidates from other parties.

Neither the Buckley campaign nor the Conservative Party played a role in the actual hardhat demonstrations. They both soon recognized, however, the political significance of this group and its supporters. On May 14, Conservative Party officials led a rally in midtown Manhattan wearing hardhats decorated with American flags. One press account marked this rally as the first use of the hardhat symbol by a politician.[41] Richard Nixon also believed in the political potency of this group. On May 26, he met with Peter Brennan, president of the Building and Trade Council of Greater New York. Brennan presented the president with a hardhat labeled "Commander in Chief." James Buckley's pro-war views and support of the Nixon administration made him a natural favorite of the hardhats. By July, Buckley volunteers distributed buttons containing no words, but depicting a hardhat and a flag. On a policy level, the Buckley campaign searched for issues to attract the hardhat vote. William Rusher advised a strong stand against the recent proliferation of pornography to win their support.[42] The campaign's policy committee recommended using the candidate's support of the war to stress the New Left's humiliation of the country.[43] By the fall, the Buckley campaign explicitly emphasized his connection with the hardhats. In a speech in Rochester, Buckley praised the construction workers, calling their final rally a "moving demonstration of their love of country."[44] In September, on his way to a rally on Wall Street, Buckley visited the World Trade Center construction site. When the workers presented him with a hardhat, he promptly put it on and kept it on while he addressed an enthusiastic crowd on Wall Street.[45] Two days later, his campaign released a new film for rallies and fundraisers. As the film showed a peaceful hardhat demonstration, Buckley's voice on the soundtrack proudly announced his association with the rally. Not all politicians found the hardhats so agreeable. In the last week of the campaign, Charles Goodell ventured to the same World Trade Center construction site. The workers drowned out his speech by singing "Good-bye Charlie" to the tune of "Good Night Ladies." The *New York Times'* account also ran a photograph showing a construction worker booing Goodell. The worker wore a hardhat adorned with a Buckley sticker.[46]

By the end of the summer, James Buckley was a viable third-party candidate. He had established a professional campaign organization capable of raising significant amounts of money. He had managed to limit his identification with the Conservative Party, while forestalling a major rebellion by the rank and file. He had also found ways to reach out to large numbers of voters from other parties. These accomplishments inspired a wave of favorable press coverage that further bolstered his campaign. In the *New York Times*, Richard Reeves described him as a "good candidate" with "a crewcut boyishness that women find attractive and campaign managers find salable."[47] Columnist Anthony Lewis cited his intelligence and charm as formidable strengths.[48] Some press coverage highlighted the seeming "man bites dog" nature of a conservative politician competing in the liberal state of New York. Soon, however, reporters abandoned this theme to focus on the spectacle of a wide-open three-way race.

DIVIDED REPUBLICANS

In the spring of 1970, Charles Goodell's primary concern was not James Buckley, but his Democratic opponent, Richard Ottinger. Ottinger was a low-key congressman from Westchester with a strong anti-war position and a sizable family fortune. As a well-financed candidate attractive to the state's liberal voters, he threatened Goodell's ability to assemble a multiparty liberal electoral coalition. The senator used his personal connections with Democrats to help assemble this coalition. He met with Senator George McGovern in Washington to get advice on the campaign's television ads.[49] He also spoke with Paul O'Dwyer, who lost to Ottinger in the Democratic Senate primary, to solicit guidance.[50] Goodell also pursued the Liberal Party cross-endorsement. The senator's anti-war legislation made him a leading GOP dove and an attractive candidate to the Liberal Party. He assured Chairman Donald Harrington that his congressional record was consistent with the party's objectives and that he would "run a vigorous campaign on the Liberal Party ticket right up to election day."[51] The drive produced results. On May 11, the Liberal state committee, following the direction of party leaders, overwhelmingly selected Senator Charles Goodell as its nominee.

Goodell's electoral coalition also assumed his ability to retain Republican support. Major elements in the state GOP, however, were no longer willing to support a liberal candidate out of party loyalty. A number of Republican officials, both upstate and in New York City's suburbs, remained hostile, even after Goodell became the party's nominee. A party committeeman from Fishkill sent a letter titled "Is Charles Goodell a Republican?" to five hundred of his colleagues across the state. The letter outlined the senator's betrayal of the party's principles and described the rebellion of numerous local Republicans to his candidacy.[52] So much of this criticism continued to focus on Goodell's ideological transformation that his being an "instant liberal" became a national joke. Representative Mo Udall, preparing for a congressional basketball game in Washington, D.C., explained that his team of Democrats would employ the "Goodell shift." The team would line up on the far right until the captain shouted, "Senate." At that point, one player would sprint to the far left for a basket.[53]

Goodell's estrangement from his party impaired his ability to raise money. Late in 1969, George Hinman advised Goodell that he had alienated many traditionally Republican campaign contributors.[54] The senator and his staff believed, however, that Nelson Rockefeller's help would overcome this problem. Throughout the 1960s, Rockefeller contributed personally to, and helped raise money for, the state's Republican candidates. During the 1969 New York City mayoral race, two well-known political columnists reported that John Lindsay had rejected financial support from Rockefeller. Goodell assured the governor that he was a different kind of candidate. "Nelson, please know that I would happily accept the contribution," Goodell joked, "and that you will never read about it in Evans and Novak."[55] Shortly after securing the GOP nomination, Goodell's campaign acknowledged this dependence, announcing it planned to meet the fundraising goal of three million dollars principally through the governor and his friends.[56] But despite Goodell's predicament and the governor's role in securing the nomination for him, Rockefeller neither contributed significantly to nor helped raise money for the Goodell campaign. The state GOP, sensitive to Rockefeller's wishes, contributed only two hundred fifty thousand dollars, a fraction of what the campaign needed. The governor realized that the state GOP would never unite behind Goodell. Faced with conducting a re-election campaign with a divided party, Rockefeller positioned himself between Goodell and James Buckley in order to be able to attract supporters of both candidates. Backing Goodell financially would have jeopardized his neutrality.

Even prior to 1970, Nelson Rockefeller showed signs that he was no longer the same paragon of liberal Republicanism. In addition to not assisting John Lindsay's re-election campaign, the governor managed to work harmoniously with an increasingly conservative legislature. Since the fall of 1969, Rockefeller had stressed a fiscal conservatism in short supply in his earlier state budgets. Press reports speculated that the governor, reading the polls, was courting the state's "silent majority." This development even raised the possibility of cooperation between Rockefeller and the Conservative Party. At the suggestion of their mutual friend, Henry Kissinger, William Buckley called on the governor in early 1970. As a member of the Nixon administration, Kissinger had an interest in preventing the president's supporters, including both Rockefeller and Buckley, from battling one another. According to the letter Buckley wrote Kissinger following the meeting, he had told the governor that "the time had come for a major elected Republican figure in New York politics to baptize the Conservative Party."[57] Buckley tried to tempt the governor with the prospect of the Conservative nomination, and its ability to attract Democratic voters. Rockefeller rejected a formal alliance with the party, but promised to give Charles Goodell only limited support. According to Buckley, the governor assured him, "I really am a conservative you know," then added with a wink, "I've got a lot to conserve."[58]

While Nelson Rockefeller rejected the possibility of a Conservative Party nomination, he willingly assumed the posture of a more conservative candidate. The governor replaced promises of expanded social services, which had been the hallmarks of his three earlier statewide campaigns, with calls for fiscal restraint and a crackdown on drug offenders. While his move to the right made sense politically, Rockefeller sometimes seemed uncomfortable with the strategy. When the governor visited the World Trade Center construction site, workers cheered his appearance and presented him with a hard hat. With uncharacteristic coyness, the governor waved the hat enthusiastically, but declined to wear it. Only after the workers chanted, "Put on the hat," did the governor acquiesce and don the year's symbol of conservatism.

Blocked from traditional GOP funding sources and hampered by party critics, Goodell was forced to stress his Republican roots. The senator's campaign released an analysis concluding that in Senate votes he supported President Nixon more regularly than Barry Goldwater.[59] Relying on this study, the campaign wrote all GOP county chairmen extolling the senator's party loyalty.[60] When an editorial in an upstate paper questioned Goodell's place in the party, his campaign responded with a lengthy letter arguing that the senator "has proven time and again his credentials as a Republican."[61] Despite this effort, however, the senator found few allies within the party. Herbert Brownell, advisor to Thomas Dewey and Dwight Eisenhower's attorney general, refused to become involved in the race because of Goodell's criticism of Nixon. In Onodaga County, the GOP congressional nominee condemned Goodell for his embrace of "irresponsible liberalism."[62] Only Jacob Javits and John Lindsay provided reliable Republican support for Goodell. Given John Lindsay's conditional status in the GOP, however, the mayor provided little help with Republican voters. Lindsay further limited his usefulness to Goodell when, late in the campaign, he endorsed Democratic gubernatorial nominee Arthur Goldberg over Nelson Rockefeller.

By the summer, the Goodell campaign recognized that Buckley's candidacy threatened the senator's ability to attract GOP voters. In a July 8 memo, campaign manager Brian Conboy informed Goodell that "the Buckley movement Upstate is getting momentum as a result of the constant carping by certain Republican county leaders and office holders."[63] Later that month, Conboy ordered the first opposition research on Buckley.[64] The campaign also tasked Group Research, a private organization that monitored right-wing groups, to look at the backgrounds of key Buckley staff.[65] Goodell's staff, hoping to find evidence of extremism, even investigated any potential connection between the Buckley campaign and the John Birch Society.[66] None of these efforts helped in the campaign, however. Goodell responded to the Conservative challenge the way liberal Republican candidates had since the early 1960s. He attacked Buckley as outside the respectable political mainstream, referring to him at one point as "the negative knight of the hard right."[67] While this strategy worked in the past, Goodell now confronted a state where conservatism had become more acceptable. The search for a John Birch Society connection indicated the staleness of his approach. Never a significant political force in the state, by 1970 the Society had dropped out of sight and no longer served as the political bogeyman it had in the early 1960s. Goodell was left trying to alarm an electorate that was no longer frightened by conservatism.

On the afternoon of August 21, Nelson Rockefeller and his aides met with his campaign's pollster, Samuel Lubell, at the governor's Manhattan office. Lubell's most recent polling data showed Rockefeller narrowly trailing Democratic candidate Arthur Goldberg. The pollster offered his client hope, however. He explained that in this campaign, Rockefeller's supporters differed dramatically from those in past elections. In the current race, the governor attracted fewer Jewish and black New Yorkers. In their place, he added conservative voters, principally from New York City's suburbs.[68] Finding a state increasingly polarized along ideological lines, Lubell counseled the governor to concentrate on his new conservative constituency. Rockefeller should assure voters that he would not raise their taxes and he should express opposition to unpopular welfare programs. Like the construction workers, but using very different language, the pollster told Rockefeller to put on the hardhat. Lubell also informed the governor that these voters overwhelmingly supported James Buckley for the Senate. To the New Yorkers that the governor needed to win re-election, Charles Goodell was an anathema.

Lubell's presentation at that August meeting confirmed, rather than transformed, the direction of Rockefeller's campaign. The campaign already showed signs of an informal alliance with James Buckley. When several upstate Republican organizations began working for the Conservative nominee, Rockefeller made no attempt to stop them. In July, two political committees with anonymous sponsorship began conducting business from a mid-Manhattan office. Both the "Silent Majority Mobilization Committee" and "Concerned New Yorkers for Buckley, Rockefeller and Levitt" (the Democratic nominee for comptroller) proclaimed a nonpartisan, ideologically conservative approach to politics. Both committees worked to elect Rockefeller as governor and Buckley as senator. The two candidates denied providing financial support to the seemingly well-funded committees, but speculation centered on the governor, given his record of prodigious campaign spending.[69] The state board of elections also inadvertently boosted the impression that the two men were running together. Faced with an overcrowded ballot, the board combined the temporary parties created by Buckley and Rockefeller on a single row.

Just as the informal Rockefeller-Buckley alliance excluded Charles Goodell, it also marginalized Conservative gubernatorial nominee Paul Adams. In 1962 and 1966, Conservatives viewed the race for governor as critical to their party's existence, and identified Rockefeller as their primary target. In 1970, the significance of the Senate race eclipsed that of the gubernatorial campaign for Conservatives. Adams consistently criticized the governor, principally on state spending and taxes, but few other Conservatives joined him. James Buckley endorsed Adams, but refused to denounce the governor throughout the campaign. Buckley even predicted voters would split their ballots and characterized this approach as healthy.[70] The candidate also refused to sanction Clif White when the campaign manager announced he was going to vote for Nelson Rockefeller. Downplaying White's seeming disloyalty, Buckley responded, "I leave it to him how he votes in other races."[71] Conservatives may have provided more active support to Rockefeller. On October 8, William Buckley sent John Mitchell a poem set to appear in the next issue of *National Review*. Buckley described the work as "discharging the terms of the Buckley/Rockefeller/Mitchell treaty."[72] Later that month, the magazine published the poem, titled "The Alternative is Goldberg." After outlining the necessity of preventing Democratic gubernatorial nominee Arthur Goldberg from being elected, the poem ended with the couplet:

> And so, despite the trauma and the shock,
> November, I'll be voting for the Rock.[73]

However significant Buckley's reference to a treaty with Rockefeller, the poem and the letter to Mitchell demonstrated a willingness of Conservatives to support the GOP in everything but the Senate race.

New York's Senate campaign, and the crossing of party lines it promoted, influenced all of the state's political races in 1970. A Rockefeller aide even suggested to a Nixon advisor that the administration invite Dan Mahoney to the White House to discuss the state's congressional races.[74] Conservative leaders correctly predicted that Buckley's popularity encouraged Republican congressional and legislative candidates to accept cross-endorsement. More importantly, the state GOP no longer presented any obstacles to Republicans who wished to align with the Conservative Party. Since Nelson Rockefeller had put on the hardhat himself, he could not prevent other Republican assembly and state senate candidates from doing so also. As a result, Conservatives cross-endorsed 108 Republican congressional and legislative candidates across the state. Not only was this the most ever, it represented the first time that the party's cross-endorsements outnumbered its independent candidates. Several congressional races demonstrated an unprecedented level of cooperation between the two parties. In the Sixteenth Congressional District in Staten Island and Brooklyn, a Republican city councilman withdrew from the race once the local GOP decided to cross-endorse the Conservative nominee. On Long Island, the Conservative candidate did the same for the Republican nominee. The Senate race even influenced how races with independent Conservative nominees were run. Independent Conservative candidates across the state tried to replicate Buckley's critique of Goodell in their own races. The Conservative Party challenger to Republican congressman Hamilton Fish Jr. warned of the incumbent's "creeping Goodellism."[75] Republicans with liberal records shunned this potentially destructive comparison. Peter Peyser, the GOP congressional candidate in Westchester, struggled to keep his campaign from being linked to the controversial senator.

The unprecedented cooperation between the two parties in legislative and congressional races, however, alienated some Conservatives. In one upstate county, members of the Conservative Party executive committee charged state headquarters with selling out to the GOP. In a letter sent to local party members, the committeemen solicited support for Fred Roland in the Conservative primary for the district's congressional seat. Roland faced Martin McKneally in this primary, the incumbent Republican and the first congressman to endorse James Buckley. State Conservative leaders backed McKneally despite Roland's record of service to the party. Members of the county committee suspected a corrupt Conservative-Republican bargain that included Nelson Rockefeller's promising to make Kieran O'Doherty a judge. Looking to spark a party rebellion against McKneally, the letter asked, "Can we prostitute this party to 'win' with a candidate who repudiates every principle that we believe in?"[76] Local Conservatives, however, chose McKneally in the party primary, another triumph for Dan Mahoney and party headquarters in their effort to align with Republicans.

WHITE HOUSE INTEREST

Richard Nixon looked to the 1970 election as an opportunity to increase Republican representation in Congress and to increase conservative representation in the Republican Party. The Senate offered the prime opportunity since a pickup of three seats gave the GOP control of the chamber. Nixon's southern strategy in the 1968 presidential campaign, while blunted by George Wallace's third-party candidacy, suggested a future for the party at odds with liberal Republicanism. Nixon even flirted with the idea of making this ideological shift official. In the summer of 1970, following a discussion with the president, H. R. Haldeman noted that, "[c]onsideration should be given to the technical and political pluses of making the big play, of changing the Party name to the Conservative Party."[77] Nixon watched events in New York for potential political opportunities. Nixon had wanted to intervene to harm John Lindsay's chances in the 1969 New York City mayoral race, and had stayed out of the campaign only because John Marchi trailed so badly that White House action seemed futile. The 1970 Senate race had the potential to be different. When the president and his political advisors looked ahead to that race in December 1969, John Mitchell cited the party's one million votes in 1968 as evidence of the need to monitor events closely.[78] Over the 1969 Christmas holidays, Nixon read and loved Kevin Phillips's *The Emerging Republican Majority*.[79] Phillips, now a White House advisor, asserted that in order to win elections Republicans needed to attract white ethnics, usually of Irish, Italian, or Eastern European ancestry. He used William F. Buckley's 1965 mayoral campaign to prove his point. Nixon accepted Phillips's analysis and began devising ways to court this "silent majority," including a potential coalition with the Conservative Party.

For its part, the Conservative Party embraced Nixon wholeheartedly during these years, defending the president's conduct of the war, controversial Supreme Court selections, and virtually all his policy initiatives. James Buckley's nomination presented the president with an attractive electoral option in 1970. Buckley, courting the state's Republican voters, continually proclaimed that he was the more reliable supporter of the president in the race. He made his support of Nixon a central part of his campaign. In contrast, Charles Goodell remained a persistent critic of the president. In April, Goodell declared he was unsure whom he would support for president in 1972, explaining that he would back Nixon only if the president handled the Vietnam War properly.[80] For the White House, the disparity between Goodell and Buckley could not have been clearer.

Despite a recent history of cooperation between the Nixon administration and the Conservative Party, and James Buckley's suitability to build on this cooperation, the White House understood the problems associated with supporting a Conservative nominee. In 1968 and 1969, Nixon advanced the alliance between the two state parties only by encouraging Conservative cross-endorsement of Republican candidates. Backing a third-party challenger to an incumbent GOP senator, a far more drastic step, exposed the administration to charges of party disloyalty. In the beginning of 1970, the White House looked for a Republican alternative to Goodell. Kevin Phillips wrote

Nixon suggesting Cliff White replace Goodell as the GOP nominee. Nixon leaked the idea to sympathetic journalists, and the proposal wound up in John Chamberlain's column in *U.S. News & World Reports*. White, however, refused to become a candidate.[81] With no prospective GOP primary challenger, the White House saw few attractive options. Harry Dent, monitoring Senate races for the administration, wrote, "I don't like the idea of being anything with Goodell, but we probably can't avoid that."[82] Even after James Buckley declared his candidacy, the White House resisted backing the Conservative nominee. Presidential assistant Peter Flanigan wrote Pat Buchanan that the White House, despite preferring Buckley, could not back him against a Republican candidate. Flanigan tried to temper the approach, however, by adding that "our neutrality with regard to Buckley's [campaign] is not armed."[83] Acting on his own, Buchanan met secretly with William Rusher over the summer to discuss election strategy.[84] But at this stage of the campaign, the most the White House would do was to refuse to support any candidate. Presidential advisor Murray Chotiner, handicapping Republican electoral prospects in an interview with the *New York Times*, pointedly refused to offer any kind words concerning Goodell.[85] Nixon's isolation of Goodell proved popular with the national GOP. At a meeting between the president and leading conservative Republicans, Barry Goldwater asked Nixon how hard he planned to work for the GOP Senate nominee in New York. When Nixon answered that, due to the confusing nature of the race, nothing would be done in New York, the politicians laughed in agreement.[86]

The Buckley campaign, however, needed more than neutrality from the White House. The candidate wanted some sign of approval from Nixon to help win over the state's Republican voters. An early campaign memo prepared by pollster Arthur Finkelstein pledged, "Buckley's campaign must and will be tied to Nixon."[87] Conservatives, recognizing the White House's hesitation, set out to demonstrate the acceptability of their candidate to the president. As he had so many times before, William Buckley interceded for the party. In July, after responding to a presidential request with advice on how to increase the number of conservative writers published in the *Paris Tribune*, Buckley brought up his brother's candidacy. Quoting from a letter he had sent a personal friend, Buckley explained that "Jim is and has always been a registered Republican. The Conservative Party is merely a vehicle of protest." Buckley's use of the word "merely" would have enraged Conservative Party loyalists and taxed all of Dan Mahoney's peace-keeping skills. The editor, however, understood the administration's concerns. He concluded his letter with a promise: "Upon arriving in the Senate, he [James Buckley] would be indistinguishable from any other Republican," he wrote.[88] Following up on this private communication, Buckley used his syndicated column to calm White House fears about the third-party status of his brother's candidacy, stressing the difference between the New York Conservative Party and third parties in other states.[89]

Nixon knew that supporting a third-party challenger against an incumbent Republican senator would create controversy, and did not intend to expend political capital for a noncompetitive candidate. In June, however, the Republican primary for a House seat in Westchester County encouraged the president. According to H. R. Haldeman, Nixon was elated when early primary returns showed liberal congressman Ogden Reid trailing a conservative challenger. Reid eventually won the GOP primary, but Nixon interpreted the closeness of the race as a "good anti-peace-candidate sign" that "may give Buckley a real chance."[90] By early August, Nixon told his closest aides that he would provide overt support if Buckley demonstrated the potential to win.[91] On August 26, the White House received the results of a requested poll showing Democratic nominee Richard Ottinger with 32 percent of the New York vote, James Buckley second with 26 percent, and Charles Goodell trailing badly with 15 percent.[92] The following day, Haldeman gave Nixon the data, adding his assessment that Goodell had no chance of winning. Nixon decided at that point "to go all out to elect Buckley."[93] On September 9, the president held a meeting in the Oval Office with his top political aides. Speechwriter William Safire recounted the meeting in his memoir of his White House years. Nixon directed his advisors to abandon the normal procedure of backing all Republican candidates in New York. He attributed the decision to Goodell's failure to support the administration and the senator's inability to mount a credible candidacy. "We are dropping Goodell over the side," Nixon bluntly told the group.[94]

WHITE HOUSE INTERVENTION

Having decided to intervene in the New York Senate race, Richard Nixon chose John Mitchell, who had ties to the state's Conservatives and Republicans, to head the effort.[95] The administration also moved to publicize subtly its new stand. When several prominent New York Republicans asked about the president's preference in the senate race, Murray Chotiner responded that the administration was confident New Yorkers would choose "the person they believe to be best qualified by training, experience and knowledge, and who will work in harmony with the Nixon administration."[96] No political observers interpreted "work[ing] in harmony with the Nixon administration" as a reference to Charles Goodell, and Chotiner made no attempt to contradict the impression that the administration preferred Buckley.

On September 15, Nixon brought Bill Buckley to the White House to discuss the New York race along with Haldeman and Mitchell. Nixon quickly declared his support of James Buckley and his contempt for Charles Goodell, and, according to Haldeman's account of the meeting, "offered all kinds of backroom help and a lot of advice."[97] This "backroom help" varied from encouraging support for the Conservative nominee from Republican county chairmen and congressmen to halting federal funds to the state until Nelson Rockefeller "plays our game re Buckley."[98] Nixon also identified money as Buckley's principal challenge. The group determined the campaign needed at least one million dollars—referred to as the "basic kitty"—and needed it quickly.

Several days after this meeting, Bill Buckley called the White House to report he had accomplished two unspecified assignments he received from the president.[99] At the same time, the White House began to actively support James Buckley's campaign. H. R. Haldeman asked Charles Colson to try to get union president Peter Brennan and the leaders of other hardhat unions in New York to support Buckley. Colson reported back that these groups already backed Buckley, if not always publicly. "Our friends," he assured Haldeman, "are very cooperative in this effort."[100] Haldeman also asked assistant Ken Cole to work on Nelson Rockefeller. The day Nixon committed his administration's resources to Buckley, Nelson Rockefeller, perhaps uncomfortable with his conversion to conservatism, seemed to abandon his neutrality and embrace Charles Goodell. At a GOP fundraising dinner in New York City, the governor, wearing a Goodell button, predicted the senator would be elected and pledged to campaign with him.[101] On September 24, Cole gave Haldeman a status update. "Your instructions to stop feeding any more aid into the State of New York until Governor Rockefeller gets himself straightened out on the position he is going to take on the Senate race has been carried out," he reported.[102] When John Ehrlichman asked, Haldeman told him that John Mitchell had delivered this ultimatum to Rockefeller.[103] Whether it was Mitchell's warning or Goodell's consistently discouraging poll numbers, Rockefeller soon abandoned his public support of the senator. At a party dinner in Rochester, the governor made it a point not to arrive until Goodell had finished speaking, and then failed to mention the senator in his own remarks.

The Nixon administration also worked behind the scenes to provide the Buckley campaign the funding it needed to be competitive. By the fall of 1970, the White House had an existing effort to ensure adequate funding for key Senate races. In "Operation Townhouse," former and current White House employees solicited contributions from major Republican donors.[104] Jack Gleason, who headed the operation from a Dupont Circle townhouse in Washington, D.C., had worked at the White House until leaving in the spring of 1970 to run Operation Townhouse. While Gleason bragged he handled over ten million dollars, the actual amount appears to have been closer to three million dollars. A group of senior White House staff, including H. R. Haldeman and Donald Rumsfeld, collectively known as the "Appropriations Committee," determined where to send the money. Gleason used a variety of methods to transfer this money, even traveling across the country to hand cash personally to candidates. For the most part, however, he distributed the money through political committees established in the District of Columbia. The Corrupt Practices Act of 1925, the only federal law regulating campaign contributions at the time, did not require District of Columbia committees to report their contributors. This loophole allowed the White House to shield its role in arranging these contributions.

At the time Operation Townhouse began business in the spring of 1970, Nixon was unwilling to support Charles Goodell and unconvinced of the wisdom of backing James Buckley. By late summer, however, that assessment had changed. When Haldeman informed the president that polls showed that Buckley could win but Goodell could not, an ecstatic Nixon contacted three people. He called former New York governor Tom Dewey with the news. He had Haldemen call Pat Buchanan to get word to the Buckley campaign. And finally, he had Haldeman call John Mulcahy in Ireland.[105] Although he spent a great deal of time in his homes in Ireland, Mulcahy was a New York native. He had sold his business, the Quigley Company, to Pfizer in 1968 for several hundred thousand shares of the larger company's stock. The wealthy former businessman contributed handsomely to Nixon's 1968 presidential campaign and gave over one and a half million dollars to Operation Townhouse in 1970.[106] While the specifics of his role in the New York race remain hazy, Mulcahy served as the Nixon administration's funding solution to the Buckley campaign's money problem.

Several years later, in a letter to the Watergate special prosecutor, Mulcahy admitted contributing three hundred thousand dollars to the Buckley campaign. He sent the money, not to Buckley's campaign, but to Jack Gleason in Washington with the understanding that the sum of three hundred thousand dollars would be divided up into one hundred checks of three thousand dollars each. Each of these smaller checks would then be transferred to one of the one hundred different D.C. committees.[107] Gleason's records indicate that Gleason divided Mulcahy's three hundred thousand dollars among these committees. Under the heading "Amount—$3,000 for each Committee," Gleason's records list one hundred committees with names such as "Alabama Citizens for Buckley" and "Montana Friends for Buckley"[108] A number of other Nixon contributors also assisted the Buckley campaign. In his files, John Dean, who became the custodian of the Operation Townhouse records in 1973, included a two-thousand-dollar check from Thomas Pappas to the "Buckley for Senate TV Committee," a political committee based in the District of Columbia. Pappas, a Greek-American businessman with close ties to Spiro Agnew, provided the administration with hush money when the Watergate burglars were arrested.[109]

Political committees in the District of Columbia could shield the identity of their donors, but had to report their own contributions to political candidates. By late fall, the Buckley campaign disclosed the existence of the D.C. committees but not the extent of the financial assistance they provided. The Goodell camp objected but misunderstood the purpose of the committees. The senator's campaign charged that the committees were being used to hide the extreme right's role in funding James Buckley. In reality, the committees were intended to obscure, at the White House's behest, the role of mainstream Republicans in helping a third-party candidate against a GOP incumbent. Following the election, reports filed by the Buckley campaign revealed that D.C. committees contributed more than four hundred fifty thousand dollars. An especially convoluted set of transactions clouded the role of these committees. Buckley's financial reports reveal the presence of over one hundred D.C. committees with names such as "Housewives for Law and Order." These committees contributed to a similar number of committees based in New York City with names such as "Cayuga County Citizens for Buckley." The "county" committees then transferred the money to the main campaign committee. In addition, some D.C. committees, including the "Buckley for Senate TV Committee," donated funds directly to the principal Buckley campaign committee. The four hundred fifty thousand dollars contributed by all D.C. committees represented almost one third of all money raised by the Buckley campaign. The evidence indicates that the Nixon administration raised this money, obscured its origins by running it through a series of sham committees, and then delivered it to James Buckley.

While the White House shielded its role in financial assistance, it sought ways to publicly demonstrate its allegiance to Buckley. Aiming to insulate the president from any potential political fallout, the administration used Vice President Spiro Agnew for this job. Agnew was already a controversial political figure. His alliterative attacks on liberals in the news media inspired the political right and enraged the left. Beginning in September, under instructions from Nixon, the vice president made a series of speeches across the country attacking congressional Democrats as "radical liberals." Nixon also assigned speechwriters Pat Buchanan and William Safire, as well as senior aide Bryce Harlow, to assist Agnew. The vice president's speeches soon added veiled references to "radical liberals" within the GOP. Eager to include Goodell in his attacks, Agnew repeatedly raised the possibility with Nixon. Finally, in late September, the president approved Agnew's explicitly denouncing Goodell, stressing the need to convey the idea that the White House wanted Goodell defeated, but to do so subtly.[110] In the coming weeks, Agnew delivered the White House's message, but found subtlety a more demanding assignment.

On September 30, in a television interview in Minot, North Dakota, the vice president publicly and explicitly criticized Charles Goodell. Agnew denounced the New York senator as a radical liberal who had left the GOP. In a speech later that day in Salt Lake City, he charged that Goodell "had strayed beyond the point of no return."[111] The following day, Agnew's office confirmed that the vice president planned to attend a New York City fundraiser for candidates who supported the president. While the Buckley campaign denied any official connection to the event, Clare Booth

Luce's role as one of its hosts suggested that the money was intended for the Conservative nominee. On October 5, the vice president attended this private fundraising luncheon at the Waldorf-Astoria. Before a well-heeled crowd of one hundred, many wearing Buckley buttons, the vice president spoke for ten minutes on the need to elect candidates who would support the president once in Washington. Agnew never mentioned James Buckley, but advised his audience not to support either Goodell or Richard Ottinger, Buckley's only opponents. Immediately following the vice president's speech, one of the event's hosts, George Champion, the former chairman of Chase Manhattan Bank, bluntly told the crowd that the Buckley campaign needed funds. Although no money was collected at the lunch, guests were handed envelopes addressed to the finance division of the Buckley campaign as they left the ballroom.[112]

Spiro Agnew's initial refusal to refer explicitly to Buckley reflected the subtlety requested by the president. His inability to maintain this approach, however, soon made news. On October 8, at a private meeting with newspaper editors, the vice president told the group that if it compared Goodell's statements in the House with his more recent remarks, "you will find he is truly the Christine Jorgensen of the Republican Party."[113] Jorgensen, born George rather than Christine, gained national attention by traveling to Denmark in 1950 to undergo a sex change operation. The comment created an immediate uproar. Virtually all aggrieved parties, including Jorgensen, demanded an apology. Agnew refused to retreat, and dismissed Jorgensen as a publicity-seeker.[114] The controversy, however, convinced the president that Agnew was no longer an effective advocate in the Senate race. In a White House meeting immediately following the Jorgensen controversy, Nixon told Haldeman, with regard to the New York race, "VP [was] now overdoing it. Move on to other things."[115]

Throughout most of the campaign, Charles Goodell contended that the White House remained neutral in the Senate race at his request. The senator even implied that the administration wanted to do more to support him but respected his wishes and remained uninvolved. In a radio interview on September 13, just two weeks prior to being denounced by the vice president, Goodell insisted that the president supported his candidacy and might send Agnew to New York to campaign for him.[116] The White House's public campaign forced Goodell to revise this position. The senator maintained that the president supported him, but that rogue members of the administration were acting independently in opposing him. On September 25, Goodell named two Nixon aides, Murray Chotiner and Charles Colson, as "men of the far right [who] have infiltrated a few positions in the White House staff" and were working against him.[117] When, at the end of September, Agnew called him a "radical liberal," Goodell added the vice president to the list of disloyal members of the administration subverting the president's desire to support him. Goodell characterized Agnew as a loose cannon and asked the president to muzzle him.[118] Goodell even assured a reporter that Nixon played no role in the attacks. "I think if the President were to intervene directly, he would have done it in a more intelligent way," he explained.[119] Years after the race, the senator recalled his initial confidence that Agnew and the White House aides opposed him without the president's approval. Only at the very end of the campaign did Goodell accept that the president directed this opposition.[120]

With Agnew no longer an effective surrogate, Nixon weighed how best to intervene against Goodell. Throughout the final weeks of the campaign, the president continually considered personally endorsing Buckley. At one point, Nixon feared that the Liberal Party, recognizing the futility of the Goodell campaign, would transfer its endorsement to the Democratic candidate, Richard Ottinger. He prepared to travel to New York in response and endorse Buckley formally. "[I] have to go for all the chips," he explained to Haldeman.[121] While the president went so far as to have John Ehrlichman call Bill Buckley about the plan, he abandoned it when the Liberal Party remained committed to Goodell. The White House identified alternative methods to demonstrate its support for Buckley. Charles Colson devised one way to associate Nixon with the Buckley campaign.[122] A White House aide informed William Rusher that, following a visit to Connecticut, the president would arrive at the Westchester Airport on the afternoon of October 12. The aide, probably Colson himself, explained that any pro-Buckley demonstrators who greeted the president would be allowed close enough to be photographed. Rusher passed this information on, and the Buckley campaign made the necessary arrangements. One thousand Buckley supporters, many waving signs proclaiming their loyalties, greeted President Nixon upon his arrival at the Westchester Airport. Not only did Nixon allow himself to be photographed with the demonstrators, he offered some encouraging, if subtle, words. When asked if he supported Buckley, Nixon replied, "I appreciate the fact that he's for me."[123] The resulting press coverage linked Buckley and Nixon. In his diary, Haldeman predicted that the event "should solve the current q[uestion] of a Buckley endorsement."[124] The next day, the Buckley campaign further exploited this public relations bonanza when anonymous sources in the campaign leaked the White House's role in staging the airport rally. This leak prompted a new round of stories linking Nixon with Buckley.[125]

The White House struggled to find the optimal way to characterize the relationship between the president and Buckley. On October 16, H. R. Haldeman and several other political aides sketched out a response to questions concerning the New York race for Nixon's press secretary, Ron Ziegler.[126] If asked about the vice president's attendance at the New York fundraiser, they instructed Ziegler to explain that when Agnew informed Nixon about the event, the president had no objections. The press secretary could then explain that because Buckley supported the administration's major policy positions and Goodell opposed them, the president would refrain from his usual endorsement of the Republican nominee.[127] To the White House's frustration, no reporter asked Ziegler about New York politics. By October 19, Haldeman asked Ziegler to make the statement proactively, explaining that Nixon "wants [us] to help Buckley as much as we can."[128] On October 21, Ziegler simply issued the statement, minus the explanation of Agnew's attending the fundraiser. The Buckley campaign, however, contacted the White House to complain that the statement was so understated that most New Yorkers failed to recognize it as an endorsement. Hoping to attract some still-hesitant Republican voters, the campaign lobbied for a straightforward endorsement by Nixon himself.[129] The White House, however, resisted taking this final step.

Richard Nixon's support of Buckley created difficulties for Nelson Rockefeller. Following John Mitchell's ultimatum to the governor to "get himself straightened out on the Senate race," Mitchell and Rockefeller had reached an understanding that required a measure of public neutrality. Rockefeller believed the White House broke this agreement when the vice president injected himself into the race at the end of September. On October 1, unable to reach the president, Rockefeller asked Mitchell for a cease-fire.[130] The attorney general made excuses, disingenuously claiming, "we don't control the Vice President."[131] The administration's indifference to the governor's concerns forced Rockefeller to go public with his attempt to arrange a cease-fire. His public declarations, however, seemed aimed at protecting his re-election campaign from criticism rather than offering any real protection to Goodell. Behind the scenes, Rockefeller maintained a cooperative relationship with the White House. On October 10, when the governor received additional polling data showing Goodell running a distant third, he passed the information on to Nixon.[132]

Abandoned by his state party, Charles Goodell prepared to step up the battle with the White House. Following Ron Ziegler's carefully worded nonendorsement, Goodell charged that Nixon "has now joined the forces of purging."[133] In the face of this escalation in hostilities, the senator purchased a thirty-minute block of television time for what his campaign called a major announcement. Speculation focused on the possibility that, recognizing he could not win, Goodell planned to pull out of the race and throw his support to Democratic nominee Richard Ottinger. Goodell's campaign encouraged this speculation to create interest in the senator's television appearance. These rumors triggered a frantic series of weekend meetings at the White House. In the hours before Goodell's television appearance, both Nixon and Haldeman spoke to Bill Buckley about potential responses if the senator withdrew.[134] The Conservative Party also flooded Goodell headquarters with anonymous calls feigning support and urging the senator to remain in the race.[135] On Sunday, October 25, Goodell's live half-hour broadcast, titled "Senator Goodell on President Nixon," began with film clips of Vice

President Agnew criticizing the senator and Ron Ziegler announcing the president did not support him. Goodell then appeared, announcing that he would not withdraw and attacking "the hardhatted political militants in the White House who desired my political demise."[136] Citing his commitment to New York and its residents, Goodell vowed to fight on and to win, even claiming new momentum for his campaign. The White House offered no response to the broadcast. While Goodell's withdrawal required a contingency plan, his denunciation of the administration presented no problems.

A CONSERVATIVE SENATOR

As the 1970 election neared, Charles Goodell, now openly antagonistic to the Nixon administration, pressed his case as an independent Republican. James Buckley remained a loyal supporter of Nixon and silent on Nelson Rockefeller's candidacy. Buckley's campaign also used a late infusion of money from the D.C. committees to purchase television and radio time in upstate cities. Rockefeller, convinced of the wisdom of neutrality in the Senate race through a combination of polling data and White House pressure, steered clear of his controversial running mate. Goodell repeatedly asked the governor for a "dramatic display of support," but Rockefeller refused these appeals.[137] In light of this lack of support, historian Arthur Schlesinger Jr. lamented in a letter to the *New York Times* that the current Rockefeller seemed a very different man from the politician who faced down conservatives at the 1964 GOP convention. Schlesinger predicted that the governor's re-election "would be welcomed with satisfaction in Washington as proof that even the most disobedient state in the Union had yielded to the politics of fear."[138] On the weekend before the election, Rockefeller announced he would campaign for a day with the full Republican slate of candidates, including Goodell. Given his reluctance to take similar steps earlier, Rockefeller's decision served only to announce that the election outcome was settled. Meanwhile, Richard Nixon continued to wrestle with personally endorsing Buckley. On the Sunday before the election, the president decided to travel to New York and endorse Buckley himself. Haldeman, fearing the potential backlash cost of such a dramatic move, had John Mitchell talk Nixon out of it.[139] Instead, Nixon settled for a telephone conversation with Bill Buckley about the campaign.[140]

On November 3, New Yorkers elected James Buckley to the U.S. Senate. The Conservative nominee received 39 percent of the vote, topping Richard Ottinger by one hundred thousand votes and Charles Goodell by seven hundred thousand votes. This relatively low winning percentage prompted some critics to question the significance of Buckley's victory. Calling the election "a step backward for New York," the *New York Times* pointed to Goodell and Ottinger's winning over 60 percent of the vote as evidence that New Yorkers did not support Buckley or his views.[141] Conservatives unanimously rejected this assessment. At his campaign headquarters, Buckley, perhaps swept up by the excitement of the evening, reflected on the occasion with uncharacteristically immodest words. After outlining the limitations of the politics of the past, the senator-elect exclaimed, "The American people want a new course, they want a new politics—and I am the voice of that new politics."[142] Spiro Agnew, watching the returns in a Washington, D.C., hotel suite with members of the Cabinet, framed the result in less polite terms. Secretary of the Interior Walter Hickel recounted that when one network projected Buckley defeating Goodell, the vice president strode toward the television set and proclaimed, "We got that son of a bitch."[143] Offering a more positive interpretation, Barry Goldwater sent a telegram to the senator-elect with his congratulations and the appraisal "America now has hope."[144] Many observers characterized the Conservative victory as ushering in a new era for the state's political parties. Bill Buckley asserted that with his brother's election "people will no longer think, as they have been trained to think, of Conservatives as a batch of Birchers and congeries of crackpots."[145] Chairman Dan Mahoney looked to translate the victory into increased influence. He warned of a possible power struggle with the GOP unless Republicans provided Conservatives with policy-making positions in state government.[146]

In the state's other major race, Nelson Rockefeller handily defeated Arthur Goldberg to win his fourth term as New York's governor. Given Rockefeller's ideological shift, his re-election bolstered the perception of a conservative tide sweeping across the state. A friend of Mayor Lindsay, quoted anonymously following the election, interpreted Rockefeller's victory after he shifted to the right and Goodell's defeat after he moved to the left as the end of liberal republicanism in the state.[147] In a campaign virtually ignored by the press and his party, Conservative gubernatorial nominee Paul Adams managed to win four hundred twenty-one thousand votes. While far behind the two major candidates, Adams's total surpassed Goldberg's votes on the Liberal line, thus maintaining Row C for the Conservative Party. In a letter to the defeated candidate, Dan Mahoney thanked the college professor for his service to the party and acknowledged the difficulty of running in the face of "Rockefeller's very sharp move to the right."[148]

New Yorkers made few changes in the state's congressional and legislative races. While the GOP lost one seat in the state senate, it retained its majority with a thirty-two to twenty-five advantage. The assembly remained unchanged with seventy-nine Republicans and seventy-one Democrats. More importantly for the Conservative Party, its cross-endorsements continued to play a critical role in numerous races. The party endorsed a majority of Republicans elected to both state houses and provided the margin of victory in several legislative elections. In addition, Conservatives Rosemary Gunning and Charles Jerabek won re-election to the assembly. In the House of Representatives, Republicans picked up two seats, but still trailed Democrats twenty-four to seventeen in the state delegation. Conservatives provided the margin of victory in the state's most publicized race where Republican Norman Lent defeated Democratic incumbent Allard Lowenstein. The congressional elections also produced a future national conservative political star. Erie County sent former Buffalo Bills quarterback Jack Kemp to the House with the help of Conservative cross-endorsement. The party's achievement in these races rested on an unprecedented level of support for its congressional and legislative candidates. Conservative nominees, both cross-endorsed Republicans and independent candidates, averaged just over ten percent of the vote in their races. Observers credited the impact of the Buckley campaign and the increasing popularity of conservatism for this improvement.

The Buckley victory was not duplicated across the country. Richard Nixon failed to achieve his goal of a Republican Senate and considered the election something of a disappointment. Defeating two of the Democratic "radical liberals," Joseph Tydings of Maryland and Albert Gore Sr. of Tennessee, and the single Republican in this group offset the disappointment to some degree. Privately, Nixon drew an encouraging lesson from the election. At a discussion with his political advisors, he speculated that the election showed that blue-collar workers, mostly Catholic and suburban, were helping to form a new majority. Nixon cited James Buckley's victory an example of this transformation.[149]

The White House wasted no time acknowledging the significance of Buckley's election. On the weekend following the election, Dan Mahoney, Kieran O'Doherty, and Bill Buckley traveled to Walker Cay, a private island in the Bahamas owned by Robert Abplanalp. A wealthy businessman who invented the aerosol valve, Abplanalp also owned the adjacent island of Grand Cay, which he made available to Richard Nixon. On the afternoon of Sunday, November 8, Mahoney and O'Doherty flew by helicopter to meet with the president on Grand Cay. The group spoke for over an hour in a session that the White House characterized as primarily social, but Mahoney conceded concerned politics. Following the meeting, the Conservative chairman reported that Nixon expressed an interest in how James Buckley attracted so many traditionally Democratic voters. The group also discussed presidential politics, with Mahoney assuring Nixon that he could carry New York State in 1972. Left unmentioned was whether this optimistic assessment required Nixon to accept Conservative cross-endorsement. According to Haldeman's diary, Nixon was pleased with the meeting and "very impressed" by Mahoney and O'Doherty.[150] At about 6:30 P.M., Bill Buckley arrived on Grand Cay to have dinner with the president while Mahoney and O'Doherty returned to their hotel on Walker Cay. Over dinner, the two men discussed domestic politics, paying special attention to Nixon's 1972 re-election campaign.[151] In order to build up the vice president as the administration's conservative answer to just re-elected California governor

Ronald Reagan, they decided Agnew would appear on Buckley's television program, *Firing Line*. Nixon and Buckley also determined that, given the Conservative Party's enhanced status, it was appropriate to find a federal position for Kieran O'Doherty.[152]

The presidential meeting in the Bahamas made news back in New York. Demonstrating the star power that accompanied election to the Senate, the *Daily News* ran the front-page banner headline, "Nixon meets Buckley Aides."[153] Press accounts contained little in the way of specifics, but characterized the meeting as representative of the state's new political realities.[154] The characterization proved accurate. New York Conservatives had achieved many of their goals. They had been accepted by a Republican president who now wanted to know their political secrets. Nelson Rockefeller had shifted his political views to appeal to the party and its members. A Conservative candidate was making plans to be sworn in as a member of the United States Senate. Most Republican members of the legislature wanted the party's cross-endorsement. Over the next several years, the relationship between the White House and the Conservative Party would prove more contentious than either side expected as 1970 came to close. The damage that the Conservative Party had inflicted on liberal state Republicans, however, was permanent. There were still liberal Republicans in the state, most prominently Senator Jacob Javits, but there was no doubt that the New York GOP had been pushed significantly to the right by a splinter party.

SIX

DISPUTED LINES

During its initial years, the New York Conservative Party struggled to overcome its status as a political outcast. This condition brought with it a number of obstacles and challenges for the third party. Outsider status, however, also provided a clarity of purpose. The New York Conservative Party opposed the liberal state GOP and the liberal wing of the national Republican Party at every opportunity. By the early 1970s, this situation had changed considerably. As a result of its achievements in the late 1960s and the 1970 election, Conservatives were no longer political outcasts. They had made significant gains in winning acceptance from both the state and national GOP. The party's challenge now was how to build on these accomplishments when it could no longer play the role of rebellious outsider. Or, to put it more simply: Would success spoil the Conservative Party? During the early 1970s, the party struggled with how to continue to pursue its ideological agenda without endangering its recent achievements.

This dilemma for the Conservative Party came at a critical stage in the ideological reshuffling of the two major parties. Conservatives had carved out a greater role in the national and state Republican Party. At the same time, however, the GOP still did not display anything close to a consistent conservative ideology. It was a party still in the midst of a painful transition. The early 1970s produced numerous examples of liberal and conservative Republicans struggling over the proper relationship between party loyalty and ideological beliefs. The Conservative Party, which in the 1960s had helped to set in motion this GOP move to the right, now sometimes pulled its punches in this battle. The party remained committed to its goal of an ideologically conservative GOP, but chose to be more restrained in how to pursue this goal so as not to endanger its accomplishments.

SENATOR BUCKLEY

After campaigning as the legitimate Republican candidate, James Buckley did not anticipate any problems joining the GOP Senate minority. In the weeks following the election, Buckley downplayed any potential difficulty, telling reporters that he considered himself a New York Conservative and a national Republican. Buckley saw no conflict in these dual allegiances because he viewed the Conservative Party as the state branch of the national GOP.[1] Some Republican senators, however, expressed reservations at accepting a representative of a third party. In December 1970, GOP Senate Minority Leader Hugh Scott of Pennsylvania said that he hoped Buckley considered his obligations to the Conservative Party to be discharged. Buckley, looking to avoid a showdown, maintained he could fulfill his responsibilities to both parties.[2] The Senate's requirement that each member designate an official party affiliation, usually a formality for new senators, exposed the complexities of Buckley's dual allegiances. Clif White, who managed the senator's 1970 campaign, counseled Buckley against designating himself a Conservative. He warned that this option would damage Buckley's ability to work with Senate Republicans as well as his prospective 1976 re-election campaign. Instead, White recommended Buckley list himself as a Republican-Conservative.[3] Kieran O'Doherty sent Buckley a series of memos summarizing how twentieth-century third-party senators designated themselves. Refraining from offering any explicit advice, O'Doherty merely informed Buckley that the majority of these senators retained their third-party affiliation once in office.[4]

This private debate became public when columnists Rowland Evans and Robert Novak devoted a column to Buckley's predicament. The team characterized Buckley's decision as critical to his political future because a Conservative designation promised an ideologically confrontational career while a Republican designation portended a more moderate approach. They described a bitter struggle between the senator's Republican supporters led by White and Conservative Party leaders led by Mahoney and O'Doherty. The columnists, however, overstated the significance of the controversy and the intensity of feeling it produced.[5] While both sides looked to protect their interests, neither wanted to go to war over the issue. Buckley finally decided to compromise by designating himself a Conservative-Republican senator, a decision all his supporters accepted.

Buckley's party designation carried no guarantee that Senate Republicans would accept him into their ranks. Senate Republicans still needed to admit him to the GOP conference before he could receive committee assignments from and caucus with Republicans. In late November 1970, a member of Jacob Javits's staff advised the senator to consider opposing Buckley's admission into the conference because "to regard Buckley as anything but the enemy—a powerful enemy because of his close ties with the President and—no surprise!—with the Governor, would be courting disaster."[6] Javits agreed with the analysis and announced that he might oppose Buckley's admission.[7] The *New York Times* editorial board also urged Javits and Senate Republicans to reject Buckley's application because accepting ideological conservatives into the party would doom the GOP to a future of electoral defeats.[8] In January 1971, Javits told the press he planned to express his concerns about Buckley to the Republican conference, although he stopped short of announcing his opposition. The senator cited Buckley's decision to designate himself as a "hyphenated Republican" as the cause for his concern.[9] In mid-January, however, the state GOP intervened. Chairman Charles Lanigan, an ally of Governor Rockefeller, wrote Javits that it was in everyone's best interests for Buckley to be admitted into the conference.[10] Lanigan asked Javits to reverse his position and support Buckley's application. This appeal demonstrated the state GOP's view that the new senator's conservatism did not disqualify him for membership in the party. While Javits refused to acquiesce to Lanigan's request, he refrained from any active opposition to Buckley's admission. As a result, Senate Republicans voted thirty-six to three to permit Buckley to join the GOP conference. Republicans went on to select the new senator for the Republican Senatorial Campaign Committee, where he became a popular speaker at party fundraisers across the country. These actions supported Buckley's position that he could be a New York Conservative and a national Republican, an indication of how the GOP was moving to the right.

The ideological realignment that would make the state GOP more consistently conservative required two parallel changes. First, the state GOP needed to accept conservatives such as James Buckley. Second, liberal Republicans needed to reconsider their party affiliation. The departure of a number of prominent GOP liberals from the party demonstrated that this second change was beginning to occur. During the 1965 New York City mayoral race, William Buckley enjoyed needling his Republican opponent that while he had nothing against him, John Lindsay did not belong in the GOP. Throughout that campaign and his entire political career, Lindsay defended his Republican credentials and the vitality of the GOP liberal wing. By 1971, however, the mayor's confidence seemed misplaced. Having won re-election on the Liberal Party line, Lindsay staffed his second administration with members of the Liberal and Democratic parties. The divisiveness of the 1970 campaign ended any chance Lindsay had to regain his status as a full-fledged Republican. When Spiro Agnew declared war on "radical liberals" in the GOP, Lindsay knew where he fit. In the gubernatorial race, the mayor's personal dislike for Nelson Rockefeller and the governor's ideological shift to the right prompted Lindsay to endorse Arthur Goldberg, the Democratic and Liberal Party nominee for governor. The mayor reassured his GOP supporters, however, "I am a Republican and intend to remain a Republican."[11]

At war with Governor Rockefeller and President Nixon, heading an administration with few Republicans, and finding an ever-decreasing number of ideologically compatible Republicans, John Lindsay had few reasons to remain in the GOP. Press reports soon identified another reason for Lindsay to change political parties: to facilitate running for President in 1972.[12] Becoming a Democrat would deliver the mayor from having to face Nixon in a series of GOP primaries, and would allow him to appeal to the more liberal voters of the Democratic Party. Lindsay, however, initially resisted because longtime Republican supporters, men such as John Hay Whitney, Herbert Brownell, and Jacob Javits, urged him to remain in the GOP. Despite these entreaties, however, the mayor concluded it was time to go. On August 11, 1971, Lindsay summoned two election officials to Gracie Mansion so that he and his wife could switch their enrollments from the Republican to the Democratic Party. Because Lindsay attributed his switch to the failure of progressivism in the Republican Party, a number of leading state Republicans defended the ideological breadth of their party. Nelson Rockefeller, Jacob Javits, and New York Attorney General Louis Lefkowitz issued a joint statement declaring the party to be broad-based and healthy. They blamed Lindsay's move on his ambition to move beyond City Hall.[13] The Ripon Society, a longtime supporter of Lindsay, lamented the mayor's decision and promised to keep fighting for liberal candidates and policies within the GOP.[14]

To observers outside the Republican Party, however, Lindsay's move seemed a recognition of reality. Supporters of liberal republicanism expressed regret at this state of affairs. A *New York Times* editorial agreed with the mayor that the GOP had moved so far to the right as to become unacceptable to Lindsay. The editorial blamed the recent actions of Richard Nixon and Nelson Rockefeller for this harmful development.[15] In contrast, the Conservative Party celebrated both John Lindsay's decision and the state GOP's growing lack of hospitality toward it liberals. From its inception, the Conservative Party had sought to drive liberal politicians—particularly Nelson Rockefeller, John Lindsay, and Jacob Javits—out of the state GOP. Rockefeller had already been forced to move right to ensure his re-election in 1970. Now, John Lindsay announced that he could no longer remain a Republican. Only Jacob Javits remained as a liberal Republican committed to preventing a more ideologically conservative GOP.

Following Lindsay's switch, two less prominent liberal Republicans, one a private citizen and one a public official, demonstrated these changes in their party by defecting. In May 1972, Jackie Robinson wrote a heartfelt and pained letter to his political mentor, Nelson Rockefeller. Beginning in the late 1950s, Robinson had supported Rockefeller in gubernatorial and presidential campaigns, advised the governor informally, and served in a variety of appointive positions. By the early 1970s, however, the move to the right by the GOP and the governor had disheartened Robinson. He informed Rockefeller that he could no longer offer his support. "I cannot fight any longer, Governor, for, I believe you have lost the sensitivity and understanding I felt was yours when I worked with you," he explained.[16] Responding in an equally anguished letter, Rockefeller confided that life would be easier if he had indeed lost his sensitivity and understanding. Rather, times had changed, and the limits imposed by the poor financial conditions of state and local governments and the ensuing taxpayer revolt forced a retrenchment of liberal policies. The governor explained that he and the party had to change or suffer at the polls. Rockefeller, concluding the letter on personal note, hoped that he and Robinson could remain friends.[17]

While Robinson's decision to leave the GOP saddened Rockefeller, the defection of a Republican congressman angered him. Ogden Reid was not just any Republican congressman. He was a personal friend who represented the governor's home district in Westchester County. In addition, Reid came from a family long associated with the GOP, and specifically its liberal wing. His grandfather had helped found the party and gone on to become its vice-presidential nominee in 1892. Reid himself had served as President Eisenhower's ambassador to Israel and owned the *New York Herald Tribune*, widely regarded as the voice of liberal Republicanism until its demise in 1966. Elected to Congress in 1962, Reid compiled a liberal voting record that won him a majority of his district's support, but created animosity among some local Republicans. This animus produced a primary challenge in 1970 from a conservative Republican that nearly toppled the congressman. Given this vulnerability, Reid considered following John Lindsay's example and switching to the Democratic Party.

Attorney General John Mitchell attempted to persuade the congressman to remain a Republican.[18] Governor Rockefeller also spent several weeks urging his friend not to switch parties. Reid, however, decided to become a Democrat. The governor exploded when Reid informed him. Frustrated by his inability to prevent the defection, he told Reid, "I feel like a Goddamn fool." Rockefeller also explained, "We will have to do our best to beat you . . . but that's life."[19] On March 21, having weathered the governor's fury, Reid publicly announced he was becoming a Democrat, or as a *Daily News* headline phrased it, he intended "To Do a Lindsay."[20] Reid explained his decision by citing his inability to support Richard Nixon's re-election, although some Republicans noted Reid's potential as a candidate for the 1974 Democratic gubernatorial nomination. The *New York Times* editorial board wished Reid well, but expressed concern about the viability of the two-party system given the demise of progressive republicanism in the state.[21] The abandonment of the GOP by lifelong Republicans such as Reid, Robinson, and Lindsay demonstrated that the ideological reshuffling of the parties had begun. An increasing number of liberals judged the Democratic Party their only viable home. Having long identified more ideologically homogeneous parties as a major goal, Conservatives embraced this change.

PRESIDENTIAL PROBLEMS

As 1971 began, the New York Conservative Party and the Nixon administration enjoyed a close relationship forged in the last months of the Buckley campaign. James Buckley, the most visible demonstration of the party's allegiance to Nixon, consistently and vocally supported the administration. In a fundraising letter, Dan Mahoney boasted of a private meeting he and Kieran O'Doherty had had with Nixon, implying that the party now enjoyed the access and influence to achieve its ideological goals.[22] With an eye on the 1972 presidential race, Nixon returned this goodwill. As promised at the meeting in the Bahamas following the 1970 election, the president appointed Kieran O'Doherty as a consultant to the Department of Commerce to assist with a study of the franchising industry. The *Ripon Forum*, the publication of liberal Republicans, sarcastically applauded the appointment, calling O'Doherty "an expert in franchising splinter parties."[23]

Increased public support from the White House did not preclude less benign private activities, however. During these years, the administration relied on White House aide Tom Charles Huston, a staunch ideological conservative, to gather intelligence about his colleagues on the right. Shortly after Buckley's election, H. R. Haldeman suggested that Huston use Republican National Committee chairman Rogers Morton as a conduit for information about the senator-elect and the Conservative Party.[24] A skeptical Huston counseled against using a Republican Party official because Buckley planned to retain some independence from the GOP and some of his staff actually believed in the idea of a third party. Instead, Huston suggested a surreptitious approach. "I will have a reliable source in his [Buckley's] senate office," he advised Haldeman, "and I have reopened direct channels to his key people in New York."[25] The White House remained eager to maintain both its support of Senator Buckley and the Conservative Party and its plans to secretly monitor its new friends.

Most ideological conservatives began 1971 supporting the Nixon administration. New policy initiatives adopted by the president soon proved troubling, however. Conservatives balked at Nixon's military spending reductions and arms control negotiations with the Soviet Union. Ever since his 1960 "Treaty of Fifth Avenue" with Nelson Rockefeller, conservatives believed Richard Nixon was an opportunist, willing to compromise principle for political expediency. Most conservatives put aside these suspicions to support him in the 1968 presidential race. Nixon's objectionable policy initiatives in 1971, however, awakened these misgivings. Many conservatives felt the president crossed a line in July when he announced plans to visit China the following year and meet with Mao Zedong and other communist leaders. At that point, a group of conservatives took action.

William Buckley invited a dozen major figures in the conservative movement to his Manhattan townhouse to discuss the president's unacceptable policies.[26] The group included conservatives from the *National Review* editorial staff, national organizations such as the American Conservative Union, and Dan Mahoney. Several participants endorsed a dramatic rupture with Nixon as the best way to express their displeasure. Both Mahoney and Buckley, however, backed the interim step that carried the day.[27] On July 29, the group, now dubbed the Manhattan 12 because of its meeting place and number of members, issued a statement suspending its support for the president. The statement cited the administration's failures with the economy, but argued, "These domestic considerations, important as they are, pale into insignificance alongside the tendencies of the administration in foreign policy."[28] Specifically, the Manhattan 12 condemned Nixon's overtures to China, his failure to respond to recent Soviet aggression, and the deterioration of the military.

In the 1960s, the Conservative Party would have rushed to support Buckley's attempt to discredit liberal republicanism. The party's growing acceptance within Republican circles, however, served as a check on its militancy in this and similar disputes. The Conservative Party carefully kept its distance from the Manhattan 12's rebellion. James Buckley refused to join his brother in his criticism of the president. The senator explained that while he shared many of the group's concerns, he was "not prepared to join them in a declaration of non-support."[29] Dan Mahoney also signed the initial Manhattan 12 statement as an individual, not as the official Conservative Party representative. Interviewed by the *Daily News*, Serphin Maltese, now Conservative Party executive director, made clear that Mahoney did not speak for the party.[30] For its part, the Nixon administration worked to ensure the Conservative Party did not formally join the Manhattan 12 rebellion. The president directed "[John] Mitchell to talk to Mahoney to make sure the Conservative Party doesn't get off track in New York."[31] Other members of the administration, including Henry Kissinger, met with the chairman and Senator Buckley to shore up Conservative support.

Richard Nixon attempted to defuse the Manhattan 12 rebellion during the summer and fall of 1971. He undercut his effort, however, by continuing to adopt polices at odds with conservative positions. Over the next few months, Nixon implemented wage-and-price controls and announced a trip to Moscow to sign an arms control treaty. The Manhattan 12 concluded that its suspension of support had failed to deter to Richard Nixon from adopting liberal policies, and looked to increase pressure by sponsoring a conservative challenger to the president. The group recognized the long odds of toppling a sitting president, but believed a conservative challenger could still force the administration to the right. Dan Mahoney advised his colleagues to resist the lure of a primary challenger and instead consider opening a Washington, D.C., office for lobbying and public relations.[32] Intent on a more confrontational course, however, the Manhattan 12 searched for someone to challenge Richard Nixon. Most major conservative politicians, including Ronald Reagan, Barry Goldwater, and John Tower, supported Nixon's re-election. Bill Buckley declined the group's invitation to become a presidential candidate.[33] The group then turned to Congressman John Ashbrook, a Republican from Ohio and chairman of the American Conservative Union. A contingent from the Manhattan 12 met with Ashbrook in New York City to offer its support in a challenge to Richard Nixon in the GOP primaries. The congressman, fearful of inviting congressional redistricting or another form of retribution, asked for time to consider his decision.[34]

Already facing a primary challenge from the left in the person of California Congressman Pete McCloskey, the White House moved to prevent a similar threat from the right. Patrick Buchanan advised targeting Dan Mahoney, identifying him as one of the group's moderates open to a possible accommodation.[35] The presidential speechwriter also suggested extending a White House social invitation to Kieran O'Doherty, now at the Commerce Department, as a first step in enlisting him to prevent a primary challenge.[36] Nixon also dispatched members of his staff to dissuade the Manhattan 12 from sponsoring an Ashbrook candidacy. On December 15, Vice President Agnew invited Bill Buckley and William Rusher to his suite at the Waldorf-Astoria Hotel. Agnew tried to allay one conservative concern by assuring the two men that the administration planned to increase defense spending. He also pledged to demand the replacement of John Ehrlichman, the president's chief domestic policy advisor, who was unpopular with conservatives. Finally, Agnew urged the men to drop the challenge because an Ashbrook candidacy would force him off the ticket.[37] Rusher and Buckley assured Agnew that this was neither their intention nor their expectation. The Manhattan 12 maintained its course of action. On December 29, John Ashbrook announced he would challenge Richard Nixon in the New Hampshire and Florida Republican primaries. The congressman cited the president's failure to fulfill his conservative campaign promises from 1968 as the reason for his candidacy.[38]

President Nixon's domestic and foreign policy initiatives in 1971 eventually convinced the Conservative Party to officially enter the fray. Five months after the Manhattan 12 suspended support of the president, the party endorsed the Manhattan 12's action. The party's statement took Nixon to task for a foreign policy insufficiently anti-communist and an economic policy too Keynesian.[39] At the end of January, the Conservative Party executive committee also voted unanimously to endorse John Ashbrook in the GOP primaries. Its announcement thanked the congressman for stepping forward "to provide political expression for the widening conservative discontent with the performance of the Nixon administration."[40] Conservative Party members volunteered to help in the New Hampshire primary. In February, Serf Maltese went to New Hampshire to direct the congressman's campaign in that state. Finding an organization without any resources, Maltese even used his personal credit card to make needed purchases.[41] Meanwhile, Dan

Mahoney provided the campaign strategic advice and helped identify potential supporters in later primary states.[42] He even touted Ashbrook's candidacy at Conservative Party events across the state. At a party meeting in Hicksville, Long Island, Mahoney called the congressman's campaign a sign of "the changing of the guard of leadership in the conservative movement."[43]

With a conservative challenger a reality, one member of the Nixon administration attempted to call in the Conservative Party debt to the White House. Presidential assistant Peter Flanigan criticized William Buckley for supporting a primary challenge to the president who had helped elect his brother in 1970. "I would not have dreamed it possible," Buckley responded, "that any favor done by you to someone to whom I have biological ties—or by Mr. Agnew, or by Mr. Mitchell, or by Mr. Kissinger, or by Mr. Nixon—carried the implication that I was thereupon bound, athwart the interests of conscience and constituency, to adopt the role of a double agent."[44] Refusing to back down, Flanigan repeated that, given the President's intervention in the 1970 race, "it would seem to me appropriate that all Buckleys, not just the Senator, evidence a sense of gratitude and loyalty in response thereto."[45] Expressing embarrassment at having to be so direct, Buckley ended the exchange in a final letter to Flanigan making plain that "the backing of my brother by Richard Nixon in November of 1970 gives his administration zero claim on me to back his policies when I disapprove of them."[46] Buckley also used *National Review* and his syndicated column to warn Nixon that he could not carry New York State without the support of the Conservative Party.[47]

The Ashbrook campaign, however, proved strikingly unsuccessful. It never raised significant funds or won the backing of any prominent conservatives beyond the Manhattan 12. The congressman received only about 10 percent of the vote in the New Hampshire primary, won by Richard Nixon with 68 percent. In reality, the congressman's showing was even more discouraging because liberal Republican Pete McCloskey received almost twice as many votes as Ashbrook. A week later in the Florida primary, Ashbrook managed to finish ahead of McCloskey, but still won only 9 percent of the vote to Nixon's 87 percent. This second disappointing result eliminated Ashbrook from future primaries. Serf Maltese left the campaign to return to New York. Despite the high hopes of the Manhattan 12, the challenge never overcame the problems of a largely unknown candidate, little money, and no real organization.

Having overcome its initial caution to join the unsuccessful Manhattan 12 challenge, the Conservative Party needed a rationale for returning to the Nixon camp. Party leaders decided to demand a reliable conservative presence in the administration, and conditioned their support on the ticket's number-two spot. At the time, Nixon was reportedly considering replacing Spiro Agnew with John Connally, a recent Democratic addition to the Cabinet. In an interview with the *New York Times*, Kieran O'Doherty warned that if Nixon replaced Spiro Agnew as his running mate, it would foreclose any chance of a Conservative endorsement of the Republican national ticket.[48] Agnew remained a bright star within an administration that had proved disappointing for ideological conservatives. New York Conservatives had felt a special bond with the vice president as far back as his controversial appearance at the 1968 party dinner. Since then Agnew had served as the most visible connection between the administration and the party. This relationship reached its apex with Agnew's very public intervention on behalf of James Buckley in the 1970 Senate race. More broadly, the vice president and the party shared many of the same friends and enemies. When Agnew spoke out against a biased liberal media, for example, Conservatives, long antagonistic to the *New York Times*, cheered him. In August, Nixon, aware of the political price of changing running mates, announced Agnew would remain on the ticket. Conservative leaders declared victory and moved to align the party with the Nixon campaign. In September, despite some sentiment that the president did not deserve the Conservative label, the party's executive committee voted to cross-endorse Richard Nixon.[49]

Throughout 1972, Richard Nixon never publicly criticized the Conservative Party for its support of John Ashbrook. The president remained convinced that his future electoral prospects required a coalition that included his conservative critics. In New York, Nixon considered the Conservative cross-endorsement critical to carrying the state. A memo briefing the vice president on state politics indicated that "since many disaffected Democrats in New York find it difficult to vote Republican, it is believed that the third line will prove valuable this fall."[50] To secure this cross-endorsement, the White House actively courted party leaders. In May, Nixon appointed Kieran O'Doherty to the Foreign Claims Settlement Commission. According to the *Wall Street Journal*, "The job pays $36,000 a year, but there is almost nothing to do."[51] Nixon also rewarded James Buckley with the high-profile assignment of seconding his nomination at the Republican National Convention. The Nixon administration's most significant act, however, was what it did not do. It never punished the Conservative Party for backing a primary challenge. This act of political forgiveness—uncharacteristic for the Nixon White House—demonstrated the value the White House placed on Conservative cross-endorsement.

Following the Conservative vote in August to endorse Nixon, the state GOP began negotiating with the third party on the issue of cross-endorsement. Nelson Rockefeller threatened to block cross-endorsement if James Buckley did not reverse his position and support a Senate revenue-sharing bill that the governor viewed as beneficial to the state.[52] Dan Mahoney managed to get word to William Buckley, who was sailing in the Bahamas, about the impasse in the negotiations. Buckley contacted H. R. Haldeman's office by radio and blamed the breakdown of negotiations on Rockefeller's demand that Senator Buckley support the ideologically unacceptable revenue-sharing bill. "Jim is not disposed to play a public role as victim of Rockefeller's disciplinary expedition," Buckley informed Haldeman.[53] The editor maintained that only the personal intervention of the previously inaccessible John Mitchell could resolve this impasse. For the first time, a Republican presidential nominee—most likely through Mitchell's personal intervention—made a concerted effort in support of the Conservative Party on the issue of cross-endorsement. Facing an engaged and resolute White House, the governor and the state GOP dropped their conditions and allowed Conservatives to cross-endorse the Republican presidential electors. A political briefing prepared for Spiro Agnew later in the campaign revealed that "Rockefeller gave in on the question of the third line only after great pressure was brought to bear and it is believed that he is privately unhappy about it."[54] Despite Rockefeller's unhappiness and the need for "great pressure," the White House prevailed. In November, Richard Nixon became the first presidential candidate ever to appear on the Conservatives' Row C.

Nixon's intervention produced joint nomination of electors, but some friction between the parties surfaced in the final stages of the campaign. Conservatives faulted the state GOP's failure to embrace Spiro Agnew's presence on the ticket. A staff memo warned Agnew that his role in the campaign was the principal contentious issue between New York Republicans and Conservatives. It explained, "A number of Conservatives have complained that the literature and other materials distributed through the state re-election operation are geared exclusively to the top of the ticket and that 'Nixon-Agnew' as opposed to 'Nixon' material is simply not available in New York except through the 'Conservatives for Nixon-Agnew' operation."[55] Conservatives distributed two million pieces of Nixon-Agnew literature and announced to the press that this material sought to correct the state GOP's unwillingness to back the vice president in the campaign. Investigating this charge, a *New York Times* reporter visited a Nixon campaign office in Manhattan and found little evidence of Agnew's presence on the ticket.[56] Conservative support for Agnew never wavered. At a party function in October, 1972, attendees greeted Agnew wearing buttons reading "12 More Years" to declare their preference for the current and the next two presidential elections.[57]

The parties' disagreement on Agnew's desirability did not compromise their effort to re-elect Richard Nixon. On election day, in his third outing as the Republican presidential candidate, Nixon finally won New York State as part of his national landslide. With 59 percent of the vote, his margin of victory was so large that he did not need the three hundred sixty thousand votes he received on Row C to carry the state. In a testament to the bipartisan nature of the victory, Nelson Rockefeller sent Dan Mahoney a thank-you note for his work on behalf of Nixon's re-election. Either poor staff work or a continuing animosity sabotaged the gesture, however, as the note was mistakenly addressed to Daniel M. Mahoney rather than J. Daniel Mahoney.[58]

DEPARTURES

In 1965, the Conservative Party used the New York City mayoral race to demonstrate its ability to attract Democratic voters through its advocacy of law-and-order and other social issues. Four years later, the party used the mayoral race to begin forcing John Lindsay out of the Republican Party. In contrast, the 1973 New York City mayoral race proved a dispiriting affair. Despite qualms on the part of Dan Mahoney and Kieran O'Doherty, the party endorsed Bronx Democratic Congressman Mario Biaggi. Biaggi had served with distinction with the New York City Police Department before becoming a member of Congress. He was popular with his largely Italian working-class constituents thanks to his ties to the community and an emphasis on constituent services. Longstanding ethical questions undermined his mayoral campaign, however. During the campaign, press reports revealed that, despite his repeated denials, the congressman had invoked the Fifth Amendment when testifying before a federal grand jury. The subsequent scandal ensured that Biaggi never competed seriously for the mayoralty and effectively silenced the party during the campaign. By election day, Conservatives were more relieved than disappointed when Biaggi finished fourth with approximately 11 percent of the vote.

Conservatives were more disappointed that fall when Spiro Agnew resigned the vice presidency as part of a *nolo contendere* plea on bribery charges. Conservatives relied on the vice president in a number of ways. Agnew and his staff provided the surest way for the party to voice its concerns to the administration. Dan Mahoney enjoyed a personal friendship with the vice president that included such perks as flying to moon launches on Air Force 2.[59] Agnew also served as an emblem of Conservative influence in the political world, especially because the party fought to keep him on the ticket in 1972. The party struggled to come to terms with the fall of a national conservative, political ally, and friend. At the 1973 anniversary dinner, party leaders had television sets wheeled into the grand ballroom of the Waldorf-Astoria so attendees could watch the now-disgraced vice president explain his actions in an interview. Following this unusual opening act, William Buckley addressed the dinner and tried to make sense of the week's events. As he had at the 1964 dinner when Barry Goldwater's defeat was virtually certain, the editor warned the crowd not to confuse the fate of a single person with the future of conservatism.[60]

While Spiro Agnew's resignation disheartened Conservatives and seemed to stall their plans for the national GOP, it represented a political opportunity for Nelson Rockefeller. Almost immediately, members of the governor's staff let it be known that he would accept appointment as vice president as long as he did not have to recuse himself from running for president in 1976.[61] As part of this quasi-campaign, Rockefeller directed state GOP chairman Richard Rosenbaum to encourage Republican governors to speak out in favor of his selection as vice president.[62] The lobbying effort failed, however, when Nixon chose Michigan congressman and House Minority Leader Gerald Ford as his vice president. In his memoirs, Nixon wrote that, while he considered Rockefeller and California governor Ronald Reagan for the job, he rejected them both as too ideologically divisive for the party.[63]

Despite this succession of political setbacks, the Conservative Party was cheered when, on December 11, Nelson Rockefeller announced his resignation as New York State's governor. Rockefeller explained that he intended to leave office with a little over a year remaining in his fourth term in order to lead two self-financed committees studying critical national issues. Despite the governor's denial, speculation focused on Rockefeller's making this move to position himself for a 1976 presidential run. More immediately, Rockefeller's resignation promoted his longtime Lieutenant Governor Malcolm Wilson, and made Wilson the incumbent for the 1974 gubernatorial campaign. All these considerations probably motivated Rockefeller. His stated rationale, leading the two policy committees, likely did play a role. Always confident in his ability to solve problems, Rockefeller no doubt expected these groups to influence public policy. The governor also acted to reward Malcolm Wilson's years of political loyalty. In addition, a politician who spent so much time, effort, and money trying to become president certainly had that office in mind when resigning the governorship. Nelson Rockefeller also recognized, however, the changed political context in which he operated. As governor, he enjoyed developing and implementing large-scale programmatic solutions to the state's problems. New York's limited fiscal resources and increasingly skeptical electorate made this style of governing obsolete. Rockefeller did not enjoy the increased restrictions of this new political world. The year before, when Jackie Robinson accused him of betraying his liberal values, the governor responded that circumstances, not he, had changed. Rockefeller defended himself in the concluding paragraph of that letter to his friend: "All I can say is that I am doing my best in a difficult period," he wrote.[64] Resigning allowed Rockefeller to move on to the next period in his life.

Nelson Rockefeller's official resignation on December 18 prompted numerous assessments of his fifteen-year tenure as governor. Many of these evaluations remarked on the ideological changes that took place during that period. The *New York Times* editorial board saluted the governor's many accomplishments but expressed regret over his shift to the right. The paper bemoaned that the governor's ambition "caused him to abandon his lifelong identification with progressive Republicanism and embark on the generally backward-looking policies that have turned the past three years of his current term into such a decline."[65] The Conservative Party agreed that the governor's ambition propelled him to move to his right. The party, however, also suspected that his transformation was superficial and that Rockefeller remained "a maverick Republican for whom 1976 is unlikely to be a year of personal celebration."[66]

None of the examinations of Nelson Rockefeller's legacy focused on the impact of his departure on the relationship between the state's Conservative and Republican parties. Rockefeller had defined and shaped both parties. For Republicans, Rockefeller won statewide elections and helped the rest of the GOP ticket. He dispensed the party's patronage, chose its candidates, and determined its overall direction. Rockefeller and his family bankrolled the New York Republican Party, ensuring a compliant state GOP. Nelson Rockefeller also symbolized the New York GOP for the rest of the country, creating a national presence for the state Republican Party. Less apparently but no less significantly, the Conservative Party also depended on Nelson Rockefeller. The party came into existence largely as a response to Rockefeller's domination of the state's politics. Opposing Rockefeller's policies, budgets, and re-election campaigns defined the party. Nelson Rockefeller's national status also made the party more important to conservatives outside the state, some of whom contributed financially to support the New York third party. The governor's resignation diminished the national significance of both the New York Republican and Conservative parties.

A CONSERVATIVE GOVERNOR?

Lieutenant Governor Malcolm Wilson, Rockefeller's longtime second in command, succeeded him as New York State's governor in 1973. Although Wilson had won four statewide elections as Rockefeller's running mate, the two men were very different. Nelson Rockefeller was an effusive, enthusiastic campaigner who drew energy from the rallies and walking tours that characterized the politics of the time. Though it was rumored that he employed his customary greeting of "Hi ya, fella" to disguise an inability to remember people's names, Rockefeller loved interacting with the voters. In contrast, the quieter and more contained Wilson excelled at behind-the-scenes politics, such as negotiations with party officials and the intricacies of the state budget process. First elected to the state legislature in 1938, Wilson was described by Rockefeller's biographer as "someone who, set down at random on any acre of New York State, could find his way to the local committeeman's house."[67] In addition, the new governor, a man of Albany, possessed few of Rockefeller's connections to international leaders in politics, much less in business or the arts. Rockefeller used his privately financed brain trust—labeled a "government in exile" by his critics—to address the major problems of the time, everything from drug abuse to world hunger. In contrast, Wilson focused on New York State and seldom displayed the grand vision of his predecessor.

Rockefeller and Wilson also enjoyed divergent ideological reputations. Throughout most his tenure as governor, Rockefeller represented the liberal wing of the GOP, with Wilson viewed as far more conservative than his boss. Given Rockefeller's domination of state politics, Wilson's conservatism seldom found expression in public. Many of Rockefeller's conservative critics, however, considered the lieutenant governor a reliable ally behind the scenes. Malcolm Wilson also sympathized with Conservative Party goals and shared the party's viewpoint on most policy issues. Party leaders relied on Wilson for information and access to an often hostile administration. Dan Mahoney, a neighbor of Wilson in Westchester County, even became a personal friend. Since Rockefeller's fourth term was widely rumored to be his last, Wilson and Conservatives regarded the next gubernatorial election as an opportunity to demonstrate the full extent of this alliance.[68] Following the 1970 election, Malcolm Wilson advocated, at least privately, a broad alliance between the two parties. Conservative leaders viewed a Wilson candidacy and administration as manifestations of their success in making the state GOP ideologically acceptable. For his part, Wilson considered a union with the Conservative Party as a source of potential strength within the GOP and in a general election. As early as the spring of 1971, Kieran O'Doherty predicted that Wilson would seek, and the party would grant him, the Conservative gubernatorial nomination.[69]

Malcolm Wilson effectively secured the Republican gubernatorial nomination when his major challenger, State Assembly Speaker Perry Duryea, was indicted on charges of vote-siphoning. The Conservative Party endorsement proved more challenging, however. The party initially embraced Wilson, confident that he planned a conservative administration. In February 1974, the new governor addressed the party's annual seminar for state legislators held in Albany. "I do not find myself among strangers," he told the enthusiastic crowd.[70] Within months, however, this relationship had deteriorated. Conservatives believed Wilson had abandoned his conservative principles in a quest to be a popular governor. They were particularly upset with Wilson's proposed spending increases for a wide variety of state programs, including an 11 percent raise in welfare benefits. After courting the party's support for more than a decade, the governor seemed to be moving to the left once in office, much as Richard Nixon had done in 1971. As the party's designating convention in June approached, many Conservatives balked at backing Wilson. Even brothers-in-law Dan Mahoney and Kieran O'Doherty differed on the issue, with the more temperamental O'Doherty opposed to endorsing Wilson and Mahoney favoring the nomination of his friend.[71]

Conservatives faced no disunity in the state's other prominent race. Senator Jacob Javits remained the type of liberal Republican politician that had inspired the creation of the Conservative Party. The national and state GOP had moved right in recent years, but Javits resisted this change at every opportunity. In 1974, with the senator seeking a fourth term, the Conservative Party's only decision concerned the most effective strategy to defeat him. The year prior to the election, Conservative leaders had considered sponsoring a Republican to oppose Javits in the GOP primary, where he seemed potentially vulnerable. Some members of the Nixon White

House, upset over Javits' anti-war statements, reportedly urged Congressman Jack Kemp to contest the nomination.[72] According to a briefing on New York State prepared for Vice President Agnew, Javits was so worried about a primary challenge from the right "that he has informed Governor Rockefeller that he will vote pretty much as the governor wants in Washington for the next two years in return for assistance in his effort to win re-election."[73] Weakened by Watergate and Agnew's resignation, however, the White House could not sponsor an effective challenge to Javits in the way it had against Charles Goodell four years earlier. Within New York, former Governor Rockefeller and current Governor Wilson discouraged any state Republicans from opposing the senator because of its potentially divisive impact. An undeterred Conservative Party, however, established the "1974 Fund to Defeat Jacob Javits" to help finance a challenge. The party sent out fundraising appeals under this fund's letterhead, hoping to capitalize on the dislike that conservatives across the country had for New York's senior senator. Despite being conducted by the right's leading authority on direct mail, Richard Viguerie, the nationwide fundraising campaign raised a disappointing fifty-four thousand dollars. Without an ally in the White House or Albany and pressed for cash, Conservatives abandoned the idea of a Republican primary challenge.

Without a Republican candidate to sponsor, the Conservative Party needed to identify its own nominee. Several years earlier, when the party polled its members to determine their preference for this race, Conservatives picked William Buckley. Dan Mahoney sent the poll results to Buckley, joking, "When can we get together to firm up the details?"[74] Buckley again refused the party's invitation to become a candidate. Another nationally prominent conservative, however, expressed interest in the nomination. Roy Cohn first gained national attention as an aide to Joseph McCarthy during the senator's anti-communist hearings in the early 1950s. In the more than twenty years since leaving McCarthy's employ, Cohn had added to this notoriety by practicing law in New York City with unparalleled tenacity, flamboyance, and—according to his numerous detractors—recklessness. While Cohn had little connection with the Conservative Party, his law partner, Thomas Bolan, had worked with the party since its inception. In early 1974, Cohn, who often publicly toyed with seeking elective office, expressed interest in running on the Conservative Party ticket. Initially, the lawyer expressed interest in challenging Manhattan District Attorney Robert Morgenthau. Then, in May, Cohn told a *New York Times* reporter what appeared to be a complete fabrication: that the Conservative Party was interested in him as its Senate candidate.[75]

At the time Roy Cohn made this statement, Conservative Party leaders had already approached Barbara Keating about the Senate nomination. Keating had never run for elective office, but benefited from a compelling personal story as the recent widow of a Marine killed in Vietnam raising a family on her own. Given her lack of experience and limited campaign skills, Keating's candidacy demonstrated that the party had few strong statewide candidates to call upon once all members of the Buckley family declined to run. Cohn, upon learning of the party's interest in Keating, called his friend Bill Buckley to set up a meeting with Dan Mahoney. Cohn dismissed Keating's candidacy and accused Mahoney of fielding a weak nominee as part of a deal with Richard Nixon in exchange for Kieran O'Doherty's federal patronage job. "Trouble with you, Dan," Cohn concluded, "is you've got an unemployable brother-in-law."[76] Mahoney ignored Cohn's political analysis and turned down the lawyer. After Cohn left the meeting, Mahoney confided to Buckley another reason for his reluctance. The previous year, Cohn had rented Buckley's sailboat and hired Dan Mahoney's son to serve as first mate. While at sea, the young Mahoney discovered Cohn having sex with another man. The chairman told Buckley that the party could never nominate "someone like that."[77]

By the spring of 1974, Malcolm Wilson recognized the seriousness of Conservative dissatisfaction with his performance. After working for more than a decade to maintain a good relationship with the third party, Wilson saw the alliance endangered when he most needed it. Accordingly, Wilson began an active campaign to win the Conservative gubernatorial nomination. The governor appointed several Conservatives to patronage jobs and began attending party functions. Most importantly, Wilson persuaded the Nassau County GOP to drop a recently instituted cross-endorsement ban. Republicans in Nassau County, a traditional center of Conservative strength, had implemented the ban several years earlier to try to check rising Conservative strength. In June, Wilson asked Nassau Republican Chairman Joseph Margiotta to end the county's prohibition.[78] In exchange for this concession, Wilson chose Nassau County executive Ralph Caso as his lieutenant governor nominee. The three-way deal was set. With one of its own on the state ticket, the Nassau County GOP agreed to drop its cross-endorsement ban. With an end to the cross-endorsement ban in a critical county, Conservative leaders agreed to endorse the governor. And, having brokered this deal, Malcolm Wilson believed he had secured the Conservative cross-endorsement needed to win in November. David Bullard, a longtime party activist, however, threatened the deal by challenging the governor for the third party's gubernatorial nomination. The Conservative state committee endorsed Wilson, but gave Bullard enough votes to force a party primary if he chose. Before Bullard could determine his course of action, however, national events overtook the state campaign.

WATERGATE

When the Watergate break-in first became a major political story in 1973, New York Conservatives dismissed its importance and defended the president.

Kieran O'Doherty framed the issue not as a legal or ethical matter, but as a political battle waged by a liberal media.[79] In a late November 1973 fundraising letter, Conservatives charged liberal senators such as George McGovern and Jacob Javits with using the scandal to advance their own political agenda. The letter promised that a donation would "let the President, the U.S. Congress and the national media know that the average American does not want the Watergate mess to be used as a cover-up in an attempt to overthrow the results of the 1972 election and to discredit conservatives."[80] Party leaders also defended the president publicly. Serf Maltese formed "Americans for Responsibility and Patriotism" to demonstrate support for Richard Nixon. Maltese also solicited donations for a newspaper advertisement by warning that the far left was out to bring Nixon down.[81] The advertisement ran in the *Daily News* on the president's birthday. Signed by over 150 individuals, most with a connection to the Conservative Party, it wished the president a happy birthday and repeated the charge that the media and Nixon's political enemies were working to overturn the 1972 election.[82]

Senator James Buckley initially echoed his party's support of the president. "I am as proud today as I was in 1972 to support him [Nixon] for president," he wrote in a May 1973 column for the *New York Times*.[83] Soon, however, the senator reversed his position, and, with characteristic disregard for the political implications, planned to address the issue publicly. Buckley's supporters viewed this quality as evidence of his operating on a higher plane and nicknamed him, "the sainted James Buckley." Buckley's detractors, not all on the left, saw it as evidence of an accidental politician who failed to master his craft.[84] In the case of Watergate, Buckley appeared unaware or unconcerned of the political consequences of making a dramatic shift. When he told his staff that he planned to call for Richard Nixon's resignation, they argued that it would destroy his political base in New York. Dan Mahoney also tried to dissuade the senator from taking this public position for the same reason.[85] Undeterred by these warnings, on March 19 Buckley called for Richard Nixon's resignation. The statement refrained from criticizing Nixon or expressing outrage over the Watergate scandal. Instead, Buckley focused on how the scandal created a "crisis of the regime" that had paralyzed and demoralized the country. He argued that impeachment offered no relief no matter the outcome, and asked Nixon to resign as a service to the nation.[86]

Reaction to Buckley's statement centered on its political impact. Nixon's detractors, still principally Democrats at this point, claimed a convert to their cause. The president's supporters rejected Buckley's analysis out of hand. In New York State, Malcolm Wilson criticized the senator's statement. George Clark, the chairman of the Brooklyn GOP and a Conservative ally, wrote Buckley a one-sentence letter, "DUMB, DUMB, DUMB, AND EXTREMELY DUMB."[87] One Nixon aide joked, "Bring back Charlie Goodell."[88] Privately, Dan Mahoney sent Bill Buckley a parody of the event. Written to resemble a party news release, the document began, "Some months ago, when President Nixon selected Representative Gerald R. Ford rather than Senator James Buckley to succeed Spiro T. Agnew as Vice President of the United States, Senator Buckley confided to key Conservative party leaders, 'I'll get even with that son of bitch if it's the last thing I do.' "[89] Despite this joke, the Conservative Party faced a serious dilemma in light of Buckley's move. Maintaining its steadfast defense of the president undercut the position of its most visible representative. Joining Buckley in calling for the president's resignation aided its political opponents and sabotaged its relationship with the GOP. In deference to the senator's vulnerability, the party replaced its defense of the president with a near silence on Watergate. Publicly, Dan Mahoney praised Buckley's courage in making the statement, but added that it did not represent the party's position. The chairman, however, seldom explained the party's actual position.

Richard Nixon's resignation on August 8, 1974, and Gerald Ford's subsequent inauguration promised an end to a difficult period for New York's Conservatives and Republicans. Ford's selection of vice president, however, ended this peace. Ford quickly narrowed the field to Nelson Rockefeller and George Bush, the current chairman of the Republican National Committee and a former member of Congress. The new president's advisors recommended Bush because the former governor was sixty-five and "his name was anathema to conservatives."[90] Ford rejected this advice, believing Rockefeller's experience and national reputation provided the country with the reassurance it needed. On August 20, he named Nelson Rockefeller as his vice president, subject to congressional approval. The president's decision demonstrated his failure to recognize the changing ideological nature of the GOP. In his memoirs, Ford professed a lack of concern over Rockefeller's liberal reputation, considering it a reflection of New York State and believing the governor had moderated his views in his final term.[91] The analysis of Ford's staff proved on target: Rockefeller's name was still anathema to conservatives. The party's increasingly conservative character guaranteed Ford would face an ideological rebellion. Rockefeller's appointment energized the conservative movement and created animosity toward the Ford administration and the Republican Party in general. Some on the right identified Rockefeller's appointment as a critical moment in the conservative movement's history. Richard Viguerie wrote that the New Right—the label applied to conservatism with its political victories in the late 1970s and early 1980s—began in reaction to Ford's appointment of Rockefeller. According to Viguerie, Ford's decision mobilized conservatives because it "revealed the true colors of the so-called 'moderate' Republicanism by choosing to use the very symbol of everything we Conservatives had always opposed."[92]

Throughout its history, the Conservative Party had used its homegrown opposition to Nelson Rockefeller as a way to play a role in the national conservative movement. Conservatives traditionally characterized Rockefeller as a threat and themselves as an effective tool in neutralizing that threat. This time, however, was different. The party did not participate in the revolt against Rockefeller's vice-presidential nomination. In fact, the Conservative Party offered only a muted reaction to the event. William Buckley praised Rockefeller for his experience and his realization—albeit somewhat late in life—of the need to limit government spending.[93] The party's executive committee waited over a month before it adopted a resolution opposing Rockefeller's confirmation by Congress. The blandly worded measure argued that since Rockefeller's principles and policies were at variance with the outcome of the 1972 presidential race, Congress should reject him.[94] This resolution, as well as the party's overall response, contrasted sharply with the party's slashing attacks of the 1960s. During that earlier period, the party's vigorous assault on Republicans rallied its troops, attracted converts, and received media attention. By 1974, New York Conservatives were constrained from such open hostility. Eager to protect their relationship with the White House and Jim Buckley's re-election prospects, Conservatives offered only *pro forma* public opposition to Rockefeller's appointment. While constrained in their public reaction, Conservatives supported opposition to the Rockefeller appointment behind the scenes. Shortly after Ford assumed the presidency, Dan Mahoney sent an editor at *National Review* an earlier anti-Rockefeller article he had written. Mahoney urged the magazine editor to use the information about the former governor in a campaign against his appointment. "Conservatives should take a hard line in behalf of their interests and positions," Mahoney argued, "rather than relax into a sense of inevitability about the post-Nixon Republican party."[95]

Bill Buckley's support of Rockefeller's appointment ensured that *National Review* would not publish Dan Mahoney's anti-Rockefeller article. *National Review*'s publisher, William Rusher, however, agreed with Mahoney on the need to work against Rockefeller's confirmation. Rusher provided Rockefeller's opponents in Congress, such as Senator Jesse Helms and Representative Trent Lott, with evidence of the former governor's unsuitability for high office.[96] Both politicians encouraged Rusher in this crusade. At one point, Senator Helms even predicted, "I think the gent [Rockefeller] has had it."[97] This assessment proved overly optimistic, however, partly because only a limited number of conservatives joined with Rusher. A far more impressive list of conservatives failed to oppose Rockefeller. Barry Goldwater, Ronald Reagan, and John Tower were conspicuously absent from this campaign. James Buckley and the Conservative Party also chose not to risk political exposure by fighting the nomination.

Although conservatives failed to mount a consequential opposition to Nelson Rockefeller, his confirmation by Congress did not go smoothly. Congressional committees scoured Rockefeller's personal and political financial history. This review revealed a singular political career where Rockefeller used his immense wealth to assist his allies, secure the loyalty of his employees, reward his friends, and, at times, wound his enemies. Several aspects of Rockefeller's financial dealings attracted criticism. As governor, Rockefeller bestowed large sums of money on current and former employees, including Henry Kissinger, to reward and encourage service. After the revelation that advisor William Ronan had received $625,000, one reporter joked that Rockefeller was the only American politician on the "give." In the 1970 gubernatorial race, Rockefeller had also financed a negative biography of his Democratic opponent, Arthur Goldberg. While the book was little more than an unfriendly cut-and-paste job, the governor had financed it through a complex set of financial transactions that included his brother Laurence, a Philadelphia law firm, and the conservative publisher Arlington House, which had published Dan Mahoney's history of the Conservative Party. While unsettling to many, Rockefeller's actions had not violated any laws, partly because no one had anticipated the need to legislate against politicians giving away their own money. In addition, Rockefeller helped his cause by being a cooperative and effective witness before Congress. Through a combination of extensive financial disclosure and personal charm, he managed to defuse the negative reaction to his appointment. On December 11, Senator Buckley joined eighty-nine of his colleagues in voting to confirm Rockefeller. A week later, the House of Representatives followed the Senate's lead and voted overwhelmingly to confirm the former governor. Nelson Rockefeller became vice president of the United States. Ford's decision and the subsequent confirmation battle re-energized the national conservative movement. The New York Conservative Party, however, had remained largely on the sidelines despite its history of participation in similar clashes.

A COSTLY DEFEAT

In 1974, as Watergate unraveled Richard Nixon's presidency, New York Republicans and Conservatives prepared for a difficult gubernatorial election. Malcolm Wilson had secured the Conservative gubernatorial designation but still faced a potential primary challenge. After considering his options, David Bullard concluded that the governor had strayed too far from conservative principles and announced he would run in a Conservative primary. While little known and politically inexperienced, Bullard created problems for Malcolm Wilson and Conservative leaders. Wilson wanted the Conservative nomination but did not want to have to run in a primary to win it. He feared that campaigning for Conservative votes could jeopardize his appeal to political moderates in the general election. Conservative leaders feared Wilson would decline to enter their party's primary, thus conceding the nomination to Bullard and ruining plans for bipartisan cooperation. To encourage his challenger to withdraw, the governor touted his conservative fiscal credentials and released a list of policies that saved the state money. Wilson also met privately with Bullard at the executive mansion in Albany. Following this meeting and the governor's pronouncement of his fiscal achievements, Bullard dropped out of the race, praising Wilson's conservative credentials. Reporters sensed a political deal, but Bullard denied any arrangement. "Our reward is in paradise not in Albany," he insisted.[98] Conservative leaders celebrated Wilson's cross-endorsement. After over a decade of struggle with Republicans and members of their own party, Dan Mahoney and Kieran O'Doherty achieved a formal alliance with the New York GOP in a statewide race.

The New York Senate race presented none of these difficulties for the Conservative Party. The party, having fended off the potentially controversial candidacy of Roy Cohn, nominated Barbara Keating. Her campaign represented the party respectably, but remained largely irrelevant in the battle between the two major candidates. The Democratic nominee, former U.S. attorney general Ramsey Clark, and incumbent GOP senator Jacob Javits treated Keating with the kind of patronizing deference still accorded women candidates in 1974. The current Conservative senator, James Buckley, unwilling to provoke GOP animosity by assisting Keating, remained uninvolved in the race. Keating, as the only candidate opposed to abortion, however, attracted a new ally for the party: the state's anti-abortion movement. Right-to-life activists donated funds allowing her to run television commercials focused exclusively on her anti-abortion position.[99] While some members of the Conservative Party worried about the influence of this alliance, most approved of Keating's political partner.

Even though most New York Republicans had reassessed their attitudes toward the Conservative Party, Javits retained his adversarial approach. Beginning in 1973, the senator opposed White House re-appointment of Kieran O'Doherty to the Foreign Claims Settlement Commission. Since the position required Senate approval, the Nixon administration eventually acquiesced to Javits's opposition.[100] The senator also objected to the party's fundraising vehicle, the 1974 Fund to Defeat Jacob Javits. He complained to Francis Valeo, the Secretary of the Senate, that because the organization referred to a specific candidate and race, it was subject to the reporting requirements of the Federal Election Campaign Act of 1971. Valeo agreed with Javits' interpretation and ordered Dan Mahoney to produce all relevant financial information or face prosecution.[101] Thomas Bolan, Roy Cohn's law partner, represented the party and argued that the fund was merely a way for the Conservative Party to conduct its normal fundraising, and thus not covered by the federal law.[102] Valeo rejected the argument and again demanded compliance. The party's subsequent disclosure, more embarrassing than damaging, revealed that the appeal failed to cover expenses.

As the fall campaign began, the Conservative Party mobilized to assist Malcolm Wilson. Dan Mahoney served as a key informal advisor to the governor, although, in deference to Wilson's need to attract moderate voters, he maintained a low profile. Still, the party made the governor's appearance the highlight of its annual dinner.[103] It also created "Conservatives for Wilson-Caso" to urge party members to back the governor at the polls. Under the auspices of this organization, Mahoney warned that Wilson was under attack by the liberal news media and needed Conservative help.[104] An October political scandal, however, threatened to tarnish this cross-party alliance. On October 8, the *Daily News* alleged that David Bullard pulled out of the race for the Conservative Party gubernatorial nomination after striking a deal with Malcolm Wilson. According to the story, the two men met secretly at an Albany airport motel, where Bullard reportedly agreed to withdraw after the governor promised a mixture of campaign money and patronage to the Conservative Party. The subsequent public meeting between the two men was a ruse to obscure the private arrangement.[105] The story behind the story proved equally compelling. Shortly after pulling out of the race, David Bullard received a phone call from Michael Blair, a thirty-five-year-old editor of a weekly upstate newspaper, the *Lowville Journal Republican*, and the former interim chairman of the Lewes County Conservative Party. Blair believed that Conservative leaders were too willing to embrace any type of Republican candidate and had lobbied party members to deny Wilson the Conservative nomination.[106] Blair contacted Bullard for an explanation of his withdrawal. In the course of four conversations over the next several months, Bullard explained that he withdrew only after he managed to negotiate an arrangement beneficial to the Conservative Party.[107] Unbeknownst to Bullard, Blair tape-recorded these conversations, and, following their last talk, supplied the *Daily News* with the tapes.

Wilson and Bullard denied any political deal. Both men acknowledged meeting to discuss the race, but characterized the talks as innocent. According to their accounts, they met to determine whether their political differences were surmountable, discovered significant common ground, and resolved to work together. A state Board of Elections preliminary investigation, begun shortly after the initial newspaper story appeared, sputtered when all of the principals denied the allegations and no directly contradictory evidence emerged. By the end of October, the Board of Elections determined that neither Bullard nor Wilson had broken any laws, and the story disappeared. The scandal, however, damaged both the Wilson campaign and the Conservative Party. Dan Mahoney acknowledged the scandal's impact in a testy response to Bullard's complaints on party strategy. The chairman angrily scolded Bullard for complaining "at the same time the *Daily News* was running a major series of articles seriously damaging to the Wilson campaign as a result of your recorded conversations with Blair."[108] A background paper prepared by the New York Republican state committee also concluded that the scandal had a negative impact on the Wilson campaign.[109] The episode made Malcolm Wilson seem like a cynical political operator at a time when public sensitivity in that area was high due to Watergate. In addition, Wilson devoted time and energy to fending off these charges during a critical period of the campaign. The scandal made the Conservative Party appear to be an unreliable political partner. Republican candidates needed to factor in this lack of dependability when determining the value of working with the Conservative Party.

Across the country on election day, voters, unwilling to consign Watergate to the past, dealt the Republican Party one of the worst defeats in its history. The election proved especially frustrating for New York Conservatives because the anti-Republican response to Watergate overwhelmed virtually all other political considerations. Creating a more ideologically conservative Republican Party meant nothing if the GOP could not win elections. New York voters joined in the national trend of punishing GOP candidates. Democrat Hugh Carey handily defeated Malcolm Wilson to become governor. Republicans lost five seats in the House of Representatives to give Democrats a lopsided twenty-seven to twelve advantage in the state delegation. Perhaps most painfully, Republicans also lost control of the state assembly as Democrats picked up eighteen seats. Amidst these defeats, the GOP maintained control of the state senate despite losing three seats. While the Conservative Party managed to retain Row C, the election proved costly for Conservatives. Malcolm Wilson's defeat denied party leaders the governing alliance they wanted with the state GOP. In congressional and legislative races, Conservative cross-endorsement failed to prevent Republican losses. As a result of these defeats, Conservatives suffered a loss of influence in Washington and Albany due to the GOP's reduced representation in the House and loss of control of the state senate. Finally, in the midst of these Republican losses, the GOP candidate Conservatives most wanted to defeat, Jacob Javits, won re-election. Over a decade earlier, Conservatives had created a party to end the careers of liberal Republicans such as Javits. Now, despite the party's opposition, Javits had won re-election in 1962, 1968, and 1974. Conservatives had successfully forced the state GOP to the right over the previous decade. But as long as Jacob Javits served in the United States Senate as a proud liberal Republican, Conservatives could not consider this achievement complete. The redrawing of party lines to create a more conservative GOP remained a goal yet to be fully achieved.

SEVEN

FINISHING THE JOB

The Conservative Party identified the re-election of Senator James Buckley as its primary goal in the 1976 election. Buckley's electoral prospects depended on GOP support, and the Conservative Party's commitment to Buckley limited its ability to defy the Republican Party. When former California governor Ronald Reagan challenged President Gerald Ford for the GOP nomination in 1976, the Conservative Party was forced to choose between support of the nation's leading conservative and loyalty to the national GOP. The party's refusal to support Reagan's challenge demonstrated a willingness to compromise ideological principle for short-term gain. This concession to political expediency failed to produce the desired results as Gerald Ford and James Buckley were both defeated. These setbacks proved unexpectedly beneficial, however. The defeat of President Ford and Senator Buckley in 1976 liberated the Conservative Party. It no longer needed to consider every action in light of its possible impact on James Buckley's political future. Freed from this restrictive loyalty to the national GOP, Conservatives could return to a more consistent advocacy of their ideological interests. This independence restored vitality to the party and allowed it to pursue its long-term goals of driving liberal Republicans from the state GOP and helping ideological conservatives gain control of the national Republican Party. By the end of 1980, New York Conservatives had accomplished both of these goals and finished the job they had started some two decades earlier.

CONSERVATIVE CHALLENGES

One of the Conservative Party's initial obstacles to gaining the acceptance of national conservatives was its status as a third party working in opposition to the GOP. New York Conservatives repeatedly justified their third party by explaining that the unique structure of state politics required a novel response. By 1975, a group of prominent ideological conservatives abandoned their objection to a third party. These conservatives concluded that pursuing a conservative agenda within the GOP was futile. They objected to President Ford's pursuit of détente, his reliance on deficit spending, his amnesty program for draft evaders, and, most of all, his appointment of Nelson Rockefeller as vice president. They especially feared that the GOP would nominate a Ford-Rockefeller ticket in 1976. Consideration of a national third party became even more serious in February 1975 when the American Conservative Union and the Young Americans for Freedom hosted the Conservative Political Action Conference in Washington, D.C. Five hundred conservatives attended the event to examine the feasibility and wisdom of operating outside the GOP. Most Republican office holders urged remaining within the GOP, but numerous conservatives advocated moving beyond the two-party system. Foremost among these was William Rusher, who used the conference to promote his soon-to-be-published book, *The Making of a New Majority Party*. Rusher's work argued that Republican indifference to conservatives necessitated the formation of a new party. Third-party proponents also cited the New York State success story as evidence of their plan's viability. When M. Stanton Evans, chairman of the American Conservative Union, addressed the conference, he explicitly called for the creation of a national party modeled on the New York Conservative Party.[1] In offering the Conservative Party as a model, however, Evans failed to acknowledge how cross-endorsement assisted New York's minor parties.

A potential national third party placed James Buckley in a difficult position. As a senator elected on a third-party ticket, Buckley seemed a likely ally. At the same time, the senator needed the endorsement and active support of the state GOP in his re-election campaign the following year. Challenging the national Republican Party, especially when Nelson Rockefeller's appointment constituted a central grievance for conservatives, jeopardized his ability to secure this backing. In an effort to defuse the situation, Buckley organized his own meeting of conservatives. The event, held in St. Michael's, a small town on Maryland's Eastern Shore, brought together third-party advocates such as Senator Jesse Helms and William Rusher, members of Congress intrigued by the idea such as Representative Trent Lott, and conservatives loyal to the GOP such as Clif White. Because many of the same individuals had just attended the Conservative Political Action Conference, some observers mistakenly concluded Buckley's meeting was part of the third-party effort.[2] In reality, the senator designed the group to increase conservative visibility and power within the GOP. Buckley hoped that his group, by winning concessions from the Ford administration and the GOP, would make a national third party unnecessary. The meeting concluded with a statement warning President Ford not to take conservative support for granted and a call for an open Republican convention in 1976. Buckley also announced that he would head an ongoing committee chartered to monitor and influence the Ford administration.[3]

In contrast to the group's stern public warnings, Buckley privately reassured the president of its less hostile intentions. Prior to the St. Michael's meeting, the senator promised the White House that it would not lead to the creation of a third party.[4] Immediately following the event, Buckley looked to arrange a meeting with the president to assure him of the group's loyalty to the GOP.[5] The senator also told a White House aide that while William Rusher and Stanton Evans advocated a third party at the St. Michael's meeting, "a majority of those present favored working within the party structure."[6] Buckley again contacted the White House when the *Washington Post* cast his group as hostile to Ford. Charging the *Post* had twisted the truth, he wrote Ford, "I very much regret that the article gave the impression of a negative view of your administration."[7] Buckley even sent a copy of this letter to Nelson Rockefeller. Gerald Ford treated James Buckley with a comparable amount of consideration, and demonstrated throughout 1975 that he valued the New York senator. When Buckley recommended Kieran O'Doherty for a place on the Postal Rate Commission, Ford appointed the party leader to the position. One study of the Ford presidency even speculated that the desire to keep Buckley in his camp may have influenced Ford's response to the New York City fiscal crisis.[8] While the evidence is not conclusive, Ford consistently solicited Buckley's advice on the issue and often followed the senator's hard line concerning any federal assistance to the city.[9]

Early in 1975, Gerald Ford declared that, while he wanted the support of conservative Republicans, he was not prepared to dump Nelson Rockefeller as his vice president to secure it.[10] The rising militancy of conservatives and the likelihood of a challenge by Ronald Reagan for the Republican presidential nomination increased the cost of his decision, however. By the fall, some important policy differences between Ford and Rockefeller also strained their political partnership. Most prominently, Rockefeller began to advocate more federal aid to alleviate New York City's fiscal crisis than the administration did. On October 28, Gerald Ford met with Nelson Rockefeller in the White House to discuss their political future. In his memoir, Ford recalled that he never asked Rockefeller to remove himself from the ticket, rather that Rockefeller had volunteered after Ford outlined the challenges they faced in winning the GOP nomination due to conservative criticism.[11] Recollecting the meeting differently, Rockefeller claimed the president asked him to withdraw his name because of opposition from GOP conservatives.[12] On November 3, 1975, Gerald Ford held a prime-time news conference. Ford announced a reshuffling of his Cabinet and told the country that he had acceded to Nelson Rockefeller's request to not be considered for the 1976 Republican vice presidential nomination. Rockefeller's withdrawal meant that his political career would come to an end at the completion of his vice-presidential term. Sending Rockefeller into political retirement had always been a goal of the Conservative Party. But the party's faithfulness to the national GOP and the Ford White House during this period meant that the pressure that forced Rockefeller's decision came from conservatives outside the state.

The Conservative Party's loyalty to Gerald Ford also restricted its actions in the fight for the Republican presidential nomination. In October of 1975, Ronald Reagan spoke at the Conservative Party's thirteenth anniversary dinner.[13] Dan Mahoney introduced the former governor as the next president of the United States. The crowd loved Reagan's stump speech attacking the size and wastefulness of the federal government and rewarded him with numerous standing ovations. The enthusiastic Conservatives even forgave him for mistakenly thanking deceased Hollywood actor Dan Duryea, rather than New York Assembly Speaker Perry Duryea, for attending the event. One account of the dinner concluded, "It is certain the Conservative Party will support him [Reagan]."[14] Conservatives, however, unwilling to alienate the national GOP, defied this prediction. Ronald Reagan's campaign initially planned a statewide challenge in New York's presidential primary.[15] It reassessed this decision, however, when the Conservative Party failed to assist. Twelve years earlier, a far weaker Conservative Party searched for every way possible to promote Barry Goldwater's candidacy. Now, the party shunned a similarly conservative presidential candidate in an effort to protect itself. With the New York GOP committed to Gerald Ford and with no help coming from Conservatives, the Reagan campaign dropped the plan of a statewide primary challenge and ran only a small number of delegates.[16]

Like his party, James Buckley, torn between ideological sympathy for the challenger and practical considerations favoring the incumbent, remained uninvolved in the nomination fight. Over the course of late 1975 and early 1976, Buckley and Nelson Rockefeller met several times to discuss national and state politics. According to both men, the vice president made it clear that Buckley would not receive the Republican Senate nomination until he backed Gerald Ford for president. The reality was less clear. Buckley initially declared himself neutral in the Ford-Reagan battle. Both the White House and the state GOP, however, protected the senator from a potential challenger. In 1975, Westchester Congressman Peter Peyser announced his candidacy for the Republican Senate nomination. Calling Buckley out of touch with the people of the state, the congressman criticized the senator on a number of issues, including his opposition to federal aid to New York City during its recent fiscal crisis.[17] Shortly before Peyser announced his candidacy, however, longtime Rockefeller loyalist George Hinman had asked him not to run for the Senate because it would divide the state GOP. Peyser rejected this advice, announced his candidacy, and told the *New York Times* that no Rockefeller aide tried to dissuade him from running.[18] Hinman responded with a scathing letter to Peyser calling him a liar unfit for public office. Hinman subsequently released the letter to the press, publicly embarrassing the candidate.[19] Peyser misinterpreted state GOP warnings to Buckley as evidence of the party's being prepared to abandon his re-election campaign. Peyser expected the state GOP to rally to his side against a hyphenated Republican. In reality, the state GOP never considered shifting its support from Buckley because he was a Republican incumbent deserving of protection. Richard Rosenbaum, the New York GOP chairman, bluntly told reporters, "Peter Peyser is on his own."[20]

Peyser expected the Ford administration to support him over the ideologically conservative Buckley. In June 1975, Peyser contacted an aide to President Ford to explain that he was the more appropriate Republican candidate.[21] In December 1975, Peyser pledged to the White House that he would try to pressure Buckley into supporting the president.[22] In April 1976, Peyser contacted President Ford in an unsuccessful attempt to gain funding from the Republican Senate Committee.[23] Despite these appeals, the White House never made the slightest move to back Peyser. Shortly before the state GOP designated its Senate candidate in the spring of 1976, Peyser also implored Nelson Rockefeller to intervene. The congressman claimed that local Republicans wanted to back him, but were waiting for some sign from the vice president. He warned the vice president, "I honestly feel we are watching the death of the Republican Party in New York unless someone like yourself is willing to again step in and give the Party a chance for a new life."[24] Rockefeller, however, was no more willing to intervene than the president. He responded with a short impersonal letter explaining his policy not to become involved in Republican primaries.[25] With Peyser's campaign unable to attract support, the Republican State Committee voted overwhelmingly to designate Buckley as the party's candidate. Although Peyser's vote fell below the 25 percent threshold required to trigger a primary, he refused to abandon his challenge. The congressman pledged to conduct a petition drive to compel a September GOP primary.

In presidential politics, Gerald Ford entered the GOP convention with a slight lead in delegates over Ronald Reagan. As Republicans gathered in Kansas City, Reagan gambled by choosing a liberal Republican, Pennsylvania Senator Richard Schweiker, as his running mate, but the move failed to attract the delegates Reagan needed to overtake Ford. Caught between his need to maintain strong ties to the Ford White House and his ideological sympathy for Ronald Reagan's challenge, Senator James Buckley briefly entered the presidential race. Buckley, encouraged by Senator Jesse Helms and Congressman Phil Crane, began a quasi-campaign for the presidency. Limited by a low-key manner often at odds with the demands of his profession and ideologically similar to one of the competitive presidential candidates, Buckley offered little to the convention. Still, on August 10, Buckley informed reporters that several prominent conservatives had approached him about becoming a compromise presidential candidate. He explained that while he refused to commit to such a candidacy, he also did not dismiss the possibility.[26] In his statement, the senator failed to explain clearly why he was considering running. He also left unanswered why another steadfast conservative represented a compromise candidate or even why a convention that appeared ready to nominate Ford—if only narrowly—needed a compromise candidate at all.

Buckley's presidential flirtation infuriated state GOP leaders. New York Republicans uniformly criticized Buckley's move as ill-advised and counterproductive. Asked about the matter on *Meet the Press*, Nelson Rockefeller's anger so distracted him that a panelist had to remind him of the senator's name.[27] State GOP chairman Richard Rosenbaum threatened to deny Buckley the party's Senate nomination unless he ended his presidential campaign.[28] Tom Wicker's *New York Times* column predicted that Buckley's move presaged a national conservative third party, although he failed to spell out how one event led to the other.[29] The *Times* editorial board expressed uncertainty over what the move meant to accomplish, but remained confident that it would reveal "a cynicism now growing rampant in right-wing circles."[30] On August 16, Buckley acknowledged a lack of support for his quasi-candidacy and abruptly ended his campaign. Buckley intended his short-lived candidacy to advance the conservative cause without provoking the retribution that outright support for Ronald Reagan would have provoked. Buckley hoped to draw enough support to force a second ballot that might help Ronald Reagan's candidacy. Never more than a curious sideshow, however, Buckley's campaign failed to influence the convention. Gerald Ford withstood Reagan's challenge to win the GOP presidential nomination at the convention.

REPUBLICAN SETBACKS

James Buckley, Dan Mahoney, and Keiran O'Doherty may have come to terms with the realities of political compromise, but some Conservatives balked at cross-endorsing Gerald Ford. John Bellport, who later won election to the state assembly as a Conservative, wrote Dan Mahoney, "Our precious Row 'C' should not be sullied by the placing of less-than-conservative candidates on our line." Demonstrating the skepticism of many in the party toward its leaders, Bellport added the dig that he hoped his suggestions would be considered rather than "discarded due to a prior arrangement with the Republicans."[31] David Bullard urged all members of the party's state committee to declare independence from the GOP by naming a favorite-son candidate or endorsing a minor-party candidate. Mahoney and O'Doherty wanted the party to cross-endorse Gerald Ford in their continuing effort to protect James Buckley's candidacy. Buckley, who endorsed Ford following the GOP convention, asked all members of the Conservative executive committee to also support the president. He acknowledged that many Conservatives were less than enthusiastic about the president, but warned that the country could not afford a Carter administration.[32] The White House, for its part, continued to work actively to secure the Conservative nomination. "There is a considerable effort being made," an internal administration memo to the president concluded, "to get the Conservative New York State Party to endorse your campaign."[33] When the state committee met in a midtown Manhattan hotel to award the party's presidential nomination, however, Conservative opposition to Ford remained strong, especially among delegates from Long Island. "Ford is a captive of the liberal wing of the Republican Party," charged Henry Paolucci, a longtime party activist.[34] He advocated that the party refrain from nominating anyone for president. After some debate, the committee narrowly rejected the blank line option by a vote of 140 to 137. The committee then selected Ford over an obscure Long Island state committeeman by a 145 to 114 vote. Mahoney and O'Doherty delivered the party's nomination to Ford, but only by the narrowest of margins.

The allegiance of James Buckley and the Conservative Party to the state and national GOP was returned in kind. While Peter Peyser gathered enough petition signatures to force a Republican primary, leaders, activists, and financial contributors refused to back the challenge. Buckley simply ignored the congressman and coasted to an easy victory in the GOP primary. The following year, Peyser left the party to become a Democrat. Buckley's victory guaranteed that, like Gerald Ford, the senator had the Conservative and Republican nominations in the general election. A few members of the party, most prominently Jacob Javits, however, still refused to support the Republican nominee in the general election. In September, citing Buckley's response to the New York City fiscal crisis, Javits announced that he would not campaign for Buckley and might not even vote for him.[35] Some local Conservative organizations also complained to their party headquarters that the GOP in their area failed to back Buckley.[36] Still, an overwhelming majority of Republicans supported the senator. Nelson Rockefeller, who withheld his backing for Buckley until the senator endorsed Gerald Ford, strained credibility with the enthusiasm of his eventual endorsement. Rockefeller explained that while the Conservative Party had been formed to end his and Jacob Javits's political careers, "it really turned out to be a tremendous asset to both of us." He continued, "They did for us what it would have been hard for us to do for ourselves—established our position in the center."[37]

The Buckley campaign faced a number of challenges in the general election. Buckley's call for Nixon's resignation continued to trouble some supporters of the president. His opposition to federal assistance in response to New York's fiscal crisis alienated many of the city's voters. And his brief presidential campaign during the GOP convention hurt his political image. Moderates accused Buckley of disloyalty for his initial reluctance to back Ford, while conservatives blamed him for never supporting Reagan. Almost all observers considered the effort amateurish and pointless. Buckley might have survived these problems were it not for the outcome of the Democratic Senate primary. Out of a five-candidate field, there was no doubt whom the Buckley campaign hoped to face. Dan Mahoney wrote the state's local

Conservative leaders shortly before the Democratic primary: "It appears that Bella Abzug may win the Democratic primary," he explained. "If she does, she would seem to be the candidate that would arouse the maximum antagonism from Regular or Al Smith Democrats."[38] The chairman went on to propose a Buckley campaign event featuring prominent Democrats abandoning their party's nominee. Putting aside the issue of how many "Al Smith Democrats" remained nearly a half-century after the governor's last campaign, Mahoney's analysis was sound. Abzug's policy positions and personal manner alienated many moderate voters. Against a political opponent with these limitations, Buckley could win a majority of the state's voters.

Except Bella Abzug lost the Democratic primary. In addition, she lost to a very different type of Democrat, former United Nations ambassador Daniel Patrick Moynihan. A veteran of both the Johnson and Nixon administrations and a current Harvard professor, Moynihan emerged as a potential candidate by providing a spirited defense of Israel while United States ambassador at the United Nations. His victory in the Democratic primary scrambled the ideological fault lines of the race. Moynihan emerged as part of a group of formerly liberal, even leftist, Democrats. These mostly New York City writers and intellectuals completed a public migration across the ideological spectrum by the mid-1970s. Dubbed neoconservatives, they advocated a more vigorous foreign policy and a continued—if revamped—role for the government domestically. Because Moynihan shared many of this group's views including a willingness to criticize liberal social welfare programs, his Senate campaign came to be seen as a manifestation of this new type of conservatism. In his *New York Times* column, William Safire called the race the first time a traditional conservative, Buckley, faced a neoconservative, Moynihan. Safire, who as a Nixon speechwriter in 1970 played an active role in the White House's backing of Buckley over Charles Goodell, praised both candidates, but endorsed Moynihan.[39] Norman Podhoretz, arguably the preeminent neoconservative, actively campaigned for the Democrat. Moynihan's neoconservative credentials protected him from being depicted as another liberal Democrat. The fact that Democratic voters chose Moynihan rather than Abzug as their candidate demonstrated the increased popularity of conservatism. For Buckley, however, it presented a formidable challenge.

Despite the many concessions the party made on his behalf, James Buckley failed to retain his Senate seat as Daniel Moynihan captured 54 percent of the vote. The alliance of Conservatives and Republicans also failed to carry the day in the presidential race as Gerald Ford lost New York State to Jimmy Carter by a margin of 52 percent to 47 percent. New York's forty-one electoral votes provided Carter with his margin of victory in the national election. Republicans also suffered disappointments in the state's legislative and congressional elections. In the legislature, Republicans added one seat to their majority in the state senate and cut into the Democratic assembly majority by picking up two seats. Republicans failed, however, to reverse the Watergate losses of 1974.

No race rivaled the Buckley loss in significance to the Conservatives, however. The party had made a number of compromises to protect James Buckley and had nothing to show for it. In the period between Buckley's election in 1970 and his defeat in 1976, the Conservative Party evaluated every situation for its potential impact on the senator's re-election prospects. The result was a more cautious party hesitant to challenge the GOP or Republican presidential administrations. The New York Conservative Party's failure to support Ronald Reagan's challenge of President Ford represented the most important example of the party's caution. Conservatives created a third party in the early 1960s to force the ideological realignment of the two major parties. They knew that conservative candidates like Reagan needed to succeed in order to affect this realignment. And yet, the party supported Gerald Ford's renomination. Reagan's narrow loss to Ford at the convention could not help but raise troubling questions about how the outcome might have been different had the party committed to him as it had to Goldwater in 1964. The 1976 election results allowed Conservatives to consign these doubts to the past. The party no longer needed to compromise its ideology out of political necessity. Without a Conservative in the Senate, the Conservative Party in New York could get on with its work.

Conservatives soon turned their focus to the next statewide election, the 1978 gubernatorial race. The GOP hoped to recapture the governor's mansion in 1978, and considered Conservative support critical to statewide success. Both leading candidates, Senate Majority Leader Warren Anderson and Assembly Minority Leader Perry Duryea, courted Conservative cross-endorsement. As moderate-to-conservative politicians, Anderson and Duryea already reflected the influence of the Conservative Party on state politics. During his earlier statewide campaigns, Nelson Rockefeller proposed new state programs and boasted of recently implemented initiatives. In contrast, Duryea and Anderson both eschewed additional expenditures and pledged to control state spending and taxes. Conservatives, aided by the state's budget problems, had shifted acceptable candidate behavior from expanding to reducing the role of the state. The two politicians also changed their positions on the most contentious social issue of the time in order to attract Conservative support. Prior to 1978, both politicians supported limited state funding of abortions. When the legislature considered the issue that spring, however, Anderson and Duryea voted against state funding. The press found no evidence of a *quid pro quo*, but speculated that a desire to win Conservative endorsement persuaded both men to make this switch.[40]

In May, frustrated by an ineffectual campaign, Warren Anderson pulled out of the gubernatorial race, leaving Perry Duryea the presumptive GOP nominee. The Conservative Party, despite Duryea's commitment to fiscal conservatism and his reversal on abortion funding, still hesitated to endorse him. Conservatives soon focused their concern on Duryea's choice of a lieutenant governor running mate, former Yonkers congressman Bruce Caputo. The party's objections to Caputo ranged from the congressman's political record to his refusal to disavow a run for the Senate in 1980. Conservative leaders also wanted an incentive in exchange for the party's endorsement, similar to their success four years earlier in getting Malcolm Wilson to end Suffolk County's cross-endorsement ban in exchange for the party's endorsement. In 1978, Conservatives again looked to the sympathetic suburbs of Long Island for a political reward. The party proposed that, in exchange for its endorsement of Duryea and Caputo, the GOP would cross-endorse its candidate in Suffolk County's First Congressional District. With Democratic incumbent Otis Pike retiring and a GOP edge in registration, a Conservative-Republican candidate had a realistic chance of winning the seat. Also, as Suffolk County's leading Republican, Perry Duryea was in a position to deliver the district's GOP nomination.

Convinced that his gubernatorial campaign required Conservative cross-endorsement to succeed, Duryea agreed. Local Republicans, however, objected to the "back-room deal" that traded away a valuable nomination, and threatened to scuttle the agreement.[41] Conservatives moved cautiously, given the fragility of the Republican commitment. Party leaders refused to nominate Duryea until they received a written commitment from local Republicans pledging to respect the deal. Duryea prevailed on the Suffolk County GOP chairman to write a letter promising his organization would support a Conservative congressional candidate. Only after Duryea aides personally delivered this letter did Conservative leaders agree to cross-endorse the candidate.[42] A small number of dissident Conservatives, however, objected to the bartering of their party's gubernatorial nomination. David Bullard, whose opposition to Conservative cross-endorsement undermined Malcolm Wilson's 1974 gubernatorial campaign, again challenged the party's leadership by becoming a candidate. This time, however, Bullard failed to spark a rebellion among his fellow Conservatives. His inability to attract support demonstrated the extent to which cooperation between the two state parties had been accepted. A smaller and smaller segment of the Conservative rank and file objected to reaching this type of accommodation with Republicans. At the Conservative convention, Duryea won 81 percent of the vote, leaving Bullard short of the 25 percent required to force a primary.

Perry Duryea's subsequent campaign displayed close cooperation between the Conservative and Republican Parties. As in previous years, Dan Mahoney led the alliance, serving as a key advisor to the Duryea campaign. By the fall, the Conservative Party printed and distributed 1.5 million pieces of literature urging New Yorkers to vote for Duryea on its Row C.[43] The Conservative-GOP alliance also extended beyond the top of each party's ticket. Conservatives mounted independent challenges in only 18.9 percent of all legislative and congressional races, the lowest percentage in the party's history. Still, the gubernatorial race demonstrated there were limits to what a Republican-Conservative alliance could deliver. While Conservatives and Republicans not working together guaranteed defeat, an alliance between the two parties did not ensure victory. Just as in 1974, a cross-endorsed gubernatorial candidate failed to win election. Perry Duryea, an attractive candidate backed by both the Republican and Conservative parties, lost his gubernatorial bid by eight percentage points.

On the positive side for Conservatives, the party provided the margin of victory for the only Republican candidate who won statewide election, Ned Regan in the state's comptroller race. Additionally, Conservatives sent a representative to Congress, as Long Island voters overwhelmingly elected Conservative William Carney to the House of Representatives. Upon being elected, Carney announced he would join the House GOP caucus once he took office.[44] James Buckley's identical announcement following his election to the Senate eight years earlier had set off a political controversy and a battle with Jacob Javits. In 1978, however, no member of the state or national GOP raised any objections. In the state's legislative races, Conservative cross-endorsement provided the margin of victory for thirteen Republican state senators and assemblymen. Since the five state senators elected due to Conservative votes produced the GOP majority, the Conservative Party boasted it had saved the senate for the Republican Party. The election's mixed results demonstrated that the increasingly routine nature of the cooperation between the Conservatives and Republicans promised enough electoral victories to maintain the support of both parties.

THE LAST LIBERAL

On January 26, 1979, Nelson Rockefeller suffered a fatal heart attack at one of his midtown Manhattan townhouses. The news shocked most New Yorkers, given the former governor's vigor and seeming good health. In the days following Rockefeller's death, attention focused on the compromising nature of his final hours and his staff's cover-up of these circumstances. Eventually, however, most commentary shifted to analyzing his political life and legacy. Rockefeller, despite his numerous strengths and resources, never achieved his primary political goal of becoming president. Most observers concluded that, given his ideological viewpoint, Rockefeller belonged to the wrong political party, a fact that contributed to his failure to win the White House.[45] These analyses, however, failed to appreciate the scope of political change during Rockefeller's political life. Rockefeller was first elected governor of New York in 1958, when conservatives—at least as they would come to be defined by the 1970s—were a minority in the national and state GOP. Rockefeller, along with other liberal Republicans, belonged to a political party that supported their views and encouraged their ambitions. Two decades of victories by conservatives across the country and in New York State, however, transformed the GOP into the party in which Rockefeller seemed so out of place by the time of his death. That a number of these transformative victories came at Rockefeller's expense only demonstrated his central role in this realignment.

Despite his withdrawal from public life the previous year, Nelson Rockefeller's death affected state politics. Twice since the reform of the state's nominating process in 1967, Rockefeller blocked disgruntled Republicans from challenging Jacob Javits in a GOP Senate primary. In his autobiography, Javits credited Rockefeller with squelching political challenges from within the party. Many political observers expected Rockefeller to suspend his retirement to help longtime political ally Jacob Javits run for re-election in 1980. Javits also expected Rockefeller to assist him again in the 1980 campaign. "I am sure he [Rockefeller] would have done this for me had I appealed to him at the right time and he had been around to do it," Javits later wrote.[46] Rockefeller's death, however, left Javits facing a re-election campaign deprived of the governor's protection for the first time.

Presented with a changed political landscape, the Conservative Party looked to capitalize on Javits's new vulnerability. The party's inability to prevent Javits's re-election to the Senate three times remained its most important frustration. In 1979, the Committee to Retire Jacob Javits, an official Conservative Party campaign organization, aggressively began raising money. A committee letter from Dan Mahoney explained how, without Nelson Rockefeller, the race was wide open. "Javits is completely vulnerable to this challenge," Mahoney explained, "He has never faced a Republican primary. He will be seventy-six years old next May. He can be taken."[47] In previous elections, Rockefeller's effective enforcement of GOP loyalty thwarted Conservative attempts to induce any ideologically conservative Republican politicians to take on Javits. Now, party leaders hoped to recruit Buffalo congressman, former professional football player, and longtime Conservative favorite Jack Kemp as a candidate. As early as March of 1979, Serf Maltese referred to Kemp as the party's leading choice in the Senate race.[48] While eager to run should Javits retire, Kemp hesitated to challenge an incumbent Republican senator. James Buckley, however, expressed an interest in re-entering politics to oppose Javits. In May 1979, Buckley announced a possible Senate run in either New York or Connecticut, and soon shifted his voter registration to Connecticut in preparation for a race there.[49] With their preferred candidate unwilling to commit and their past hero leaving the state, Conservatives feared again being unable to find a Republican willing to challenge Javits in the primary.

But the 1980 Senate election demonstrated a changed Republican Party. In a testament to Javits's increased vulnerability without Rockefeller's protection, three Republicans emerged to compete for the GOP nomination. In October, James Eagan, a Queens lawyer active in local GOP politics, became the first Republican to challenge Javits. Next, Bruce Caputo, former Westchester congressman and 1978 Republican and Conservative lieutenant governor nominee, entered the race. Finally, Hempstead presiding town supervisor Alfonse D'Amato expressed interest in the Senate nomination. While D'Amato's job required him to oversee a city of almost eight hundred thousand residents, the Long Island politician was little known outside Nassau County. Some political insiders even doubted that D'Amato was serious about actually running.[50] All three Republican challengers recognized the value of Conservative backing in a GOP primary and courted the third party. In September, the Eagan campaign contacted Conservative officials asking for help in defeating Javits.[51] Bruce Caputo tried to overcome the doubts Conservatives had had when he ran for lieutenant governor in 1978. "I believe I have the name recognition, support in the polls, experience, fund raising capacity, and state wide organization to do the job better than any prospective candidate," he wrote a Conservative Party leader.[52]

Al D'Amato, however, pursued the Conservative Party cross-endorsement most vigorously. "It had been clear to me all along that the Conservatives were the key to a challenge against Javits," he later recalled.[53] D'Amato unabashedly pursued Conservatives. The candidate crisscrossed the state, meeting informally with local Conservative leaders, often in restaurants or taverns. When Conservatives like Congressman Bill Carney held fundraisers, D'Amato made sure to purchase tickets.[54] D'Amato and his wife personally courted state party leaders. He later recalled a lengthy dinner at a New York City Italian restaurant with Dan Mahoney, Serf Maltese, and their spouses: "We told jokes and I played the piano til three o'clock in the morning," D'Amato remembered. "We wound up closing the place."[55] While D'Amato stressed the personal rapport that produced this alliance, Conservatives also recognized qualities in the Long Island politician that made him an attractive candidate. First, D'Amato had a history of working with the party, including appointing Conservatives to patronage positions in the Hempstead government. Second, his record as a campaigner and an elected official demonstrated an ability to win and maintain the support of the middle-class voters Conservatives valued. Third, because D'Amato could count on the backing of the Suffolk and Nassau County Republican Parties, he seemed capable of forcing a GOP Senate primary. Finally, D'Amato gave every sign of being willing to confront Javits aggressively, a characteristic the party prized in a challenger.

In January 1980, Conservative leaders announced that the party, hoping to maximize its impact on the GOP nominating process, would decide which Republican challenger to back within the next month or two.[56] Events during the next few weeks clarified the race. First, Jacob Javits announced that he would seek a fifth Senate term. He also disclosed that he had been diagnosed with a progressive muscular disorder. In his autobiography, Javits explained that, while he seriously considering retiring given his medical condition, he decided to fight on because as the last prominent liberal New York Republican, he felt "anathema to the ultraconservatives in the Republican Party and to the leaders of the New York Conservative Party."[57] Once Javits declared his intention to seek re-election, Jack Kemp decided not to run for the Republican Senate nomination. Kieran O'Doherty promptly informed the press that party leaders were leaning toward backing D'Amato.[58] D'Amato, eager to make this preference official, continued to meet with local Conservatives across the state and supply them with information concerning the flaws in Bruce Caputo's congressional voting record. These local Conservatives then wrote members of the party's state committee explaining that, while Bruce Caputo refused to support adequate military appropriations or to oppose an extension of the deadline for the Equal Rights Amendment, Al D'Amato would uphold the Conservative position on these and all other issues.[59] In March, the Conservative state committee met to award an informal endorsement that would, for all practical purposes, commit the party to a candidate. Suffolk County chairman John O'Leary asked members of the state committee if they wanted to back "a Johnny-come-lately Conservative or a real Conservative like Al D'Amato."[60] The committee backed D'Amato over Bruce Caputo by a two-to-one margin, with Jim Eagan receiving only minimal support.

In June, New York's political parties held their conventions to designate their Senate candidates. Although D'Amato entered the Conservative convention with the party's informal endorsement—one newspaper referred to it as the party's "official informal endorsement"—Bruce Caputo refused to concede the nomination.[61] According to D'Amato, Caputo attempted to win over the Conservative convention by employing a series of parliamentary stalling techniques while spreading rumors that D'Amato was tied to organized crime.[62] Party leaders and rank-and file members remained committed to D'Amato, however, and formally selected him as their Senate nominee. At its convention, the Liberal Party nominated Jacob Javits as expected. Finally, New York Republicans met to choose their Senate nominee. Without doubt, Javits would win a majority of delegates. Less certain, however, was whether the senator could prevent a challenger from reaching the 25 percent threshold needed to force a September primary. Conservatives had spent the preceding months enhancing D'Amato's chances at the GOP convention. First, the party used its links to conservatives beyond the state to help D'Amato raise four hundred thousand dollars.[63] D'Amato spent part of this money to run television commercials aimed at convincing Republican convention participants that he was a serious candidate. The commercials, created by the producer of Bill Buckley's television show, cast D'Amato as the real Republican in the race. In addition, four Republican state legislators, all of whom had received Conservative cross-endorsement, wrote committee members with survey results that found that Jacob Javits had provided no coattails for his fellow GOP candidates in the 1974 election. They argued that, in contrast, Al D'Amato had always helped the rest of the GOP ticket in Nassau County.[64]

Jacob Javits also spent the months preceding the convention demonstrating his Republican credentials. Javits pledged to back Ronald Reagan should the California governor win the GOP presidential nomination. He also used fellow GOP officeholders to vouch for his partisan loyalty. Letters from leading Republicans in Congress and the state legislature to members of the GOP state committee linked Javits's renomination to the GOP's ability to gain control of the senate and the state assembly.[65] Overall, however, New York Republicans found few effective ways to help the incumbent senator. Without Rockefeller, the state party could not protect Javits. "It's tougher without Nelson," Javits conceded.[66] On June 19, Republicans gathered at the Waldorf-Astoria Hotel to select a Senate candidate. Recognizing his failure to generate any support, Bruce Caputo withdrew from the race prior to the voting. The committee then designated Jacob Javits as its nominee, but with only sixty-four percent of its vote. Republicans gave Al D'Amato the remaining thirty-six percent, guaranteeing a GOP primary. After eighteen years, the Conservative Party finally succeeded in producing a primary challenger to liberal Republican Jacob Javits.

The state GOP also proved ineffective in preventing a meaningful presidential primary. In 1976, the New York GOP asked all presidential candidates to refrain from entering the state's primary because it wanted its delegates to remain uncommitted. With Nelson Rockefeller still a powerful force in the 1976 election, Gerald Ford and Ronald Reagan respected the party's wishes and ran only a small number of delegates in the New York primary. Republican voters chose uncommitted delegates in the state primary, and, in the midst of a nearly evenly divided convention, Nelson Rockefeller delivered New York's delegation to Gerald Ford. Four years later, the New York GOP wanted to implement this same strategy. Republican state chairman Kilbourne, however, could not impose this plan. In late 1979, the Reagan campaign announced it would not respect Kilbourne's ban on running delegates in the state primary.[67] Several GOP county chairmen, led by Brooklyn chief George Clark, assembled slates of Reagan delegates in defiance of their state party. George Bush subsequently announced that he would also field delegate slates across the state. By New York State's March 23 presidential primary, even the state GOP's supposedly uncommitted delegates were moving towards supporting Ronald Reagan. Newspapers estimated that the former governor controlled the state delegation with support from at least 100 of the 123 delegates.[68] This assessment ultimately proved to have understated support for Reagan. The Republican convention nominated Reagan with all but two New York delegates voting for him.

In 1976, the Conservative Party practiced neutrality during the presidential nomination season. Despite its natural affinity for Ronald Reagan, the party stayed neutral to protect James Buckley's re-election prospects.

Now freed of these constraints by Buckley's defeat, the party looked to join forces with the 1980 Reagan campaign. In 1979, the party informally endorsed Reagan for president in the following year's campaign. In October, Dan Mahoney wrote John Sears, then Reagan's campaign manager, to arrange the candidate's appearance at a party fundraiser.[69] In January 1980, Reagan attended a Conservative Party fundraiser at the trendy Manhattan disco Regine's. Addressing a very supportive crowd, Reagan reminisced about the 1960s and 1970s when conservatives struggled through difficult times. Pledging that those days were gone forever, he promised, "We have entered a new phase—putting the majority together."[70] The event raised forty thousand dollars for the party and helped cement the relationship between Conservatives and Reagan.

THE FINAL CHAPTER

As the September Republican primary approached, Jacob Javits struggled to capitalize on his significant strengths as a candidate and neutralize his equally important weaknesses. Javits's four Senate terms meant that virtually every New Yorker knew him, with most considering him a serious and hard-working legislator. He also counted many loyalists in the state GOP, bolstered by decades of recommendations for federal appointments. In addition, many New York Republicans respected Javits's campaign record of winning three terms in the House and four terms in the Senate without an electoral defeat. On the negative side, the senator's manner often bordered on imperious, and an overriding caution on controversial issues frustrated even supporters. Finally, his liberal legislative record was at odds with the beliefs of many in his party. In the past, Javits's ability to avoid Republican primaries facilitated his general election strategy of courting liberal non-Republican voters while expecting GOP voters to remain loyal to their party's nominee. In 1980, however, Javits needed to make his case to Republican voters in a primary, when both the state and national parties were more conservative than in the past. A staff memo prepared for a debate advised him "to use the word 'conservative' in describing his position on reducing government spending and the scope of the Federal bureaucracy."[71] In addition, the Javits campaign ran one television commercial featuring Barry Goldwater's somewhat ambivalent endorsement: "I disagree with Jack Javits on just about everything, but I want him back in the United States Senate."[72] Javits's first GOP primary was also plagued by questions about his health. Throughout his political career, Javits projected a vigorous image symbolized by his passion and skill in tennis. Now at seventy-six and affected by a motor neuron condition, Javits seemed a very different man. Even supporters expressed some concern about the wisdom of electing someone with a degenerative disease who would be eighty-two at the end of his Senate term. Javits's television commercials stressed that neither the senator's age nor his health limited the value of his experience. Finally, the senator directed most of the campaign's one million dollars toward an effort to telephone Republicans across the state urging them to vote for him in the GOP primary.

During the primary campaign, Al D'Amato proved he was the aggressive and effective challenger the Conservative Party wanted. While he did not raise as much money as Javits, D'Amato collected about 75 percent of the incumbent's cash total, ensuring a serious challenge.[73] D'Amato also ran a controversial advertising campaign focusing on Javits's two major vulnerabilities. First, like previous candidates backed by Conservatives, D'Amato characterized himself as the race's legitimate representative of the GOP. His early television commercials called him "a Republican who is a Republican."[74] A fundraising letter cast the race as being between "a make-believe Republican and a real one."[75] While D'Amato's framing of this issue was not original, it proved especially effective because of conservative successes within the GOP. In the presidential race, Javits endorsed the party's nominee, Ronald Reagan, but never managed any convincing words of support for Reagan's major policy initiatives, including the former governor's call for a major tax cut. In contrast, D'Amato campaigned on a platform indistinguishable from that of the popular presidential candidate. D'Amato also used the Liberal Party's cross-endorsement against the senator. Liberals were considering incumbent Democrat Jimmy Carter or Republican Congressman John Anderson, running as an independent, as their presidential nominee. In July, D'Amato asked Javits to forbid his name from appearing on any line headed by Carter or Anderson because "the Republican Party electorate demands nothing less of all its candidates this year than our unqualified and undivided support for Ronald Reagan."[76] D'Amato undoubtedly realized that Javits would never renounce his Liberal nomination, but recognized the issue's potential to complicate the senator's campaign. When Javits failed to respond to his letter, D'Amato wrote local GOP leaders across the state charging that Javits's decision diminished Reagan's chances of carrying New York State in November and indicated a willingness to run a divisive campaign detrimental to all GOP candidates.[77] Changes in New York politics made D'Amato's challenge potent. In the 1960s, Republicans who accepted Conservative cross-endorsement were vulnerable to attack. By 1980, the Conservative nomination was a non-issue, but the Liberal endorsement provoked criticism.

Second, D'Amato attacked Javits on a more personal and controversial front. Some forty years younger than Javits, D'Amato raised the issue of the incumbent's age and health. In August, the D'Amato campaign ran a television commercial that listed the senator's various departures from Republican orthodoxy. The ad's conclusion, however, drew all of the attention. Accompanying the picture of a crumpled Javits campaign poster, the ad concluded, "And now, at age 76 and in failing health, he wants six more years."[78] While Javits charged the ads were unfair, he found no way to reassure concerned voters on this issue. D'Amato used the health issue as part of his effort to woo moderate Republicans. He used the more constant theme of his primary campaign—that Javits was too liberal—to energize his base.

The Conservative Party mobilized its organization to turn out GOP voters for Al D'Amato in the September 9 Republican primary. In mid-August, Dan Mahoney urged all county chairmen to redouble their efforts in anticipation of the GOP primary. He promised that state headquarters would supply local leaders with poll watcher certificates and everything else needed "to make a maximum effort to 'man the polls.' "[79] Two days later, the party issued an emergency special request for Conservatives to compile primary voter lists from three of New York City's boroughs.[80] The party intensified its efforts as the campaign drew to a close. Serf Maltese explained the significance of the GOP primary to local party leaders. "Make no mistake about it," he wrote, "this is one of the most important days since the formation of our Party in 1962. Each and every one of you must give a maximum effort to insure that Conservative-Republican Al D'Amato triumphs over liberal Jacob Javits."[81] Javits, to demonstrate his standing in the national GOP, brought in Republicans such as former president Gerald Ford and fellow senators including Ted Stevens, Alan Simpson, and John Danforth to campaign across the state in the final days before the primary. While some newspaper polls showed D'Amato edging ahead of Javits with potential GOP voters, Javits's stature, experience, and unblemished electoral record led many to believe he might still prevail in a tight race. On primary day, however, the senator could not overcome the dual problems of being more liberal than most members of his party and in increasingly frail health. He won only about 44 percent of the Republican vote as New York Republicans chose Alfonse D'Amato as their Senate nominee. Jacob Javits, deprived of a sympathetic national party and Rockefeller's political muscle, lost his first statewide primary. The vote validated the Conservative Party's choice of candidate and its overall strategy. It also demonstrated that liberal Republicans could no longer compete effectively within the state.

Javits remained in the race even without the Republican nomination. Fulfilling a pledge he made during the campaign, Javits prepared to run in the general election as the Liberal Party nominee. Some of the senator's supporters shrugged off the primary loss, hoping that the campaign would be a repeat of the 1969 New York City mayoral race. In that campaign, John Lindsay lost the Republican primary to John Marchi, but went on to win the general election as the Liberal Party candidate. There were important differences, however. Unlike Lindsay, Jacob Javits faced a statewide electorate with little history of backing Liberal Party nominees. Also, despite his difficult first term, Lindsay retained enough glamour and promise to rally a significant portion of the electorate to his side. Javits, in contrast, appeared to be a man who had overstayed his time on the political stage. Finally, and most importantly, politics in New York had changed since the 1960s. Far more of the state's voters had grown receptive to conservatism in general and to conservative candidates such as Al D'Amato and Ronald Reagan.

Initially, the senator's campaign responded to the primary loss as a manageable problem. Javits's campaign promised to secure a second ballot line by creating a paper party in the hope of attracting New Yorkers uncomfortable with voting for the Liberal Party nominee.[82] Javits, however, soon found his candidacy crippled by three interrelated problems: the loss of party assistance, an inability to raise money, and declining poll numbers. Almost immediately, the campaign conceded that the requirement to create a second ballot line—twenty thousand petition signatures from registered voters who did not vote in the Democratic or Republican primaries—was beyond its organizational capacity.[83] Fundraising also proved more difficult than the campaign anticipated. Javits's campaign estimated that the candidate needed one million dollars to run a competitive race. Prior to the GOP primary, the Republican Senatorial Campaign Committee (RSCC) had pledged seven hundred seventy thousand dollars to Javits for the general election. The RSCC allocated the money, however, expecting Javits to win the GOP nomination. When Al D'Amato protested, the Javits campaign offered to divide the money equally. D'Amato refused this settlement, and forced the RSCC to give him the entire sum. Denied the RSCC money, Javits never approached his fundraising goal of one million dollars. Additionally, unlike a decade earlier when John Lindsay won re-election, there was no longer a group of liberal Republican donors to tap. The ideological reshuffling of the two major parties in the 1970s drove the financial patrons of liberal republicanism into the Democratic Party. A month after the primary and just three weeks before the election, the senator's campaign had raised only two hundred thousand dollars.

As a result of these setbacks, Javits understandably began losing support. A number of unions, traditional allies of the senator, abandoned Javits to back Elizabeth Holtzman. By October, virtually no Republican elected officials remained committed to the senator. Javits's poll numbers began to decline until he was a distant third in the race. Javits had no way to reverse this erosion of support. The traditional sources of liberal Republican support were ineffectual now. The Ripon Society, for example, still backed the senator's re-election, but was politically inconsequential. The society's endorsement of Javits as the "last vestige of human dignity in the Republican Party" highlighted its marginal status in GOP circles.[84] Since Liberals chose John Anderson as their presidential candidate, Javits shared that party's line with another liberal Republican who could not win the support of the GOP. In a statement that seemed to betray the futility of his own campaign, Javits dismissed Anderson's chances. "I don't think the American people are prepared to abandon the two-party system," he said.[85] Instead of supporting Anderson, Javits remained committed to Ronald Reagan, even campaigning for the former governor in Jewish areas of Florida. In the month leading up to the election, the Javits campaign grew increasingly dispirited. The candidate, citing his health problems, drastically limited his public campaigning. At a mid-October meeting with the *New York Times* editorial board, Javits complained about his inability to communicate with voters, admitting, "I feel a lot of frustration."[86] On October 30, the *Times*, a longtime supporter of Javits, ran an editorial arguing that, while the senator was the best candidate, his failure to attract support meant that he should withdraw from the race. This sentiment grew more common, and Javits spent the final stage of his campaign denying he was going to drop out of the race or justifying his decision to stay in it.

With both the GOP and Conservative nominations, Alfonse D'Amato suffered from none of the problems that plagued Jacob Javits. Most importantly, D'Amato's campaign raised sufficient funds due in part to the RSCC donation. The candidate spent most of this money on television commercials to rehabilitate his image following the nasty primary fight. Many of these ads featured D'Amato's mother and stressed the candidate's immigrant heritage and humble origins. His expensive media campaign also helped him appear less confrontational and more reassuring. The Conservative Party's importance diminished significantly during this stage of D'Amato's campaign. The party, however, had provided critical help earlier in the campaign. In March, its all-but-official endorsement made D'Amato the principal Republican challenger to Javits. In June, its ties to local GOP leaders facilitated D'Amato's winning enough support from the Republican executive committee to force a primary. And, finally, in September, it provided the manpower and organization to mobilize the Republican voters D'Amato needed to win the GOP primary. The Conservative nomination helped D'Amato win the Republican primary.

In the fall campaign, the Conservative Party shifted its focus to other races, especially for the presidency. Conservatives, for the first time, enjoyed the ideal situation in a presidential campaign. Ronald Reagan was an ideologically suitable candidate who not only accepted the party's cross-endorsement, but coordinated his campaign to their mutual benefit. Reagan, even as the Republican presidential nominee, helped Conservatives raise money. Conservatives sent out a fundraising letter in which the nominee asked for contributions so the party could help him carry New York State in the November election. In a testament to the party's level of acceptance, Reagan even referred to Dan Mahoney as "an old friend of mine" in this letter.[87] Along with the Reagan letter, the party included a short note from vice-presidential nominee George Bush that shared this friendly tone.[88] There were additional signs of this alliance. For example, one Conservative Party leader, Tom Bolan, served as an important fundraiser for the Reagan campaign. In 1964, the party accepted a clandestine role in order to assist Barry Goldwater's presidential campaign. By 1980, Conservatives enjoyed being a visible and integral part of Ronald Reagan's campaign.

Most of the state's congressional and legislative races demonstrated similar cooperation between the Conservative and Republican Parties. The general rule of Conservative cross-endorsement of Republican nominees remained in effect in 1980. A potential primary threat to Representative Bill Carney, the only Conservative in Congress, threatened this comity. John J. Hart, a local lawyer, tried to make Carney's Conservative affiliation an issue with Republican voters. The Republican Party's response demonstrated the strength of the interparty alliance. Both local GOP figures and prominent state Republicans such as Jack Kemp came to Carney's aid. With this backing and the advantage of incumbency, the congressman handily won the GOP primary. As conservatives increased their cooperation with the GOP, they also cast off the few remaining ideologically acceptable Democrats. The Queens Conservative Party, for example, withdrew its customary support of Democratic congressman, Leo Zeferetti.[89] Local Republicans rewarded Conservatives for this move by cross-endorsing their candidate, Paul Atanasio. The state legislative races also consistently demonstrated the bipartisan alliance as Conservatives joined with Republicans to help the GOP try to retake the assembly and to protect its majority in the state senate.

The Conservative-Republican coalition triumphed on election day in 1980. Alphonse D'Amato bested Democratic nominee Elizabeth Holtzman by approximately one hundred thousand votes. Underfunded and abandoned, Jacob Javits won barely 10 percent of the vote. Javits chose not to offer a concession, but admitted to a crowd of supporters, "There's been a great political overturn in our country tonight."[90] In the presidential race, Ronald Reagan carried New York on his way to winning forty-five states and the White House. For Conservatives, the nature of these victories constituted even better news. The votes from its ballot line provided the margin of victory for both Reagan's New York victory and D'Amato's election, an unprecedented achievement. The Republican-Conservative coalition produced some additional gains in the rest of the state's races. Republicans picked up four congressional seats to reduce the Democratic advantage to twenty-two to seventeen in the state delegation. Conservatives managed to elect only one of their two party members running for Congress. William Carney easily won re-election, while Paul Atanasio lost a close race. In the legislative races, New Yorkers maintained the status quo, returning the Republican majority to the state senate and the Democratic majority to the assembly.

AFTERMATH

With Ronald Reagan's election as president in 1980, conservatism achieved national political ascendancy. Although less complete than Franklin Roosevelt's remaking of American politics in the 1930s, the "Reagan Revolution" still ushered in a period in which conservative politicians and policies prevailed. The new president wasted no time thanking the New York party that played a role in this transformation. At a testimonial dinner in honor of Dan Mahoney in the spring of 1981, Ronald Reagan sent a lengthy letter spelling out Chairman Mahoney's role in the party's success and the national significance of this success. The president closed his message with the playful postscript "And I want you to know here at the White House, 'Boss Mahoney,' we await your orders."[91] On a more substantive level, party leader Tom Bolan acted as the patronage liaison with the new administration, finding employment for numerous Conservatives. Reagan appointed former senator James Buckley as undersecretary of state, then head of Radio Free Europe, and finally to the Court of Appeals for the District of Columbia Circuit. The new president also rewarded the two party's founders. Initially, Reagan appointed Kieran O'Doherty to serve on the Postal Rate Commission. When some major direct-mail companies protested the appointment, however, O'Doherty became counsel to the House Post Office Committee. In 1986, on Al D'Amato's recommendation, Reagan appointed Dan Mahoney to the Court of Appeals for the New York Circuit. This appointment ended an era. Mahoney stepped down after twenty-four years as Conservative Party chairman.

In reality, the events of 1980 and not Mahoney's resignation as chairman six years later represented the true end of an era for the Conservative Party. With the 1980 election, the party achieved the primary goals it had identified at its inception nearly twenty years earlier. On the most basic level, Dan Mahoney and Kieran O'Doherty formed a third party because they believed the state GOP consistently ignored conservative Republicans. Republican leaders typically nominated statewide candidates capable of attracting liberal voters from outside the party. They calculated that conservative Republicans would vote for the liberal nominee out of party loyalty. This strategy helped win statewide office for Thomas Dewey, Jacob Javits, and Nelson Rockefeller in the 1940s and 1950s. It also created the frustration and resentment among conservative Republicans that led to the creation of the Conservative Party. From its inception, the party attempted to force the state GOP to abandon this strategy by providing conservative Republicans a way to express their displeasure at the polls. By 1980, the party's success at achieving this goal was evident. The GOP could not take the state's ideologically conservative voters for granted. Frustrated conservative Republicans could support the third party to punish the state GOP.

Political developments distinct from the creation of the Conservative Party would also have given conservative voters more influence within the state GOP. New York's use of party conventions to nominate statewide candidates would have been replaced by a more democratic primary process in keeping with changes outside New York. That reform would have given conservative voters power within the GOP that more accurately reflected their numbers. In addition, no one could replicate the mix of charm, celebrity, personal wealth, and institutional power that Nelson Rockefeller used to dominate the state GOP. Accordingly, the party would have become less disciplined, and thus a more hospitable home for conservatives, once Rockefeller relinquished his role as head of the state GOP. The Conservative Party, however, accelerated and enhanced the transformation that made the state GOP more conservative. It took the Conservative Party nearly two decades to bring about this change. It would have taken longer, and been less comprehensive, without its labors.

By 1980, Conservatives also achieved their goal of institutional cooperation between the two state parties. In the 1960s, New York Conservatives and Republicans were in open warfare. Conservative Party leaders were shocked by the GOP's initial hostility. They expected ideologically conservative Republicans to welcome their assistance. But the state GOP imposed strict party discipline and denied Conservatives any alliance. In the mid-1960s, Conservative gains at the polls started to earn the party some GOP support. Bill Buckley's New York City mayoral campaign in 1965 and Conservative support of the Civilian Review Board Referendum the following year generated interest and approval for the party. Both these campaigns, although limited to New York City, had statewide impact. The tremendous press attention afforded the 1965 mayoral race and the 1966 referendum introduced the Conservative Party to voters across the state. In addition, the growing popularity of law and order, along with other social issues, helped Conservatives win over a growing percentage of the state's voters. This success translated into increased support for Conservative candidates at the legislative, congressional, and statewide level. Republican politicians across the state began to recognize the potential threat presented by the growing Conservative vote, and began to consider the possibility of an accommodation with the Conservatives. This growing desire for cooperation emerged first in the suburban counties of Long Island, but it soon spread to parts of New York City as well as upstate. Throughout the 1960s, however, Nelson Rockefeller and the state GOP blocked this interparty alliance, despite the objections of some county GOP organizations.

Pressure from national Republican leaders forced the state GOP to cooperate with the Conservative Party. Richard Nixon applied the full resources of the national Republican Party and the White House to support the Conservative Party. His decision to replace liberal Republican Senator Charles Goodell with Conservative James Buckley altered New York politics. Nelson Rockefeller was a perceptive-enough politician to recognize that polls and his president demanded a new approach. By the 1970s, the New York Republican Party allowed at least partial cooperation with Conservatives. Local county organizations forged cooperative relationships with their Conservative counterparts, and cross-endorsement of statewide candidates began. Throughout the decade, the parties cross-endorsed most of the state's senatorial and gubernatorial candidates and all of its presidential electors. The Conservative-Republican alliance did not guarantee victory. The lack of cross-endorsement, however, ensured defeat. The Conservative Party would run its own candidate against an ideologically unacceptable GOP nominee, thus guaranteeing the defeat of both in the general election. The clearest evidence of this dynamic is that no Republican statewide candidate has won without Conservative cross-endorsement since 1974. The Conservative Party's ability and willingness to impose a political price on the GOP should it drift too far to the left gave it something approximating a veto of Republican candidates by 1980.

The last Republican candidate to win a statewide race in New York without Conservative cross-endorsement was also the party's last prominent liberal, Jacob Javits. Senator Javits was New York's final symbol of liberal republicanism. The Conservative Party had successfully purged every other prominent liberal from the state GOP. John Lindsay's defeat in the 1969 Republican mayoral primary started the shift. In the early 1970s, Lindsay and most other prominent Republicans defected to the Democratic Party. Nelson Rockefeller remained a Republican, but moved far enough to the right that few observers still considered him a liberal by the time he left the governor's mansion. Dan Mahoney and Kieran O'Doherty founded the Conservative Party to force liberals out of the state GOP. By the mid-1970s, the party had succeeded in achieving this goal, with the exception of Jacob Javits. The defeat of the state GOP's last prominent liberal completed this job.

New York Republican leadership also reflected the Conservative Party's success in transforming the state GOP. In 1981, New York Republicans chose an ideological conservative, George Clark, as their new state chairman. Formerly the head of the Brooklyn GOP, Clark rose to prominence within the state by opposing Nelson Rockefeller. In 1973, he scuttled the governor's plan to have Robert Wagner run for New York City mayor as the Republican nominee. In 1976, Clark defied Rockefeller and supported Ronald Reagan for president. By 1981, however, Nelson Rockefeller and every other prominent liberal Republican was gone. The party had grown more conservative, and needed a leader who shared this ideological focus. Already enjoying a good relationship with the Conservative Party, the new state chairman promised a "firm friendship" with its leaders.[92]

The 1980 election also demonstrated Conservative Party success in its most far-reaching goal, the realignment of the two national parties along ideological lines. New York Conservatives identified this as a goal from the very inception of the party. They rejected the broad ideological coalitions within the national Republican and Democratic parties as detrimental to their interests and those of the country. Conservatives believed that both broad coalitional parties ignored the views of their conservative members. They blamed both parties for stifling conservatism, and for harming the country by denying voters a choice between candidates with contrasting ideological viewpoints. Or as George Wallace phrased it in his 1968 independent presidential campaign, "There's not a dime's worth of difference" between the two parties.[93] By 1980, with the liberal wing of the Republican Party decimated and Ronald Reagan elected president, the national GOP was now the ideologically conservative party. The political reshuffling of the previous two decades realigned the parties along ideological lines. The Republican Party was now the home for conservatives, and the Democratic Party was for the nation's liberals.

Jacob Javits's changing fortunes demonstrated the extent of this transformation. In 1964, the senator, along with other liberal Republicans, refused to support the candidacy of Barry Goldwater, judging his conservatism too extreme for the party. By the time of the general election in 1980, Javits was no longer the arbiter of all things Republican. Instead, his membership in the GOP had become the issue. Al D'Amato's charges that Javits was "a make-believe Republican" resonated with GOP voters. By the time of the general election, Javits was running as the Liberal Party candidate and trying to bolster his Republican credentials by campaigning for Ronald Reagan. In the Republican Party of 1980, there was a place for a conservative like Reagan, but not for a liberal like Jacob Javits. The parties had been redrawn along ideological lines.

The New York Conservative Party did not transform the country's two major parties on its own. This was a complex process which took place in different ways in different parts of the country. The migration of southern white conservatives from the Democratic to the Republican Party during this period is only the most studied cause of this change. This ideological reshuffling of the parties, however, could not have been accomplished as long as a vital liberal wing existed within the national GOP. And the annihilation of that wing could not have occurred as long as liberal Republicans dominated the New York GOP.

The Conservative Party's contributions to this transformation did not guarantee it a prominent place in the new American politics. The 1980 election began conservatism's ascendancy and the New York Conservative Party's decline. Within the state, the party retained its power to keep the GOP from abandoning conservative principles, but it mattered less beyond the state's borders after 1980. Previously, the conservative movement needed the party to confront the state's liberal giants. National conservatives viewed the New York GOP, and politicians such as Nelson Rockefeller, Jacob Javits, and John Lindsay, as the cause of many of their problems. They viewed the New York GOP as the political arm of an eastern establishment that tyrannized conservatives. National conservatives assisted the third party as a way to overthrow this tyranny. With this revolution complete by 1980, the state was no longer central to the battles that would determine the fate of conservatism. New York Conservatives were no longer of critical importance to the movement. The south and the west would provide the electoral base and the leadership for conservatism. In the 1960s and 1970s, however, the New York Conservative Party did more than the routine political tasks of drafting platforms, raising money, identifying candidates, and running campaigns. It also pursued the overall goal of making the GOP more consistently conservative. By 1980, the party had successfully transformed the state Republican Party in this way, thus making the national GOP reliably conservative. New York Conservatives had helped redraw America's party lines.

NOTES

INTRODUCTION

1. Andy Logan, "Around City Hall: Sundance," *New Yorker*, 21 August 1971, 69.

2. "Transcript of Mayor's Statement on Party Switch," *New York Times*, 12 August 1971, 26.

3. "The Conversion of John Lindsay," *Time*, 23 August 1971, 7.

4. "Why You Should Enroll Conservative," (campaign literature), 1962, Series 2, Box 4, Folder 6, Conservative Party Papers of New York State, M.E. Grenander Department of Special Collections and Archives, University at Albany Library, Albany, New York.

5. William F. Buckley Jr., "Exit Lindsay," *National Review*, 10 September 1971, 1011.

6. For further explanation of these terms see "Fusion Candidacies, Disaggregation, and Freedom of Association," *Harvard Law Review* 109 (1996): 1302–17.

7. Peter H. Argersinger, " 'A Place on the Ballot': Fusion Politics and Antifusion Laws," *American Historical Review* 85 (April 1980): 287–306.

8. "The Constitutionality of Anti-Fusion and Party-Raiding Statutes," *Columbia Law Review* 47 (1947): 1211.

9. Richard Hofstadter, *The Age of Reform: From Bryan to F.D.R.* (New York: Knopf, 1956), 97.

10. Phyllis Schlafly, *A Choice Not an Echo* (Alton, Ill.: Pere Marquette Press, 1964).

11. Theodore H. White, "The Lindsay Choice Now: To Preach or to Run," *Life*, 20 August 1971, 66–67; "John Lindsay: A Switch in Time," *Newsweek*, 21 August 1971, 15–16; "The Conversion of John Lindsay," *Time*, 23 August 1971, 7–9.

CHAPTER 1

1. J. Daniel Mahoney, *Actions Speak Louder* (New Rochelle, N.Y.: Arlington House, 1968), 14–16.

2. John A Wells, ed., *Thomas E. Dewey and the Two-Party System* (Garden City, N.Y.: Doubleday, 1966), 9.

3. Ibid.

4. Douglas Dales, "Mayor Puts Off Senate Decision," *New York Times*, 29 August 1956, 16.

5. "Rockefeller It Is—But Can They Be So Sure?" *National Review*, 30 August 1958, 149.

6. David Rockefeller, *Memoirs* (New York: Random House, 2002), 180.

7. Douglas Dales, "Rockefeller Best, Javits Contends," *New York Times*, 30 November 1959, 16.

8. Leo Egan, "Rockefeller Challenges Nixon to Speak Up on National Issues," *New York Times*, 9 June 1960, 1.

9. Leo Egan, "Pre-Convention Strategy," *New York Times*, 30 May 1960, 30.

10. Warren Weaver, Jr., "Rockefeller's Future," *New York Times*, 17 October 1960, 23.

11. Vincent Leibell, Jr., "A Message to New York Republicans," Series 7, Box 11, Folder 20, Conservative Party Papers.

12. Newton H. Fulbright, "The Conservative Party in New York State," *U.S.A.*, 13 January 1967, 2–3.

13. William F. Buckley Jr., *Cruising Speed: A Documentary* (New York: Bantam, 1972), 41.

14. William H. Honan, "Mayor Goes the 'Fusion' Tradition One Better," *New York Times*, 8 November 1981, sec. 4, p. 7.

15. The group consisted of Bob Sanders and Paul Cheney, who were both lawyers, investment counselor Dick Doll, and Paul Franklin, a banker.

16. Mahoney, *Actions Speak Louder*, 19.

17. While New York has sixty-two counties, election law allows the two smallest counties to be counted as one for this purpose.

18. Charles G. Nitsche, "A History of the Conservative Party of New York State," (master's thesis, Niagara University, 1968), 13.

19. Rusher to L. Brent Bozell, 28 September 1961, Reel 3, William A. Rusher Papers, Manuscripts Division, Library of Congress, Washington, D. C.

20. J. Daniel Mahoney to Buckley, 22 May 1962, Box 19, William F. Buckley Jr. Papers, Manuscripts and Archives, Sterling Memorial Library, Yale University, New Haven.

21. Mahoney to Rusher, 14 June 1961, Reel 10, Rusher Papers.

22. Mahoney to Buckley, 26 July 1961, Box 13, Folder "Conservative Party of New York State (1961)," Buckley Papers.

23. Buckley to E. V. Rickenbacker, 28 July 1961; Buckley to Lemuel R. Boulware, 11 August 1961; Buckley to Raymond Moley, 10 August 1961; Buckley to F. R. Courdert, 28 July 1962; Box 13, Folder "Conservative Party of NY," Buckley Papers.

24. Boulware to Buckley, 15 August 1961, Box 13, Folder "Conservative Party of NY," Buckley Papers.

25. Buckley to Mahoney, 18 August 1961, Box 13, Folder "Conservative Party of NY," Buckley Papers.

26. Rusher to L. Brent Bozell, 28 September 1961, Box 21, Folder 15, Rusher Papers.

27. Kieran O'Doherty to Frank Meyer, 8 November 1961, Series 7, Box 14, Folder 76, Conservative Party Papers; Buckley to J. Daniel Mahoney, 2 January 1962, Box 19, Folder "Conservative Party," Buckley Papers.

28. John Cummings, "Rightists Form Anti-Rocky Party," *Newsday*, 15 November 1961, 3.

29. O'Doherty, (letter to the editor), *Newsday*, 20 November 1961, Reel 8, Rusher Papers.

30. James Desmond, "Bob Aims Own Knife at Splitup of State Pie," *New York Daily News*, 16 November 1961, 10.

31. Clayton Knowles, "Rightists Seeking Own State Party," *New York Times*, 16 November 1961, 27.

32. Frederick S. Dennin to J. Daniel Mahoney, 15 August 1962; Mahoney to Dennin, 21 August 1962; Series 1, Box 1, Conservative Party Papers.

33. Earl Mazo, "New State Party of Hard-Core Rightists Out to Beat Liberals Rockefeller & Javits," *New York Herald Tribune*, 16 April 1962, 1.

34. John Cummings and Robert Mayer, "GOP to Rightists: Stick with the Party," *Newsday*, 16 November 1961, 5.

35. Warren Weaver, Jr., "Rockefeller Bids G.O.P Widen Base," *New York Times*, 18 April 1962, 27.

36. M. Ahearn to William Ronan, (memo), 18 July 1962; William Ronan to Rockefeller, (memo), 24 July 1962, Record Group 15, Reel 90, Nelson A. Rockefeller Papers, Rockefeller Archives Center, North Tarrytown, New York.

37. Clayton Knowles, "Javits to Run Again; Calls on Democrats to Debate With Him," *New York Times*, 17 July 1962, 1.

38. Hinman to Rockefeller, (memo), 29 August 1962, Series J.2, Subseries 1, Box 93, Folder 642, Rockefeller Papers.

39. Raymond Moley, "Splinter-Party Folly," *Newsweek*, 22 January 1962, 84.

40. Goldwater to Moley, (telegram), 16 January 1962, Box 19, Folder "Goldwater, Barry M.," Raymond Moley Papers, Hoover Institution Archives, Stanford University, Palo Alto, Cal.

41. Buckley to J. Daniel Mahoney, 28 February 1962, Box 19, Folder "Conservative Party," Buckley Papers.

42. Buckley to Goldwater, 18 May 1962, Box 20, Folder "Goldwater, Barry M. (1962)," Buckley Papers.

43. Hugh Morrow to Rockefeller, (memo), Series J.2, Subseries 1, Box 20, Folder 118, Rockefeller Papers.

44. George Hinman to Rockefeller, (memo), 16 June 1962, Series J.2, Subseries 4, Box 93, Folder 642, Rockefeller Papers.

45. George Hinman to Rockefeller, (memo), 25 July 1962, Series J.2, Subseries 4, Box 93, Folder 642, Rockefeller Papers.

46. Hinman to Rockefeller, (memo), 31 August 1962, Series J.2, Subseries 4, Box 93, Folder 642, Rockefeller Papers.

47. Douglas Caddy, (letter to the editor), *Wall Street Journal*, 9 March 1962, 14.

48. David Jaquith to Hanighen, 8 August 1962, Series 7, Box 11, Folder 70, Conservative Party Papers.

49. Hanighen to Jaquith, 10 August 1962, Series 7, Box 11, Folder 70, Conservative Party Papers.

50. "In New York: The Conservative Party," *National Review*, 27 February 1962, 119–20.

51. Smant, Kevin J., *Principles and Heresies: Frank S. Meyer and the Shaping of the American Conservative Movement* (Wilmington, Del.: ISI Books, 2002), 85.

52. William Rusher to William Buckley, (memo), 3 October 1962, Reel 4, Rusher Papers.

53. Mahoney, *Actions Speak Louder*, 34–37.

54. Conservative Party Organization Manual, [1962], Series 7, Box 14, Folder 108, Conservative Party Papers.

55. Mahoney, *Actions Speak Louder*, 94.

56. Douglas Dales, "Conservatives Fight State Law on County Nominating Petitions," *New York Times*, 11 August 1962, 28.

57. "Nominations Law Upheld by Court," *New York Times*, 18 August 1962, 19.

58. Mahoney, *Actions Speak Louder*, 78.

59. George Sokolsky, "The Conservative Party," *Washington Post*, 12 July 1962, A21; Confidential Memo to L. Judson Morhouse, 2 July 1962, Record Group 15, Series 22, Subseries 3, Box 33, Folder 974, Rockefeller Papers.

60. Clayton Knowles, "Race is Dropped by Conservative," *New York Times*, 20 July 1962, 15.

61. "Conservatives a 'Shadow Party,' Pell Charges in Quitting Group," *Ticonderoga Sentinel*, 26 July 1962.

62. Editorial, " 'Conservatives' Uncovered," *Ticonderoga Sentinel*, 26 July 1962, 8.

63. Conservative Party Special Bulletin, 3 August 1962, Series 2, Box 2, Folder 13, Conservative Party Papers.

64. Morhouse to Javits, 3 August 1962, Series 5, Subseries 2, Box 13, Folder "Conservative Party, 1962," Jacob K. Javits Collection, Special Collections Department, Frank Melville Jr. Memorial Library, State University of New York at Stony Brook.

65. William A. Rusher, *The Rise of the Right* (New York: William Morrow, 1984), 131–32.

66. "Conservative Party Leader Resigns," *Rochester Democrat and Chronicle*, 9 October 1962, 25.

67. Editorial, "Splinters Weaken 2-Party System," *Rochester Democrat and Chronicle*, 10 October 1962, 20.

68. Leonard Ingalls, "Conservative Party Candidate Picked to Oppose Rockefeller," *New York Times*, 14 July 1962, 1.

69. "The Conservative Party," (anonymous memo), 21 July 1962, Reel 5, Rusher Papers.

70. Morhouse to "Country Chairmen," (memo), 8 August 1962, Record Group 4, Series J.1, Subseries 1, Box 57, Folder 625, Rockefeller Papers.

71. Gordon Howe to Carl Spad, 17 July 1962, Record Group 15, Series 22, Subseries 3, Box 33, Folder 974, Rockefeller Papers.

72. Morhouse to McManus, (memo), 10 July 1962, Record Group 15, Reel 167, Rockefeller Papers.

73. Morhouse News Release, 13 September 1962, Series 5, Subseries 2, Box 13, Folder "Conservative Party, 1962," Javits Papers.

74. Nitsche, "History of the Conservative Party," 24.

75. Mahoney, *Actions Speak Louder*, 86–87.

76. "GOP Launches Drive Today to Block Conservative Vote," *Syracuse Post-Standard*, 25 September 1962, 1.

77. State Headquarters to All Club Chairmen, (memo), 27 September 1962, Series 2, Box 2, Folder 14, Conservative Party Papers.

78. Mahoney, *Actions Speak Louder*, 90.

79. Nitsche, "History of the Conservative Party," 24.

80. "Democrats Demand Rockefeller Answer Conservative Charges," *New York Times*, 28 September 1962, 21.

81. Douglas Dales, "G.O.P. Ends Suit on Conservatives," *New York Times*, 2 October 1962, 31.

82. Mahoney, *Actions Speak Louder*, 105.

83. Clayton Knowles, "9,000 Conservatives at Rally Jeer Cuba Action as Too Timid," *New York Times*, 23 October 1962, 28.

84. Douglas Dales, "O'Doherty Is Paid by Conservatives," *New York Times*, 1 November 1962, 20.

85. "Jaquith Tells Why He Seeks Birch Help," *New York Times*, 31 July 1962, 14.

86. J. Daniel Mahoney to the Editor of the *Ticonderoga Sentinel*, 8 August 1962, Series 2, Box 2, Folder 14, Conservative Party Papers.

87. "The Conservative Party," (campaign literature), 1962, Conservative Party, Inc. Papers, George Arents Research Library for Special Collections, Bird Library, Syracuse University.

88. State Headquarters to all Club Chairmen, (memo), 27 September 1962, Series 2, Box 2, Folder 13, Conservative Party Papers.

89. Clayton Knowles, "9,000 Conservatives at Rally Jeer Cuba Action as Too Timid," *New York Times*, 23 October 1962, 28; Mahoney, *Actions Speak Louder*, 104.

90. Speech by O'Doherty, (press release), 22 October 1962, Series 7, Box 7, Folder 5, Conservative Party Papers.

91. Luther F. Bliven, "Crowd at Garden Yells 'We Want Jaquith,' " *Syracuse Post-Standard*, 23 October 1962, 6; "Conservatives Hail Response at Rally," *New York Times*, 24 October 1962, 35.

92. Anonymous Confidential Memo, 18 October 1962, Box 155, Folder 1, Rusher Papers.

93. Robert D. Novak, *The Agony of the G.O.P.* (New York: Macmillan, 1965), 71–72.

94. Peter Kihss, "G.O.P Bid Spurned by Conservatives," *New York Times*, 20 September 1962, 25.

95. Mahoney to "Friend," October 1962, Reel 5, Rusher Papers.

96. Warren Weaver Jr., "Eisenhower Says G.O.P. Furnished Impetus on Cuba," *New York Times*, 30 October 1962, 1.

97. Editorial, "The New York Conservatives," *New York Times*, 31 October 1962, 36.

98. All numerical information concerning election returns and party nominations is derived from the relevant edition of the *Manual for the Use of the Legislature of the State of New York*. The manual, published every two years by New York's Department of State, contains complete information on all elections within the state from the presidential to assembly level.

99. Ralph de Toledano, (news release), 12 November 1962, Box 156, Folder 2, Rusher Papers.

100. "Alive and Kicking," *National Review*, 20 November 1962, 376–77.

101. Homer Bigart, "Election Returns Are a Blow to the Right Wing," *New York Times*, 8 November 1962, 19.

102. Richard H. Rovere, "Letter from Washington," *New Yorker*, 17 November 1962, 203–6.

103. James Desmond, *Nelson Rockefeller: A Political Biography* (New York: Macmillan, 1964), 311–12.

104. James P. Kalteaux to Morhouse, 14 December 1962, Record Group 15, Series 22, Subseries 3, Box 35, Folder 1024, Rockefeller Papers.

105. J. Gregory Merriam to Morhouse, 26 December 1962, Record Group 15, Series 22, Subseries 3, Box 35, Folder 1024, Rockefeller Papers.

106. Donald D. Vole to Morhouse, 10 December 1962, Record Group 15, Series 22, Subseries 3, Box 35, Folder 1024, Rockefeller Papers.

CHAPTER 2

1. State Chairman to Club Chairmen, (memo), 14 November 1962, Series 2, Box 2, Folder 13, Conservative Party Papers.

2. New York Department of State, (press release), 20 March 1964, Series 2, Box 3, Folder 36, Conservative Party Papers.

3. Richard H. McDonnell, "A History of the Conservative Party of New York State, 1962–1972" (Ph.D. dissertation, Pennsylvania State University, 1975), 66.

4. Robert A. Schoenberger, "Conservatism, Personality, and Political Extremism," *American Political Science Review* 62, no. 3 (September 1968): 873.

5. "Interview with the Governor of New York: Where Rockefeller Stands," *U.S. News & World Report*, 23 September 1963, 76–83.

6. Art Richardson to George Hinman, Carl Spad and Malcolm Wilson, (memo), 12 April 1963, Record Group 15, Series 22, Subseries 3, Box 33, Folder 974, Rockefeller Papers.

7. Pillion to Wilson, 26 December 1962; Pillion to Robert Grimm, 26 December 1962; Pillion to A. H. Kirchofer, Box 2, Folder "December 1962," John R. Pillion Papers, Rare and Manuscript Collections, Carl A. Kroch Library, Cornell University, Ithaca, New York.

8. Wilson to Pillion, 11 January 1963, Box 53, Folder "Conservative Party/Splinter Parties," Pillion Papers.

9. Rockefeller to Pillion, 22 January 1963, Box 53, Folder "Conservative Party/Splinter Parties," Pillion Papers.

10. Mahoney, *Actions Speak Louder*, 164–65.

11. "Missionary Mahoney," *New York Times*, 28 June 1963, 28.

12. "Coming of Age," *National Review*, 16 July 1963, 10.

13. Conservative Party Memorandum, 1963 Series No. 4, 22 October 1963, Reel 16, Rusher Papers.

14. St. George, (press release), 12 January 1963, Box 54, Folder "Press Releases 1963," Katherine St. George Papers, Rare and Manuscript Collections, Carl A. Kroch Library, Cornell University, Ithaca, New York.

15. Conservative Party Memorandum, 1963 Series No. 1, 29 March 1963, Series 2, Box 4, Folder 12, Conservative Party Papers.

16. Mahoney to Derounian, 21 January 1963, Series 1, Box 1, Folder "Correspondence 1963/4," Conservative Party Papers.

17. Mahoney to Derounian, 11 August 1963, Series 1, Box 1, Folder "Correspondence 1963/4," Conservative Party Papers.

18. Mahoney, *Actions Speak Louder*, 170–71.

19. Warren Weaver, Jr., "Bid to G.O.P. Made by Conservatives," *New York Times*, 28 August 1963, 1.

20. "Conservative Party Stirrings," *New York Times*, 30 August 1963, 20.

21. William Rusher to J. Daniel Mahoney, 30 August 1963, Box 17, Folder 1, Rusher Papers; Mahoney, David Jaquith, and Kieran O'Doherty, "Conservatives' Stand," Letter to the Editor, *New York Times*, 18 September 1963, 38.

22. Conservative Party Press Release, 7 November 1963, Series 7, Box 8, Folder 10, Conservative Party Papers.

23. Wayne J. Thorburn, "The Conservative Party of New York State: The Pressure Party in a Cross-Endorsement System" (Ph.D. dissertation, University of Maryland, 1974), 70–71, 161–62.

24. State Chairman to Club Chairmen, (memo), 23 November 1962, Series 2, Box 2, Folder 13, Conservative Party Papers.

25. William Rickenbacker, David Jaquith and Kieran O'Doherty, 12 April 1963, Series 2, Box 4, Folder 12, Conservative Party Papers.

26. Mahoney to Henry L. Day, 16 January 1962, Series 1, Box 1, Folder 1, Conservative Party Papers. Document is misdated and appears to be from January 1963.

27. Robert Yarnall to Mahoney, 3 February 1963, Series 7, Box 11, Folder 20, Conservative Party Papers.

28. Conservative Party Memorandum, 1963 Series No. 4, 22 October 1963, Reel 16, Rusher Papers.

29. Mahoney to White, 9 September 1963, Series 7, Box 11, Folder 20, Conservative Party Papers.

30. Mahoney, *Actions Speak Louder*, 193–94.

31. Wick to Mahoney, 24 January 1963; Mahoney to Wick, 15 February 1963; Series 7, Box 11, Folder 70, Conservative Party Papers.

32. Kent Courtney, *Nelson Rockefeller's Candidacy* (New Orleans: Conservative Society of America, 1963).

33. Courtney to Buckley, 9 April 1963, Box 25, Folder "General Correspondence 1963," Buckley Papers.

34. Mahoney to Courtney, 28 May 1963, Box 25, Folder "General Correspondence 1963," Buckley Papers.

35. Warren Weaver Jr., "Rockefeller and '64," *New York Times*, 14 April 1963, Section IV, p. 10.

36. "83 Protestant Ministers Say 'No' to Rocky," *Human Events*, 8 June 1963, 152–53.

37. Peter Kihss, "Rockefeller Says Rightists Imperil G.O.P. and Nation," *New York Times*, 15 July 1963, 1.

38. Mahoney, *Actions Speak Louder*, 167–68.

39. Robert Stephen Goldner, "Minor Party Politics and the Two-Party System: A Case Study: The New York Conservative Party" (master's thesis, Brown University, 1974), 20–1.

40. "Conservatives Brand Rocky a Big Spender," *Chicago Tribune*, 27 January 1964, 15.

41. "Rockefeller Called Fiscal Phony;" (editorial), "The Record Speaks," *Manchester Union Leader*, 27 January 1964, 1.

42. Mahoney to Dean Burch, 25 January 1964, Reel 19, Rusher Papers.

43. Graham Molitor to Roswell Perkins, (memo), 14 May 1964, Record Group 15, Series 22, Subseries 2, Box 29, Folder 888, Rockefeller Papers.

44. Mahoney to Dean Burch, 7 March 1964, Box 12, Folder "Congressional District Information," F. Clifton White Papers, Rare and Manuscript Collections, Carl A. Kroch Library, Cornell University, Ithaca, New York.

45. State Chairman to Finance Committee, (memo), Series 2, Box 4, Folder 12, Conservative Party Papers.

46. Mahoney to David H. Jaquith et al., (memo), 22 January 1964, Box 12, Folder "Congressional District Information," White Papers, Cornell University.

47. Mahoney to Dean Burch, 7 March 1964, Series W, Box 11, Folder 7, Barry M. Goldwater Papers, Arizona Historical Foundation, Hayden Library, Arizona State University, Tempe.

48. Rita Bree to F. Clifton White et al., (memo), 7 January 1964, Box 155, Folder 8, Rusher Papers.

49. "Meeting at Hotel Shelburne," (notes), 9 June 1964, Box 90, Folder "Goldwater for President," Marvin Liebman Papers, Hoover Institution Archives, Stanford University, Palo Alto, Cal.

50. Mahoney to Kitchel, 24 January 1964, Box 15, Folder "Conservative Party," White Papers, Cornell University.

51. Mahoney to White, (memo), 11 April 1964, Box 15, Folder "Conservative Party of New York," F. Clifton White Papers, Archival Collections, John M. Ashbrook Center for Public Affairs, Ashland University, Ashland, Ohio.

52. Dennison Kitchel to White, (memo), 16 April 64; Mahoney to White, 27 April 1964, Box 15, Folder "Conservative Party of New York," White Papers, Ashbrook Center.

53. Mahoney to White, 9 June 1964, Box 15, Folder "Conservative Party of New York," White Papers, Ashbrook Center.

54. Mahoney to White, 17 June 1964, Box 12, Folder "Congressional District Information," White Papers, Cornell University.

55. Mahoney, *Actions Speak Louder*, 197.

56. St. George to Thomas Moore, 7 April 1964; St. George to Lena M. Johnston, 18 May 1964; Box 59, Folder "1964 Campaign-Conservative Party," St. George Papers.

57. Waterman to Dan Mahoney, 23 March 1964; Waterman to Mahoney, 24 March 1964; Series 2, Box 4, Folder 12, Conservative Party Papers.

58. Mahoney, *Actions Speak Louder*, 237–38.

59. "Rockefeller Keeps 87 of Delegates," *New York Times*, 13 July 1964, 17.

60. Jacob K. Javits, "Why the GOP Must Beat Goldwater," *New York Post*, 12 July 1964, 25.

61. Theodore H. White, *The Making of the President 1964* (New York: Atheneum, 1965), 210–13.

62. Joseph W. Sullivan, "Goldwaterites Hope Miller Will Gain City Votes," *Wall Street Journal*, 17 July 1964, 1.

63. Marvin Liebman, *Coming Out Conservative: An Autobiography* (San Francisco: Chronicle Books, 1992), 168–69.

64. Edwin McDowell, "Goldwater-Miller Ticket," *Arizona Republic*, 1.

65. J. Daniel Mahoney to John T. McCarty, 31 July 1964, Box 53, Folder "M-N," William E. Miller Papers, Rare and Manuscript Collections, Carl A. Kroch Library, Cornell University, Ithaca, New York.

66. Earl Mazo, "Javits Bars Aid for Goldwater, Joining Keating," *New York Times*, 22 July 1964, 1.

67. Earl Mazo, "Goldwater View is 'Frightening' to Rockefeller," *New York Times*, 18 July 1964, 1.

68. Earl Mazo, "Javits Bars Aid for Goldwater, Joining Keating," *New York Times*, 22 July 1964, 1.

69. Arnold Rampersand, *Jackie Robinson: A Biography* (New York: Knopf, 1997), 387.

70. Edwin Waterman to Rita Bree, 10 August 1964, Box 11, Folder "Rennselaer," White Papers, Cornell University.

71. Earl Mazo, "State G.O.P. to Shun Rightists," *New York Times*, 16 July 1964, 18.

72. Mahoney to Young, 29 July 1964, Series 7, Box 8, Folder 11, Conservative Party Papers.

73. Young Statement, (press release), 29 July 1964, Record Group 4, Series J.2, Subseries 4, Box 94, Folder 648, Rockefeller Papers.

74. Mahoney to John T. McCarty, 31 July 1964, Box 53, Folder "M-N," Miller Papers.

75. Mahoney, *Actions Speak Louder*, 234–35.

76. Samuel R. Pierce, Jr. to Luce, Letter, 4 November 1963, Clare Booth Luce Papers, Manuscripts Division, Library of Congress, Washington, D. C.

77. Earl Mazo, "Mrs. Luce Weighs Senate Race on State's Conservative Ticket," *New York Times*, 6 August 1964, 13.

78. Earl Mazo, "Goldwater Gets Rockefeller Plea," *New York Times*, 13 August 1964, 1.

79. Karl Hess, *In a Cause that Will Triumph: The Goldwater Campaign and the Future of Conservatism* (Garden City, N.Y.: Doubleday, 1967), 209–10. Hess includes a transcript of this private meeting of Republican leaders as an appendix in his book.

80. Hess, *In a Cause that Will Triumph*, 216.

81. Rockefeller News Conference, (transcript), 12 August 1964, Box 21, Folder "Campaign 1964," Joseph E. Persico Papers, M. E. Grenander Department of Manuscripts and Special Collections, University Library, University at Albany, Albany, New York.

82. *Let's Find Out*, (radio transcript), 16 August 1964, Series 2, Box 485, Folder 27, Kenneth B. Keating Papers, Department of Rare Books and Special Collections, Rush Rhees Library, University of Rochester, Rochester, New York.

83. Mahoney to Rockefeller, 14 August 1964, Series 7, Box 11, Folder 20, Conservative Party Papers.

84. Keating, (press release), 18 August 1964, Series 2, Box 489 Folder 14, Keating Papers.

85. Ronald Sullivan, "Goldwater Asks Mrs. Luce's Help," *New York Times*, 21 August 1964, 1.

86. Conservative Party News Release, 23 August 1964, Box 15, Folder "Conservative Party," White Papers, Cornell University.

87. "Layhmond Robinson, "Mrs. Luce Will Run for Senate if Conservatives Nominate Her," *New York Times*, 23 August 1964, 1.

88. William F. Buckley Jr., "Clare Booth Luce's Candidacy Struck Down by Scorpions," *Los Angeles Times*, 2 September 1964, sec. 2, p. 6.

89. Layhmond Robinson, "Mrs. Luce Scored by 2 G.O.P. Chiefs," *New York Times*, 24 August 1964, 1.

90. Murray Kempton, "The Hosts of Unreason," *New Republic*, 12 September 1964, 11.

91. "Keating on Tour of Upstate Areas," *New York Times*, 25 August 1964, 26.

92. Editorial, "Helping Goldwater—or Kennedy?" *New York Times*, 24 August 1964, 26.

93. Buckley to Luce, 24 August 1964, Box 220, Folder 1, Luce Papers.

94. Luce, (press release), 30 August 1964, Box 223 Folder 3, Luce Papers.

95. Mahoney, *Actions Speak Louder*, 242.

96. Hinman and McHugh Statement, 30 August 1964, Series 5, Subseries 2, Box 13, Folder "1964 Campaign," Javits Papers.

97. Layhmond Robinson, "Keating Chosen by Republicans in Show of Unity," *New York Times*, 1 September 1964, 1.

98. Ronald Sullivan, "State G.O.P. Sees Johnson Sweep; Shuns Goldwater," *New York Times*, 16 September 1964, 1.

99. Joseph A. C. Wadsworth to Edwin L. Hotchkiss, 30 September 1964, Box 235, Folder 81, Ogden R. Reid Papers, Manuscripts and Archives, Sterling Memorial Library, Yale University.

100. Mary C. Brennan, *Turning Right in the Sixties: The Conservative Capture of the GOP* (Chapel Hill: University of North Carolina Press, 1995), 97.

101. Mary McAniff to Richard Nathan, (memo), 6 October 1964, Box 35, Folder 12, Graham T. Molitor Papers, Rockefeller Archive Center, North Tarrytown, New York.

102. Stan Hinden, "Nixon Booed Backing Ken," *Newsday*, 1 October 1964, 3.

103. Conservative Party Campaign Literature, Series 7, Box 8, Folder 20, Conservative Party Papers.

104. Paolucci Campaign Literature, Series 7, Box 8, Folder 20, Conservative Party Papers.

105. Paolucci Interview, *WINS News Conference*, (radio transcript), 4 October 1964, Series 7, Box 8, Folder 20, Conservative Party Papers.

106. Walter Carlson, "Party Lines Are Mixed in the 17th District," *New York Times*, 27 October 1964, 23.

107. Barbara Carter, *The Road to City Hall: How John V. Lindsay Became Mayor* (Englewood Cliffs, N.J.: Prentice-Hall, 1967), 115.

108. Russ Walton to F. Clifton White, (memo), Box 4, Folder "Personal," White Papers, Cornell University.

109. White to Howard Goldson, 28 September 1964, Box 3, Folder "New York," White Papers, Cornell University.

110. Peter Byrnes to Rita Bree, (memo), Box 11, Folder "Byrnes, Peter," 23 September 1964, White Papers, Cornell University.

111. Ronald Sullivan, "Goldwater Forces Assail Rockefeller, *New York Times*, 6 October 1964, 1.

112. John Judis, *William F. Buckley, Jr.: Patron Saint of the Conservatives* (New York: Simon & Schuster, 1988), 230–32.

113. Peter Byrnes to Regional and County Chairmen, 26 October 1964, Box 11, Folder "Steuben," White Papers, Cornell University.

114. A. K Gage, (memo), Box 11, Folder "Field Reports," White Papers, Cornell University.

115. Mickel to "New Yorkers for Goldwater-Miller," 26 October 1964, Box 11, Folder "Schoharie," White Papers, Cornell University.

116. Murray Kempton, "Goldwater's Triumph in the Empire State," *The New Republic*, 14 November 1964, 7.

117. Earl Mazo, "Nixon Terms Rockefeller 'Divider' as G.O.P. Quarrels," *New York Times*, 6 November 1964, 1.

CHAPTER 3

1. Editorial, "Road Ahead for the G.O.P.," *Washington Post*, 6 November 1964, sec. 1, p. 20.

2. Warren Weaver, Jr., "Keating Assays Defeats in State," *New York Times*, 25 November 1964, 22.

3. Jacob K. Javits, "The Road Back for the G.O.P.," *New York Times*, 15 November 1964, sec. 6, p. 28–29.

4. John V. Lindsay, "The New G.O.P," *Atlantic*, January 1965, 39–43.

5. Godfrey Hodgson, *The World Turned Right Side Up: A History of the Conservative Ascendance in America* (Boston: Houghton Mifflin, 1996), 106–14.

6. Earl Mazo, "Goldwater Sees Need to Realign 2 Major Parties," *New York Times*, 15 November 1964, 1.

7. "3rd Party Backed by Conservatives," *New York Times*, 2 May 1965, 64.

8. Mahoney to *Newsday*, 4 May 1965, Series 2, Box 5, Folder 45, Conservative Party Papers.

9. Mahoney to James Gilroy, 7 January 1965, Series 7, Box 5, Folder 17, Conservative Party Papers.

10. Kevin P. Phillips, *The Emerging Republican Majority* (New Rochelle, N.Y.: Arlington House, 1969), 87.

11. Conservative Party Bulletin, December 1964, Box 29, Folder "Conservative Party 1964," Buckley Papers.

12. Conservative Party News Release, 8 January 1965, Series 2, Box 5 Folder 26, Conservative Party Papers.

13. Mahoney to Rockefeller, 3 February 1965, Record Group 15, Office Records, Reel 101, Rockefeller Papers.

14. "Javits Seeks Fusion Movement to Oust Wagner," *New York Times*, 7 December 1964, 26.

15. Thomas P. Ronan, "Lindsay Says He Will Run," *New York Times*, 14 May 1965, 1.

16. "Conservatives Turn Quickly on Lindsay, *New York World-Telegram and Sun*, 4 November 1964, 12.

17. *Searchlight*, (WNBC-TV transcript), 30 May 1965, Series 2, Box 4, Folder 12, Conservative Party Papers.

18. Thomas P. Ronan, "Lindsay is Facing Full Opposition of Conservatives," *New York Times*, 31 May 1965, 1.

19. William F. Buckley Jr., "Mayor, Anyone?" *National Review*, 15 June 1965, 498.

20. Mike McGrady, "Buckley: The Pessimistic Hopeful," *Newsday*, 21 August 1965, 2W.

21. Vincent J. Cannato, *The Ungovernable City: John Lindsay and the Struggle to Save New York* (New York: Basic Books, 2001), 36–37.

22. Judis, *William F. Buckley*, 237.

23. William F. Buckley Jr., *The Unmaking of a Mayor* (New Rochelle, N.Y.: Arlington House, 1966), 121–23. Buckley's prediction of one vote referred to his secretary since, having missed the deadline to change his registration from Connecticut to New York, he would not be eligible to vote in the November election.

24. Richard L. Madden, "Lindsay Seeking No Help from the National G.O.P.," *New York Times*, 27 May 1965, 1.

25. Frank Lynn, "The Power of Rockefeller Money," *New York Times*, 9 October 1974, 30.

26. Richard L. Madden, "Lindsay Seeking No Help from the National G.O.P.," *New York Times*, 27 May 1965, 1.

27. *New York Times*, 25 October 1965, 28.

28. "Buckley vs. Buckley: William F. Buckley Interrogates Himself Before the National Press Club," 4 August 1965, Box 318, Folder 206, Conservative Party Papers.

29. Mahoney, *Actions Speak Louder*, 285. In assessing Mahoney's attribution of the statement to Lindsay, Jonathan Schoenwald wrote, "While there is no compelling reason to believe that the quotation is not true, Mahoney, one of the founders of the Conservative Party, had many axes to grind and used his book to get in his licks whenever possible." Schoenwald, *A Time for Choosing: The Rise of Modern American Conservatism* (New York: Oxford University Press, 2001), 296.

30. Buckley to Robert Strausz-Hupe, 16 July 1965, Series 5, Subseries 2, Box 18, Folder "Mayoralty 1965 (1)," Javits Papers.

31. Eric Swenson to George Lindsay and Robert Price, (memo), 3 October 1965, 97-M-160, Box 13, Buckley Papers.

32. Mahoney to Buckley, et al., (memo), 12 July 1965, Series 2, Box 3, Folder 37, Conservative Party Papers.

33. Rusher to Arthur Andersen, et al., (memo), 15 September 1965, Series 2, Box 3, Folder 37, Conservative Party Papers.

34. Buckley Campaign Literature, Box 322, Folder 248, Buckley Papers.

35. James L. Buckley, *If Men Were Angels: A View from the Senate* (New York: Putnam, 1975), 15–16.

36. Mahoney to Buckley et al., (memo), 16 July 1965, Box 296, Folder 45, Buckley Papers.

37. Neal Freeman to Buckley, (memo), 6 August 1965, Box 297, Folder 46, Buckley Papers.

38. Buckley to Conservative Party Officials, (memo), 8 September 1965, Series 2, Box 3 Folder 37, Conservative Party Papers.

39. Luce to Goldwater, 7 July 1965, Box 225, Folder 4, Luce Papers.

40. Goldwater to Buckley, 20 July 1965, Box 35, Folder "Goldwater, Barry," Buckley Papers.

41. Buckley to Goldwater, 23 July 1965, Box 35, Folder "Goldwater, Barry," Buckley Papers.

42. Goldwater to William Middendorf, 9 June 1965, Box 35, Folder "Goldwater, Barry," Buckley Papers.

43. Hodgson, *The World Turned Right Side Up*, 108–11.

44. Liebman to Arthur Andersen, et al., (memo), 28 August 1965, Box 63, Folder "WFB," Liebman Papers.

45. James Buckley to "Fellow Conservative," Series 2, Box 3, Folder 37, Conservative Party Papers.

46. Arthur C. Nielsen, Sr. to Charles Edison, 4 August 1965, Box 9, Folder "Fundraising Letters," Liebman Papers.

47. Charles Edison to Arthur C. Nielsen, Sr., 20 September 1965, Folder "Fundraising Letters," Liebman Papers.

48. Nitsche, "History of the Conservative Party," 48.

49. Schoenwald, *A Time for Choosing*, 180–3.

50. Cannato, *Ungovernable City*, 38.

51. Judis, *William F. Buckley, Jr.*, 237.

52. Lindsay for Mayor News Release, 21 October 1965, Part 1, Series 1, Box 104, Folder "Javits on Radical Right," John V. Lindsay Papers, Manuscripts and Archives, Sterling Memorial Library, Yale University, New Haven.

53. David Murray, "Lindsay on Buckley—'Doctrine of Hate,' " *New York Post*, 15 October 1965, 3.

54. Marvin Liebman to Mahoney, 27 October 1965, Box 8, Folder "Buckley for Mayor," Liebman Papers.

55. Richard Witkin, "Beame Obtains Badillo Support, Averting a Split," *New York Times*, 11 October 1965, 1.

56. Courtney to "Fellow American,"18 October 1965, Box 309, Folder 142, Buckley Papers.

57. "Beware of Lindsay," (pamphlet), 18 October 1965, Box 309, Folder 142, Buckley Papers.

58. Richard Witkin, "Rightists Fight Lindsay by Mail," *New York Times*, 25 October 1965, 1.

59. Buckley, *Unmaking of a Mayor*, 314–17.

60. Buckley to Goldwater, (telegram), 15 October 1965, Box 35, Folder "General Correspondence 1965," Buckley Papers.

61. Buckley for Mayor News Release, 25 October 1965, Box 310, Folder 148, Buckley Papers.

62. Woody Klein, "Hate Tactics Hit Lindsay," *New York World-Telegram and Sun*, 9 September 1965, 1.

63. Douglas Robinson, "Lindsay Alleges Violence by Foes," *New York Times*, 10 September 1965, 1.

64. Buckley, *Unmaking of a Mayor*, 266.

65. Cannato, *Ungovernable City*, 54–55.

66. Costello News Release, 15 October 1965, Box 309, Folder 146, Buckley Papers.

67. Paul L. Montgomery, "Buckley Assails Liberal 'Attack' on His Religion," *New York Times*, 18 October 1965, 1.

68. Bruce Felknor to Robert Price, 20 October 1965, Series 5, Subseries 2, Box 18, Folder "Mayoralty 1965 (1)," Javits Papers.

69. Thomas P. Ronan, "Buckley Accuses Lindsay of Smear," *New York Times*, 21 October 1965, 53.

70. Robert Price to Bruce Felknor, 24 October 1965. Series 5, Subseries 2, Box 18, Folder "Mayoralty 1965 (1)," Javits Papers.

71. Marvin Liebman to Arthur Andersen et al., (memo), 3 November 1965, Box 297, Folder 46, Buckley Papers.

72. Editorial, "Lindsay's Astounding Victory," *New York Times*, 3 November 1965, 38.

73. "Mayor John Lindsay, New GOP Hope?" *Newsweek*, 15 November 1965, 31–36.

74. "A Second Mandate to Republicans: A Ripon Society Report and Analysis of the 1965 Elections," Box 3, Folder 187, Ripon Society Papers, Rare and Manuscript Collections, Carl A. Kroch Library, Cornell University, Ithaca, New York.

75. Richard L. Madden, "Lindsay Promises Nonpartisan Role as a Fusion Mayor," *New York Times*, 6 November 1965, 1.

76. "Lindsay, Fusion and the Future," *Life*, 12 November 1965, 4.

77. Judis, *William F. Buckley, Jr.*, 255.

78. Richard Reeves, "Goldwater a Big Hit at Buckley Dinner," *New York Herald Tribune*, 12 November 1965, 14.

79. Joseph Alsop, "Thank You, Mr. Buckley," *New York Herald Tribune*, 8 November 1965, 20.

80. Carter, *The Road to City Hall*, 70.

81. Buckley, *Unmaking of a Mayor*, 376–77; Mahoney, *Actions Speak Louder*, 303–6.

82. Shana Alexander, "Even Better than Batman," *Life*, 5 August 1966, 22.

83. Donald J. Devine, "Conservative Hari-Kari," *New Guard*, March 1966, 12.

84. Freeman to Buckley, (memo), 28 April [1966], Box 39, Folder "Freeman, Neal," Buckley Papers.

85. J. Daniel Mahoney, "Conservative Hari-Kari: A Rejoinder," *New Guard*, October 1966, 24.

86. Thomas P. Ronan, "Attack on Mayor Renewed by Fino," *New York Times*, 15 May 1967, 50.

87. Clayton Knowles, "Bronx Insurgents Open Battle on Fino," *New York Times*, 10 July 1967, 22.

88. "Mayor's 'Bright Young Men' Criticized," *New York Times*, 22 April 1967, 30.

89. News release, 15 June 1967, Record Group 15, Series 35, Subseries 3, Box 20, Folder 254, Rockefeller Papers.

90. "Three Contests," *National Review*, 12 July 1966, 664.

91. Casey campaign literature, SPE XMS 90.10, Folder "William Casey for Congress," Tanya M. Melich Papers. M. E. Grenander Department of Special Collections and Archives, University of Albany Library, Albany, New York.

92. William F. Buckley Jr., "Something's Going On—It's Hard to Tell What," *Los Angeles Times*, 15 June 1966, sec 2, p. 6.

93. Casey to Javits, 11 June 1966, Box 20, Folder "William Casey 1966," Javits Papers.

94. Tanya Melich to Casey, (memo), 17 May 1966, SPE XMS 90.10, Folder "William Casey for Congress," Melich Papers.

95. M. Stanton Evans, *The Future of Conservatism: From Taft to Reagan and Beyond* (New York: Holt, Rinehart & Winston, 1968), 141.

96. Raymont, Henry, "Miller to Aid Rockefeller in Re-election Campaign," *New York Times*, 24 April 1966, 1.

97. Richard Witkin, "Governor Rejects Aid from Miller," *New York Times*, 30 April 1966, 1.

98. Ronald Maiorana, "L.I. Conservatives Plan to Sue Republican as Political Deserter," *New York Times*, 6 June 1966, 26.

99. State Headquarters to County Chairman, (memo), 21 April 1966, Series 2, Box 5, Folder 78, Conservative Party Papers.

100. Waterman to Marty Burgess, 6 May 1966, Series 2, Box 3, Folder 43, Conservative Party Papers.

101. Liebman to Buckley, 1 June 1966, Box 101, Folder "Committee of Public Safety," Liebman Papers.

102. Liebman to Arthur Anderson and James Buckley, (memo), 3 June 1966, Box 101, Folder "Committee of Public Safety," Liebman Papers.

103. Liebman to Milbank, 14 June 1966, Box 101, Folder "Committee of Public Safety," Liebman Papers.

104. Edison letter, Series 7, Box 5, Folder 30, Conservative Party Papers.

105. Buckley to "New York City Conservatives," Memo, 22 June 1966, Box 101, Folder "Committee of Public Safety," Liebman Papers.

106. Ruth Cowan, "The New York City Civilian Review Board Referendum of November 1966: A Case Study of Mass Politics" (Ph.D. dissertation, New York University, 1970), 366.

107. Richard Dougherty, "Conservatives, PBA Out to Kill Board," *New York World Journal Tribune*, 27 September 1966, 10.

108. Cowan, "The New York City Civilian Review Board Referendum," 366.

109. Sidney Zion, "Civilian Review Board: FAIR Fights for It," *New York Times*, 11 September 1966, sec. IV, 6.

110. Bernard Weinraub, "Lindsay to Fight Police Issue Vote," *New York Times*, 9 July 1966, 1.

111. FAIR pamphlet, Series 5, Subseries 2, Box 19, Folder "CRB (2)," Javits Papers.

112. "Adams Campaigns in Northern Bronx," *New York Times*, 23 October 1966, 87.

113. Editorial, "The Police Review Fight," *New York Daily News*, 26 October 1966, 59.

114. "*NR* Interview with Dan Mahoney: Do the Big City Police Have Popular Support?" *National Review*, 6 September 1966, 880–82.

115. Cannato, *Ungovernable City*, 178.

116. Terence Smith, "Adams Charges Roosevelt Deal," *New York Times*, 5 October 1966, 33.

117. Rowland Evans and Robert Novak, "New York Backlash," *Washington Post*, 3 October 1966, A21.

118. 1966 Gubernatorial Campaign Archives, Record Group 4, Series J.1, Subseries 3, Box 60, Folder 661, Rockefeller Papers. Document contains only a reference to the Wilson memo.

119. Wells, ed., *Thomas E. Dewey and the Two-Party System.*

120. Louise Boyer to Rockefeller, (memo), 25 August 1966 Record Group 4, Series J.1, Box 59, Folder 653, Rockefeller Papers.

121. Louise Boyer to Rockefeller, (memo), 31 October 1966 Record Group 4, Series J.1, Box 59, Folder 653, Rockefeller Papers.

122. Louise Boyer to Rockefeller, (memo), 28 September 1966 Record Group 4, Series J.1, Box 59, Folder 653, Rockefeller Papers.

123. Editorial, "A Million Minor-Party Votes," *New York Times*, 10 November 1966, 46.

124. "Victory in Defeat," (advertisement), *New York Times*, 23 November 1966, 10.

125. Mahoney, *Actions Speak Louder*, 340.

126. Newton H. Fulbright, "The Conservative Party in New York State," *U.S.A.*, 13 January 1967, 1.

127. Richard Witkin, "The Liberals' Outlook," *New York Times*, 17 December 1966, 24.

128. Edward T. Rogowsky, Louis H. Gold and David W. Abbott, "Police: The Civilian Review Board Controversy," in *Race and Politics in New York City: Five Studies in Policy-Making*, ed. Jewel Bellush and Stephen M. David (New York: Praeger, 1971), 70.

CHAPTER 4

1. Richard M. Nixon, *RN: The Memoirs of Richard Nixon*, (New York: Touchstone, 1990), 266.

2. J. E. Marans, B. Gorenstein and J.R. Price to Javits, (memo), 13 January 1967, Box 4, Folder "J," Ripon Society Papers.

3. Kieran O'Doherty, "A Letter to Conservatives," *The New York State Conservative*, August 1967, 2.

4. Mahoney, *Actions Speak Louder*, 348.

5. Conservative Party Bulletin to County and Club Chairmen, 12 September 1967, Box 85, Folder "Conservative Party," Liebman Papers.

6. Rusher, *Rise of the Right*, 198–200.

7. Judis, *William F. Buckley, Jr.*, 279.

8. Buchanan to Buckley, 8 March 1966, Box 40, Folder "Nixon, Richard," Buckley Papers.

9. Buckley to William Rusher, (memo), 17 March 1967, Box 40, Folder "Nixon, Richard," Buckley Papers.

10. "Mr. Nixon's Reply," *National Review*, 5 April 1966, 304.

11. Rusher, *Rise of the Right*, 201.

12. Staff Memo to Javits, 17 April 1967, Box 20, Folder "1968 Campaign (2)," Javits Papers.

13. Richard Witkin, "Nixon Will Speak at Javits Dinner," *New York Times*, 30 November 1967, 41.

14. Richard Witkin, "Tribute to Javits Draws 3,000 Here," *New York Times*, 12 December 1967, 1.

15. Clayton Knowles, "Conservatives 'Startled' by Nixon Backing Javits," *New York Times*, 15 December 1967, 34.

16. Phillips to Buckley, 13 March 1967, Box 45, Folder "Phillips, Kevin," Buckley Papers.

17. "Javits Going," *National Review Bulletin*, 28 March 1967, 5.

18. Neal Freeman to Buckley, (memo), 24 March 1967, Box 43, Folder "Freeman, Neal," Buckley Papers.

19. Judis, *William F. Buckley, Jr*, 310–11.

20. Buckley to Neal Freeman, 2 May 1967, Box 43, Folder "Freeman, Neal," Buckley Papers.

21. Buckley to Mahoney, 21 March 1967, Box 43, Folder "Conservative Party of New York," Buckley Papers.

22. Mahoney to Buckley, 4 April 1967, Series 10, Box 2, Folder 4, Conservative Party Papers.

23. Clayton Knowles, "Group Formed to Draft Buckley to Oppose Javits in '68 Primary," *New York Times*, 4 September 1967, 16.

24. Clayton Knowles, "Buckley Rejects Race with Javits," *New York Times*, 5 September 1967, 28.

25. McDonnell, "History of the Conservative Party,"183–84.

26. Dan Mahoney to William Buckley, (memo), 30 January 1968, Box 52, Folder "Mahoney, J. D," Buckley Papers.

27. James F. Clarity, "Conservative Bid Linked to Miller," *New York Times*, 10 March 1968, 3.

28. "Wanted Legitimate Republican," (public notices), *New York Times*, 3 March 1968, 91.

29. Mahoney to James Buckley, 12 March 1968, Box 52, Folder "Mahoney, J. D," Buckley Papers.

30. Buckley Opening Statement, Series 7, Box 3, Folder 107, Conservative Party Papers.

31. Unsigned Memo, Box 20, Folder "1968 Campaign (2)," Javits Papers.

32. Richard Aurelio to Javits, (memo), 2 April 1968, Box 19, Folder "1968 Campaign (6)," Javits Papers.

33. Javits to "Fellow New Yorker," 11 June 1968, Box 18, Folder "1968 Campaign (3)," Javits Papers.

34. Aurelio to Javits, (memo), 21 June 1968, Box 19, Folder "1968 Campaign (6)," Javits Papers.

35. Richard L. Madden, "Javits Camp Tries to Lure Dissident Democrats into Supporting Senator's Race," *New York Times*, 11 July 1968, 23.

36. M. Stanton Evans, "Nelson Rockefeller: 'Reluctant' Candidate," *Human Events*, 27 April 1968, 7a.

37. Nitsche, "History of the Conservative Party," 62.

38. Mahoney to John Ashbrook, et al., (memo), 11 March 1968, Box 48, Folder "Buckley, J. L.–Senate Race," Buckley Papers.

39. M. Stanton Evans, "Nelson Rockefeller: 'Reluctant' Candidate," *Human Events*, 27 April 1968, 5a.

40. Mahoney, *Actions Speak Louder*, 347.

41. McDonnell, "History of the Conservative Party," 127.

42. James Griffin to Mrs. Michael Maduras, Jr., 20 September 1968, Series 2, Box 6, Folder 45, Conservative Party Papers.

43. George J. Marlin, *Fighting the Good Fight: A History of the New York Conservative Party* (South Bend, Ind.: St. Augustine's Press, 2002), 143–44.

44. Charles E. Goodell, Oral History Collection of Former Members of Congress, Library of Congress, Washington, D.C., 35.

45. J. Daniel Mahoney to James Buckley, et al., (memo), 16 July 1968, Box 48, Folder "Buckley, J. L.–Senate Race," Buckley Papers.

46. Buckley, (press release), 17 July 1968, Series 10, Box 1, Folder 4, Conservative Party Papers.

47. Richard Aurelio to Javits, 26 July [1968], Box 18, Folder "1968 Campaign (3)," Javits Papers.

48. Wells to Javits, (memo), 28 July 1968, Record Group 15, Series 35, Subseries 1, Box 3, Folder 57, Rockefeller Papers.

49. Javits to Charles Schoeneck, Jr. and Robert Douglass, 12 August 1968, Box 18, Folder "1968 Campaign (3)," Javits Papers.

50. Will Lissner, "Jackie Robinson Splits with G.O.P. over Nixon Choice," *New York Times*, 12 August 1968, 1.

51. Wells to Rockefeller, (memo), 19 August 1968, Record Group 15, Series 35, Subseries 1, Box 3, Folder 57, Rockefeller Papers.

52. Ibid.

53. James F. Clarity, "Nixon Pact Asked by Conservatives," *New York Times*, 17 August 1968, 12.

54. Thomas P. Ronan, "One Slate Pushed by Conservatives," *New York Times*, 21 August 1968, 32.

55. Wells to Rockefeller, (memo), 19 August 1968, Record Group 15, Series 35, Subseries 1, Box 3, Folder 57, Rockefeller Papers.

56. Rockefeller, (handwritten notes), Record Group 15, Series 35, Subseries 1, Box 3, Folder 57, Nelson A. Rockefeller Papers.

57. James F. Clarity, "Governor and Javits Tell Nixon They Oppose Conservative Plan," *New York Times*, 22 August 1968, 27.

58. Nixon and Rockefeller, (joint statement), 21 August 1968, Record Group 15, Series 35, Subseries 1, Box 3, Folder 57, Rockefeller Papers.

59. William Buckley spoke about the campaign while interviewing Jacob Javits on *Firing Line* in 1969. See *Firing Line* Transcript, September 1969, Box 453, Folder 172, 16–19, Buckley Papers.

60. Buckley to Nancy Reagan, 27 August 1968, Box 53, Folder "Reagan," Buckley Papers.

61. Mahoney to Members of the Republican State Committee, 28 August 1968, Box 103, Folder "JLB Senatorial Campaign," Liebman Papers.

62. Clayton Knowles, "Nixon Approves Conservative Bid," *New York Times*, 29 August 1968, 28.

63. Clayton Knowles, "Nixon Denies Backing Conservative Party on Joint Electors," *New York Times*, 30 August 1968, 8.

64. Editorial, "The G.O.P. Electors," *New York Times*, 4 September 1968, 46.

65. Conservative Party News Release, 4 September 1968, Box 85, Folder "Conservative Party," Liebman Papers.

66. Editorial, "The G.O.P Stands Firm," *New York Times*, 6 September 1968, 42.

67. "Javits Knifes Nixon," *Human Events*, 14 September 1968, 579.

68. Maurice Carroll, "Conservatives Won't Run Rival Nixon Elector Slate," *New York Times*, 9 September 1968, 1.

69. Ibid.

70. Rockefeller to Nixon, (telegram), 8 October 1968, Record Group 15, Series 35, Subseries 1, Box 3, Folder 57, Rockefeller Papers.

71. Rowland Evans and Robert Novak, "Accord with Conservative Party May Cost Nixon New York State," *Washington Post*, 30 October 1968, A25.

72. Editorial, ". . . and Conservatives' Sacrifice," *New York Times*, 10 September 1968, 46.

73. Javits, (speech transcript), 14 October 1968, Box 42, Folder "10/16/68," Javits Papers.

74. "Agnew Ridicules a 3-Way Debate," *New York Times*, 15 October 1968, 34.

75. Michael Clendenin, "Agnew: Disorder is Top Danger," *New York Daily News*, 15 October 1968, 5.

76. "New York: RFK's Successor," *Newsweek*, 16 September 1968, 36.

77. Editorial, "The Conservatives' Gain . . ." *New York Times*, 10 September 1968, 46.

78. Goodell, Oral History, 31–32.

79. "SSK" to Javits, et al., (memo), 8 July 1968, Box 18, Folder "1968 Campaign (3)," Javits Papers.

80. Liebman to "All Concerned," (memo), 21 March 1968, Box 15, Folder "Conservative Party (1965)," White Papers, Ashbrook Center.

81. Richard Aurelio to Jacob Javits, (memo), Box 184, Charles E. Goodell Papers, Rare Books and Manuscripts, New York Public Library.

82. Maurice Carroll, "3 in Senate Race Find Foraging for Funds is a Big Part of Game," *New York Times*, 12 August 1968, 25.

83. Buckley to Organizing Committee, (memo), 14 October 1968, Box 103, Folder "Republicans for Buckley," Liebman Papers.

84. Buckley Press Release, 22 October 1968, Series 10, Box 1, Folder 7, Conservative Party Papers.

85. "Buckley on L.I., Attacks Javits," *New York Times*, 31 October 1968, 33.

86. Luce and Rusher, (telegram), 10 September 1968, Box 103, Folder "JLB Senatorial Campaign," Liebman Papers.

87. James Buckley to Alisa Mellon Bruce, 20 November 1968, Reel 21, Rusher Papers.

88. Advertisement, *Syracuse Herald Journal*, 1 November 1968, 13; *Syracuse Post Standard*, 2 November 1968, 11; *Rochester Democrat and Chronicle*, 4 November 1968, 8B.

89. O'Doherty to Rusher, 11 November 1968, Reel 23, Rusher Papers.

90. Buckley, (*Newsmakers* transcript), 6 October 1968, Series 10, Box 1, Folder 3, Conservative Party Papers.

91. "Buckley on L.I., Attacks Javits," *New York Times*, 31 October 1968, 33.

92. Edward C. Burks, "9 Upstate Chiefs Challenge Javits," *New York Times*, 25 October 1968, 21.

93. Advertisement, *New York Times*, 28 October 1968, 50.

94. Dick Weston to Nancy Shuker, (memo), 5 September 1968, Box 22, Folder 1968 Campaign (6)," Javits Papers.

95. Javits, (speech transcript), 29 October 1968 Box 25, Folder "1968 Press Releases," Javits Papers.

96. Hampton to Griffin, 28 September 1968, Series 7, Box 11, Folder 40, Conservative Party Papers.

97. Griffin to Hampton, 1 October 1968, Series 7, Box 11, Folder 40, Conservative Party Papers.

98. Sydney H. Schanberg, "Javits Assisted by Liberal Wing," *New York Times*, 7 November 1968, 40.

99. Confidential Memo, 20 May 1970, Box 169, Folder 3, Rusher Papers.

100. Sydney H. Schanberg, "Javits In," *New York Times*, 6 November 1968, 1.

101. James D. Griffin to Conservative-Endorsed Legislators, (memo), 7 March 1968, Series 2, Box 5, Folder 12, Conservative Party Papers.

102. "Albany Curbs State Spending," *The New York State Conservative*, July 1969, 3.

103. Rowland Evans and Robert Novak, "N. Y. Conservative Party Threatened by New Bill," *Washington Post*, 18 December 1968, A21.

104. James Griffin to Paul Adams, 18 November 1968, Series 7, Box 1, Folder 10, Conservative Party Papers.

105. William Rusher to William Buckley, (memo), 11 November 1968, Reel 22, Rusher Papers.

106. Steven V. Roberts, "State G.O.P. Gets Patronage Role," *New York Times*, 15 December 1968, 42.

107. This account is drawn largely from *Will: The Autobiography of* G. *Gordon Liddy* (New York: St. Martin's Press, 1980), 123–24.

108. Jeb Stuart Magruder, *An American Life: One Man's Road to Watergate* (New York: Pocket Books, 1975), 200.

109. R. W. Apple, "Rockefeller Got No Nixon Job Bid," *New York Times*, 28 November 1968, 31.

110. Ogden R. Reid, "Do Republicans Have the Courage to Become the Majority Party?" *Look*, 13 May 1969, 76–78+.

111. Richard Reeves, "Lindsay Declares He Will Run Again for a 'Better City,' " *New York Times*, 19 March 1969, 1.

112. Claiborne Edmunds, Jr. to Aurelio, 13 February 1969, Series 12, Box 226, Folder "Campaign in NYC," Lindsay Papers.

113. Chris McNickle, *To Be Mayor of New York: Ethnic Politics in the City* (New York: Columbia University Press, 1993), 224.

114. Kevin P. Phillips, "John V. Lindsay's Electorate," Box 310, Folder 152, Buckley Papers.

115. Anthony Proisendorf, "Conservatives Consider Primary Fight," *New York Post*, 4 December 1968, 6.

116. 1969 Mayoralty Race, (memo), 21 March 1969, Series 7, Box 3, Folder 70, Conservative Party Papers.

117. Richard Reeves, "Here Comes the Next Mayor," *New York Times*, 2 November 1969, sec. VI, p. 25.

118. Gloria Steinem, "Nelson Rockefeller: The Sound of One Hand Clapping," *New York*, 11 August 1969, 26.

119. Rusher to May Preston Davie, Box 27, Folder 7, 11 April 1969, Rusher Papers.

120. Mahoney to ACU Board of Directors, (memo), 24 April 1969, Box 133, Folder 1, Rusher Papers.

121. James Buckley to Rusher, 26 May 1969, Box 169, Folder 11, Rusher Papers.

122. "For the Record," *National Review*, 3 June 1969, 514.

123. Editorial, "The Governor's Silence," *New York Times*, 23 May 1969, 46.

124. Ken Cole to Peter Flanigan et al., (memo), 28 April 1969, White House Subject Files [WHSF], White House Central Files [WHCF], Confidential Files, Box 39, Folder "LG/A-Z," Richard M. Nixon Presidential Materials, National Archives, College Park, Maryland.

125. Peter Flanigan to Ken Cole, (memo), 14 May 1969, WHSF, WHCF, Confidential Files, Box 39, Folder "LG/A-Z," Nixon Presidential Materials.

126. Harry Dent to Nixon, (memo), 20 June 1969, WHSF, Staff Members and Office Files [SMOF], President's Office Files: President's Handwriting, Box 2, Folder "June 1969," Nixon Presidential Materials.

127. Joseph Kraft, "The Nixon Administration View of Lindsay," *New York*, 29 September 1969, 8–9.

128. Harvey Aronson, "The Man Who Manages the Mayor," *New York*, 9 June 1969, 37–40.

129. Aurelio to Lindsay, (memo), 24 May 1969, Series 12, Box 226, Folder "Campaign in NYC," Lindsay Papers.

130. John Lindsay, (news release), 18 June 1969, Box 137, Folder "Post-Primary Statement," Lindsay Papers.

131. Editorial, "Marchi for the Republicans," *New York Times*, 18 June 1969, 46.

132. William E. Farrell, "Minority Parties Gain Major Role," *New York Times*, 19 June 1969, 37.

133. Goldwater to Buckley, 21 June 1969, Box 61, Folder "Goldwater," Buckley Papers.

134. Cannato, *Ungovernable City*, 412.

135. Buchanan to Nixon, (memo), 20 June 1969, WHSF, SMOF, President's Office Files: President's Handwriting, Box 2, Folder "June 1969," Nixon Presidential Materials.

136. Javits to William Nelson, 25 July 1969, Box 22, Folder "Lindsay Campaign 1969," Javits Papers.

137. Wells to Rockefeller, 23 June 1969, Record Group 15, Series 35, Subseries 1, Box 4, Folder 73, Rockefeller Papers.

138. Rockefeller to Wells, 24 June 1969, Record Group 15, Series 35, Subseries 1, Box 4, Folder 73, Rockefeller Papers.

139. Alexander Butterfield to John Ehrlichman, (memo), 1 July 1969, WHSF, WHCF, Confidential Files, Box 39, Folder "LG/A–Z," Nixon Presidential Materials.

140. Harry Dent to John Ehrlichman, (memo), 8 July 1969, WHSF, WHCF, Confidential Files, Box 39, Folder "LG/A–Z," Nixon Presidential Materials.

141. Tod Hullin to John Ehrlichman, (memo), 15 July 1969, WHSF, WHCF, Confidential Files, Box 39, Folder "LG/A–Z," Nixon Presidential Materials.

142. Goldwater to Buckley, 21 June 1969, Box 56, Folder 5, Buckley Papers.

143. Rusher to Buckley, (memo), 7 July 1969, Box 72, Folder 9, Goldwater Papers.

144. Rusher to Ashbrook, 25 July 1969, Box 7, Folder 10, Rusher Papers.

145. Richard Reeves, "Lindsay Is Planning 'Urban Party,' " *New York Times*, 19 June 1969, 1.

146. Advertisement, *New York Daily News*, 28 October 1969, 17.

147. Paul L. Montgomery, "Lindsay Says War Is City Issue," *New York Times*, 27 September 1969, 1.

148. Haldeman, (diary entry), Haldeman Diaries, Box 1, Folder "Volume 3," Nixon Presidential Materials.

149. Dent to Nixon, (memo), 17 October 1969, WHSF, SMOF, President's Office Files: President's Handwriting, Box 2, Folder "June 1969," Nixon Presidential Materials.

150. Haldeman, (diary entry), Haldeman Diaries, Box 1, Folder "Volume 3," Nixon Presidential Materials.

CHAPTER 5

1. Initially, Goodell faced the possibility of having to run in 1969 and 1970. A suit in federal court contended that the governor's appointment power was temporary and so required an election in 1969 for a one-year term, followed, in 1970, by another election for a full Senate term. The federal courts, however, upheld the Governor's power to make an appointment for the remainder of the term. As a result, Goodell did not face an election until 1970.

2. Paul Hoffman, "The End of Liberalism," *The Nation*, 12 April 1971, 457.

3. Rockefeller to Goodell, 18 December 1968; Goodell to Rockefeller, 31 December 1968, Box 299, Goodell Papers.

4. Confidential Memo, 8 June 1969, Box 297, Goodell Papers.

5. W. H. St. Thomas to Goodell, 23 June 1969, Box 177, Goodell Papers.

6. Confidential Memo, 8 June 1969, Box 297, Goodell Papers.

7. Roland Powell, "New Image of Goodell," *Buffalo Evening News*, 19 July 1969, B4.

8. Bill Kovach, "Goodell Calls for Pullout," *New York Times*, 26 September 1969, 1.

9. Donald Campbell to Goodell, 29 October 1969, Box 177, Goodell Papers.

10. John Bouck to Beverly Rodman, 6 January 1970, Box 176, Goodell Papers.

11. *Firing Line*, (transcript), Box 452, Folder 158, Buckley Papers.

12. "News & Views: A Word for Goodell" *Commonweal*, 17 October 1969, 60.

13. Clayton Knowles, "Speno Will Seek Goodell's Seat," *New York Times*, 6 November 1969, 1.

14. "Marchi Confident of Defeating Goodell," *New York Times*, 27 November 1969, 48.

15. Marchi to Vincent Palmer, Jr., 2 December 1969, Box 177, Goodell Papers.

16. Harry Dent to Richard Nixon, (memo), WHSF, SMOF, Harry Dent, Box 9, Folder "New Political Group," Nixon Presidential Materials.

17. Martin Tolchin, "Goodell Praised by Rockefeller," *New York Times*, 7 November 1969, 1.

18. David Jaffe, 5–6, John Marchi Oral History Project, College of Staten Island.

19. Memo to Goodell, 21 March 1970, Box 174, Goodell Papers.

20. Thomas Poster, "Goodell Enters Race Formally," *New York Daily News*, 25 March 1970, 24.

21. Judis, *William F. Buckley, Jr.*, 311–12.

22. Buckley, *If Men Were Angels*, 20.

23. Ibid.

24. Rusher, *The Rise of the Right*, 235.

25. Mahoney to William Buckley, (memo), 22 May 1970, Box 132, Folder 7, Buckley Papers.

26. Mahoney to James Buckley, (memo), 3 July 1970, Series 7, Box 4, Folder 4, Conservative Party Papers.

27. Ibid.

28. Buckley to Mahoney, (memo), 8 July 1970, Box 169, Folder 3, Rusher Papers.

29. Arthur Finkelstein, "Quick Thoughts," Box 169, Folder 4, Rusher Papers.

30. McDonnell, "History of the Conservative Party," 164.

31. Lynn Dane to Arnold Steinberg, 18 August 1970, Series 7, Box 4, Folder 3, Conservative Party Papers.

32. "200 at Conservative Picnic Upstate Attend Buckley," *New York Times*, 13 September 1970, 46.

33. Gus Bliven, "The Political Front," *Syracuse Post Standard*, 11 September 1970, 6.

34. Thomas Poster, "Marchi Urges GOP: Bolt & Back Buckley," *New York Daily News*, 30 April 1970, 48.

35. "5 New York G.O.P. Men at Buckley Reception," *New York Times*, 3 June 1970, 30.

36. Kevin P. Phillips, (press release), 2 August 1970, Box 169, Folder 1, Rusher Papers.

37. Goldwater to William Buckley, 30 June 1970, Box 72, Folder 9, Goldwater Papers.

38. Goldwater to William Buckley, 28 July 1970, Box 72, Folder 9, Goldwater Papers.

39. William Buckley to James Buckley, 3 August 1970, Box 293, Folder 2, Buckley Papers.

40. Buckley to Tower, 29 July 1970, Box 169, Folder 3, Rusher Papers.

41. Fred J. Cook, "Hard-Hats: The Rampaging Patriots," *The Nation*, 15 June 1970, 717.

42. Rusher to James Buckley, (memo), 30 June 1970, Box 169, Folder 3, Rusher Papers.

43. Neal Freeman to Arnold Steinberg, (memo), Box 169, Folder 5, Rusher Papers.

44. "Republicans and Hard Hats," *National Review*, 22 September 1970, 989.

45. Richard Reeves, "Goodell Shifts Campaign Chief," *New York Times*, 3 September 1970, 27.

46. Alfonso A. Narvaez, "Goodell Booed by 'Hard Hats,' " *New York Times*, 31 October 1970, 1.

47. Richard Reeves, "Buckley Serious Contender," *New York Times*, 12 July 1970, sec. 4, 6.

48. Anthony Lewis, "The Charm of Mr. Buckley," *New York Times*, 25 July 1970, 22.

49. Goodell's Schedule, 29 June 1970, Box 177, Goodell Papers.

50. Marilyn Russell to Brian Conboy, (memo), 2 July 1970, Box 176, Goodell Papers.

51. Goodell to Harrington, 28 March 1970, Box 178, Goodell Papers.

52. Everett Johnson, "Is Charles Goodell a Republican?" 27 June 1970, Series 7, Box 1, Folder 12, Conservative Party Papers.

53. Fred L. Zimmerman, "'Instant Liberalism' Helps Sen. Goodell," *Wall Street Journal*, 13 May 1970, 20.

54. Memo on Brian Conboy-George Hinman conversation, 31 December 1969, Box 174, Goodell Papers.

55. Goodell to Rockefeller, 27 October 1969, Box 182, Goodell Papers.

56. Fred L. Zimmerman, " 'Instant Liberalism' Helps Sen. Goodell," *Wall Street Journal*, 13 May 1970, 20.

57. Buckley letter; Kissinger to Buckley, 26 February 1970, Box 274, Folder 2399, Buckley Papers.

58. William F. Buckley Jr., "Nelson Rockefeller, RIP," *National Review*, 2 March 1979, 319.

59. Goodell Press Release, 19 August 1970, Box 197, Goodell Papers.

60. Letter to GOP County Chairman, Box 174, Goodell Papers.

61. Robert Sweet to Andrew Wolfe, 26 August 1970, Box 177, Goodell Papers.

62. Richard Gambetta to Brian Conboy, 15 September 1970, Box 177, Goodell Papers.

63. Conboy to Goodell, (memo), 8 July 1970, Box 297, Goodell Papers.

64. Conboy to Tanya Melich, (memo), 27 July 1970, Box 188, Goodell Papers.

65. Diane Abelman to Wesley McCune, 26 August 1970, Box 184, Goodell Papers.

66. Handwritten Notes, Box 184, Goodell Papers.

67. Goodell Press Release, 19 August 1970, Box 177, Goodell Papers.

68. Transcript of Staff Meeting, 21 August 1970, Record Group 15, Series 16, Subseries 5, Box 22, Folder 346, Rockefeller Papers.

69. McDonnell, "History of the Conservative Party," 161.

70. Clayton Knowles, "Buckley Predicts Splits on Ballots," *New York Times*, 10 September 1970, 57.

71. WABC-TV Interview with James Buckley, (transcript), 12 July 1970, Goodell Papers.

72. Buckley to Mitchell, 8 October 1970, Box 205, Folder 1592, Buckley Papers.

73. W. H. Von Dreele, "The Alternative is Goldberg," *National Review*, 20 October 1970, 1098.

74. Murray Chotiner to Peter Flanigan, (memo), 27 April 1970, WHCF, Subject Files-States, Box 12, Folder 2, Nixon Presidential Materials.

75. William E. Farrell, "Congressional Race: Reapportioned 9-County 28th District Favors the G.O.P. Candidate," *New York Times*, 2 October 1970, 21.

76. Frank Murano et al. to Fellow Conservatives, Series 7, Box 6, Folder 24, Conservative Party Papers.

77. H. R. Haldeman, "General Political Notes," 13 July 1970, WHSF, SMOF-Haldeman, Box 292, Folder Political (1970 Election) (1)," Nixon Presidential Materials.

78. Harry S. Dent, Memorandum for the President, 3 December 1969, WHSF, SMOF-Dent, Box 9, Folder "New Political Group," Nixon Presidential Materials.

79. Dan T. Carter, *The Politics of Rage: George Wallace, the Origins of the New Conservatism and the Transformation of American Politics* (New York: Simon & Schuster, 1995), 380.

80. WCBS-TV "Newsmakers," (transcript), 12 April 1970, Box 176, Goodell Papers.

81. F. Clifton White and William J. Gill, *Why Reagan Won: A Narrative History of the Conservative Movement, 1964–1981* (Chicago, Regnery Gateway, 1981), 144.

82. Harry Dent to Hugh Sloan, (memo), 9 January 1970, WHCF, Subject Files-States, Box 12, Folder 2, Nixon Presidential Materials.

83. Flanigan to Buchanan, (memo), 9 April 1970, WHCF, Subject Files-States, Box 12, Folder 2, Nixon Presidential Materials.

84. Smant, *Principles and Heresies*, 286–87.

85. "Chotiner, Long a Nixon Aide, Cautious on G.O.P Prospects," *New York Times*, 11 June 1970, 29.

86. Harry S. Dent, *The Prodigal South Returns to Power* (New York: John Wiley & Sons, 1978), 190.

87. Arthur Finkelstein, "Quick Thoughts," Box 169, Folder 4, Rusher Papers.

88. Buckley to Nixon, 16 July 1970, Box 19, Folder "CP," Buckley Papers.

89. William F. Buckley Jr., "Nixon and the New York Election," *National Review*, 28 July 1970, 805.

90. H. R. Haldeman, (diary entry), 23 June 1970, Box 1, Folder 5, Nixon Presidential Materials.

91. H. R. Haldeman, (diary entry), 5 August 1970, Box 1, Folder 6, Nixon Presidential Materials.

92. Alan D. Monroe to Larry Higby, 26 August 1970, WHSF, SMOF-Haldeman, Box 374, Folder "New York State Study," Nixon Presidential Materials.

93. H. R. Haldeman, (diary entry), 27 August 1970, Box 1, Folder 6, Nixon Presidential Materials.

94. William Safire, *Before the Fall: An Inside View of the Pre-Watergate White House* (New York: Belmont Tower), 318.

95. Rowland Evans Jr. and Robert D. Novak, *Nixon in the White House: The Frustration of Power* (New York: Viking, 1972), 321–22.

96. Robert B. Semple, "A 'Neutral' Nixon Is Reported to Favor Buckley Over Goodell," *New York Times*, 24 September 1970, 1.

97. H. R. Haldeman, (diary entry), 15 September 1970, Box 1, Folder 6, Nixon Presidential Materials.

98. H. R. Haldeman, (meeting notes), 15 September 1970, WHSF, SMOF-Haldeman, Box 42, Folder "July–Sept. 1970," Nixon Presidential Materials.

99. Patrick Buchanan to H. R. Haldeman, (memo), 18 September 1970, WHSF, SMOF-Haldeman, Box 64, Folder "Sept. 1970," Nixon Presidential Materials.

100. Colson to Haldeman, (memo), 21 September 1970, WHSF, SMOF-Colson, Box 1, Folder "1969–1970," Nixon Presidential Materials.

101. Richard Mathieu, "Rocky Declares His Firm Support for Sen. Goodell," *New York Daily News*, 16 September 1970, 5.

102. Cole to Haldeman, (memo), 24 September 1970, WHSF, WHCF, Confidential Files, Box 61, Folder "CF-ST," Nixon Presidential Materials.

103. Haldeman to Cole, (handwritten note), 24 September 1970, WHSF, SMOF-Colson, Box 1, Folder "1969–1970," Nixon Presidential Materials.

104. J. Anthony Lukas, *Nightmare: The Underside of the Nixon Years* (New York: Viking, 1976), 110–11.

105. H. R. Haldeman, (diary entry), 27 August 1970, Box 1, Folder 6, Nixon Presidential Materials.

106. Interview of John Mulcahy, 13 November 1970, Box 1, Watergate Special Prosecution Force Papers, National Archives, College Park, Maryland.

107. Judah Best to Roger Whitten, 14 December 1973, Box 7, Watergate Special Prosecution Force Papers.

108. List of Buckley Committees, Box 2, Watergate Special Prosecution Force.

109. Anthony Summer with Robbyn Swan, *The Arrogance of Power: The Secret World of Richard Nixon* (New York: Penguin, 2000), 284.

110. Evans and. Novak, *Nixon in the White House*, 332.

111. Frank Lynn, "Agnew Opposes Goodell," *New York Times*, 1 October 1970, 1.

112. Gene Spagnoli, "Spiro Bucks for Buckley," *New York Daily News*, 6 October 1970, 5.

113. "Agnew Attacks Goodell Anew," *New York Times*, 9 October 1970, 49.

114. "Miss Jorgensen Asks Agnew for an Apology," *New York Times*, 11 October 1970, 46; "Agnew Won't Apologize for Jorgensen Remark," *New York Times*, 13 October 1970, 38.

115. Lawrence Higby, (handwritten notes), 9 October 1970, WHSF, SMOF-Haldeman, Box 52, Folder "Oct.–Dec. 1970," Nixon Presidential Materials.

116. "Let's Find Out," (WCBS radio transcript), 13 September 1970, Box 175, Goodell Papers.

117. "Goodell Rips 'Rightist' Aides," *Newsday*, 25 September 1970, 3.

118. Frank Lynn, "Goodell Appeals to Nixon to Cool Agnew Rhetoric," *New York Times*, 3 October 1970, 1.

119. Transcript of "News Closeup," WNEW, 18 October 1970, Box 184, Goodell Papers.

120. Goodell, Oral History Collection of Former Members of Congress, 45–46.

121. Lawrence Higby, (handwritten notes), WHSF, SMOF-Haldeman, Box 52, Folder "Oct.–Dec. 1970," Nixon Presidential Materials.

122. H. R. Haldeman, (diary entry), 12 October 1970, Box 1, Folder 6, Nixon Presidential Materials.

123. "Nixon Comments of Buckley," *New York Times*, 13 October 1970, 38.

124. H. R. Haldeman, (diary entry), 12 October 1970, Box 1, Folder 6, Nixon Presidential Materials.

125. Alfonso A. Navarez, "White House Tip Given Buckley on Nixon's Visit," *New York Times*, 14 October 1970, 35.

126. H. R. Haldeman, (diary entry), 16 October 1970, Box 1, Folder 6, Nixon Presidential Materials.

127. Draft Statement by Ron Ziegler, WHSF, SMOF-Haldeman, Box 42, Folder "Oct.–Dec. 1970," Nixon Presidential Materials.

128. H. R. Haldeman, (diary entry), 19 October 1970, Box 1, Folder 6, Nixon Presidential Materials.

129. H. R. Haldeman, (diary entry), 26 October 1970, Box 1, Folder 6, Nixon Presidential Materials.

130. Karl E. Meyer, "Rocky as Peacemaker," *Washington Post*, 7 October 1970, A21.

131. "New York: Rock of Ages," *Newsweek*, 19 October 1970, 43–44.

132. Rose Mary Woods to Nixon, note, 22 October 1970, WHCF, Subject Files-States. Box 13, Folder "New York," Nixon Presidential Materials.

133. Francis X. Clines, "Goodell Assails Nixon 'Intervention' in Race," *New York Times*, 23 October 1970, 48.

134. H. R. Haldeman, (diary entry), 25 October 1970, Box 1, Folder 6, Nixon Presidential Materials.

135. Marlin, *Fighting the Good Fight*, 175.

136. "Senator Goodell Address," (transcript), 25 October 1970, Box 183, Goodell Papers.

137. C. Gerald Fraser, "Governor Spurns Goodell Aid Plea," *New York Times*, 29 October 1970, 1.

138. Arthur Schlesinger, Jr., (letter to the editor), *New York Times*, 30 October 1970, 40.

139. H. R. Haldeman, (diary entry), 1 November 1970, Box 1, Folder 6, Nixon Presidential Materials.

140. H. R. Haldeman, (diary entry), 3 November 1970, Box 1, Folder 6, Nixon Presidential Materials.

141. Editorial, "Senator-Elect Buckley," *New York Times*, 4 November 1970, 46.

142. Maurice Carroll, "Rockefeller and Buckley Elected," *New York Times*, 4 November 1970, 1.

143. Walter J. Hickel, *Who Owns America?* (Englewood Cliffs, N.J.: Prentice-Hall, 1971), 274.

144. Goldwater to James Buckley, (telegram), Box 72, Folder 9, 4 November 1970, Goldwater Papers.

145. McCandlish Phillips, " 'Evangelizing' by Buckley Pays Off at Last," *New York Times*, 5 November 1970, 71.

146. Frank Lynn, "Aftermath of Defeat," *New York Times*, 4 November 1970, 18.

147. Richard Reeves, "Realignment in State Likely," *New York Times*, 4 November 1970, 1.

148. Mahoney to Adams, 10 December 1970, Series 7, Box 1, Folder 13, Conservative Party Papers.

149. Theodore H. White, *The Making of the President 1972* (New York: Atheneum, 1973), 49–50.

150. H. R. Haldeman, (diary entry), 9 November 1970, Box 1, Folder 6, Nixon Presidential Materials.

151. H. R. Haldeman, (handwritten notes), 9 November 1970, WHCF, Subject Files-States, Box 12, Folder 2, Nixon Presidential Materials.

152. Dan Mahoney to John Mitchell, 22 December 1970, Box 192, Folder 14, Buckley Papers.

153. *New York Daily News*, 9 November 1970, 1.

154. Robert B. Semple, Jr., "President Meets 3 State Leaders of Conservatives," *New York Times*, 9 November 1970, 1.

CHAPTER 6

1. Charles Lam Markmann, *The Buckleys: A Family Examined* (New York: William Morrow, 1973), 306–7.

2. Richard L. Madden, "Buckley Doubts Seating Problem," *New York Times*, 2 December 1970, 27.

3. White to Buckley, (memo), 12 January 1971, Box 30, Folder "Buckley-Before Election," White Papers, Ashbrook Center.

4. O'Doherty to Buckley, (memo), Box 117, Folder "CP," 14 January 1971, Buckley Papers.

5. Rowland Evans and Robert Novak, "Buckley's Tag," *New York Post*, 16 January 1971, 29.

6. Paul [Leventhal] to Javits, (memo), 23 November 1970, Box 297, Goodell Papers.

7. Richard L. Madden, "Javits May Oppose a G.O.P. Label for Buckley," *New York Times*, 25 November 1970, 29.

8. Editorial, "A Prodigal Son," *New York Times*, 28 November 1970, 26.

9. Javits Press Release, 19 January 1971, Box 48, Folder "1/19/71," Javits Papers.

10. "State Party Chiefs Urged Javits to Accept Buckley," *New York Times*, 29 January 1971, 12.

11. Lindsay Press Release, 19 October 1970, Box 256, Folder "Correspondence," Lindsay Papers.

12. Rowland Evans and Robert Novak, "Man Without a Party," *Washington Post*, 11 March 1971, A19.

13. Steven R. Weisman, "Lindsay's Switch Draws Regrets," *New York Times*, 13 August 1971, 26.

14. "The Lindsay Switch: Hell No, We Won't Go," *Ripon Forum*, September 1971, 3.

15. Editorial, "Lindsay the Democrat," *New York Times*, 12 August 1971, 32.

16. Robinson to Rockefeller, 2 May 1972, Series P-Ann C. Whitman-Politics, Record Group 4, Box 16, Folder 392, Rockefeller Papers.

17. Rockefeller to Robinson, 8 May 1972, Record Group 4, Series P-Ann C. Whitman-Politics, Box 16, Folder 392, Rockefeller Papers.

18. Richard L. Madden, "Rep. Reid Quitting G.O.P." *New York Times*, 22 March 1972, 1.

19. Transcript of Rockefeller's telephone conversation, 20 March 1972, Record Group 15, Series 16, Subseries 5, Box 30, Folder 487, Rockefeller Papers.

20. "Reid, GOP Vet, to Do a Lindsay," *New York Daily News*, 22 March 1972, 5.

21. Editorial, "Democrat Reid," *New York Times*, 22 March 1972, 46.

22. Mahoney to "Key Party Supporters," (memo), Series 2, Box 4, Folder 12, Conservative Party Papers.

23. "New York: Hire an Expert," *Ripon Forum*, July 1971, 5.

24. Haldeman to Patrick Buchanan and Huston, (memo), 30 November 1970, WHSF, SMOF-Haldeman, Box 293, Folder "Political," Nixon Presidential Materials.

25. Huston to Haldeman, (memo), 1 December 1970, WHSF, SMOF-Haldeman, Box 293, Folder "Political," Nixon Presidential Materials.

26. Judis, *William F. Buckley, Jr.*, 328–42.

27. Ibid., 329.

28. William Rusher News Release, 29 July 1971, Box 168, Folder 1, Rusher Papers.

29. Buckley News Release, 1 August 1971, Box 13, Folder 5, Rusher Papers.

30. Thomas Poster, "Conservatives Launch Bid to Keep Spiro," *New York Daily News*, 29 July 1971, 28.

31. H. R. Haldeman, *The Haldeman Diaries: Inside the Nixon White House* (New York: Putnam, 1994), 332.

32. Mahoney to "The Manhattan Twelve," (memo), Box 193, Folder 1432, Buckley Papers.

33. Robert Sherrill, "Why John Ashbrook is Running for President of the United States," *Saturday Review*, 3 June 1972, 16.

34. "Ashbrook Weighs Race in Primary," *New York Times*, 8 December 1971, 30.

35. Buchanan to John Mitchell and H. R. Haldeman, (memo), 3 December 1971, WHSF, SMOF-Buchanan, Box 3, Folder "Haldeman 1971," Nixon Presidential Materials.

36. Buchanan to Charles Colson, (memo), 10 December 1971, WHSF, SMOF-Buchanan, Box 1, Folder "December 1971," Nixon Presidential Materials.

37. Rusher, (file memo), 21 December 1971, Box 274, Folder 2491, Buckley Papers.

38. Marjorie Hunter, "Ashbrook Enters Presidency Race," *New York Times*, 30 December 1971, 1.

39. Conservative Party News Release, 9 December 1971, Series 7, Box 4, Folder 68, Conservative Party Papers.

40. Conservative Party Press Release, 25 January 1972, Series 2, Box 7, Folder 8, Conservative Party Papers.

41. Marlin, *Fighting the Good Fight*, 193.

42. Mahoney to Ashbrook, 28 January 1972, Box 168, Folder 6, Rusher Papers.

43. Betti Logan, "LI Backing for Ashbrook," *Newsday*, 21 January 1971, 10.

44. Buckley to Flanigan, 3 January 1972, Box 168, Folder 6, Rusher Papers.

45. Flanigan to Buckley, 6 January 1972, Box 274, Folder 2402, Buckley Papers.

46. Buckley to Flanigan, 16 February 1972, Box 274, Folder 2402, Buckley Papers.

47. Cato, "Letter from Washington," *National Review*, 21 January 1972, 16; William F. Buckley Jr., "Nixon and the Conservative," *Los Angeles Times*, 26 March 1972, sec. 8, p. 7.

48. Frank Lynn, "Agnew Role Vital to Conservatives," *New York Times*, 19 July 1972, 21.

49. Conservative Party Executive Committee Meeting, (notes), 30 August 1972, Series 2, Box 6, Folder 51, Conservative Party Papers.

50. David Keene to Agnew, (memo), 10 October 1972, Series 3, Subseries 111, Box 3, Spiro T. Agnew Papers, Archive and Manuscripts, McKeldin Library, University of Maryland, College Park, Maryland.

51. "Nod to Conservatives," 26 May 1972, *Wall Street Journal*, 1.

52. Thomas P. Ronan, "Nixon Is Stalled on 2d Ballot Line," *New York Times*, 27 August 1972, 35.

53. Buckley to Haldeman, (transcribed message), 28 August 1972, Box 117, Folder "Conservative Party," Buckley Papers.

54. David Keene to Agnew, (memo), 10 October 1972, Series 3, Subseries 111, Box 3, Agnew Papers.

55. David Keene to Agnew, (memo), 10 October 1972, Series 3, Subseries 111, Box 3, Agnew Papers.

56. Frank Lynn, "G.O.P. Tactics Keep Agnew in Shadow," *New York Times*, 13 October 1972, 21.

57. Thomas Ronan, "Agnew Appeals for Moral Order," *New York Times*, 14 October 1972, 16.

58. Rockefeller to Daniel M. Mahoney, 12 November 1973, Record Group 15, Series 35, Subseries 3, Box 11, Folder 144A, Rockefeller Papers.

59. Mahoney to Edward J. Kiernan, 28 December 1972, Series 1, Box 1, Conservative Party Papers.

60. Maurice Carroll, "Buckley Scores Agnew Position," *New York Times*, 16 October 1973, 37.

61. Frank Lynn, "Rockefeller Said To Be Available," *New York Times*, 11 October 1973, 33.

62. Francis X. Clines, "Governor Pushed for Vice President," *New York Times*, 12 October 1973, 25.

63. Nixon, *RN*, 926.

64. Rockefeller to Robinson, 8 May 1972, Series P-Ann C. Whitman-Politics, Record Group 4, Box 16, Folder 392, Rockefeller Papers.

65. Editorial, "Governor Bows Out . . . ," *New York Times*, 12 December 1973, 46.

66. Conservative Party News Release, 11 December 1973, Series 3, Box 1, Folder 2, Conservative Party Papers.

67. Reich, *Life of Nelson A. Rockefeller*, 713.

68. McDonnell, "A History of the Conservative Party," 164.

69. Paul Hoffman, "New York's GOP: The End of Liberalism," *The Nation*, 12 April 1971, 457–61.

70. Thomas Ronan, "Rockefeller to Go on Stump," *New York Times*, 6 February 1974, 28.

71. Frank Lynn, "Money Game a Puzzle to Campaigners," *New York Times*, 6 May 1974, 25.

72. Michael Kramer, "Early Warnings," *New York*, 5 February 1973, 8.

73. David Keene to Agnew, (memo), 28 October 1973, Series III, Subseries 11, Box 4, Folder "Suffolk County, New York, 3/29/73," Agnew Papers.

74. Mahoney to Buckley, (memo), 6 April 1971, Box 192, Folder 14, Buckley Papers.

75. John Corry, "The Metamorphosis of Roy Cohn," *New York Times*, 12 May 1974, 36.

76. Nicholas von Hoffman, *Citizen Cohn*, (New York: Doubleday, 1988), 361.

77. Ibid.

78. Francis X. Clines, "State G.O.P. to Fill Out Slate," *New York Times*, 7 June 1974, 39.

79. Kieran O'Doherty, (television editorial reply transcript), 30 August 1973, Series 2, Box 4, Folder 12, Conservative Party Papers.

80. 1974 Fund to Defeat Jacob Javits Letter, 24 November 1973, Series 1, Box 1, Folder 8, Conservative Party Papers

81. Maltese to "Friend," Series 7, Box 2, Folder 15, Conservative Party Papers.

82. Americans for Responsibility and Patriotism Letter, Series 7, Box 2, Folder 15, Conservative Party Papers.

83. James L. Buckley, "The Benefit of Doubt," *New York Times*, 9 May 1973, 47.

84. F. Clifton White with Jerome Tuccille, *Politics as a Noble Calling* (Ottawa, Ill.: Jameson Books, 1995), 198.

85. Mahoney to Henry Shephard, 15 April 1974, Series 1, Box 2, Conservative Party Papers.

86. Buckley, (news release), 19 March 1974, Series 10, Box 1, Folder 11, Conservative Party Papers.

87. Clark to Buckley, 19 March 1974, Box 1, Folder "Clark, George," James L. Buckley Papers, St. John's University, Queens, New York.

88. "Heat Lightning on the Right," *Newsweek*, 1 April 1974, 24.

89. Mahoney, (news release), 19 March 1974, Series 1, Box 2, Conservative Party Papers.

90. Gerald R. Ford, *A Time to Heal: The Autobiography of Gerald R. Ford* (New York: Berkley, 1979), 139.

91. Ibid., 140.

92. Paul Gottfried and Thomas Fleming, *The Conservative Movement* (Boston; Twayne, 1988), 79.

93. William F. Buckley Jr., "Notes on Rocky," *New York Post*, 24 August 1974, 24.

94. Conservative Party News Release, 17 September 1974, Series 2, Box 6, Folder 54, Conservative Party Papers.

95. Mahoney to Daniel Oliver, 14 August 1974, Box 192, Folder 1419, Buckley Papers.

96. Rusher to Helms, 7 October 1974, Box 39, Folder 1; Rusher to Lott, 7 October 1974, Box 55, Folder 5, Rusher Papers.

97. Helms to Rusher, 18 October 1974, Box 39, Folder 1, Rusher Papers.

98. "Bullard Leaves Governor Race," *New York Times*, 29 June 1974, 19.

99. Les Brown, "Anti-Abortion Spot Seen as Editorial," *New York Times*, 9 November 1974, 63.

100. David Wimer to Alexander Haig, (memo), 13 August 1974, WHCF Name File—O'Doherty, Box 2368, Gerald R. Ford Presidential Papers, Gerald R. Ford Presidential Library, Ann Arbor, Michigan.

101. Valeo to Mahoney, 10 July 1974, Series 7, Box 4, Folder 28, Conservative Party Papers.

102. Bolan to Valeo, 19 July 1974, Series 7, Box 4, Folder 28, Conservative Party Papers.

103. Calle Fricke and Thomas Bolan to "Fellow Conservative," 9 September 1974, Series 2, Box 1, Folder 6, Conservative Party Papers.

104. Mahoney and Raymond Thek to "Fellow Conservative," 29 October 1974, Series 2, Box 4, Folder 14, Conservative Party Papers.

105. Sam Roberts, "Report a Wilson-Conservative Deal," *New York Daily News*, 8 October 1974, 3.

106. Blair to "Conservative Party Chairmen," Series 2, Box 6, Folder 53, Conservative Party Papers.

107. "The Blair-Bullard Tapes," New York Republicans State Committee Background Paper, Series 5, Subseries 2, Box 40, Folder "New York Republican State Committee," Javits Papers.

108. Mahoney to Bullard, 4 November 1974, Box 192, Folder 1423, Buckley Papers.

109. "The Blair-Bullard Tapes," New York Republicans State Committee Background Paper, Series 5, Subseries 2, Box 40, Folder "New York Republican State Committee," Javits Papers.

CHAPTER 7

1. R. W. Apple Jr., "Conservative Party Taken Up with Talk of 3rd Party," *New York Times*, 15 February 1975, 13.

2. Rusher, *The Rise of the Right*, 271–72.

3. Lou Cannon and David S. Broder, "Conservative Unit to Watch Ford, Rocky," *Washington Post*, 4 March 1975, A1.

4. Jack March, (handwritten notes), 6 February 1975, WHCF Name File—Buckley, James, Box 434, Ford Library.

5. William Kendall, (schedule), 4 March 1975, WHCF Name File—Buckley, James, Box 434, Ford Library.

6. William Kendall to Ford, (briefing paper), 15 April 1975, WHCF File, Box 2, Ford Library.

7. Buckley to Ford, 4 June 1975, Box 1, Folder "Ford, Gerald R.," James Buckley Papers.

8. John Robert Greene, *The Presidency of Gerald R. Ford* (Lawrence: University Press of Kansas, 1995), 95.

9. Jim Cavanaugh to Jim Cannon, (memo), 29 October 1975, Box 12, Folder "Vice President, 10/75–11/75," James M. Cannon Papers, Ford Library.

10. "Ford Asks '76 Aid of Conservatives," *New York Times*, 16 February 1975, 1.

11. Ford, *A Time to Heal*, 318.

12. Greene, *The Presidency of Gerald R. Ford*, 159–60.

13. Frank Lynn, "Conservative Party to Support Reagan over Ford for 1976," *New York Times*, 21 October 1975, 1.

14. "Out of the West," *New Yorker*, 3 November 1975, 7–8.

15. Frank Lynn, "Reagan Mapping Big Effort Here, *New York Times*, 3 December 1975, 29.

16. Maurice Carroll, "Three Slates of Reagan Delegates Here Are Trying to Get on Primary Ballot," *New York Times*, 25 January 1976, 32.

17. Frank Lynn, "Peyser to Challenge Buckley Next Year," *New York Times*, 2 December 1975, 1.

18. Martin Tolchin, "Peyser Will Run for Buckley Seat," *New York Times*, 7 March 1975, 39.

19. Frank Lynn, "Rockefeller Aide Assails Peyser," *New York Times*, 14 March 1975, 36.

20. John T. McQuiston, "State G.O.P. to Send Delegates to Convention 'Uncommitted,'" *New York Times*, 12 November 1975, 23.

21. Jack Calkins to Robert T. Hartmann, (memo), 27 June 1975, Box 2, Folder "New York," John T. Calkins Files, Ford Library.

22. Leo to Bo [Calloway], (memo), 9 December 1975, Box 2, Folder "New York," John T. Calkins Files, Ford Library.

23. Peyser to Ford, 26 April 1976, Box 33, Folder 3, Peter Peyser, Special Collections and Archives, Case Library, Colgate University, Hamilton, New York.

24. Peyser to Rockefeller, 8 June 1976, Record Group 26, Series C, Box 179, Folder "Political Affairs," Rockefeller Papers.

25. Rockefeller to Peyser, 9 June 1976, Record Group 26, Series C, Box 179, Folder "Political Affairs," Rockefeller Papers.

26. Frank Lynn, "Buckley Reports a Presidency Bid," *New York Times*, 11 August 1976, 13.

27. Andy Logan, "Around City Hall: Parables," *New York Times*, 27 September 1976, 61.

28. Jules Witcover, *Marathon: The Pursuit of the Presidency, 1972–1976* (New York: Viking, 1977), 481.

29. Tom Wicker, "The Paradox in Kansas City," *New York Times*, 13 August 1976, 23.

30. Editorial, "The Buckley Caper," *New York Times*, 13 August 1976, 22.

31. Bellport to Mahoney, 20 August 1976, Series 2, Box 2, Folder 18, Conservative Party Papers.

32. David Bullard to Mahoney, 13 January 1976, Series 7, Box 10, Folder 19, Conservative Party Papers.

33. Review of Major New York Races, (briefing paper), Box 22, Folder "1976/10/12–13," David Gergen Files, Ford Library.

34. Glenn Fowler, "Conservative Party, by 140 to 137, Stops Bid to Keep Ford Off Ticket," *New York Times*, 19 September 1976, 34.

35. Gene Spagnoli, "Javits Nixes Buckley," *New York Daily News*, 21 September 1976, 3.

36. Jack McCarthy to Barbara Keating, 5 October 1976, Series 7, Box 12, Folder 31, Conservative Party Papers.

37. Martin Tolchin, "Rockefeller Offers Aid to Buckley and Praises Conservative Party," *New York Times*, 22 September 1976, 80.

38. Conservative Party Bulletin, 25 August 1976, Series 2, Box 2, Folder 19, Conservative Party Papers.

39. William Safire, "Demo Demosthenes," *New York Times*, 7 October 1976, 51.

40. Howard A. Scarrow, *Parties, Elections, and Representation in the State of New York* (New York: New York University Press, 1983), 71.

41. Amanda Harris, "Suffolk GOP Backs Conservative," *Newsday*, 10 June 1978, 11.

42. Frank Lynn, "The Power of the Conservatives," *New York Times*, 2 July 1978, sec 21, p. 18.

43. Serphin Maltese, (memo), 30 October 1978, Series 2, Box 6, Folder 20, Conservative Party Papers.

44. John T. McQuiston, "L.I. Conservative a First in House," *New York Times*, 9 November 1978, sec. 2, p. 8.

45. "Nelson Aldrich Rockefeller: Remembered," *New York Times*, 28 January 1979, sec. 4, p. 2.

46. Jacob K. Javits with Rafael Steinberg, *Javits: The Autobiography of a Public Man* (Boston: Houghton Mifflin, 1981), 500.

47. Mahoney to "Fellow Conservative," Series 7, Box 5, Folder 30, Conservative Party Papers.

48. Joyce Purnick, "Senate 1980: See How They Run," *New York*, 19 March 1979, 45.

49. "James Buckley Shifts Registration to Connecticut," *New York Times*, 24 August 1979, sec. 2, p. 5.

50. Frank Lynn, "D'Amato's Senate Bid Puzzles Politicians," *New York Times*, 16 December 1979, sec. 21, p. 1.

51. Wilfred Dalton to "Conservative Leader," 20 September 1979, Series 5, Subseries 2, Box 34, Folder "Jim Eagan, 1980," Javits Papers.

52. Caputo to James O'Doherty, 27 February 1980, Series 2, Box 6, Folder 40, Conservative Party Papers.

53. Alfonse D'Amato, *Power, Pasta and Politics: The World According to Senator Al D'Amato* (New York: Hyperion, 1995), 79–80.

54. Margaret Dillon to Serphin Maltese, 19 December 1979, Series 7, Box 5, Folder 65, Conservative Party Papers.

55. D'Amato, *Power, Pasta and Politics*, 84.

56. Frank Lynn, "Conservatives to Endorse Republican for Javits Seat," *New York Times*, 14 January 1980, sec. 2, p. 3.

57. Javits with Steinberg, *Javits*, 493.

58. Frank Lynn, "D'Amato Gains Support for Race to Unseat Javits," *New York Times*, 27 February 1980, sec. 2, p. 3.

59. John P. McGloine to Conservative State Committeeman, 15 February 1980; Dale Nicholson to "Fellow Conservative," 19 February 1980, Series 2, Box 6, Folder 40, Conservative Party Papers.

60. Dick Zander, "D'Amato Gets Conservative Nod," *Newsday*, 23 March 1980, 5.

61. Ibid.

62. D'Amato, *Power, Pasta and Politics*, 85.

63. Frank Lynn, "This Time, Javits Has No Shortage of Rivals," *New York Times*, 15 June 1980, sec. 4, p. 6.

64. John D. Caemmerer et al. to "Fellow Republican," Series 5, Subseries 1, Box 36, Folder "1980 Campaign (2)," Javits Papers.

65. Warren Anderson and James Emery to "State Committee Member," 11 June 1980; Howard Baker et al. to "Republican State Committee Members," 11 June 1980, Series 5, Subseries 1, Box 36, Folder "Campaign 1980 (1)," Javits Papers.

66. Martin Tolchin, "The Last Hurrah of Jack Javits," *New York Times*, 25 May 1980, sec. 6, p. 48.

67. Maurice Carroll, "Reagan's Aides Veto New York Proposal," *New York Times*, 13 December 1979, 21.

68. Frank Lynn, "Reagan Is Given G.O.P. Backing from New York," *New York Times*, 25 April 1980, 18.

69. Mahoney to Sears, 17 October 1979, Series 2, Box 4, Folder 11, Conservative Party Papers.

70. Murray Kempton, "Reagan Treads Cautiously on Friendly Turf," *New York Post*, 16 January 1980, 25.

71. Tully Plesser to Javits, (memo), 28 August 1980, Series 5, Subseries 1, Box 37, Folder "1980 Campaign (3)," Javits Papers.

72. Maurice Carroll, "Javits, in Ads, Concedes His Illness and Age Are Issues in the Primary," *New York Times*, 16 August 1980, 23.

73. Maurice Carroll, "Two Candidates Report Spending Over $1 Million," *New York Times*, 29 August 1980, sec. 2, p. 4.

74. Frank Lynn, "D'Amato TV Ads Begin and Draw 'Misstatement' Charge from Javits," *New York Times*, 11 June 1980, sec. 2, p. 8.

75. D'Amato to "Republican," Series 5, Subseries 2, Box 33, Folder "Alfonse D'Amato, 1980," Javits Papers.

76. D'Amato to Javits, 7 July 1980, Series 5, Subseries 2, Box 33, Folder "Alfonse D'Amato, 1980," Javits Papers.

77. D'Amato to "Republican Leader," 24 July 1980, Series 5, Subseries 2, Box 33, Folder "Alfonse D'Amato, 1980," Javits Papers.

78. Maurice Carroll, "D'Amato's TV Commercial Makes a Point of Javits's Health and Age," *New York Times*, 8 August 1980, sec. 2, p. 3.

79. Mahoney Memo, 13 August 1980, Series 7, Box 7, Folder 12, Conservative Party Papers.

80. Serphin Maltese to "New York City Conservative Party Leaders," 15 August 1980, Series 2, Box 4, Folder 6, Conservative Party Papers.

81. Mahoney to "Key Supporters," (memo), 29 August 1980, Series 2, Box 2, Folder 23, Conservative Party Papers.

82. Javits with Steinberg, *Javits*, 503–4.

83. Frank Lynn, "Javits Abandons His Effort to Gain a Second Line on New York Ballot," *New York Times*, 17 September 1980, sec. 2, p. 11.

84. Ripon Society Press Release, 9 October 1980, Series 1, Subseries 2, Box 5, Folder "Campaign Materials, 1980," Javits Papers.

85. Frank Lynn, "Javits Voices 'Frustration' at Efforts to Sway Voters," *New York Times*, 22 October 1980, sec. 2, p. 1.

86. Ibid.

87. Reagan Letter, September 1980, Box 134, Folder "Conservative Party Meeting #3," Liebman Papers.

88. Bush to "Friend," September 1980, Box 134, Folder "Conservative Party Meeting #3," Liebman Papers.

89. King County Conservative Party News Release, 12 January 1980, Series 7, Box 6, Folder 10, Conservative Party Papers.

90. Clyde Haberman, "Javits, as Long Career Ends, Decides Against Concession," *New York Times*, 5 November 1980, 20.

91. Reagan to Mahoney, 7 May 1981, Series 1, Box 52, Folder "J. Daniel Mahoney, 1976–1982," Buckley Papers.

92. Maurice Carroll, "Will Success Spoil New York's Conservative Party?" *New York Times*, 22 February 1981, 38.

93. Theodore H. White, *The Making of the President 1968* (New York; Atheneum, 1969), 409.

BIBLIOGRAPHY

MANUSCRIPT COLLECTIONS

Spiro T. Agnew Papers, Archive and Manuscripts, Hornbake Library, University of Maryland, College Park, Maryland.

Warren Anderson Papers, George Arents Research Library for Special Collections, Bird Library, Syracuse University, Syracuse, New York.

James L. Buckley Papers, University Archives, St. Augustine Hall, St. John's University, Jamaica, New York.

William F. Buckley Jr. Papers, Manuscripts and Archives, Sterling Memorial Library, Yale University, New Haven, Connecticut.

Barber Conable Papers, Rare and Manuscript Collections, Carl A. Kroch Library, Cornell University, Ithaca, New York.

Conservative Party, Inc. Papers, George Arents Research Library for Special Collections, Bird Library, Syracuse University, Syracuse, New York.

Conservative Party of New York State Papers, M. E. Grenander Department of Special Collections and Archives, University Library, University at Albany, Albany, New York.

Ralph De Toledano Papers, Hoover Institution Archives, Stanford University, Palo Alto, California.

Gerald R. Ford Presidential Papers, Gerald R. Ford Presidential Library, Ann Arbor, Michigan.

Barry M. Goldwater Papers, Arizona Historical Foundation, Hayden Library, Arizona State University, Tempe, Arizona.

Charles E. Goodell, Oral History Collection of Former Members of Congress, Manuscript Division, Library of Congress, Washington, D.C.

Charles E. Goodell Papers, Rare Books and Manuscripts, New York Public Library, New York, New York.

Group Research Collection, Rare Book & Manuscript Library, Butler Library, Columbia University, New York, New York.

Jacob K. Javits Collection, Special Collections Department, Frank Melville Jr Memorial Library, State University of New York at Stony Brook, Stony Brook, New York.

Kenneth B. Keating Papers, Department of Rare Books and Special Collections, Rush Rhees Library, University of Rochester, Rochester, New York.

Marvin Liebman Papers, Hoover Institution Archives, Stanford University, Palo Alto, California.

John V. Lindsay Papers, Manuscripts and Archives, Sterling Memorial Library, Yale University, New Haven, Connecticut.

Clare Booth Luce Papers, Manuscript Division, Library of Congress, Washington, D.C.

John Marchi Oral History Project, College of Staten Island, Staten Island, New York.

Tanya M. Melich Papers, M. E. Grenander Department of Special Collections and Archives, University of Albany Library, Albany, New York.

William E. Miller Papers, Rare and Manuscript Collections, Carl A. Kroch Library, Cornell University, Ithaca, New York.

Raymond Moley Papers, Hoover Institution Archives, Stanford University, Palo Alto, California.

Graham T. Molitor Papers, Rockefeller Archive Center, North Tarrytown, New York.

Richard M. Nixon Presidential Materials, National Archives, College Park, Maryland.

Joseph E. Persico Papers, M. E. Grenander Department of Manuscripts and Special Collections, University Library, University at Albany, Albany, New York.

Peter A. Peyser Papers, Special Collections and Archives, Case Library, Colgate University, Hamilton, New York.

John R. Pillion Papers, Rare and Manuscript Collections, Carl A. Kroch Library, Cornell University, Ithaca, New York.

Ogden R. Reid Papers, Manuscripts and Archives, Sterling Memorial Library, Yale University, New Haven, Connecticut.

Ripon Society Papers, Rare and Manuscript Collections, Carl A. Kroch Library, Cornell University, Ithaca, New York.

Nelson A. Rockefeller Papers, Rockefeller Archives Center, North Tarrytown, New York.

William A. Rusher Papers, Manuscript Division, Library of Congress, Washington, D.C.

Katherine St. George Papers, Rare and Manuscript Collections, Carl A. Kroch Library, Cornell University, Ithaca, New York.

Watergate Special Prosecution Force Papers, National Archives, College Park, Maryland.

F. Clifton White Papers, Archival Collections, John M. Ashbrook Center for Public Affairs, Ashland University, Ashland, Ohio.

F. Clifton White Papers, Rare and Manuscript Collections, Carl A. Kroch Library, Cornell University, Ithaca, New York.

NEWSPAPERS AND MAGAZINES

Albany Times-Union
Arizona Republic
Atlantic
Battle Line
Buffalo Evening News
Chicago Tribune

Christian Science Monitor
Commonweal
Empire State Report
Human Events
Life
Look
Los Angeles Times
Manchester Union Leader
The Nation
National Review
National Review Bulletin
New Guard
The New Republic
New York
New York Daily News
New York Herald Tribune
New York Post
New York State Conservative
New York Times
New York World Journal Tribune
New York World-Telegram and Sun
New Yorker
Newsday
Newsweek
The Reporter
Ripon Forum
Rochester Democrat and Chronicle
Saturday Review
Syracuse Herald Journal
Syracuse Post-Standard
Ticonderoga Sentinel
Time
U.S. News & World Report
Wall Street Journal
Washington Post

BOOKS, DISSERTATIONS, AND JOURNAL ARTICLES

Alan, Mohamed B. *Third Party Politics in the United States: A Select Bibliography*. Monticello, Ill.: Vance Bibliographies, 1989.

Alexander, Joe. *Nelson Rockefeller: A Biography*. New York: Harper & Row, 1960.

Alitt, Patrick. *Catholic Intellectuals and Conservative Politics in America, 1950–1985*. Ithaca: Cornell University Press, 1993.

Allen, Gary. *The Rockefeller File*. Seal Beach, Cal.: '76 Press, 1976.

Amy, Douglas J. "Entrenching the Two-Party System: The Supreme Court's Fusion Decision." In *The U.S. Supreme Court and the Electoral Process*, edited by Douglas K. Ryden, 142–63. Washington, D.C.: Georgetown University Press, 2000.

Andrew, John A. *The Other Side of the Sixties: Young Americans for Freedom and the Rise of Conservative Politics*. New Brunswick, N.J.: Rutgers University Press, 1997.

Argersinger, Peter H. " 'A Place on the Ballot': Fusion Politics and Antifusion Laws." *American Historical Review* 85 (April 1980): 287–306.

Arian, Asher, Arthur S. Goldberg, John H. Mollenkopf, and Edward T. Rogowsky. *Changing New York Politics*. New York: Routledge, 1991.

Bachrack, Stanley D. *The Committee of One Million: "China Lobby" Politics, 1953–1971*. New York: Columbia University Press, 1976.

Bell, Daniel, ed. *The Radical Right*. Garden City, N.Y. Anchor, 1964.

Benjamin, Gerald and T. Norman Hurd, ed. *Rockfeller in Retrospect: The Governor's New York Legacy*. Albany: Nelson A. Rockefeller Institute of Government, 1984.

Berman, William C. *America's Right Turn: From Nixon to Bush*. New York: Hill & Wang, 1994.

Beyle, Thad L., ed. *State Government: CQ's Guide to Current Issues and Activities*. Washington, D.C.: Congressional Quarterly, 1990.

Bibby, John F. and L. Sandy Maisel. *Two Parties—or More? The American Party System*. Boulder, Col.: Westview Press, 1998.

Bjerre-Poulsen, Niels. "Organizing the American Right, 1945–1964." Ph.D. diss., University of California, Santa Barbara, 1993.

———. *Right Face: Organizing the American Conservative Movement, 1945–65*. Copenhagen: Museum Tusculanum Press/University of Copenhagen, 2002.

Blumenthal, Sidney. *The Rise of the Counter-Establishment: From Conservative Ideology to Political Power*. New York: Times Books, 1986.

Brennan, Mary L. *Turning Right in the Sixties: The Conservative Capture of the GOP*. Chapel Hill: University of North Carolina Press, 1995.

Brock, David. *Blinded by the Right: The Conscience of an Ex-Conservative*. New York: Crown, 2002.

Brooke, Edward William. *The Challenge of Change: Crisis in Our Two-Party System*. Boston: Little Brown, 1966.

Buckley, James L. *If Men Were Angels: A View From the Senate*. New York: Putnam, 1975.

Buckley, William F. Jr. *Up from Liberalism*, 2nd ed. New York: Bantam Books, 1965.

———. *The Unmaking of a Mayor*. New Rochelle, N.Y.: Arlington House, 1966.

———. *Cruising Speed: A Documentary*. New York: Bantam Books, 1972.

Cannato, Vincent J. "John Lindsay's New York and the Crisis of Liberalism." Ph.D. diss., Columbia University, 1998.

———. *The Ungovernable City: John Lindsay and the Struggle to Save New York*. New York: Basic Books, 2001.

Capell, Frank A. *The Strange Case of Jacob Javits*. Zarephath, N.J.: The Herald of Freedom, 1966.

Caro, Robert A. *The Power Broker: Robert Moses and the Fall of New York*. New York: Vintage Books, 1975.

Carter, Barbara. *The Road to City Hall: How John Lindsay Became Mayor*. Englewood Cliffs, N. J.: Prentice-Hall, 1967.

Carter, Dan T. *The Politics of Rage: George Wallace, the Origins of the New Conservatism, and the Transformation of American Politics*. New York: Simon & Schuster, 1995.

Chafe, William H. *Never Stop Running: The Struggle to Save American Liberalism*. New York: Basic Books, 1993.

Citron, Casper. *John V. Lindsay and the Silk Stocking Story*. New York: Fleet, 1965.

Collier, Peter and David Horowitz. *The Rockefellers: An American Dynasty*. New York: Holt, Rinehart & Winston, 1976.

Connery, Robert H. and Gerald Benjamin. *Governing New York State: The Rockefeller Years*. New York: Academy of Political Science, 1974.

Connery, Robert and Gerald Benjamin. *Governor Rockefeller of New York: Executive Power in the Statehouse*. Ithaca: Cornell University Press, 1979.

"The Constitutionality of Anti-Fusion and Party-Raiding Statutes." *Columbia Law Review* 47 (1947): 1207–14.

Cooney, John. *The American Pope: The Life and Times of Francis Cardinal Spellman*. New York: Times Books, 1984.

Costikyan, Edward. "Politics in New York City: A Memoir of the Post-War Years." *New York History* 74 (October 1993): 415–34.

Courtney, Kent. *Nelson Rockefeller's Candidacy*. New Orleans: Conservative Society of America, 1963.

Cowan, Ruth. "The New York Civilian Review Board Referendum of November 1966: A Case Study of Mass Politics." Ph.D. diss., New York University, 1970.

Crawford, Alan. *Thunder on the Right: The "New Right" and the Politics of Resentment*. New York: Pantheon Books, 1980.

Dallek, Matthew. *The Right Moment: Ronald Reagan's First Victory and the Decisive Turning Point in American Politics*. New York: Free Press, 2001.

D'Amato, Alfonse. *Power, Pasta and Politics: The World According to Senator Al D'Amato*. New York: Hyperion, 1995.

Dean, John, III. *Blind Ambition: The White House Years*. New York: Simon & Schuster, 1976.

Dent, Harry S. *The Prodigal South Returns to Power*. New York: John Wiley, 1977.

———. *Cover-Up: The Watergate in All of Us*. San Bernardino, Cal.: Here's Life Publishers, 1986.

Desmond, James. *Nelson Rockefeller: A Political Biography*. New York: Macmillan, 1964.

de Toledano, Ralph. *The Winning Side: The Case for Goldwater Republicanism*. New York: Putnam, 1963.

Disch, Lisa Jane. *The Tyranny of the Two-Party System*. New York: Columbia University Press, 2002.

Donovan, Robert J. *The Future of the Republican Party*. New York: New American Library, 1964.

Dudman, Richard. *Men of the Far Right*. New York: Pyramid Books, 1962.

Dullea, Henrik. "Charter Revision in the Empire State: The Politics of New York's 1967 Constitutional Convention." Ph.D. diss., Syracuse University, 1982.

Dwyre, Diana and Jeffrey M. Stonecash. "Where's the Party?: Changing State Party Organizations." *American Politics Quarterly* 20 (July 1992): 326–44.

Edsall, Thomas Byrne and Mary D. Edsall. *Chain Reaction: The Impact of Race, Rights, and Taxes on American Politics.* New York: W. W. Norton, 1991.

Edwards, Lee. *The Conservative Revolution: The Movement that Remade America.* New York: Free Press, 1999.

Ellis, David M. *New York: State and City.* Ithaca: Cornell University Press, 1979.

Ellis, David M., James A. Frost, Harold C. Syrett, and Harrry J. Carmen. *A History of New York State.* Ithaca, N.Y.: Cornell University Press, 1967.

Ellsworth, Ralph E. and Sarah M. Harris. *The American Right Wing.* Washington: Public Affairs Press, 1962.

Epstein, Benjamin R., and Arnold Forster. *The Radical Right: Report on the John Birch Society and Its Allies.* New York: Random House, 1967.

Evans, M. Stanton. *The Liberal Establishment.* New York: Devin-Adair, 1965.

———. *The Future of Conservatism: From Taft to Reagan and Beyond.* New York: Holt, Rinehart & Winston, 1968.

Evans, Rowland and Robert D. Novak. *Nixon in the White House.* New York: Viking, 1972.

Feigert, Frank B. "Conservatism, Populism and Social Change." *American Behavioral Scientist* 17 (1973): 272–78.

Filler, Louis. *Dictionary of American Conservatism.* New York: Philosophical Library, 1987.

Firestone, Bernard J. and Alexej Ugrinsky, eds. *Gerald R. Ford and the Politics of Post-Watergate America.* Westport, Conn.: Greenwood, 1993.

Ford, Gerald R. *A Time to Heal: The Autobiography of Gerald R. Ford.* New York: Harper & Row, 1979.

Forster, Arnold and Benjamin R. Epstein. *Danger on the Right.* New York: Random House, 1964.

Freedman, Samuel G. *The Inheritance: How Three Families and the American Political Majority Moved from Left to Right.* New York: Touchstone, 1998.

Freeman, Joshua B. "Hard-hats: Construction Workers, Manliness, and the 1970 Pro-War Demonstrators." *Journal of Social History* 26 (Summer 1993): 725–44.

"Fusion Candidacies, Disaggregation, and Freedom of Association." *Harvard Law Review* 109 (April 1996): 1302–17.

Gaertner, Samuel Lawrence. "A Telephoned Call for Help: Does the Race of the Victim Affect the Helping Behavior of New York City Liberal and Conservative Party Members." Ph.D. diss., City University of New York, 1970.

Gargan, John J. "Conservative Success in Liberal New York." In *The Future of Political Parties,* edited by Louis Maisel and Paul Sacks, 165–92. Beverly Hills, Cal.: Sage, 1975.

Gavin, William F. *Street Corner Conservative.* New Rochelle, N. Y.: Arlington House, 1975.

Gervasi, Frank. *The Real Rockefeller: The Story of the Rise, Decline and Resurgence of the Presidential Aspirations of Nelson Rockefeller.* New York: Atheneum, 1964.

Gilder, George F. and Bruce K. Chapman. *The Party that Lost Its Head.* New York: Knopf, 1966.

Gillespie, J. David. *Politics at the Periphery: Third Parties in Two-Party America.* Columbia: University of South Carolina Press, 1993.

Goldner, Robert S. "Minor Party Politics and the Two-Party System. A Case Study: The New York State Conservative Party." Master's thesis, Brown University, 1974.

Goldwater, Barry M. *The Conscience of a Majority*. Englewood Cliffs, N.J.: Prentice-Hall, 1970.

Goldwater, Barry M. with Jack Casserly. *Goldwater*. New York: Doubleday, 1988.

Goret, Mark. "A History of the Bronx Conservative Party." *Bronx County Historical Society Journal* 23 (Spring 1986): 8–12.

Gottfried, Paul, and Thomas Fleming. *The Conservative Movement*. New York: Twayne, 1993.

Greene, John Robert. *The Limits of Power: The Nixon and Ford Administrations*. Bloomington: Indiana University Press, 1992.

———. *The Presidency of Gerald R. Ford*. Lawrence: University Press of Kansas, 1995.

Haldeman, H. R. *The Haldeman Diaries: Inside the Nixon White House*. New York: Putnam, 1994.

Harr, John Ensor and Peter J. Johnson. *The Rockefeller Conscience: An American Family in Public and Private*. New York: Charles Scribner's Sons, 1991.

Hasen, Richard L. "Entrenching the Duopoly: Why the Supreme Court Should Not Allow States to Protect Democrats and Republicans from Political Competition." In *Supreme Court Review 1997*, edited by Dennis J. Hutchinson, David J. Strauss, and Geoffrey R. Tone, 331–71. Chicago: University of Chicago Press, 1998.

Hess, Karl. *In a Cause That Will Triumph: The Goldwater Campaign and the Future of Conservatism*. Garden City, N.Y.: Doubleday, 1967.

Hess, Stephen and David S. Broder. *The Republican Establishment: The Present and Future of the G.O.P.* New York: Harper & Row, 1967.

Hevesi, Alan G. *Legislative Politics in New York State: A Comparative Analysis*. New York: Praeger, 1975.

Hickel, Walter. *Who Owns America?* Englewood Cliffs, N.J.: Prentice Hall, 1971.

Hitchens, Christopher. *The Trial of Henry Kissinger*. London: Verson, 2001.

Hofstadter, Richard. *The Age of Reform: From Bryan to F.D.R.* New York: Knopf, 1956.

———. *The Paranoid Style in American Politics and Other Essays*. New York: Vintage, 1967.

Hodgson, Godfrey. *The World Turned Right Side Up: A History of Conservative Ascendancy in America*. Boston: Houghton Mifflin, 1996.

Huckshorn, Robert J. *Party Leadership in the States*. Amherst: University of Massachusetts Press, 1976.

Huebner, Lee W. and Thomas E. Petri, ed. *The Ripon Papers, 1963–1968*. Washington, D.C.: National Press, 1968.

Janson, Donald and Bernard Eismann. *The Far Right*. New York: McGraw Hill, 1963.

Javits, Jacob K. *Order of Battle: A Republican's Call to Reason*. New York: Atheneum, 1964.

Javits, Jacob K. with Rafael Steinberg. *Javits: The Autobiography of a Public Man*. Boston: Houghton Mifflin, 1981.

Jewell, Malcolm E. and David M. Olson. *Political Parties and Elections in American States*. Homewood, Ill.: Dorsey Press, 1978.

Josephson, Emanuel M. *The Truth about Rockefeller: Public Enemy No. 1*. New York: Chedney Press, 1964.

Joyner, Conrad. *The Republican Dilemma: Conservatism or Progressivism*. Tucson: University of Arizona Press, 1963.

Judis, John. *William F. Buckley Jr.: Patron Saint of the Conservatives*. New York: Simon & Schuster, 1988.

Kelly, David. *James Burnham and the Struggle for the World: A Life*. Wilmington, Del.: ISI Books, 2002.

Kessel, John H. *The Goldwater Coalition: Republican Strategies in 1964*. Indianapolis: Bobbs Merrill, 1968.

Kessner, Thomas. *Fiorello H. LaGuardia and the Making of Modern New York*. New York: McGraw Hill, 1989.

Klatch, Rebecca E. *A Generation Divided: The New Left, the New Right, and the 1960s*. Berkeley: University of California Press, 1999.

Klein, Milton, ed., *The Empire State: A History of New York*. Ithaca: Cornell University Press, 2001.

Kramer, Daniel C. *The Days of Wine and Roses Are Over: Governor Hugh Carey and New York State*. Lanham, Md.: University Press of America, 1997.

Kramer, Michael S. *"I Never Wanted to be Vice-President of Anything!": An Investigative Biography of Nelson Rockefeller*. New York: Basic Books, 1976.

Kruschke, Earl R. *Encyclopedia of Third Parties in the United States*. Santa Barbara, Cal.: ABC-CLIO, 1991.

Lasky, Victor. *Arthur J. Goldberg: The Old and the New*. New Rochelle, N.Y.: Arlington House, 1970.

Liddy, G. Gordon. *Will: The Autobiography of G. Gordon Liddy*. New York: St. Martin's, 1980.

Liebman, Marvin. *Coming Out Conservative: An Autobiography*. San Francisco: Chronicle Books, 1992.

Liebschutz, Sarah F. with Robert W. Bailey, Jeffrey Stonecash, Jane Shapiro Zacek and Joseph F. Zimmerman. *New York Politics & Government: Competition and Compassion*. Lincoln: University of Nebraska Press, 1998.

Lindsay, John V. *Journey into Politics: Some Informational Observations*. New York: Dodd Mead, 1967.

———. *The City*. New York: Norton, 1970.

Lipset, Seymour and Earl Raab. *The Politics of Unreason: Right Wing Extremism in America, 1790–1970*. New York: Harper & Row, 1970.

Lowi, Theodore J. *The End of the Republican Era*. Norman: University of Oklahoma Press, 1995.

Lukas, J. Anthony. *Nightmare: The Underside of the Nixon Years*. New York: Viking, 1976.

Lurie, Leonard. *Senator Pothole: The Unauthorized Biography of Al D'Amato*. New York: Birch Lane Press, 1994.

Magruder, Jeb Stuart. *An American Life: One Man's Road to Watergate*. New York: Pocket Books, 1975.

Mahoney, J. Daniel. *Actions Speak Louder*. New Rochelle, N.Y.: Arlington House, 1969.

Markmann, Charles. *The Buckleys: A Family Examined*. New York: William Morrow, 1973.

Marlin, George J. *Fighting the Good Fight: A History of the New York Conservative Party*. South Bend, Ind.: St. Augustine's Press, 2002.

Mason, Robert. *Richard Nixon and the Quest for a New Majority*. Chapel Hill: University of North Carolina Press, 2004.

Mayhew, David R. *Placing Parties in American Politics: Organization, Electoral Settings, and Government Activity in the Twentieth Century*. Princeton: Princeton University Press, 1986.

Mazmanian, Daniel A. *Third Parties in Presidential Elections*. Washington, D.C.: Brookings Institution, 1970.

McClelland, Peter D. and Alan L. Meyowitz. *Crisis in the Making: The Political Economy of New York State since 1945*. Cambridge: Cambridge University Press, 1981.

McDonnell, Richard H. "A History of the Conservative Party in New York State, 1962–1972." Ph.D. diss., Pennsylvania State University, 1975.

McGirr, Lisa. *Suburban Warriors: The Origins of the New American Right*. Princeton: Princeton University Press, 2001.

McLendon, Winzola. *Martha: The Life of Martha Mitchell*. New York: Random House, 1979.

McNickle, Chris. *To Be Mayor of New York: Ethnic Politics in the City*. New York: Columbia University Press, 1993.

Meehan, William F., III, ed. *William F. Buckley, Jr.: A Bibliography*. Wilmington, Del.: ISI Books, 2002.

Melich, Tanya. *The Republican War against Women: An Insider's Report from Behind the Lines*. New York: Bantam, 1996.

Miner, Brad. *The Concise Conservative Encyclopedia*. New York: Free Press, 1996.

Moley, Raymond. *The Republican Opportunity*. New York: Duell, Sloan and Pearce, 1962.

Morris, Charles R. *The Cost of Good Intentions: New York City and the Liberal Experiment, 1960–1975*. New York: Norton, 1980.

Moscow, Warren. *Politics in the Empire State*. New York: Knopf, 1948.

———. *What Have You Done for Me Lately? The Ins and Outs of New York City Politics*. Englewood Cliffs, N.J.: Prentice-Hall, 1967.

Moser, Charles A. *Promise and Hope: The Ashbrook Presidential Campaign of 1972*. Washington, D.C.: Institute of Government and Politics, 1985.

Munger, Frank J. and Ralph A. Straetz. *New York Politics*. New York: New York University Press, 1960.

Nash, George H. *The Conservative Intellectual Movement in America since 1945*. New York: Basic Books, 1975.

Nitsche, Charles G. "A History of the Conservative Party in New York State." Master's thesis, Niagara University, 1968.

Nixon, Richard M. *RN: The Memoirs of Richard Nixon*. New York: Simon & Schuster, 1990.

———. *Six Crises*. New York Pocket Books, 1962.

Novak, Robert D. *The Agony of the GOP: 1964*. New York: Macmillan, 1965.

Oudes, Bruce, ed. *From the President: Richard Nixon's Secret Files*. New York: Harper & Row, 1989.

Paone, Arthur J. *Conflict of Interest: James L. Buckley in the U.S. Senate*. Brooklyn, N.Y.: Paone, 1976.

Parmet, Herbert S. *George Bush: The Life of a Lone Star Yankee*. New York: Scribner, 1997.

Perlstein, Rick. *Before the Storm: Barry Goldwater and the Unmaking of the American Consensus*. New York: Hill & Wang, 2001.

Perry, James M. *The New Politics: The Expanding Technology of Political Manipulation.* New York: Potter, 1968.

Persico, Joseph E. *The Imperial Rockefeller: A Biography of Nelson A. Rockefeller.* New York: Simon & Schuster, 1982.

———. *Casey: From the OSS to the CIA.* New York: Viking, 1990.

Phillips, Kevin P. *The Emerging Republican Majority.* New Rochelle, N.Y.: Arlington House, 1969.

Pierce, Neal R. *The Megastates of America: People, Politics, and Power in Ten Great States.* New York: Norton, 1972.

Pilat, Oliver Ramsay. *Lindsay's Campaign: A Behind the Scenes Diary.* Boston: Beacon Press, 1968.

Podhoretz, Norman. *Breaking Ranks: A Political Memoir.* New York: Harper & Row, 1979.

Rae, Nicol C. *The Decline and Fall of the Liberal Republicans from 1952 to the Present.* New York: Oxford University Press, 1989.

Rampersand, Arnold. *Jackie Robinson: A Biography.* New York: Knopf, 1997.

Reagan, Ronald W. *A Time for Choosing: The Speeches of Ronald Reagan, 1961–1980.* Chicago: Regnery, 1982.

Reeves, Richard. *President Nixon: Alone in the White House.* New York: Simon & Schuster, 2001.

Reich, Cary. *The Life of Nelson Rockefeller: Worlds to Conquer, 1908–1958.* New York: Doubleday, 1996.

Reichley, A. James. *States in Crisis: Politics in Ten American States.* Chapel Hill: University of North Carolina Press, 1964.

———. *Conservatives in an Age of Change: The Nixon and Ford Administrations.* Washington, D.C.: Brookings Institution, 1981.

Reinhard, David W. *The Republican Right Since 1945.* Lexington: University Press of Kentucky, 1983.

Rockefeller, David. *Memoirs.* New York: Random House, 2002.

Rockwood, D. Stephen, Cecelia Brown, Kenneth Eshleman, and Deborah Shaffer. *American Third Parties Since the Civil War: An Annotated Bibliography.* New York and London: Garland Publishing, 1985.

Rogers, William. *Rockefeller's Follies: An Unauthorized View of Nelson A. Rockefeller.* New York: Stein and Day, 1966.

Rogowsky, Edward T., Louis H. Gold, and David W. Abbott, "Police: The Civilian Review Board Controversy." In *Race and Politics in New York City: Five Studies in Policy Making*, edited by Jewell Bellush and Stephen M. David, 59–97. New York: Praeger, 1971.

Roshwalb, Irving and Leonard Resnicoff. "The Impact of Endorsements and Published Polls on the 1970 New York Senatorial Election." *Public Opinion Quarterly* 35 (Fall 1971): 410–14.

Rusher, William A. *The Making of a New Majority Party.* New York: Sheed and Wand, 1975.

———. *The Rise of the Right.* New York: William Morrow, 1984.

Safire, William. *Before the Fall: An Inside View of the Pre-Watergate White House.* New York: Belmont Tower Books, 1975.

Scarrow, Howard A. *Parties, Elections and Representation in the State of New York.* New York: New York University Press, 1983.

———. "Duverger's Law, Fusion, and the Decline of American 'Third' Parties." *Western Political Quarterly* 39 (December 1986): 634–47.

Schneier, Edward and John Peter Murtagh. *New York Politics: A Tale of Two States*. Armonk, N.Y.: M.E. Sharpe, 2001.

Schoen, Douglas E. *Pat: A Biography of Daniel Patrick Moynihan*. New York: Harper & Row, 1979.

Schoenberger, Robert A. "Conservatism, Personality, and Political Extremism." *American Political Science Review* 62 (September 1968): 868–77.

———, ed. *The American Right Wing: Readings in Political Behavior*. New York: Holt, Rinehart and Winston, 1969.

———. "The New Conservatives: A View from the East" in *The American Right Wing: Readings in Political Behavior*, 280–98. New York: Holt, Rinehart & Winston, 1969.

Schoenwald, Jonathan M. "Vice and Virtue: Extremism and Moderation: The Rise of Modern Conservatism, 1957–1972." Ph.D. diss., Stanford University, 1998

———. *A Time for Choosing: The Rise of Modern American Conservatism*. New York: Oxford University Press, 2001.

Sifry, Micah. *Spoiling for a Fight: Third Party Politics in America*. New York: Routledge, 2002.

Simon, William. *A Time for Truth*. New York: McGraw Hill Books, 1978.

———. *A Time for Action*. Berkeley Books, 1980.

Smallwood, Frank. *The Other Candidates: Third Parties in Presidential Elections*. Hanover, N.H.: University Press of New England, 1983.

Smant, Kevin J. *Principles and Heresies: Frank S. Meyer and the Shaping of the American Conservative Movement*. Wilmington, Del.: ISI Books, 2002.

Smith, Richard Norton. *Thomas E. Dewey and His Times*. New York: Simon & Schuster, 1982.

Solara, Ferdinand V. *Key Influences in the American Right: A Guide to Sixty Leading Conservative, Libertarian, and Anti-Communist Organizations and Publications in the United States*. LEA Communications, 1974.

Spitzer, Robert J. "A New Political Party is Born: Single-Issue Advocacy and the Election Law in New York State." *National Civic Review* 73: (July/August 1984): 321–28.

———. *The Right to Life Movement and Third Party Politics*. Westport, Conn.: Greenwood, 1987.

———. "Multi-Party Politics in New York: A Cure for the Political System." In *State Government: CQ's Guide to Current Issues and Activities, 1989–1990*, edited by Thad Beyle, 46–50. Washington, D.C.: Congressional Quarterly, 1990.

———. "Third Parties in New York State." In *Governing New York State*, 3rd ed., edited by Jeffrey M. Stonecash, John Kenneth White, and Peter W. Colby, 103–16. Albany: State University of New York Press, 1994.

———. "Multi-Party Politics in New York." In *Multi-Party Politics in America*, edited by Paul S. Hernson and John C. Green, 125–37. Lanham, Md.: Rowman & Littlefield, 1997.

Stonecash, Jeffrey M. "Working at the Margins: Campaign Finance and Party Strategy in New York Assembly Elections." *Legislative Studies Quarterly* 13 (November 1988): 477–93.

———. "Political Cleavage in Gubernatorial and Legislative Elections: Party Competition in New York, 1970–1982." *Western Political Quarterly* 42 (March 1989): 69–81.

———. "Campaign Finance in New York Senate Elections." *Legislative Studies Quarterly* 15 (May 1990): 247–62.

———. " 'Split' Constituencies and the Impact of Party Control." *Social Science History* 16 (Fall 1992): 455–77.

Summers, Anthony with Robbyn Swan. *The Arrogance of Power: The Secret World of Richard Nixon*. New York: Penguin, 2000.

Thimmesch, Nick. *The Condition of Republicanism*. New York: Norton, 1968.

Thorburn, Wayne J. "The Conservative Party of New York: The Pressure Party in a Cross-Endorsement System." Ph.D. diss., University of Maryland, College Park, 1974.

Tolchin, Martin and Susan. *To the Victor . . . Political Patronage from the Clubhouse to the White House*. New York: Random House, 1971.

Turner, Michael. *The Vice-President as Policy Maker: Rockefeller in the Ford White House*. Westport, Conn.: Greenwood, 1982.

Underwood, James E. and William J. Daniels. *Governor Rockefeller in New York: The Apex of Pragmatic Liberalism in the United States*. Westport, Conn.: Greenwood, 1982.

Viguerie, Richard. *The New Right: We're Ready to Lead*. Falls Church, Virg.: Viguerie, 1981.

von Hoffman, Nicholas. *Citizen Cohn*. New York: Doubleday, 1988.

Wells, John A. *Thomas E. Dewey and the Two-Party System*. Garden City, N.Y.: Doubleday, 1966.

Whalen, Richard. *Catch the Falling Flag: A Republican's Challenge to His Party*. Boston: Houghton Mifflin, 1972.

White, F. Clifton. *Suite 3505: The Story of the Draft Goldwater Movement*. New Rochelle, N.Y.: Arlington House, 1967.

White, F. Clifton and William J. Gill. *Why Reagan Won: A Narrative History of the Conservative Movement, 1964–1981*. Chicago: Regnery Gateway, 1981.

White, F. Clifton with Jerome Tuccille. *Politics as a Noble Calling*. Ottawa, Ill.: Jameson Books, 1995.

White, John Kenneth, "New York's Selective Majority." In *Party Realignment and State Politics*, edited by Maureen Moakley, 210–24. Columbus: Ohio State University Press, 1992.

White, Theodore H. *The Making of the President 1960*. New York, Atheneum, 1961.

———. *The Making of the President 1964*. New York, Atheneum, 1965.

———. *The Making of the President 1968*. New York, Atheneum, 1969.

———. *The Making of the President 1972*. New York: Atheneum, 1973.

Williams, Oscar R., III. "The Making of a Black Conservative: George S. Schuyler." Ph.D. diss., Ohio State University, 1997.

Winchell, Mark R. *William F. Buckley, Jr.* Boston: Twayne, 1984.

Wise, David. The Politics of Lying: Government Deception, Secrecy, and Power. New York: Random House, 1973.

Witcover, Jules. *Marathon: The Pursuit of the Presidency, 1972–1976*. New York, Viking, 1977.

Zimmerman, Joseph Francis. *The Government and Politics of New York State*. New York: New York University Press, 1981.

INDEX